RODNEY COLLIN

a man who wished to do something
with his life

—⁓—

by Terje Tonne

THE KARNAK
PRESS

RODNEY COLLIN

a man who wished to do something with his life

Cover design: David Eidsvoll

First Edition: May 2023
ISBN: 978-1-957278-06-3
Printed in the United States of America

THE KARNAK
PRESS
Austin, Texas

In memory of Joyce Collin-Smith;
a friendship beyond time.

Rodney Collin

a man who wished to do something with his life

CONTENTS

PART 1
Rodney Collin 1909 - 1956

PART 2
Rodney Collin 1909 - 1956

APPENDIX

PREFACE

A substantial proportion of the text in the biographical material of this book refers to a text Rodney Collin (Rodney Collin-Smith) wrote after Ouspensky's death.

Because the text, which some claim Dr. Roles contributed to, can be found in two versions and both are called *Last Remembrance of a Magician*, I have refrained from using this title. Instead I refer to what I understand is Collin's text, as 'the unpublished material'. I have been given this material from the daughter of one of Ouspensky's pupils, which previously belonged to her mother. Three of the people, who have been anonymized in the text with the initials Miss H, Miss P and Miss R are allegedly Misses Hoare, Pryor and Romer.

RODNEY COLLIN

ACKNOWLEDGEMENTS

The author acknowledges the contributions made to the contents of this book by Dorine van Oyen, Heidi Aarsten, Robin Bloor, Paula Schmidt, David Eidsvoll, Cato Feness, Jan Roberg, Hege Kambo Dinh, and my patient wife Ulrike Hebel-Tonne.

PHOTOGRAPHS

Plate 1. Rodney Collin-Smith

Plate 2. Wedding photo, Marylebone, London, March 1934:
Rodney Collin-Smith and Janet Buckley

*Plate 3. Rodney Collin-Smith, Kathleen Logan Collin-Smith,
Richard "Derry" Collin-Smith*

*Plate 4. Kathleen Logan Collin-Smith, Rodney Collin-Smith,
Frederick Collin-Smith*

Plate 5. Rodney Collin-Smith, Richard "Derry" Collin-Smith, presumably Mrs. Logan

RODNEY COLLIN

Plate 6. Peter Ouspensky

PART 1
Rodney Collin
1909 – 1956

CHAPTER 1
Towards The Inner Life

If one wants to understand Rodney Collin one eventually has to look behind the outer condition of his life and into life itself and its potentiality. Although external living conditions can both contribute to and make it impossible to reach an inner aim, or even form one, the decisive steps must be taken by each individual.

Such steps reveal the human potential and anyone who takes them moves in the direction of another realm, different from the one formed by the conditions of outer life. Rodney Collin's directions in life became an endless inner journey but without disregarding the outer world. He was in it, but eventually not of it. Drawn by his extraordinary love for higher realms and seeking, above all, knowledge of universal laws, his unending quest led him to a life of contemplation, presence, and sharing what he had found on his often arduous journey. His spiritual, dramatic life has captivated a generation with a spiritual quest, arousing intense interest and bewilderment, but also rejection.

He was born on April 26th, 1909, in the coastal town of Brighton, England, as the first child of Fredrick Collin-Smith and Kathleen Logan. At the age of 50 his father had retired, as intended, from a business as a general merchant and wine importer in London, where he became fairly wealthy and, after travelling in Europe and Egypt, had settled down in Brighton. There he married Kathleen Logan, much younger than he, and a daughter of the owner of the local Royal Crescent Hotel. Before World War I he had bought a Georgian house at Marine Parade in Brighton, where the family lived, and where Rodney and his brother Derry, who was four years younger, were born.

From an early age Rodney Collin tended to explore and immerse himself in areas of knowledge that might enrich and widen his outlook on the world. He was fascinated by stone circles, megaliths, prehistoric man, former civilizations and antiques. It was presumably these and similar interests which led him to be swallowed up by books and provided him with an insight that was unusual for boys of his age. His brother remembered how they often strolled around on journeys of discovery, exploring book and antique shops, and spending time examining the dolmen in the church yard of St. Nicholas. Kathleen was a member of the local Theosophical Society and had a strong interest in astrology – possibly the source of Rodney Collin's later interests. She also worked extensively transcribing texts into the Brail system for the blind. Collin first attended the local Brighton High School. He went to boarding school at Ashford Grammar School in Kent. Learning was his great passion and he spent his free time reading, often one book a day, which probably made him one of the most frequent guests at the local library. After leaving school, he studied for three years at the London School of Economics, where he received his Bachelor of Commerce degree.

In this period, he stayed at TOC-H in Fitzroy Square, London. This was, at the time, a large international Christian charity and membership movement that originally emerged from a soldier's club in Poperinge, Belgium, during World War I. The members, people from various backgrounds, provided practical help in their community, as their goal was to seek to lighten the burdens of others through acts of service. It also ran hostels all over Britain. During the three years Collin studied in London he began to write articles for various newspapers. When he finished his studies he became a freelance writer on art and travel, contributing a weekly series of articles on weekend walks in London for the Evening Standard and the Sunday Referee. Later he became engaged with the Daily Express Encyclopaedia, both as a researcher and writer, and the secretary at the Youth Hostel Association. Eventually he became the founder and the editor of its journal, The Rucksack, which still exists today. His summer vacation of 1926 was spent with a French family in the French countryside. This stay seemed to arouse wanderlust. Each year for many of the following years he went abroad.

CHAPTER 2
Palms and Patios

In the summer of 1927 Rodney Collin travelled to Spain with some financial help from his parents. The original idea was to be away for a month, but with a blend of frugality and an ability to get small jobs along the way, he finally returned to England three months later. All the way he made careful notes that formed the basis for the manuscript, *Palms and Patios*, a set of Andalusian essays, published two years later in 1931 by Heath Cranton Limited, London.

Palms and Patios is a mix of travelogue and sharp analysis of human beings and their milieu, often contrasted by historical perspectives – a voyage of discovery by an 18-year-old English boy. He takes the reader on an extensive journey, often on foot, from Córdoba, Granada and La Veleta, across the country from Seville to Malaga and the blue Mediterranean, and further. In the last chapter, named *By Contrast*, he takes us to the small independent principality of Andorra.

The descriptions of landscapes and humans are often so vibrant that images arise unobstructed as they flow from chapter to chapter. If you are, once in a while, reminded of the author's age, you pause for a moment, astonished, before the next sentence again captures your attention and you soon forget. In his description of Andalusia in the preface, we find, as in other chapters, a curious ability to extract insights from trivial incidents:

> *To-day, the books and the travellers wrangle furiously as to whether it is paradise or purgatory. The Garden of Eden reborn on earth, some say. The seventh circle of Dante's Inferno, say others. But in reality it is neither, or, more accurately, it is a cunning admixture of the two ingredients.*[1]

By hats, contrasts, and wit, he effortlessly pinpoints characteristic cultural aspects of people:

> *The probable reason why the English, as a race, are so reserved, is that England is the home of the bowler. Now the bowler is solid, black, smug and uncommunicative; it makes no advances and rejects any made to*

---

[1] Rodney Collin, Palms and Patios (London: Heath Canton Limited, 1931), p13.

it. Even more does its rich and aristocratic relation, the topper, borne down by the weight of its own stately dignity, scorn social contact for fear of contaminating itself with the lower orders. No wonder, then, that Anglo-Saxons are reserved! The trilby, well-meaning and sociably-minded but reserved, is too shy to remedy the state of affairs. It is left to the cap, a trifle democratic, but hail-fellow-well-met, to relieve the general gloom. But the straw! Ah! The straw! It is he who makes the first smiling advances, encourages the timid, declaims or whispers, promotes witty bubbling conversation as light as himself about life and laughter and letters and love and wine and women and waltzes and all other delightful things beginning with 'l' and 'w' and most of the other letters of the alphabet.

In Malaga he is unhandicapped and free from the restraining genteel influence of bowler and top-hat. What wonderfully amusing times he does have! There he is now, with a thousand of his brothers, all nodding and shaking in the sunlight over glasses of every shape and size, glowing jewels of purple and gold and amber.[1]

Moving from hats to shoes he continues to show how ordinary street-life reveals human traits:

I would say, if it did not sound rather depreciative, that if there is one thing that the Spaniards can do really well, it is to clean shoes. Every man with any pretence at smartness (and none so smart as the Spanish dandy) is never seen with shoes that are not absolutely speckless. Miraculously, in this country where dust is inevitable, and, except in the centre of watered towns, ubiquitous, shoes remain lustrous and mahogany-like. In the bright sunlight, one can almost imagine, darting from them in electric rays, the little haloes of glory which figure so prominently in the boot-polish advertisements. And all this is the work of the shoe-shiner. Most of the day he lies asleep just round the corner, huddled up with head on arm on the pavement, or back to a wall in the shade, till the sun, creeping round, catches him up again. At which he moves a few paces farther on and devotes himself to Morpheus once more. Then when the cafés are most full, he pulls himself together and wanders round, searching for shoes which have lost their mirror-like splendour.

He works conscientiously, realizing the importance of his position, and rigorously explores every wrinkle, every nook and cranny of his pedal

---

[1] Rodney Collin, Palms and Patios (London: Heath Canton Limited, 1931), p45-46.

charges. Meanwhile, the patient, foot on stand, continues to talk, wave his hands, or drink, with the motto that one should never let one extremity know what the other doeth, or is being done by. One really industrious shoe-shiner I have seen to take a quarter of an hour over one pair. When he has finished, he collects his coppers and moves off in search of fresh game.[1]

Visiting a cathedral in Granada he lets us explore its origin and history, before revealing artistic details and the artist's deep-rooted motivation:

Here, every statue, every arch, every tiny detail of sculpture, every dark corner, is worked lovingly, carefully, as though the artist had put his whole soul into the work. [...] The Gothic builders never forgot they were building a cathedral; and a cathedral was, for them, something quite different from a palace or a town hall or a castle; it was a thing apart, into which each workman put his whole life. A Gothic cathedral is full of a million little intimate details, for every craftsman had a certain freedom in expressing himself.[2]

From time to time, someone tries to trick him to pay too much for his hotel, food, and drinks etc. The mix of his financial situation, thrift and a certain acceptance makes him sensitive and vulnerable without losing perspective, but rather enables him to describe the events with accuracy:

The mentality which will throw a starving man into prison because he steals a crust of bread, but regards it as praiseworthy to defraud a stranger on every possible occasion, seems to northerners rather unbalanced, to say the least. The only consolation is to keep one's eyes well open, and to regard the matter philosophically. Morality is, after all, only relative.[3]

Describing the city of Granada seen on the horizon, Collin puzzles out aspects of distance which are distant to our every-day mind:

Distance does lend enchantment to any view, but it is the enchant-ment of the immense, of the hugeness of bare nature. All the works of man, even the greatest, are washed over by distance, not only the hideous blotches of factories and chimneys and smoke, but also gems of supreme beauty like the Alhambra. Everything is reduced, as it were, to the highest common factor of the ages, so that the view from the Sierra is the same to-day as it must have been to a Moorish sentinel of the

[1] Rodney Collin, Palms and Patios (London: Heath Canton Limited, 1931), p48-49.
[2] Rodney Collin, Palms and Patios (London: Heath Canton Limited, 1931), p83.
[3] Rodney Collin, Palms and Patios (London: Heath Canton Limited, 1931), p98.

fifteenth century, to a Roman centurion of the first, to a Phoenician prospector of three thousand years ago, or even to a primitive savage of the forgotten ages before that. It would need a keen eye to pick out any detail in the scene, which is not ageless, and probably it will be even as unchanged in a hundred years as it is to-day.[1]

By observation he recognizes how the time-destroying atmosphere of Andalusia come to have an effect upon him:

So, in the heat of the day, it was only too easy to relapse into mere blank existence for six hours. In Andalusia time soon ceases to mean anything at all. Whereas in London one hurries frantically hither and thither to crowd every five minutes as full as possible, there five hours or five days flow timelessly by with an equal lack of effort. One soon learns the art of meditation. In the first few weeks in Spain, during those spells of quietude enforced by waiting for trains or meals, one's brain frantically works to fill in the lost time. Gradually, as the months pass, the brain bothers itself less and less, ambling leisurely alone with a vague wonder about the world in general where it had previously rushed with the greatest speed possible. I am firmly convinced that if one lived long enough in Andalusia one would reach the ideal of the Orientals and meditate comatosely upon nothing for eight hours a day.[2]

Late in the autumn he ended his three-months-long journey by climbing the Route des Pyrenees. On this stony track that took him to the heights of 8,500 feet, he experienced what seems the most dramatic adventure on his travel before he descended into Soldou, a hamlet in Andorra:

... the snow lay heavy over the mountain-sides, obliterating the faintest trace of the stony track. All around, on my eye-level, and above, the varied outlines of rocky peaks crowded precipitously, gleaming white in their banks of virgin snow. The whole landscape was white and vividly clear but for the bare black precipices of a range to the south and the dark thread of mountain stream below. Gradually, the whole scene changed. Slowly out of the east a white mist came rolling up, engulfing everything. The distant mountains dimmed, blurred to faint outline, and vanished. The world softly closed in to a thing vaguely white and barely ten yards big. I was left alone on the crest in an opaque blanket of fog. Gingerly I crept along what I supposed the track, halted, waited, shouted, and crept on again. After half an hour or so, snow and mist

[1] Rodney Collin, Palms and Patios (London: Heath Canton Limited, 1931), 102-103.
[2] Rodney Collin, Palms and Patios (London: Heath Canton Limited, 1931), 148-149.

together had deprived me of all sense of direction or position. Suddenly a dark form loomed up out of the fog. I hailed it, and the shadow acquired substance and solidified into a mountain shepherd and his dog. Stolidly he greeted me. That same morning he had come up from France. I could follow his footsteps in the snow away down to civilization. A gruff good-bye, and he etherealized into the whiteness. Down and down I scrambled and slid, and always the broad footmarks went on solitarily across the snow.

It was many hours later, as the dusk was tinging the mist with blue, that I came down into the main road far below. There is nothing quite so isolating as mist in the mountains. One is completely alone in the universe, standing on a few stones and a foot of earth in the middle of opaque space. One can imagine that the whole world has melted away into complete timelessness. There are no longer any dimensions, only a mathematical point in the white damp nothingness. Sometimes, if one waits, as wait one must, the miracle comes. The earth is reborn. It is one of the most impressive experiences one can undergo.[1]

Taking Rodney Collin's young age into account, *Palms and Patios* is unusual. His multiple approaches and the breadth of his vocabulary can partly be explained by his insatiable and extensive reading from a very early age, but primarily by the source of this excessiveness, an exceptional urge to learn and explore the world and life beyond boyhood.

---

[1] Rodney Collin, Palms and Patios (London: Heath Canton Limited, 1931), 176-177.

CHAPTER 3
Meeting Janet Buckley

R odney Collin's trip to Spain had expanded his impression of the outer world and enabled him to take a step outside the literal world that had been a dominating factor in his life. This journey, and his visit to Austria, Hungary and Czechoslovakia in 1929, with all its challenges, might have eased the sense of purposelessness that increasingly troubled him during his youth.

The question "Who am I?" constantly arose and agitated him. His engagement in the Toc-H organisation gave inspiration to his idealism and creativity but could not fulfil the deeper layers in his being. In 1930 Toc-H organized a pilgrimage to the Passion Play at Oberammergau in Germany. With an inseparable blend of a feeling for Christian mysticism, and seeing the opportunity as an omen, he decided to attend. The play takes place every ten years and is a five-hour massive theatrical production with more than a thousand local participants. Its theme is the suffering of Jesus. It was within this frame that Rodney Collin met Janet Buckley, his future wife. She was eight years older than him and also a member of Toc-H. Janet was the daughter of Berta (Terrel) and Wilfred Buckley (1873-1933) and grew up at Moundsmere Manor in Hampshire. Her father, a wealthy former Minister and passionate collector of antique glass, bequeathed his vast and unique collection to the Victoria and Albert Museum.

After Rodney and Janet returned from the pilgrimage to Oberammergau, they got involved with the Peace Pledge Union, a British pacifist non-governmental organisation who pledge its members to work for a world free from war and encourage peaceful and non-violent solutions to conflict. Among PPU's notable members were John Middleton Murry, Aldous Huxley and Bertrand Russell. Another member of PPU was the biologist Robert de Ropp. He had discovered Ouspensky earlier on and now shared his interest with them. Rodney Collin then read Ouspensky's *A New Model of the Universe*. Although the book made a significant impression on him and he felt that it contained material that would unquestionably be important for him later, he somehow seemed to know that he was not ready for it.

Meeting Janet Buckley

In the autumn of 1931, he went abroad once more, this time to the narrow belt of the east shore of the Adriatic Sea: Dalmatia, one of the four historical regions of Croatia. This was a tour on foot, an adventure he describes later that year in two articles published in the Cornhill Magazine.

As a journalist, he was far from just a portrayer of travel experiences. An article from January 19th, 1934 in *The Spectator* called *Hitlerism as a Sex Problem*, can serve as an illustration of the range of his journalistic activity. In an attempt to explain Hitler's malevolence as based on sexual disturbance, he draws lines back to World War I, but also illustrates his perspectives through historical links back to ancient times. Collin traces the reason Germany could be seduced by Hitler's ideology and propaganda back to the social climate during and after World War I. The forced absence of a normal sex life during the war led to a 'sexual starvation' that, by the end of the war, had brought many of the German male population to a neurotic state of promiscuity. The social consequences of unemployment "made German men less willing to contemplate marriages." Military zealotry, "the recognized enemy of full heterosexuality" made way for "the literary occupation with perversity, the notorious nightclubs for men only; these stories showed how deep went the underground currents."

After Germany suffered the depression in 1931 Collin saw that the "sex starvation turned ugly and flamed into fanaticism, cruelty and bitterness. Distorted sex showed itself in Jew-baiting, persecution and ultra-puritanism ... frustrations were in many cases sublimated into extreme patriotism, loyalty, and certain disciplined idealism. The turmoil spread and intensified. In the German cities these tendencies were quickly exaggerated. The Teutons have always been given to military discipline ..."

It was in such psycho-historical features that a figure like Hitler found fertile ground, and the German people found a resonance and consensus with his message. These were also the reasons why, according to Collin's analyses, "the true goal of normality, love, companionship and family – could never properly be reached."

The article is characterized by Collin's unmistakable literary depiction, where the arguments emerge through often unexpected composite images. That his way of thinking here is influenced by Sigmund Freud is obvious, but the article nevertheless appeared independent and convincing, particularly impressive in view of the fact that he was 25 years old. At a certain point Collin draws clear lines and summarises the justifications and necessity for a broader and deeper understanding of history.

Sexual inhibition and distortion are widely recognized as a root-cause of individual vagaries. Even the possibility of sexual repression on a national scale, as in the England of 1850, is now acknowledged, and the important psychological effects thereof are being investigated. But the psychoanalytical interpretation of history and politics, which should naturally follow from any acceptance of Freudianism, remains unwritten...

In 1934 Rodney Collin proposed to Janet Buckley. Janet, who was eight years older than Rodney, hesitated to marry him because of the age difference, but in March the same year they married in Marylebone, London. They spent their honeymoon on a walking trip in Cornwall, a county in South West England well known for its legendary South West Coast path. Later the same year they went to Italy and spent six weeks in Sicily.

Maurice Nicoll, an English psychologist and a former student of P. D. Ouspensky, started in 1931 to take meetings in London, in which he spoke of the Fourth Way. He was presenting a teaching, communicated to him orally by Ouspensky for ten years, that was not commonly known and had been carefully guarded in order not to be distorted. The teaching addresses the possibility of inner development through increasing consciousness, raising it above its ordinary level where will, righteous conduct, and unity become possible. In 1935 the Collins attended several meetings conducted by Maurice Nicoll in a lecture room at a Dancing School in Finchley Road in London. Dr. Nicoll's former experience, insight and ability to express himself undoubtedly gave rise to pondering, and became a topic of conversation when they left for the United States a short time later, where they travelled along the west coast and toured the Mexican border.

In 1936, seven years after reading *A New Model of the Universe*, he met Ouspensky for the first time. This meeting undoubtedly made a strong impression on him, because from then on Ouspensky's teaching became his consuming interest, to which he dedicated all his time. His personal search that had led to extensive travel and insatiable reading now found a clear direction.

Pyotr Demianovich Ouspensky and his wife Sophie Grigorievna decided in 1935 to leave Hayes House, a Victorian house in Kent, which had become too small and impractical for group work, and move to Surrey where they settled in Lyne Place. It was a substantial Queen Anne mansion with a hundred acres, including a small lake and an English Garden. It also had a farm suitable for small scale farming. Lyne Place had obviously been neglected for some time and was in need of repair. Three months after it was purchased it was brought to a state of repair suitable enough for Mr. and Madame Ouspensky to move in together, along with the other permanent residents of Hayes House. Most of the refurbishment was performed by members of Ouspensky's groups which included electricians, carpenters, architects and engineers. Among an ever-increasing circle of followers, about a hundred came to Lyne Place on the weekends to take part in practical work, together with students who were living there permanently.

The benefit of working for an individual and common aim through working collectively has been affirmed through history by spiritual and religious movements. At Gurdjieff's Institute for the Harmonious Development of Man, established in 1922 near the village of Avon on the outskirts of Fontainebleau in France, Ouspensky, and particularly Madame Ouspensky, had witnessed many of the benefits of such organisation. They were undoubtably inspired by it somehow when settling at Lyne Place. Although they were not living there, Rodney and Janet both participated regularly in the activities at Lyne. In 1937 Janet bought a house nearby, in Virginia Water, to intensify their personal work. In April the same year she gave birth to their first and only child, Chloe. Besides taking part in the practical work at Lyne, and working in Fleet Street, Rodney Collin spent considerable time at the British Museum Library, where he studied aspects of religion, science, art and philosophy that seemed most relevant to Ouspensky's lectures. The same year, he and his wife went on a short holiday to Romania before they later drove through Algeria and up to the north of the Sahara.

Part of the teaching at Lyne included the Movements, a number of demanding sacred dances that are intended for self-study and the development of a sensitivity that can receive concrete cosmic knowledge. Rodney Collin was a member of the ensemble that demonstrated some of these dances publicly in London in 1938. His participation in these sacred dances undoubtably created a deep interest, because immediately after the demonstration he travelled to Syria in hope of seeing the characteristic turning of the Mevlevi Dervishes. Although he met the sheik of the tekye in Damascus, he was unable to see the Whirling Dervishes.

CHAPTER 4
The War

In September 1939, when England declared war on Germany, Rodney Collin moved from New Pipers, Gorse Hill Rd., with his family, into Lyne Place. The Collin's former household at Egham numbered 13 people, including his mother, who by then had become a widow. Mildred Geiger, another member of the household, was associated with the work at Lyne. That same year she married Hugh Ripman, who was employed by the Maritime Commission at the US Embassy in London. They were both to become lifelong friends of Rodney and Janet and to play a prominent role in the Gurdjieff Work in America.

Shortly after the Collins had moved into Lyne Place, Janet and their daughter Chloe left for the United States to scout for a house suitable for group work. At first they hired a series of temporary properties before they found a house in Rumson on the coastline of New Jersey. However, this building proved to be unsuitable. Eventually, with the support of members from the Orage Group, including Schuyler Jackson, the unconventional literary scholar, they found a large farm at Mendham near Morristown, about 50 miles from New York City. With the help of substantial aid from Janet, who was very comfortably placed financially, they acquired the former residence of the Governor of New Jersey, Franklin Farms. Back in England, Rodney Collin, still living at Lyne, worked on censorship in the daytime and at night was part of the local air raid defence.

On January 25th, 1941 Ouspensky called a meeting at Lyne where he announced that he was leaving for America. He asked some senior members of the group to keep the work going at Lyne. Originally, he had hesitated to leave England, but had now decided to join his wife who had left with Miss R. a few weeks previously. Six days after what was to be his last meeting in England for many years, he sailed, along with Tom Forman, Rodney Collin and Lord Pentland (Henry John Sinclair) from Liverpool on the SS Georgic to New York. It was by coincidence that Collin joined them. He had secured himself a position with the British Purchasing Commission who had decided to transfer him to Bermuda where he stayed from February onwards. Day and night the boat had to zigzag to avoid

German submarine attacks, and the journey must have seemed longer and more eventful than desired for crew and passengers alike.

Although employed by the Commission which procured war materials for the UK, Collin, as a former censor, was not a part of its bureaucracy.

The Commission had a security division for communications with Canadian and US law enforcement, including military intelligence branches and immigration authorities. Collin's work on their behalf explains his various travels during the war. In 1943 he went to both Canada and Mexico. He returned to Mexico again in 1944 and 1945. It makes sense that his first-rate intellect would by valued by the intelligence service.

After his six month stay in Bermuda, Collin was transferred to the British Security organisation in New York at the Rockefeller Center. Besides guarding against the sabotage of British interests and investigating other possible enemy activities, the BCS had set up a nationwide news manipulation operation where anti-German influence was placed in American media and Collin, with his journalistic background, probably contributed to this section. Living at Franklin Farm he travelled the 50 miles to his office in New York each day.

When he travelled to America with Ouspensky, he had a unique possibility to interact with him during the journey. However, perhaps because he was a junior member of the group, it appears that a close relationship did not develop until later.

With the aid of C. S. Nott, who had also emigrated from England, Ouspensky established groups in New York to whom he eventually lectured regularly, however, establishing a firm core of serious people was not without obstacles. Nott's first initiative was to arrange a meeting at Muriel Draper's apartment at Madison Avenue. It was not a success. The audience consisted mainly of members from Orage's old group, who thought Ouspensky was intellectual, dry and uninspiring. However, Nott, who had sympathy with Ouspensky and an unwavering respect for what he stood for, continued to support him tirelessly. When the meetings became regular, they took place in a studio at 78th Street and at private homes of his pupils. The difficulty of forming a group of durable followers persisted. However, as his activities broadened, chosen people from his groups were invited to Franklin Farms for weekends, where they took part in practical work.

By the end of the war he had a large following, including members from the Gurdjieff group in New York. Although the situation at Franklin Farms was not a replica of Lyne Place, they had many common features. Madame Ouspensky was there, as in England, running and overseeing the Work activities with a firmness rarely found elsewhere. Those who could best benefit from her confrontational teaching were undoubtedly the ones who clearly knew what they wished for. When someone without sufficient self-knowledge is exposed to this way of teaching, they are bound to react and those who lack self-insight tend to blame others. There has been no shortage of discussion of the characteristics of Madame Ouspensky's teaching. The most derogatory mentions appear to be not only the least striking, but also those that most clearly reflect the source of criticism.

At Mendham, as at Lyne, Ouspensky lived a secluded life. Rarely was he seen participating in the daily activities. Neither did he attend the joint meals where Madame more often than not staged her precise confrontations based on her unparalleled perceptions of students' actions and psychological features. Ouspensky preferred to keep to himself or to his narrow circle of which Rodney Collin was a central part. Collin rarely took part in meetings in the city as he was often exhausted from his work in New York. He attended practical tasks at the farm in the evening, but he was often awake in his room when he heard Ouspensky's chauffeur-driven car come up the driveway. One such evening he must have been ready to confront some inner conflict he had in his relationship with Ouspensky, the man he somehow knew was so important to him. He rushed downstairs and flung the kitchen door open to where Ouspensky sat drinking alone and shouted:

"Why am I afraid of you?"

Whereupon Ouspensky calmly replied:

"Why do you say I?"

Joyce Collin-Smith, from whom I first heard that story told me that Rodney had said to her that this was a turning point in his life. A deep understanding obviously emerged from this incident and their relationship took on a different meaning. They spent more and more time together. Ouspensky drew him ever closer. Collin started to drive him regularly to the meetings in New York and they often spent their evenings together in restaurants or in Ouspensky's study at Franklin Farms. There were rumours that this contact was undesired by Ouspensky and that Collin took advantage of him. Such a view is a strong underestimation of Ouspensky and most likely an outgrowth of well-known human traits, envy and jealousy.

THE WAR

Marie Seton, an actress and critic of art, theatre and film, developed an interest in the Work ideas after attending lectures in London in 1936. By chance she learned that Ouspensky was in New York and eventually arranged to meet him. He knew about her participating in an earlier translation of Chekhov's play, *The Cherry Orchard*, from Russian into English, and asked her to help him with the practical arrangements for his lectures, and to organise his living conditions for the weekdays he spent in New York. Through these activities she got to spend some time with him and his circle, including Rodney and Janet Collin.

In an article first published in *Quest* in 1962, *The Case of P.D. Ouspensky*, she elaborated on her impressions of him and the situation around him. Her motive for the article, she stresses, is:

> ... *not to discredit Ouspensky, [...], but rather to induce people who are uncritical of themselves in relation to gurus to see that they themselves can unconsciously contribute to their beloved guru slipping, let us say, from 'grace'.*[1]

In the article the Collins are portrayed as a young rich married couple who contributed financially in pursuit of recognition. And "when Ouspensky was often sharp with them," is interpreted as Ouspensky's dissatisfaction and almost disgust at their seemingly insatiable pursuit. Seton appears to fail to see Ouspensky's behaviour towards the Collins as corrections and help for their inner work. It seems that Seton, in her desire to relay her perspective, ends up distorting rather than illuminating her subject.

It is a known psychological phenomenon that a fixed motivation may cast such extensive shadows that what one wishes to illuminate becomes almost invisible. In one of her many speculations, obviously directed at the Collins, she concludes that: "They lived to gain his approval and the more they hoped for it the less they got it."

Few people are free from the desire to be accepted. But to unilaterally characterise the Collins' generous financial contribution to realise Lyne Place and Franklin Farms, including daily operations and restaurant visits, as a means to be approved, testifies to a lack of insight into the depth of their commitment to inner work. Their philosophy was simple: those in the work who have financial resources and are willing to use them should use them – an attitude they shared with another of Ouspensky's followers, Maurice Nicoll. Mary Seton's opinion that people like the Collins could

---

[1] Seton, Marie. "The Case of P.D. Ouspensky." *Gurdjieff International Review* Vol. 2 No. 3: 66.

27

contribute unconsciously to Ouspensky's slipping from grace is a contention that kneels under the weight of its own lack of reasoning.

One evening in November 1946 at Franklin Farms, when Collin sat alone with Ouspensky in what he describes as a gentle and open mood, Ouspensky asked him to call Janet, his wife. Hardly speaking, the three of them simply sat together, drinking a little. In this silent atmosphere Collin experienced a rare complete trust, certainty, and respect.

When he asked a question about stopping thoughts Ouspensky said: "Ask yourself always what you want."

Collin answered: "I want to learn to self-remember."

Ouspensky said: "Well ..." before he continued: "It depends if you have a positive attitude towards me."

Then all of a sudden Ouspensky said with a gesture: "Open all bottles."

While opening the bottles on the table Collin suddenly instantly knew what it meant: "Try everything, leave nothing undone, taste all experience; [...] Find all truths, unlock all secrets ..."

Before they went to bed, Ouspensky shook their hands and said: "I hope to see you again."

This took place several months after communication with him had become not only scarce but when there had become fewer and fewer things one could talk to him about. By accepting this their sensitivity expanded.

CHAPTER 5
Abandoning the System

There can be no doubt that the last years of Ouspensky's life were the most challenging, spectacular and educational period of Rodney Collin's life. Regardless of which perspective one assumes for a description or interpretation of Collin's Work-life, Ouspensky's direct and indirect influence is clear. From one perspective they even seem inseparable. Ouspensky's role, action, understanding and level of being have often been subjects for debate. Sometimes a bystander's experience collides with rumour, speculation, half-truths, slander and historical investigations. James Moore's lax handling of historical data in this context is both problematic and unsettling, not least given that his extensive writing includes so many influential people in the Gurdjieff-Ouspensky tradition. There is no doubt that his writing must at times be considered outstanding, but his descriptions of the events at Lyne Place in 1947 are incorrect and directly misleading, even though he admits that Ouspensky worked hard in his final phase. Collin's role and contribution is, however, almost dismissed as melodramatic. It becomes particularly problematic when Collin's and Ouspensky's roles are not only hinted at erroneously, but are emphasised.

Rodney Collin was regularly in the midst of Ouspensky's activities from 1936, except for a period during the war when he was working for the British Government. After 1945 he dedicated himself entirely to work with Mr. and Madame Ouspensky. During the whole summer and autumn in 1947 he was permanently around Ouspensky until he died on October 2nd. This period was critical to Rodney Collin who was an eyewitness to the changes that took place in Ouspensky's life close to his death. No histories or historical investigations can replace an eyewitness experience.

Ouspensky had left England for the United States on January 31st, 1941. When he set out on his return journey on January 18th, 1947, it was not only against Madame Ouspensky's will, but also against the advice of his doctor. Already during the summer in 1946, at Steinway Hall, New York, he had announced that he would leave and return to England, and that Work would proceed at Mendham under Madame Ouspensky's direction. This became difficult for many of his followers in New York who did not have a direct relation to Franklin Farms at Mendham. When the meetings in New York had ceased and his weakness increased, people wondered why he would leave. In this period, he hardly spoke to anyone and was surrounded by a wall of silence. Many around him could not imagine what he could communicate to the people in England as he became increasingly weaker. His behaviour, hints and direct instructions became less comprehensible to conventional thinking, and people responded differently according to their level of being. Some found him illogical, irrational and sometimes unreasonable, others would find meaning in even his gestures.

Rodney Collin, who had joined him in England just after Easter, had to take up a temporary residency in a caravan in Lyne Place grounds, as their house in Virginia Water had been commandeered by the army who had installed a gun emplacement in their rose garden. Rodney Collin was neither shocked nor surprised by Ouspensky's behaviour as he had followed his progressive and accelerating change of methods and thoughts in the first year or two in America. Besides this, it seems unthinkable that his essential character was not deeply seized by the truth that life, in its infinite diversity can never be conceived in a system. To Rodney Collin the changes were logical consequences in a process. It had obviously become more and more difficult for Ouspensky to teach in the format of 'The System' and:

> ... *his personal answers had begun to change. They became less and less explanatory, more and more enigmatic. Each answer became, one felt, a sort of problem or puzzle to be solved, rather than a solution in itself. Very often many levels of meaning were to be seen in a single sentence, or even a phrase; which could be taken differently according to the insight of the hearer. And he used less and less the actual language of the System, though this continued in use through readings of old lectures and writings.*

Several visitors from England had, in 1944 and 1945, already noticed an evident change of communication between Ouspensky and his followers, and recognised the impossibility of logically deciphering his answers. To many of them they were like the koans of Chinese Zen. Another definite change was that he gave less instructions and made fewer demands. Right after he had given a series of lectures in Carnegie and Steinway Halls in New York in 1946, his health deteriorated rapidly. It was in this phase that Collin recognised with clarity that:

... it was a new education simply just to be with O. At this time driving him to New York, sitting with him at the studio over coffee and cakes, buying wine and calling at the barber's. For this an absolute passivity combined with clear seeing was necessary. One had not to think, but to see, and seeing to do what was right, even though it was not asked.

He saw this form of handling of ordinary life-situations as a submission of his self-will and:

... soon learned that one must have no business of one's own to fit in, no preferences or laziness. And then one must not forget nothing. O. would say: 'First we see this man' and one had to remember without asking what he had said in two sentences and the night before he would like to call on so and so. Then in mid New York he would lean back and say: 'Well, now we can go there.' And one had to know where against considering in parking anywhere and everywhere regardless of tough policemen and for external considering in drawing exactly to the curb, in walking in front so that he could follow, in watching without to watch, being there yet remaining invisible.

In the following months Rodney Collin had a clear impression of how communication with Ouspensky grew more and more difficult and challenging. Their usual communication gradually shrank and eventually fewer and fewer subjects became communicable. But, for the time, there was still a bridge over this gradually widening abyss:

Only the simplest and clearest cry could now carry across the divide, either almost childlike remarks about the cats, the wine, physical surroundings, or else something straight from the heart, with no consideration at all.

... when he spoke, one felt it necessary to understand by some kind of intuition rather than by listening to his words, which on the surface were either trivial or incomprehensible. On the other hand even the most casual remarks seemed to have a sort of hidden significance. If he said: 'Cat watches', or 'Open the bottles', cat was not only cat, bottles were not only bottles, but were a kind of cipher or symbol for some deeper truth. One dimly felt that his mind worked in a quite other way from most, images on different scales being linked together by some inner analogy: so that in remarking on the physical, he himself perceived at the same time something hidden and very significant.

31

For Collin, the gradual shift from the more conventional and accustomed way of teaching was a natural outcome and completion of a process heading for fulfilment. It was ten years since he first met Ouspensky and he now experienced moments of complete trust, respect and certainty. It seems that their relationship grew extensively as Collin's attention was moving from Ouspensky's oral teaching to his demonstration of the Work. In December 1946, on one of their last trips to New York, Ouspensky told Collin that he would like him to come to Lyne Place about Easter if he could manage it.

Ouspensky's return to Lyne Place was now fixed for January. But as his health condition was worsening with a series of heavy nose-bleeds, Rodney Collin thought it was very unlikely that he would reach England at all. Still, Ouspensky sailed on The Queen Elizabeth on January 18th, together with Miss Q. and Miss R. with the Shs. and Rm. As they were walking down the stairs leaving the Franklin House, and while the whole household was watching attentively from a distance, Ouspensky asked Collin to lend him his arm. This had never happened before in public and only once before in private. For anyone who knew how Ouspensky refused anyone who handed him his coat or even held a door open for him, this must have been a clear indication of change. When Rodney Collin drove him to the docks and installed him in his cabin, Ouspensky's last words were: "Do not forget to come there – about Easter."

When he arrived in England January 23rd, 1947, he wished to hold meetings at Colet House, the headquarters of Ouspensky's Historico-Psychological Society in London. He called Dr. Roles and told him to gather three hundred people within three weeks. When Dr. Roles wondered what he should say to them:

"Why say anything? Just ask them what they want," replied Ouspensky.

The people were gathered, and the first three meetings were held February 24th, March 5th, and 12th. Rodney Collin was not there, he arrived in England at Easter, as suggested.

These meetings were more to shock than surprise the audience. Not only did he seem to many in the audience to abandon and disclaim the structure on which his teaching was based, but he also refused to answer some questions, often insisting he did not understand. Listening to people's impressions of these meetings, what struck Collin was the incredible honesty in Ouspensky's answers:

A sort of tour de force of sincerity. Only then did honesty appear as a trait of superman, not belonging to ordinary men at all. For his honesty was so unknown, that half the hearers were left baffled, some even pitying O. for having lost his mind though all felt something intensely emotional. One couple, coming for the first time, said afterwards: 'This man tried very hard and told the truth. We never heard anyone tell the truth before.'

Every question seemed to bring the whole quintessence of his experience and then to answer in a few words – which immediately set the whole problem in quite a different and unsuspected light. Beside these answers, the old method with exact language and theoretical explanations seemed in retrospect strangely limited and pedestrian. But certainly, one had to listen in a different way; one understood less than half by the words and more by some sort of direct perception which he himself made possible.

One of the accounts from these meetings where Collin saw how Ouspensky tore away the illusion of common aim, which lies at the back of so many hypocrisies and pointed to the necessity of starting from the known, which is personal and different for everybody, and where Ouspensky neither pretended, claimed or recalled anything, went like this:

Q. We have been trying to follow out the teaching you gave us years ago.

O. I gave no teaching.

Q. You told us certain things to help us.

O. You misunderstood.

Q. Where can we begin to work now?

O. I will see what you want to know and where you want to begin and then we will see the first step.

Another sequence where Collin found Ouspensky throwing light on his own conduct and baffling the audience went like this:

Q. You told us how to begin and now you say that you gave us no teaching. I do not understand that.

O. I don't know. You see, I generally forget things that have no immediate connection with the present.

Q. Can you tell us again the way in which to change ourselves, to be less mechanical?

O. No, I can't. I can't speak. That would be mechanical. Just talk without any reason.

Q. What can I do to become better, even though I do not understand anything?

O. I would be quite satisfied to become worse. I don't know how to do this.

Q. Now can we find harmony?

O. This is my question now and I have no answer.

Many of the incidents in the last part of Ouspensky's life, including the meetings in Colet Gardens in 1947, that have often been regarded as indications and even proofs of Ouspensky's instability and degeneration, were in fact forms of preparation for himself and his closest circle. When Ouspensky abandoned the system and urged people to reconstruct it all, Rodney Collin, his most intimate pupil, did understand that this was a necessary shock, forcing people to penetrate to what they really understood and wanted in their hearts. Others saw the abandoning as an expression, not only of Ouspensky's stagnation, but took it to be a signal of the necessity to look elsewhere for what they believed was missing. Collin took the reconstruction to mean:

> *... abandoning old forms, penetrating to the truth which lay behind those forms, and creating new forms for that truth – which in their turn one day must be abandoned also. Abandoning and recreating seems to me the only way of keeping alive the hidden connection which lay behind the system. If one clings to the old, it fossilizes, and oneself inside. The idea of reconstruction seems to be endless.[1]*

Here Collin not only illustrates how truth survives through change and renewal, and portrays pitfalls, but he also indirectly points to the essence of form; its nature is to carry content. Rodney Collin felt so little surprised when Ouspensky rejected the old language, the method and the abandonment of the system, that he hardly looked for an explanation. To him the system's knowledge had become so overwhelming and so complete that in many cases, including his own, it had begun to strangle that deep inner curiosity and search in man which can only struggle with the unknown.

To Collin the abandoning was an incomplete phrase. He had himself heard Ouspensky say:

"Yes, I said abandon, not destroy," when he once was asked about it.

---

[1] Rodney Collin, *Theory of Conscious Harmony* (London: Robinson & Watkins Books Limited, 1958), 182.

CHAPTER 6
Life at Lyne Place

When Rodney Collin had arrived at Lyne in the beginning of April, he found it quiet and uncomplicated. Ouspensky stayed in his rooms with W. Miss Q., who took care of all his practical needs, and Collin observed that the rest of the household seemed to be focused on Ouspensky's invisible presence. Still he found this isolation rather strange. Collin had to take up a temporary residency in a caravan in Lyne Place grounds when he came at Easter, as their house in Virginia Water had been commandeered by the army who had a gun emplacement in their rose garden. From America, Ouspensky had written to Lyne saying that he was coming to see certain people "whom he would choose":

> *On the very day of his arrival he did in fact invite one or two people to come and sit with him or to dine. But curiously enough, after the first invitation, nearly all these people found themselves too busy to respond. Some had unavoidable duties on the farm or business in London, which they regarded as work – and so were never available when called for. Others came once, but finding that nothing was said or done, inwardly felt it rather a waste of time. Unaccepted invitations were not repeated.*

In this way Ouspensky's closed circle narrowed down to four people: Miss Q., Rodney Collin, Miss R., and W. These four eventually became almost his entire group of companions. They would take lunch and supper together in the refectory, a panelled dining room where they could overlook the garden with its ravine and a cedar-tree through the French windows. To Collin "... the whole scene seemed bathed in a mildness and beneficence, which were very striking after the harshness of America."

During these meals Ouspensky would remain silent or say little. At the end of the meal they all became silent, smoking.

At such silent moments Collin became aware of:

> *... his own awareness of the four figures sitting in easy positions about the head of the table. One lay within the sphere of physical sensation, himself; two were familiar and half-known. But the fourth, a once massive but now frail old man, with short white hair, a stubbly growth*

of white beard, and strange blue eyes, in some way escaped observation, attention fell into a void at that place.

Although Collin found Ouspensky fragile, he was more than ever impressed by a certain indefinable but very definite power. It was through Ouspensky's increasing economy with words, his turning of the small group's attention to seemingly insignificant things, and hours at a stretch of silence, that Collin recognised a growing of an extraordinary sensitivity:

> *O. would say little or nothing, but from time to time point to the cats, as though directing attention specially to them. Sometimes he might ask for something, or wish a dish set aside or a pie placed by his soup. But with such economy of words that 'Go ... take ... put' seemed to cover almost all eventualities. If something were not as required, the rest had learned to remain still, both outwardly and inwardly, curbing any impulse to move, suggest or interfere – until the solution showed itself.*

After the meal they would gather in the Green Drawing Room. At Ouspensky's request, Miss R. gathered the cats, one by one and carried them in. On one occasion Ouspensky, turning to Miss Q., said: "Do you want anything?... Shall we go and look at cats?"

It was within such circumstances that Rodney Collin recognized how his atmosphere of sensitivity gave access to a more objective view on these occasions when they, for hours and hours, got used to sitting still together in silence:

> *One's eyes fell with pleasure on the bright spots of Persian and Indian miniatures against the restful green and gold walls, or on the chestnut-tree beyond the window, on which day by day buds gave way to flowers and these to clusters of nuts. Nothing else was apparent. And yet in some way one's whole attitude of life changed at such times, all impatience vanished and one became content to exist definitely in the present. This, it later became clear, was a very definite preparation.*

His sensitivity, growing in the soil of this silence, made him extraordinarily receptive to moods. Until now he had felt that Ouspensky was engaged in an invisible agenda he was gradually unmasking. When Ouspensky, in the evenings, intensively studied photographs and postcards from Moscow and Russia, or snapshots from his Indian travels of 1913-14,

> *... he gave the impression of being very intensively at work, reconstructing another time, putting it together, remembering*

everything about it – but for a particular reason, to obtain a definite result, connected with an exact aim.

Already in 1946, when during the summer he saw Ouspensky reading vast quantities of Russian novels of his time, he had asked himself: "Where is he? What is he occupied with?" In the same period, he found him also reading a forty-volume Russian encyclopaedia – straight through. From time to time he would also approach certain people and talk with them about names of streets in Moscow and the whereabouts of shops and restaurants. Rodney Collin saw all this in the perspective of a carefully detailed reconstruction for recurrence.

In the concept of recurrence lies the opportunity for change through growth of consciousness and liberation from mechanical repetition. It does not take place in time as we in our ordinary state experience time, an experience based on and limited by our senses, but in eternity which is orthogonal to linear time. The idea of recurrence includes a multidimensional scope of a same time. Although Ouspensky never failed to express that recurrence was not a part of the system, he did not see it as a contradiction. To him recurrence was a fact. During this time Ouspensky saw Rks. Now and then and they spoke in detail about the whereabouts of shops, restaurants and names of streets in Moscow, relative to his early years in Russia. Collin was of the conviction that, even without knowing the idea of recurrence, one would understand what this is a preparation for. From these and similar observations, he concluded that Ouspensky was lessening his involvement in Franklin Farms because he was already engaged with his youth in Moscow.

Two other curious incidents, probably from September 1946, confirm what occupied Ouspensky's thoughts and attention at the time. He told Miss Q. about a dream he had had where he was a baby. When his father was speaking to him playfully, he was about to answer him when he suddenly remembered that he as a baby should not speak. He stressed the importance to Miss Q. that he knew that he must "tell them nothing." Later, one evening, together with W. and Miss Q., he made curious remarks with reference to his dream. He not only spoke of his own recurrence, but of the possibility of people being born later to relate to him in an earlier period in time. He indicated that former incidents, and buildings and places still existing, could be a link that could establish or strengthen such connection.

During April, Ouspensky became gradually sicker until a crisis on April 26th, when he had to return to bed immediately after supper. In the following days, evidently in great pain, he made tremendous efforts to dress and come down to have meals and to sit with them in the Green Room. These struggles weakened him considerably.

In the following days he could barely speak and hardly stand but at lunch on April 28th he was very much better. He called Rodney Collin soon after and had him organise messages to be sent to various people, including a telegram to F. who lived in Paris, advising him to come to see him as soon as possible. F. was obviously of particular interest to Ouspensky in his meticulous preparation for recurrence. F. was of Polish origin and was Ouspensky's one close schoolfriend and one of the figures in his novel, *The Strange Life of Ivan Osokin*. Ouspensky used to find F. a good listener in their schooldays when he wanted to converse on subjects that interested him. F., who also could recall details at length from their schooldays, was seemingly of interest to Ouspensky with his preoccupation with recurrence. When Collin was in Paris in March, Ouspensky had instructed him to find F. and persuade him to come to Lyne. In response to the last telegram F. arrived at Lyne on May 11th.

On April 28th, Dr. Roles was called at a London Hospital and told that he was urgently wanted. When he arrived at Lyne one hour later, Ouspensky wanted to know how quickly he could arrange a meeting. "In ten days" he answered, and he promised 300 people. When Collin asked how the new meeting would begin, Ouspensky replied in an almost cheerful tone:

"I don't know how it will begin, question is how it will end."

In the evening of May 7th, Ouspensky, on Miss Q.'s arm, walked onto the platform at Colet Gardens where 300 people awaited him. After pointing to where Miss Q. was to sit and finding his own seat, he asked R. what he had got. R read from some selected questions. Later there were also questions from people in the audience. In a soft voice he began to answer in short sentences or single words. He explained that what they had tried in America did not work and that it was necessary to try a different approach and that the question now was:

"What do you want?"

As he said it, it was as though no-one had heard the phrase before. Many attempted to answer, sincerely enough. Yet always he pressed them further to be more personal, exact and urgent in their demand. To those who began from some real fact, for example, from a will to renew experiences when the mind worked differently or a higher understanding came to them, he would say simply: "Continue like that."

Others remarked: "I find nothing turns out like I intended, though I spend all my time deciding what to do."

He answered: "Find what prevents it."

He was again most strict with those who echoed old ideas and to a lady who declared: "I want to stop thoughts" he almost shouted: "Why?"

And of another who said: "I want to feel my nothingness," he demanded sharply: "What does that mean?"

As always there were quite unexpected answers. One woman said: "I want to get rid of selfishness." The answer was: "And supposing that is exactly what you need?"

Now he kept repeating: "You must find examples, you must give material, then you may talk."

A few indeed began suggested methods for acquiring what they wished, exercises that might prove useful.

One man asked: "Should one try to act as though one already had what one wanted?"

"Yes, this is one method. But there are many, you must try all."

Of course, there came the inevitable rejoinder: "Won't you help us a little? Won't you suggest some method?"

He replied: "There is no method, really there is no method."

To others who had good ideas he said simply: "Try."

There were a few attempts to raise the discussion to the plane of his intention or of the meaning of this phase of the work. It was asked:

"Is it not better to think about the purpose of this group than about purely personal questions?"

He replied brusquely: "What questions are not personal?"

Then an old acquaintance essayed from the back: "We have reason to think you have knowledge that would be useful to us. How can we get it?"

And he answered enigmatically: "That is the whole thing, how can you get it?"

"Why do you make it so much harder for us than before?" a lady complained at this.

He laughed cheerfully and said: "I don't know how I could make it harder."

But when someone faltered a doubt about their "right" to conditions of help, he cried with great force:

"You have right to nothing, you have right to anything!"

Although this summary, however accurate, obviously cannot parallel the experience of witnessing Ouspensky in action, it seems to be a necessary constituent to approach an understanding of Ouspensky's direction. To Collin, the impossibility of conveying the impressions from this meeting lay in Ouspensky's ability to hold up a mirror where people could see a reflection of their own desires – false or true. Perhaps needless to say, but many people experienced his answers as if a ball was kicked to the wall and returned.

It was during this meeting, as he sat listening, an exact formulation of Collin's own aim abruptly entered his mind and this simple phrase was to act as a charm. From this moment on he felt that his problems in life dissolved as his life arranged itself. Later he came to understand that it is the true formulation of one's aim that has the magic 'Sesame' that opens doors.

On May 11th F. arrived at Lyne Place and was warmly welcomed by Ouspensky who had not seen him since 1920 in Constantinople. Rodney Collin found him to be a quiet man with the sensitivity of one who has lived in many countries and under various conditions. He also found that he talked easily with Ouspensky who stimulated F.'s memory by handing him boxes of postcards. Later he lent him *The Strange Life of Ivan Osokin* to read.

In the days that followed, Collin could not help noticing that F. was not completely puzzled or confused by the overtone of Ouspensky's welcome or his work. Approximately one week after F.'s arrival, Ouspensky announced another meeting "for F." 300 people attended this meeting. F., who could not understand the words was greatly taken by the atmosphere. He said repeatedly that he had not experienced anything like it, neither in any church or law-court.

During his stay, F. and Ouspensky had detailed conversations about their schooldays where F. remembered very well when they would walk and talk for hours. These conversations, as with everything around Ouspensky at that time, had more than a hint of the taste of recurrence. That this meeting with F. had a particular significance to Ouspensky was clear to the few who stood closest to him. The last evening of F.'s visit, after supper, Ouspensky collected himself energetically and with both hands shook F.'s hands as he looked him in his eyes and said with warm emotions:

"Goodbye my old friend."

F. returned to Paris the next morning, and Ouspensky sank into a world invisible to those around him.

It was in this period that Rodney Collin's growing understanding of how instinctive and mental habits hide insights and new and wider perspectives, when a curious change began to come over the pattern of his life:

> *O. seemed to find it difficult and after two- or three-hours rest would wake again about 9 or 10 p.m., take breakfast coffee, rise and begin another day. This would mean that Miss. R. must serve 'lunch' sometimes after midnight, after which they might sit together for an hour or two and then go back to bed again. The next day O. might wake at 10, there would be a second lunch at 2, supper at 6.30, he would retire once more and so on. In this way, two complete days became compressed into 24 hours.*

One of these nights, after having lunch at midnight, Miss Q. fell asleep on the sofa and W. was dozing, Rodney Collin describes how he:

> *For some reason remained alert and was filled with a strange awareness, sitting there, the whole house asleep in the curious pause of the small hours, facing O. for hour after hour, the two of them quite silent and quite still. [...] Awareness mounted and mounted in the silence and then suddenly gave out, drowsiness falling till the dawn whitened the cracks in the shutters, hours later. It was strange, too, falling completely out of step with ordinary life: and curious when early or later ceased to have meaning, because there was nothing to measure by. Was a meal late lunch or early supper and were they late retiring on Friday or early to bed on Saturday? All such ideas and in fact all ordinary ways of looking at the routine of life and passage of time were revealed as simply habits of thought. If a man were strong enough to create circumstances which broke such habits, quite new points of view became possible. Like everything that summer, it was a preparation. But for what?*

CHAPTER 7
The Return to America as a Stop Exercise

Not long after Rodney Collin arrived at Lyne in April, Ouspensky asked him to come with him on his return to America in September. Collin immediately agreed. Due to Ouspensky's deteriorating health there were other conditions to address and consider for the departure besides the necessity for special facilities on the ship. Both at Lyne and Mendham the whole household was focused on either his departure or his arrival. In the early morning of September 4th, the truck with all the luggage left Lyne and travelled down to the ship at Southampton. Rodney Collin, R. and H. left Lyne at about one o'clock and arrived at 3.30 p.m. R. then arranged with the transport and medical officers for Ouspensky's car to drive straight through and right to the ship's gangway.

Ouspensky's car, arriving just a few minutes later, drove through the gate and parked right at the end of the gangplank. Miss R., Miss Q. and Ouspensky, all traveling together, remained in the car. The rest of the travel companions waited patiently on the dock in quiet. It was then when Ouspensky made some remarks that seemed to indicate that he did not want to go. Miss Q. tried hard but could not persuade him. Neither could Miss R., who insisted that he must go to see Madame. At about four o'clock he called the people that were to travel with him, each in turn, and said:

"I cannot go in these conditions."

To Rodney Collin he added: "I thought to take a holiday, but I decided not."

Except for Miss Q., who made a last attempt to persuade him and Miss R. who cried and said: "Do as he says," the rest of the travellers remained silent.

A little later Ouspensky, for some reason, emerged from the car and advanced in the direction of the gangway and then returned to the car. He struggled and was obviously in great pain. All activities at Lyne and Mendham came to a halt. This incident has historically been viewed simply as if Ouspensky changed his mind because of his medical conditions. Rodney Collin saw it differently. Not only did he recognise Ouspensky's decision as a general stop to the impetus of arrangements in both England and America, but also as a created test for every individual concerned:

> *As a result of this general test and the sudden interruption of all activity, the stage was automatically set and the characters arranged for what he later proposed to do.*

That this whole event was a part of a larger play became more evident when the Daimler, with Rodney Collin sitting in the front seat, was slowly leaving the docks:

> *[...] pausing at the gate where H. was still waiting. O. called H. and leaning forward, said very directly to the four of them: 'You know, I never intended to go to America not for a minute.'*

They drove back to Lyne in the afternoon, only stopping at a wayside shop for some food which they took in the car. They enjoyed their meal in a pleasant, cheerful but quiet atmosphere, with the doors of the car open to the sunny countryside and a large tray of beer and a heap of sandwiches spread on the floor of the car. When the car drove through the lighted gate at Lyne, where the people awaited his return, darkness had fallen.

Ouspensky remained in the car for some time and Miss E. came to welcome him. As he made no hint of wanting to leave the car, some tried to tempt him with descriptions of the nice atmosphere inside with cats and the open fireplace. Eventually he went into the house where he took his hat and coat off before he very intentionally returned to the car and said:

"This is not the right Lyne, let us go and find another."

No one understood the situation and seemed just to sit calmly and wait for things to sort themselves out. After some time, he was given a glass of wine and a little later:

> *... he leaned forward in a very pleasant way and said: 'Well, what is the matter?'*
>
> *Rodney Collin replied: 'I don't seem to be able to think of anywhere better to go at the moment.'*
>
> *He said: 'Well, let's go anyway.'*

The driver, who had fallen asleep in the gravel, was wakened and they drove out in the warm dark evening. After about 20 minutes, going through Chertsey, they were back at Lyne. He left the car very energetically, went inside and had supper, whereupon he directly went to bed. The next day he appeared more energetic than in several months and he seemed very relieved. He stated that he experienced the reception as unpleasant and that he felt that it was necessary to talk to people. In addition to a longer conversation in Russian with Miss and Mrs. H., he sought out several of the residents.

These conversations seem to have been marked by deep concern for the people who, in being in contact with him, shared his fate. In the following days Ouspensky spoke in various ways about the long and difficult journey that was ahead of him and those around him. On Saturday he spoke with Mademoiselle about going straight to Paris on Monday but called Rodney Collin on Sunday to have arrangements made immediately for a return to America. Collin made inquiries on Monday and found, to Ouspensky's disappointment, that the first possible passage would be in October. The next day Australia, where Ouspensky's friend Plavin lived, had become the destination.

At least to Rodney Collin, but most probably to several of Ouspensky's closest circle, it gradually became clear that Paris, Australia and America were allegories for not yet known targets. It was at this stage that Collin found Ouspensky's search for words or pretended search for words conspicuous. It occurred to him at the time that the connection between ideas and word-memory was broken. At other times when he spoke clearly and exactly it dawned upon him that his misuse of words and forgetfulness was intentional and deliberate. He simply saw it as a training for those around him to receive and understand Ouspensky's indications in a new way. In the same period there were incidents that intensified impressions to heights not recognisable in ordinary states, as when Rodney Collin:

> ... handed him a note on the top of a sheet of a pad, he read the note and then went on to read, one by one, all the blank pages of the pad. Such actions had an extraordinary power of riveting the attention. And they began to make it clear that nothing he did was done for ordinary logical reasons. Later, it was this realisation that made intelligible much that would never otherwise have been.

CHAPTER 8
The Road Trips

The many car journeys undertaken by Ouspensky in the last period of his life have historically been wrongly attributed to Rodney Collin's inventiveness. Ouspensky's own initiative for these journeys became apparent on the evening of September 4th, after arriving at Lyne Place from Southampton. Except for two breaks, the first at 12.30 on the journey made on Thursday, September 11th, these trips were all in accordance with Ouspensky's inclinations. The first break was suggested by Rodney Collin and R. on the old road to Andover, having driven by Camberley and Basingstoke. The second break was when they later arrived at Whitchurch where they had lunch. Their meals were taken in the car, but Ouspensky would eat nothing. Collin's observation was striking:

Such initiative he simply ignored, allowing each person to do as he liked, yet himself remaining absolutely unaffected by their suggestion. Nevertheless, he looked at everything about him with great interest.

At 4.30 the car with Miss R., Rodney Collin, R. and Ouspensky arrived in the warm afternoon at Lyne after a five-and-a-half-hour trip in the English countryside.

Wednesday the 10th, the day before this outing, they had admittedly talked about the possibility of going to Stonehenge, but they had not made a final decision. Although they apparently started the trip with Stonehenge in mind, none of them seem to have made a definite choice and it is unclear whether they ever reached Stonehenge or not. Before Ouspensky went to bed that evening he said to Miss R:

"Perhaps I could go where I want tomorrow."

The next morning, September 12th, Ouspensky first called Rodney Collin, then a little later Miss P. and finally R. Together they tried to figure out where he wanted to go. As he could not remember the name of the place and only could give a vague description of the way/route there, Mrs. M. made a list of former places he had stayed which proved not to be what he was looking for. With the vague hints: 'strange way', 'safe place' and the 'more or less historic', given a little earlier by Ouspensky, the car was ready for departure after lunch. The latter formulation 'more or less historic' was taken to mean: some definite landmark in the history of the System. On this trip, beside the chauffeur, only Rodney Collin and R. were going with him. Once in the car Rodney Collin asked him where they should go:

> He leaned forward and said very firmly: 'we will go in the direction of...' and then stopped.

At the time it seemed that he hoped by speaking firmly and quickly to make the name come but later Rodney Collin came to understand this differently. The only name that had aroused his interest this morning was Wendover. When this then was suggested he said:

"Yes, we often used to go from there."

It was on this trip to Wendover that Collin sensed that there was a "greater air of purpose about the whole expedition" and he tried to become more receptive to Ouspensky's hints and proposals. The closer they came to Wendover the stronger the feeling grew in Collin that something "ought to happen." He remembered that seven years earlier he had met Ouspensky and Madame in Wendover. He also recalled everything he had been told by E. and others about Ouspensky's time in Wendover. Now, when they were approaching their target under a grey rainy sky, he made the effort to bring both these images together. However, when they reached Wendover and driving through the Wendover High Street Ouspensky lost interest and said: "It is far from here."

They parked and Rodney Collin got out and walked to the house.

When he got back, they all had sandwiches and beer in the car except Ouspensky, who would have neither. Later they drove back, viewing the Vale of Aylesbury, by the foot of the Downs, High Wycombe and Marlow and arrived by seven at Lyne. Although the trip did not seem to have led to any results, there was an undercurrent of something unsettled and Ouspensky remained resolute. After supper before going to bed he said about the driver:

"Tell the man to come again tomorrow morning."

The same evening Rodney Collin wrote:

> There is some special problem to be solved here. We have not solved it yet. But this is the most extraordinary time. All kinds of barriers are crumbling and almost anything is possible.

The third trip took place on Saturday September 13th. Although the list of places Ouspensky formerly had a relation to were studied more thoroughly that morning, no clear decision was made of where to go. Places considered were Red Spire at Dymchurch, Encombe at Sandgate, Oast House at Trottiscliffe, Wendover, the Dell at Sevenoaks, Gaddesden, Rye and Romney Marsh.

Rodney Collin and R. Had, independently of each other, come to link Ouspensky's phrase 'strange place' with Romney Marsh, a sparsely populated wetland area in the counties of Kent and East Sussex. After some time, Ouspensky had had enough of the repetition of names and places and instead repeatedly focused on 'the station' and 'where we go from'. Suggestions were made but dismissed. In the afternoon Ouspensky, R., and Rodney Collin went off in a taxi without a specific destiny. As they left Ouspensky asked where the nearest station was. When he was told Virginia Water the taxi driver was met with Ouspensky's disgust. When Chertsey was suggested Ouspensky said forcefully in a loud voice:

"Impossible."

When Collin eventually suggested Waterloo, Ouspensky agreed although it was indisputably not what he wanted.

Within two hours they were back at Lyne after having been to Waterloo and Embankment. Obviously, they found nothing of interest on this trip. In the evening Ouspensky said:

"I must go to her place."

To those present this seemed to indicate all the places where Mr. and Madame Ouspensky had together established Work. Rodney Collin and R. tried to arouse and reassemble the places and the numerous people who were a part of the history.

> During these days there was a very special sense of the whole period of the Work in England being brought back, reviewed and looked over for some reason. Perhaps the past was simply being reconstructed, perhaps something definite was being searched for there. In any case M's connection with all that was several times referred to and it was to 'Madame's place' that they were to go.

In the evening Rodney Collin and R. tried to reconstruct the places, people and incidents of these bygone times.

Sunday, September 14th, Ouspensky, Rodney Collin and R. set off in a large Buick lent from some old friend, probably Basil Tilley. The evening before Ouspensky had called Rodney Collin to his room and asked if they could leave very early the next day. When Collin asked him where he wanted to go Ouspensky referred to R. and said:

"R wrote it down right."

From this it was assumed that he wanted to go to Dymchurch and Encombe at Sandgate. When the Ouspenskys first came to England they spent their holiday at Dymchurch. At Sandgate they stayed with Mrs. P. a few years later.

After one hour they reached Sevenoaks, where the car slowed down as they were passing the front gate of 'Dell,' one of Ouspensky's former addresses. One hour later they reached Rye, where they paused. When they set off again, they drove slowly through the street of Rye passing the Old Mermaid Inn and:

> ... looked out over the flat, sunny marshes, dotted with their little churches in groves of trees. Although O. lay right back in his seat, he obviously took everything in most keenly. The trip across the marsh itself made a strong impression – there was a sharp blustery wind that kept sweeping through the reeds and trees, so that the silvery underside glinted in the bright sun.

Three hours after their departure from Lyne, they reached Dymchurch, having driven 100 miles. When they inquired about the way to Red Spire, they found that it was almost the only house in the village that was bombed during the war. They then drove along the coast and eventually past the entrance and lodge of Encombe at the seawall at Sandgate. In the Folkstone area they turned and went along the Ashford to London road.

After Maidstone they decided not to go to the Oast house at Trottiscliffe because of the heavy Sunday traffic, as people were returning from the weekend at the coast.

At 8.30 p.m., when the Buick drew up at Lyne, they had driven 200 miles.

> O. did not get out, but stayed sitting in the car. The others were by now a little prepared and accepted this more quietly and passively than before. Only when he seemed to suggest that the steps of the porch were many and difficult, did they drive through the garden to the door of the Green Drawing Room. Miss R. drew the curtains and they looked straight from the car into the brightly lighted room, with a fire burning and two cats and the Persian miniatures and new pictures of Moscow on the walls. O. looked with great interest, then remarked:
>
> 'No, I don't believe in it!'

They drove round further and looked into the best dining room where the zakouska was all laid out – as if in a stage set waiting for actors who had missed their cues.

But this was not satisfactory and they returned to the porch again. After about an hour and a half of such manoeuvres, Miss R., who was running from one door to another begging O. to come in, was almost in tears. R. too, understanding better than the rest the intense physical discomfort and exhaustion that he must be suffering after twelve hours sitting in one position, without food or drink, without moving, and with his painful sickness, began to worry, fearing that he had lost the power to move his legs.

So he aroused vexation in those with him – in one from compassion with his suffering, in another that the carefully prepared supper should spoil, in a third from physical impatience at the enforced immobility. It was at this time that he seemed to begin to do all he could to be 'unreasonable,' striving in every way to make his companions vexed with him and set them against him. For this was a test of them – to bring them to a state where they could give up every impulse of self-will and accept all. Only when one observed, it was seen that every 'unreasonableness' and every test was at the cost of his own suffering.

But this he completely hid. As through all the rest of those weeks, so great was his self-control that one could be close by him yet widen the impression that he was quite at ease. Only by a definite effort of imagination and sympathy could one come to realise what he must, for purely physical reasons, be suffering. And when one did, one had to accept this also and not rebel against it.

At this point Ouspensky appeared very cheerful and now and then laughed, seemingly at himself and his weak condition. From Rodney Collin's perspective, Ouspensky seemed to have undertaken a task, making demands upon himself, not yet seeing the outcome of it. Still at twelve o'clock in the evening he was vigorous, cheerful and laughed several times, whilst the others were petering out or exhausted. Once again Ouspensky wanted to 'move' and they drove off. This time to the Wheatsheaf. When they came back he studied the house from all sides. He was not content, so once more they took off, this time to Guildford. When they arrived at Lyne again, Ouspensky declared that he would not enter the house – not before morning.

Many times during the night the rest fell asleep. O. would leave them for a little and then cry out:

'Move, move. We must move from here'.

Then they would drive off for ten miles or so, return, doze for twenty minutes and set off again. Sometimes Miss R. came, sometimes Yosh; sometimes Miss P. was in the porch to greet them and sometimes not. But all night and indeed from then on until he was driven by exhaustion to his room, it was always:

'We must move! We cannot stay here, I had to move, had to, you understand? We must decide I begin not to like Lyne... Move, move... It is too late to go back now...'

So that there seemed constantly before them the sense of some unknown quest of great urgency and which it was the utmost danger to ignore.

Rodney Collin had by this time begun to feel that Ouspensky had started to accomplish something relative to his determined efforts and seemed ready to go on. To urge him to rest, eat or in any way change his behaviour seemed to him strangely pointless. Helped by Collin and Miss R. Ouspensky eventually came to the drawing room. Supported by Miss. R's arm he was walking around and taking in impressions of various objects in the rooms with the utmost detailed interest: Persian miniatures, photographs, small boxes, a picture from Moscow, they all were intensely studied. At about seven thirty in the morning, he returned to the Green Room from a short walk in the garden where he had studied the house, the sky, and the cedar tree. In the Green Room he studied all the pictures and other objects with the same intensity and detailed interest. Still early in the morning, Ouspensky then wanted to gather all the people in the house, but either they could not be found or they would not come.

"Well we must decide," he said.

Rodney Collin, who had carefully watched Ouspensky's gestures asked: "About the house?"

He replied: "About the house of course – everything depends on that."

Turning to Miss P. he asked her: "What is this place?"

She said: "Lyne Place."

He asked her: "What is it connected with?"

All the places and events of the last days still in their minds, she answered: "It is connected with everything."

He said: "Thats it – exactly."

It became clear during a conversation this morning about the houses they had been visiting that Gaddesden had been left out. Five minutes after, someone asked him if he wanted to go there, and he had said:

"Yes, of course."

He was back in the car again.

8.30 a.m., Monday, September 15th, Rodney Collin, Miss R., Ouspensky and R. left Lyne, this time heading for Gaddesden. They were obviously affected by the night's intense activities and impressions, when after one hour they got to West Wickham. Gaddesden had altered a lot, having become a girl's school. The lodge-keeper allowed them to drive to the playground, and eventually they were also able to enter the house, after speaking with the headmistress who said:

"How terrible it must be for you to see your old house like this – but the children really love it."

Ouspensky replied: "Very glad, very glad."

They returned by Carshalton and Esher, where they stopped and got out of the car. Sweaty and his clothing disarranged, Ouspensky walked very slowly backwards and forwards in the grass, and now and then got in and out of the car. Every step obviously demanded considerably efforts. The others were now calm and tranquil and accepted whatever occurred without resistance. By eleven they were back at Lyne where they picnicked in the car for an hour or two, parked in front of the drawing room, in an atmosphere characterized by "an extraordinary sense of peace and freedom."

When Ouspensky finally entered the house, he had been in the car almost permanently for 24 hours. To Collin these efforts were a consequence of an active will, able to penetrate the body's own limitations and attain the unattainable. Ouspensky and the small nucleus who encircled him had been challenged both psychologically and physically over an extended period.

It is understandable that they therefore chose to rest on September 16th.

Early morning on September 17th, when Ouspensky, Rodney Collin, R. and Miss R. were seated in a taxi, already ordered by Mrs. M., Ouspensky said: "Go the same way."

They first drove to the Dell at Sevenoaks. Without getting out of the car they sat watching the house and its immediate surroundings. After ten minutes they drove further to the Oast house at Trottiscliffe. Ouspensky seemed willing to travel further, but they could not conclude where to go from the various suggestions. When somebody suggested Encombe, O. replied:

"But why? That is what must be understood."

When Rodney Collin suggested that they should go home and think again, O. replied: "It is too late for that now."

It seems that this answer was a turning-point for Collin. He started to see where all these expeditions were leading. They turned back at 5 p.m. and were home by 8 p.m., but without leaving the car. They all sat, smoking, and later Mrs. R. brought them coffee and sandwiches. After a time, the taxi-driver contacted the taxi owner, as Ouspensky refused to leave the vehicle.

Collin observed that: "At another time it would have been the climax of his 'unreasonableness' but now it had no power to touch those who were with him."

No protest or explanations from the owner helped, Ouspensky totally ignored him. Finally, the owner, who had become silent and accepted the situation as beyond his power, left, taking the driver with him. After a while sitting watching the stars, it seemed that the atmosphere in the car shifted. Ouspensky became cheerful and it became possible for each of them to ask their innermost questions.

R. asked: "How can one find real I?"

He answered: "By making demands on oneself. I show you the way."

Then he approved Miss R. when she asked about physical demands.

"How shall I cast out fear?" Miss P. asked.

He said to her: "Realise that you have no existence."

Rodney Collin had no question but said: "I feel that though great forces are against us, there are also forces in our favour."

"I did not quite find that," replied Ouspensky.

Then turning to R. he cried as though there were something to be very pleased about: 'What do you say to that Roles?'

R. did not answer but spoke of something else.

One of Ouspensky's cats, Yosh, was laying between Miss P. and him.

P. said: "You said cats have astral bodies."

O. said: "Yes."

P.: "Are they born with them?"

O.: "No, kittens don't have."

P.: "Only grown cats?"

O.: "Yes."

P.: "Do dogs have astral bodies?"

O.: "Some dogs, but all cats."

P.: "The cat was a sacred animal."

O.: "Yes."

P.: "A magical animal."

O.: "Yes."

Every phrase seemed also to refer to men and to them and to the possibility of creating a new body, the greatest mystery of all. They were laughing and he suddenly said: 'If you have an astral body you must not laugh; laughter destroys something.'

It seems that at some point an intense situation arose that, at least apparently, was disconnected from the previous conversations.

Ouspensky said: "Evremov was connected with black magic." In the next moment all of a sudden: "What have you been doing all this time? Why! Confess, confess!"

Ouspensky was not only speaking louder and clearer and more excited than before but sounded both pleased and surprised.

Thinking that Ouspensky was speaking to Rodney Collin, R. turned to Collin and said while laughing:

"What have you been doing so bad?"

But Ouspensky had been speaking past Collin as if to someone invisible. He continued in a cheerful mood:

"Do you notice anything this evening?"

Rodney Collin who at this moment could not see him as he was looking forward and out of the window then heard:

"Evremov was connected with magic. He was a master of murder."

When someone exclaimed incredulously Ouspensky said:

"Yes, they think nothing of murder."

When Miss P. said that she experienced the situation as a miracle and series of dress rehearsals for an unknown play, Ouspensky said:

"This is not dress rehearsal. This is not miracle. This is preparation for preparation for a miracle."

He said more. A miracle had to happen. As it was, he knew exactly what each of them would do and say. They were all personal people. Now they had all to be different. They had to move from the place where they were. Movement, movement was what was necessary. And he added, in some unknown connection: 'Machine-guns were what made them move.'

After a long pause, Rodney Collin collected the Buick and parked it beside the taxi. As Ouspensky was about to leave the taxi, he again sat back in his seat. Then again – the same over and over again. Only after half an hour was he eventually seated in the Buick. Then, several times, he went back in the taxi. When they finally drove off it was about half past one. After an apparently short trip, with no particular direction, they were back, and Collin parked in front of the Green Room. For approximately two hours they, now and then, moved slowly around the house and to various places on the property. After some time R. got angry and said:

"You will wake everyone up."

Collin answered: "That is the ideal."

They drove to the farmyard one hour before dawn and filled up with petrol. Once all were seated the atmosphere altered:

O. made them count many times how many they were, say who they were. He made them get out of the car many times, each time counting to see that everyone was there, each time saying the names, until they were somehow aware of the presence of all at once.

At a certain point, when Ouspensky had asked them how many there is room for in the car, and they had told him that there was room for one more, Rodney Collin was sent to collect N., who was roused from bed to join them. When he came Ouspensky asked him:

"How did it all begin?"

But Collin did not understand and said nothing. Over and over Ouspensky made them count how many they were. When at last they were all sitting in the car again, he asked:

"How many cats?"

Miss R. answered: "Three."

He asked: What is their order?"

And she named them by the time they had been in the household:

"First cat, second cat, third cat."

Then he said: "Remember all must be in order – one, two, three."

Then he asked them finally: "How many are here?"

And they said: "Six and three cats."

He said: "There should be many more."

Then he said: "You must start again. You must make a new beginning. How many do you want?"

They said: "Twenty."

He said: "First six, then twenty, then add twenty more, then we see."

He said: "Remember to make of it something very big." And he said again: "Continue to be brave."

Then he got out of the car. There was a high brick wall: he hit it with his fist and cried to them: "Go through there."

It seems obvious that Ouspensky's economy with words was part of the form of his concealed language intended to break and unchain one's former associations and to make way for a possible new understanding. It is natural to assume that gestures, tone of voice, and facial expressions must also have been elements of what constituted an atmosphere that contributed to convey his directives. Bearing this in mind can help us avoid the pitfall of concluding that, merely from reading about it, one could understand what really took place. However it seems difficult not to see the law of three and the lawfulness of the six triads reflected in Ouspensky's reference to the three cats when he first said:

"Remember all must be in order – one, two, three."

And then, with reference to a new beginning, he said: "First six."

It is unthinkable that Ouspensky's closest circle was unfamiliar with the idea that no change is possible unless three forces come into play, and that chance and hazard are a part of the game. They must likewise have been familiar with the six processes, and with the fact that predictability, or rather one's ability to manoeuvre, rely on the six possible combinations of the three forces. It seems that Ouspensky, relative to a new beginning, is pointing to the necessity for the right triads, as it is within the variety of combinations of triads that our actions are determined. We will later come back to more details about the concept of triads in the chapter which discusses *The Theory of Celestial Influence*.

A little later they all got back in the car except Ouspensky, who walked alone slowly in front. Soon Rodney Collin got out and offered him his arm. Together they walked very slowly as each step for Ouspensky was obviously a painful strain. After about fifteen yards Collin, who could not bear to see how he suffered, asked:

"Need there be any more?"

Ouspensky, who still held his arm tight, said: "Don't you wish to learn?"

Collin said: "Yes."

Collin was almost terrified as Ouspensky's "face was terrible with the efforts in the first light of the dawn, grotesque with glasses and hat, as though it had nothing to do with the tremendous will and spirit that were almost tangible."

Shortly after, when they had proceeded with the slow walking, Ouspensky asked Collin:

"Do you understand that everything can only be done by effort, or do you think that things can happen right?"

Rodney Collin said: "I don't understand that things can only be done by effort. I think they can happen right."

They kept on walking step by step, Ouspensky moving in a feeble and unsteady way and several times almost falling while sweating from his forehead. Holding him with both arms after he was about to fall again, Rodney Collin said:

"Now I understand. It is enough... May the car come?"

After this Ouspensky allowed the car to come, but now it would not start. Slowly they advanced step by step towards the vehicle. Once there, Ouspensky collapsed in the front seat leaning over the control panel. Collin got into the car but had to use the weight of his body to thrust Ouspensky's further in before slamming the door.

Then he said to Collin: "Drive them all."

Once they reached the front drawing room they parked and remained in the car. After a pause Ouspensky told him:

"Remember, you may have this, have that, but cat doesn't change. There's something which doesn't alter. Before I spoke of big, now I speak of small."

When R. expressed his gratefulness for what he had done and given them and mentioned the System, Ouspensky replied:

"System is only language to hang cat on."

Again he insisted that a new beginning was necessary because: "All was such muddle that nothing worse could come," and pointed at the necessity to do what they could by telling them to start from both big and small.

After a pause, speaking of himself he said: "I did nothing. I was not strong enough. I only spoiled everything. I know that. Perhaps it will be better."

Rodney Collin then said: "Surely only results will show whether things were spoiled or not."

Ouspensky told him: "What you call results means nothing. You can do something. You have something."

Half an hour later Ouspensky wanted to move again. Night had turned into day, it was a sunny morning and with Rodney Collin behind the wheel they drove very slowly through the area of Chobham Common.

Collin had had nothing to eat or drink since lunch the day before, but still experienced this trip to be extraordinary, beautiful and clear.

Now they realised what all the movement of the last days meant, what it meant to be roused in the middle of the night, again and again, to 'move', 'move', to move at all costs, not worrying whether one can know in advance the place that one will come to.

Around two hours later they came back to Lyne where they had coffee and cakes in the car before entering the Green Room. There they were, five people sharing an atmosphere permeated with their new understanding. Afterwards they had lunch in the Green Drawing Room before calling the rest of the people at Ouspensky's request. All together they were 15 people. Those who had been with Ouspensky all night spoke briefly about what he had told them to do. How a few people must reconstruct everything, and of the necessity of being brave from the beginning. It became possible to see reconstruction in the perspective of a man's whole life, everything he had been told and learned and come across in the right order. All his experience. Later when they all had gone and they were alone Rodney Collin asked:

"Is it that everything should continue just as it is now; but within that, twenty people must begin from the very beginning, to reconstruct everything?"

Ouspensky replied: "Let it be like that."

When Ouspensky constantly subjected himself to further painful activities, such as long meetings and exhausting road trips, it can be thought of as part of his preparations to be able to master the stresses between his impending death and possible birth. It is difficult to imagine a more thorough and fundamental preparation than by creating an absolute distinction between the negative sensations of the body and the positive emotions associated with a deliberately intentional acceptance of one's life situation.

CHAPTER 9
The Curtain of Time Grows Thin

Our ordinary perception of time is confined and limited by our senses which are bound to operate in three dimensions, and our ordinary thinking about time is inextricably linked to and limited by these perceptions. Einstein's Theory of Relativity showed that time is not an absolute in itself, but relative to the observer. The way we usually conceive time is along a horizontal line determined by the three points: before, now and after. This is the line of fourth dimension. If we conceptualise that multiple lines, perpendicular to this line, designate NOW for some moments, we will see that each of these moments has a continual NOW. This is the fifth dimension.

Seeing the problem of time in perspective of dimensions allows us to think differently, beyond our ordinary categories. As our senses are a part of our psychic functions, linked to our psychology and consciousness, it follows that an expanded consciousness may change our relation to time. Expanded consciousness relative to time would facilitate a further exploration of aspects of time. When F. Schiller refers in his letters to the necessity of a certain kind of consciousness in order to be able to experience beauty, he is referring to the same dynamics and lawfulness, not in regards to time as such, but to aesthetics.[1]

In *The New Model of The Universe*, Ouspensky points out that we are under the influence of the existence of other times, both the parallel and the perpendicular, and that it enters our consciousness, though we are unaware of it. Becoming aware would then include the possibility of rearrangement and change. Viewed in this perspective many of Ouspensky's strange and mysterious remarks, particularly those referring to Evremov, can be united with his deliberate attempt to achieve some completely new level for himself while in touch with moments outside linear time.

One strange incident recalled by Rodney Collin was at the beginning of the second meeting held at Colet House in 1947. Ouspensky said:

"Some time we were meeting in New York. It was interesting because somehow it happened that many people came that I knew before. You

---

[1] Rudolf Steiner, *The Redemption of Thinking* (London: Hodder and Stoughton Ltd., 1956), 14.

know I was only six weeks in New York. People that I met in Petersburg – and they all happened to collect this day in New York ..."

He was then interrupted with an irrelevant question before he, after a short pause, continued:

"I thought of what I was going to say. It was interesting. I met many people I didn't expect. Several people quite unexpectedly without knowing one another and they met. Most of them I met in Petersburg. All sorts. Or two or three. Well, I wanted to begin in that way ..."

Neither Rodney Collin nor Miss Q. could remember any such meeting.

But Collin was reminded by this of an earlier incident that he found strange, taking place the first year in America, and that Ouspensky several times referred to. Only accompanied by his dog, a Great Dane named Helka, Ouspensky used to sit alone at the head of the table in the dining room at Franklin Farm. One day he told Collin that all his old friends from all his periods of life had come to see him – people from Petersburg and Moscow. Although Collin was uncertain whether this was the meeting Ouspensky was referring to or not, it seemed to him that this was a definite exercise in preparation for recurrence. He had even, on one occasion, found a table plan on a torn up paper where Ouspensky had placed himself at the head of the table and written the names of those he often referred to in anecdotes of his past on either side of the table.

He had many times heard him speaking of directly finding the source of esoteric knowledge in his next life. On the various occasions he had spoken of a character he called Evremov. Sometimes in loose sentences and sometimes in longer passages. This brought about an atmosphere where his closest circle felt they were most intensely facing a mystery of the unknown.

When Ouspensky had spoken of Evremov in the car late at night on September 17th, and told them of this master of murder who was connected with black magic, they could not make any sense of it. In the evening after they returned from Cobham Common he also mentioned Evremov, just as incomprehensibly. He had pointed at a picture of Moscow and told them that he and his grandmother were there and that she had expected him at the age of five to know everything about serious questions including death. Then he told them that Madame might have been there, but also Evremov. There had been the Evremov who lived earlier at Lyne, a quiet elderly railway engineer, a freemason, and a very old friend of Ouspensky, who gave Russian lessons to some people and who died in 1943. Certainly, Ouspensky had said of this Evremov:

"There's a person whom nobody takes any notice of – but he has more than anyone."

Yet there seemed at first no possibility of connection between the two. Ouspensky's characterisation of Evremov as a master of murder came to be understood as relating to the destruction of individual personality through some magical ritual. Even though there were indications, from later conversations, about the identity of Evremov not being the Evremov of Lyne, it was ambiguous.

In the morning of September 18th, Ouspensky told Rodney Collin in a private conversation to write to Madame Ouspensky and describe everything that had happened, adding:

"It was strange that Evremov should come. Tell Madame about him, she will understand."

When Collin asked him from where Evremov had come and to which period or phase he belonged the answers were vague and fleeting. Sometimes it could seem that he belonged to the work-period 1916-1917 in Moscow or Petersburg, at other times he could have been a freemason of some unclear period.

On September 20th he again spoke of Evremov, he said:

"Who was it who saw Madame yesterday? A man saw Madame and he told her about me and everything and Madame promised him she would come. He was Russian man. He came from Church – no, from that place – New York."

Miss R. said: "Do you mean Evremov?"

O.: "Probably. That man knew my mother and my grandmother and all Peter's people."

(Peter seemed sometimes to refer to himself and sometimes to Peter the Great.)

Miss R.: "Mr. O. I believe you see things in different time, out of time. The man you described must be very old if he knew your mother and your grandmother. You said he taught them and they taught you ... (pause) ... I believe that man was you and that you taught your grandmother."

O.: "Probably. You think of me and Evremov. Evremov dead – or not dead."

Miss P.: "Does that mean that when someone is strong enough, they do not disappear when they die and they can keep about and be seen by some people? ... And do people who have real knowledge have to be born, in some sort of way, from people who also have real knowledge – of a sort of 'direct blood' from someone else who knows?"

O.: "Yes, it is like that."

Miss R.: "Did your mother and grandmother have real knowledge?"

O.: "Partial knowledge. The man in the village was religious man ..."

Miss P: "It reminds me of the rhyme:

'Yesterday upon the stair,

I met a man who was not there;

He was not there again today,

How I wish he'd go away!' "

O.: "Yes, but sometimes he comes back!"

When Rodney Collin, several days later, asked him whether his grandmother was a highly developed or extraordinary woman, he told him that she was not, but was, as some women are, a channel. After this conversation Collin had a strong and intense feeling that there are periods in time where very high energy is collected and accumulated in order to be distributed to esoteric work on a large scale across time to people in need. It also struck him that it could be possible for extraordinary developed men to likewise cross time if they had somewhere to perch. And that certain women could provide a point for such reception. He seemed certain that Ouspensky's grandmother had this capacity.

On September 25th Collin experienced a strong emotional state where he felt that he understood how Evremov could belong to several different periods of time: to the period of Peter the Great, Ouspensky's childhood with his grandmother, to his period in Petersburg when he was initiated to Work, and to the appearance in the car in present time. Evremov and Ouspensky seemed to him to not be different, but still not the same. Questions about Ouspensky's grandmother's role in relation to each of them arose in him, but also the questions why and how Ouspensky alternately taught his grandmother and was taught by her.

In conjunction with this, Rodney Collin saw Ouspensky's efforts to be aimed at an earlier and different connection with esoteric knowledge, next time – in recurrence – sidestepping Gurdjieff.

CHAPTER 10
Admitting The Existence Of Miracles

It was after the night spent with Ouspensky in the car between September 17th and 18th that he found it more and more difficult to describe the events that took place in an objective way, and it gradually became problematic to define, express and transmit the range of meaning he made available:

> *They began to understand things which he wished to convey to them without being told: or in single sentences and phrases they would see some extremely subtle and illuminating significance, which they knew very well they could never have invented for themselves. Moreover, they began to feel every gesture and situation as meaningful, just as they are in a play, where nothing is introduced which does not relate directly to the plot. Sometimes again, people and even common objects, seemed to them to be demonstrating the laws of three or seven. And in the whole situation they gained the impression that O. was doing in some normally inconceivable way, moving, arranging, combining and experimenting with human material without any visible or audible direction.*

It seemed to be an indispensable factor in Ouspensky's operation and purpose that nothing said or done could be reduced to any concept that later could be revealed directly to others. Nor could it be counterchecked. That this increased communication was largely due to thought transference was indubitable to Rodney Collin. Already in the middle of August he was having experiences in this direction.

In the early summer he had decided to bring together all he understood about the enneagram. At the end of July, while writing, focusing on a specific aspect, he saw how his writing took an unexpected turn, bursting the boundaries of his original plan and embracing a greater perspective. He experienced that his own ideas were displaced in favour of new ideas that pushed forward. New ideas far beyond his own would enter him in the midst of the ordinary daily activities as he was walking in the fields, taking the train, or sitting on the underground. Later, while sitting at his desk, these new and often complicated ideas would evolve and expand in his own mind. To him it seemed that the original impulses entering him were broad abstract ideas that became furnished and completed through his own understanding.

When he later shared his experience with Ouspensky it became clear that he was well aware of his project. Before that, Collin did not know where these ideas came from and certainly had not seen Ouspensky as their source. The transmission of ideas and instructions through thought transference after September 18th apparently became more intensified and extensive. Formerly it took place in Ouspensky's immediate presence, but gradually it reached a quality where distance became insignificant. The recipient, on the other hand, had not only to have a wish to understand, but also to keep an unflagging attention in order to grasp what was conveyed. Inner criticism, doubt or any other negative attitude would consume and eradicate this influence. That this was groundwork and preparation for receiving thoughts was beyond doubt to Collin. Ouspensky, who each day brought forward new and remarkable instances, engendered gradually more and more energy.

Several of the conversations that took place in the Green Room at Lyne on September 19th were viewed by Rodney Collin and others of the small group in the perspective of thought-transference. These conversations also reflected a relationship to time beyond the ordinary linear conception, impossible to understand from an ordinary way of thinking, but creating the psychological ambience necessary for the adventure to ever new levels of understanding for the participants:

> ... from time to time those who listened did understand and both Miss P. and Miss R. would suddenly express astonishing formulations of ideas absolutely new to all of them. Miss R. herself spoke of speaking 'without knowing where it came from' and to her hearers the ideas and even the manner and clarity of their expression then had nothing to do with the Miss R. with whom they were familiar.

None of them were unfamiliar with the idea of making efforts but through efforts made individually in this atmosphere a deeper understanding of its necessity unfolded. One of the consequences of this was not only that a power was reinforced throughout the whole house, but it laid a necessary foundation for Ouspensky's further accomplishment.

When one of them spoke of the necessity of committing to such a demand that would keep her awake for the rest of her life. Ouspensky said:

"Quite right. Gradually you all come to the same conclusion."

ADMITTING THE EXISTENCE OF MIRACLES

At this point, it appears that those who were already initiated and those who were still on a preparatory level were largely exposed to the same impulses, but every now and then with some individual aspects. Clues, hints and signs given to an individual invariably revolved around their potential, and the availability of this inherent potential. To one person, however, he said:

"Something was got for you, but now it has disappeared."

During this same period he would, apparently without any prompting and often in the middle of a conversation, cry out loud:

"Remember big line …" or "Big aim … big line …"

And he had no patience with people who would ask certain questions about knowledge, how to relieve suffering, or any aspect of organisation, etc.

On September 20th he continued this uncompromising behaviour but now he took it to unprecedented heights. Throughout the day, from morning to evening, he shouted: "Aim." Whether they sat together in silence, or in the middle of a meal, or when someone would fetch something for him, this small circle of people would hear his loud and penetrating voice shout, without a hint of warning: "Aim, aim …"

What in the world had happened? What was going on? This was the man who already in 1912 had written *Tertium Organum*, exploring the fourth dimension through mathematical concepts and building a bridge between eastern mysticism and Western rationalism. Then in 1914 he published *A New Model of The Universe*, presenting the principles of the psychological method in its application to problems of science, religion and art. And not to forget his legendary book, *In Search of The Miraculous*, a 'tour de force', which later would, like no other book, help to make the Fourth Way accessible to countless people. And now, at Lyne Place, in September 1948, Ouspensky had collected all his experiences, narrowed them down, shrunk them to a size less than a nickel, and put them into action. His concoctions did not fail to have an impact on those present:

> *… all gradually came together into one single impression which possessed their minds day and night.*

Then, once more, Ouspensky removed the distinction between day and night by having meals served at the most inconceivable times, sit for some time and then go back to bed. To Rodney Collin this led to a state where everything was coming together as if it were a continuous experience and where one was living in two worlds at the same time, "one old and familiar, the other utterly unknown and mysterious."

Although it is difficult, not to say impossible, to understand the situation at Lyne in this period, one of the many marvellous events there may still serve as an attempt at illustration. One morning, when several people were gathered, Miss R. perceived them as the planets of the planetary body-types, set in an enneagram structure, and how it was imperative to a certain work in progress for them to be arranged in the right order.

With pen and paper, she tried to figure out this order. She saw Rodney Collin as Mercury, Miss P. as Venus, R. as Mars, and Ouspensky as Jupiter. When she spoke to Collin about this he told her that she herself was the Moon. She felt very strongly that something was not right, that something was missing. In that very moment she saw Ouspensky making a gesture to a place beside him on the sofa, saying sharply: "Take it." Immediately she now not only saw that the empty seat was Miss Q's missing place in the enneagram circle, but that all the people present filled the other planetary points. The triangle in this enneagram was filled with the three cats present.

All the people continually exposed to Ouspensky's influence had equally strange experiences in this same period, coloured by and in accordance with their individual nature. Passing through the remarkable circumstances of this time, Rodney Collin experienced again and again innumerable instances and patterns of what he found to be definite stages in a process of initiation conducted by Ouspensky, as when:

> ... personality was brought to the surface and accentuated to the highest degree, preparatory to being destroyed.

Where Collin himself:

> ... began to act and pose with extraordinary arrogance, 'like a cross between an Indian rajah and the Grand Lama.'

One of his features and capacities was his ability to record. When this feature was controlled by personality:

> ... it gave rise to pride of authorship, intense belief in his exclusive way of interpreting scenes and events and thus to lying and the colouring of accounts to justify himself and bolster his own importance.

He saw how he and others had three ways of meeting these temptations and opportunities. One either fell into the temptation where personality took advantage of what it liked, or one recognised the temptation and tried to resist it with more or less success. A third option, he recognised, was by accepting the temptation without reservation it became transmuted and brought an insight that was his real course, the course for which he existed. This third way he found possible only when personality was stripped by the numerous experiences he had withstood and he was filled with aspiration or an unshakable faith in Ouspensky's purpose.

This purpose had two aspects: to raise his own level, and to provide a process that would enable his closest students to raise theirs and completely transcend their old life and nature if, and only if, they could reciprocate. Miss R. played a significant role in this commencement, as she had a clear awareness of psychic influences. For Collin, her traits were a two-edged sword. When her innate sensitivity was combined with fear and ignorance, she became superstitious and her actions became irrational, in order to bypass imaginary dangers or attract imaginary luck. On the other hand there were occasions where her confidence in Ouspensky was so complete and impersonal that she was able to extract from his indication influences that bypassed the ordinary level of awareness and thus become a tool to expose 'miracles' to the small group around Ouspensky that she herself was part of.

CHAPTER 11
The Drama Unravels

In the afternoon of September 23rd Ouspensky called Rodney Collin to his bedroom and said "Look after all the cats. They are in your care." The previous evening Collin had tried, through some special efforts, to expand his understanding in a particular area and was determined to continue with this as he withdrew to the Best Dining Room at eleven o'clock. But this evening he lacked emotional force and it came to nothing.

About two o'clock he and Miss P. fetched R. and all three went to Ouspensky's bedroom. A little earlier Miss P. had become aware of Ouspensky's discomfort and her benevolence had overcome her fear of his resistance. The three of them, working together, lifted him, changed his pyjamas and bed clothes, and made him as comfortable as possible. To begin with he resisted and opposed, but accepted help when he saw that they would not relent.

When it was over, and the fire made up, they began to realise many things which they hitherto had failed to understand, and at last tried to see through his eyes rather than their own. They realised that it had been a principle for him to refuse to ask the slightest service which might alleviate his discomfort. He had made it his rule to accept everything. He accepted the physical weakness which prevented him changing his clothes, he accepted the incontinence of his illness, he accepted the discomfort, dirt and repugnance of old age and decay – he accepted all this to the utmost, with all its consequences, not attempting to mitigate it in the slightest. Indeed, he seemed deliberately to accentuate it. In a way almost incomprehensible to ordinary people, he accepted suffering. This was evidently part of his plan. At the same time he would shout and violently resist any who attempted to make things easier for him.

Up till now those who wished to do so had been immediately deterred by this apparently violent reaction. But now Miss P. had shown that when real and heartfelt sympathy simply ignored this resistance, he accepted all, and could at last be given some comfort. And they suddenly understood, to their remorse, that it was their own fear which had kept him in physical misery and them from serving him and from the understanding which might follow.

Rodney Collin and the two others spent most of that night in his bedroom and from that time decided to stay alongside him as much as possible. A little later during this period they would come to discover new and hidden sides of him. His behaviour became much clearer in light of a dream he had told them about at Mendham in 1946, in which he, as a newborn, could not speak but knew everything. It also came to mind now what he had said to a guest at Mendham during the same period:

"Have you ever thought what it like to be born? You are a little baby – you cannot speak, you cannot arrange anything. What will you do?"

Ouspensky's infantile phrases, his unintelligible language, assumed helplessness, now made some sense:

It was as though he was intentionally acting the part of a baby, learning how to live as the baby he soon expected to be.

They started to see that his rejection of help and needed comfort in one perspective was 'pantomime of infancy'. His ability to arrange his surroundings with invisible direction, his transmitting of thoughts and his speechless instructions, all pointing in the direction of preparation for the helpless condition of lying in a cradle. To Collin and the others of the small nucleus there seemed to be no doubt that Ouspensky's recurrence, in a sense, had already begun. Rodney Collin spent most of the night in Ouspensky's bedroom, together with Miss P. and R., as Ouspensky now was so sick that he needed more or less constant attendance. The day after, Friday, September 24th, he did not leave his room. A kitten that he a few days earlier had asked them to find was now brought to his room. After watching it playing around the room for a while, he demanded that Miss R. and Miss P. should take responsibility for it. It was christened 'Aim'.

In the afternoon of September 24th, Collin had the inclination to go to Ouspensky's bedroom. He entered the room very deliberately and with no hesitation sat down on the edge of an armchair facing Ouspensky, who sat on the edge of his bed. They were only five or six feet apart. For a few minutes they were simply just sitting there. Then Ouspensky started to slowly move his hands, feet and head and then began to sway his body in various directions. All small movements. For some reason unknown to Collin he felt an impulse to repeat, reflect and echo Ouspensky's movements. Like in a mirror he duplicated every movement faithfully. This went on for some time and continued as Ouspensky rose from his bed and

Collin from the edge of the chair. Gradually Ouspensky's movements became more and more violent but Rodney Collin responded conscientiously, both to the movements themselves and their intensity. Ouspensky started to thrust energetically in various directions while his arms struck out, right and left. He was also punching in the direction of Collin who uninterruptedly mirrored him. All of a sudden Ouspensky, mortally sick with a sweating face and clothes so disarranged that they were falling from him, jumped upon him and grabbed him by the throat, shouting. Holding each other's throats and both shouting, the drama was raised to an unimaginable level:

> *... gesture for gesture and blow for blow. So that they fought there, and on the floor, and kicked each other in the face and chest, and wrestled, shouting and screaming, like a man fighting his own image.*

While all this was going on, Rodney Collin was able to let it ...

> *... pass without any shadow of personal feeling. Violent action and shouting and the sensations of blows received passed through him quite without inner reaction, and he looked out from his gesticulating body with complete calm. And at the moment when O. rushed on him, waving his arms and shouting with toothless mouth, he suddenly perceived him as an exact image of certain Tibetan deities in their wrathful or destroying aspect. It was not that he recalled or resembled such images: he actually was that.*

At the climax of this mirrored fight the old man rushed forward with a bowed head and their foreheads smashed together forcefully, over and over again. Miss P. had by this time left the room, disturbed and worried, but returned shortly after. R., originally seated on the floor, quietly watching, was now concerned of the possible medical implication of the battle, besides the risk of furniture and objects being demolished. Miss R., who had started to vaguely copy their movements, was still sitting on the floor.

When the battle calmed down, the three others in the room started to imitate, but uncertainly. Then they formed a closed circle round Ouspensky, holding him and each other. They started to move and eventually moved out of the room. After a while, when they came to the landing, Ouspensky's strength weakened, and they returned to the room again where they all rested peacefully.

When Miss R. said to Ouspensky that she thought he had fought with a devil he laughed and said: "A very small devil."

Rodney Collin later came to see the smashing of their heads together as a means for stimulating some inner organs, and also as an aid and ritual to transfer a definite substance from Ouspensky. The same afternoon he became aware that a new bond had been established between them.

Later, towards nightfall, sitting with Ouspensky's head relaxing upon his chest, he became aware of "strange feelings and premonitions" seemingly connected with the weight of his head towards the area of his heart. This experience enabled him see that Ouspensky now not only was dying, but that the new life was close by. The sentence: 'All must leave here to go through there' had gradually assembled inside him and he could see that it encompassed all his understanding of what he, two days earlier, had written about death and recurrence. While sitting there, something filled him, and he had no doubt that it was communicated by Ouspensky through the actual physical contact of his head resting upon his chest. There and then the following vision formed and entered his mind:

He found himself in a garden, most of his view filled by a great chestnut tree through which the sun was shining in a dappled pattern. At the same time he was aware that just over the garden wall was a street where horses and carriages were passing; and though he could not see them he was aware of the high Russian collars of the horses and of their carriage-bells ringing gaily. There was an extraordinary sense of gaiety and happiness about the whole vision, and he knew that quite close, at the end of the garden, was a house in which marriage-preparations were going on. Here the mother and father of O. would come, and in a short while he would be conceived.

All this had that quality of certain dreams, in which one sees a scene rather vaguely, but at the same time knows a great deal about it and what is happening there. The strongest impression, however, lay in the physical sense of midsummer, and in the air of extraordinary happiness, gaiety and innocence which suffused everything. Though it was only afterwards that calculation confirmed mid-June as the time of O's conception.

Collin's conviction that this vision was related to some form of communication that was due to their physical contact was unshakable. Just as their earlier ritual struggle had left a substance in his forehead, he later knew that a substance had been transferred to his heart region. Still laying with Ouspensky's head on his breast he experienced a variety of unfamiliar sensations. Miss R. told him at the time that she perceived the three of them as father, mother and son. The parts constituting the triad of creation.

In the evening, while holding Ouspensky's hand as he was laying still on his bed, breathing rapidly and very emotionally with short gasps, and now and then shouting hoarsely, Rodney Collin echoed his shouting. At a certain moment Ouspensky uttered, in a soft and down to earth tone:

"Don't shout."

Whereupon he immediately returned to his 'feverish panting' and continued with what Collin took to be an exercise. At the end of this scene Collin could hear several sounds, seemingly coming from Ouspensky's head, as if bones were snapping. That night Rodney Collin slept in an armchair in the study beside Ouspensky's bedroom. The sensation that something of Ouspensky had entered him was definite and he felt fundamentally changed. As he woke up several times during the night, he was able to verify that it had not left him and that it seemed to have a pivotal focus between his eyebrows. When he woke up in the morning, he wrote the following to Madame Ouspensky:

"He went to Southampton, then stopped, to make circumstances for something. All happened as it had to. He gave me something that he had. Now we begin. I would like to kiss your hand – you are necessary to him, us, it. Well, it may not be possible. Be glad."

He then went to Ouspensky's bedroom and showed it to him. After reading it very closely he said to him:

"What would the others make of it?"

Recognizing the possibility for the letter to create misunderstandings when read in an ordinary state it was decided not to send it. A little later, when they were both seated on Ouspensky's bed, Collin entered a highly emotional state while looking at all the pictures on the wall. It was as if he could see into Ouspensky's life through them. Focusing on one particular motif of an empty street, he felt some great significance connected to this picture. When he asked what happened there, Ouspensky said:

"Murder in Petersburg."

Then Rodney Collin recognised two fearful and hesitating people in the street he said:

"They were very frightened. Could they not go somewhere safe?"

Ouspensky replied: "Where else could they go?"

From all this Collin could see connections with Ouspensky's initiation in Petersburg, supposedly by Gurdjieff, and that the persons in the street were Ouspensky and possibly Madame, while murder referred to the death of their old selves. He then came to remember the passage from *In Search of the Miraculous* taking place in Finland, and the undefined decision that Gurdjieff had put to Ouspensky there. Collin said:

"I thought that happened in Finland?"

Ouspensky then tossed his head a little and said: "Finland! That was mild!"

After a moment, he added: "No, it was in Petersburg."

In Finland, during conversation, Gurdjieff had, without words, put some question in front of Ouspensky, to which Ouspensky had replied. Rodney Collin now experienced the same phenomena, as a large part of their conversation comprised "an extraordinary range of half-glimpsed perceptions in which ordinary ideas of space and time played no part." He now, from the disjointed scraps of talk, felt not only that his understanding had reached a higher level, but that Ouspensky's own initiation could be seen in a considerably clearer light.

During the further conversation Ouspensky revealed detailed information about his grandmother that clarified to Collin Miss R.'s role in all this as a connection, channel and transmitter of information. As the drama now unfolded, Rodney Collin experienced a completion of his intimacy with Ouspensky, and he felt himself to be "a kind of Siamese twin in some psychic sense." A little later, in support of the other people's wish to make Ouspensky a little more comfortable, sitting on Ouspensky's bed he said:

"You must be bathed this morning."

Ouspensky then replied: "That refers to second: what is in you is seventh."

It apparently puzzled Collin that he, in his heightened state, couldn't immediately grasp the entire meaning, but it seemed to him that Ouspensky was pointing at his former attempts to transmit consciousness and that this last transmission was the seventh. However, he remained uncertain:

> ... *whether this meant that he himself represented O.'s seventh experiment, he could not be sure, and if so, he did not understand what it could mean that O.'s own physical body was 'second'.*

Still feeling the inextricable connectedness of having become Ouspensky's offspring in some psychic sense, he asked him what had happened to the others.

"Some died, some disappeared," he said.

A little later Collin, with himself in mind, asked:

"And do you watch over what happens to them?"

"Not necessarily," he answered.

Then a remarkable change took place. Rodney Collin experienced strongly that his former life had come to an end and that he had become a different man. His former identity had departed and disappeared. He had now become 'he'. He had become a different person. In this experience there was no room for pretence or artificiality. Having been occupied with the idea of recurrence for several weeks he asked:

What happens to the life of C-S? Where does it go?"

Ouspensky answered: "I do not know about that."

Collin then asked: "And his marriage, relation with his wife, all that must be made over again differently?"

"Yes," Ouspensky acknowledged.

It was right after this conversation that he went to his wife and told her without any pretence: "Your husband is dead. Make ready to marry again."

As a part of the process of his new body becoming linked to his physical body he now found that two points were already active. One between his eyebrows and one in his heart. He had a strong feeling that in order to fulfil the third connection, the sexual centre, an intense sexual act was necessary. After making love to his wife, "… it was as if to a woman he had never known before." He confirmed this necessity as: "… some psychic germination had been successfully completed."

As he left his room he was informed that a seat on a plane to America had become available the same afternoon. He went immediately to Ouspensky and sat down on his bed and said:

"Now I must go to Madame."

"Who goes to Madame?" shouted Ouspensky and in the next minute hit Rodney Collin several times in the face before he took a strangling grip around his throat.

After loosening the grip, he asked with a clear voice: "What happened?"

Collin was still laying on his back and looking at the ceiling when he answered: "A man was killed."

During the blows to his face and the strangling grip he felt a strange indifference and he had no reactions. He then was made to stand up-right and said loudly with a voice that was unfamiliar to him: "What must we do?" and then, "kill out the old man."

When he sat down again on the bed, he felt very tranquil. On an indication from Ouspensky, he rose from the bed and went over to Dr. Roles, who stood a few metres away, and hit him hard on his cheek before returning to Ouspensky's bedside again. An extraordinary gratitude and tide of love came over him and he put his arm around Ouspensky's shoulder. They looked at each other and smiled with great tenderness "the same smile".

In the midst of all this, weeping uncontrollably, sat Miss P. and Miss R. kneeling on the floor. Very quietly Ouspensky said to them:

"I cannot be accused," before he added, "Is it wrong?"

Miss R., still crying, answered: "Nothing is wrong."

A little later Ouspensky said aside to Collin in a lowered voice:

"He knew he was good for nothing."

After Ouspensky said: "Call someone," Dr. Roles fetched H.

When H. arrived he went down on his knees and looked both fearful and amazed. Ouspensky asked them all what had happened but only Miss P. could answer, saying that he had passed something of himself to Rodney Collin, adding: "the other must be killed."

Bitterly weeping she asked: "Is there a second chance?"

Very gently Ouspensky told her: "Why not?" before he took her hand.

When Miss R. offered Collin a glass of wine saying: "You are strong," he waved it away whilst Ouspensky added "nonsense," before telling the others to leave. Later, with reference to H., he said: "He saw nothing. He was not witness."

When the others had left, Collin was overwhelmed with such love and gratitude that it was almost unbearable. He kissed the hand of Ouspensky who looked at him with tenderness and said: "Do not thank me," before Rodney Collin went to his own room, crying.

CHAPTER 12
The Trip To Madame

After he returned to his room, his wife told him they had to leave for the airport in ten minutes. In these ten minutes, while dressing for the journey, he felt free and overwhelmed with pure emotions, but also helpless.

This was very different from what he had gone through in the recent phase. There had been no reason for hesitation, no problems, because there had been no alternative but 'to go on'. Each time he had said: "There is nothing else to do," and Ouspensky had nodded. Now his wife, leading the way to the car, even had to show him where to sit. He felt as though everything familiar was slipping away. He felt like a new-born child with no knowledge of who he was. What had formerly constituted parts of his identity had now simply slipped away. Name, position, past, family, friends, or any connections, had disappeared – all gone. Still he looked at his new surroundings with great interest.

At the airport, helpless and unable to make any decision, his wife had to organise everything, including his tickets, luggage, passport, and even choose which cake to put on his plate in the tea room. When he went alone through the gates into the customs hall, he was not anxious or fearful that something bad or unpleasant might happen because, whatever happened, it could not be wrong – but still he felt helpless. Being unable to make decisions, he found himself last in the queue and taking the last seat on the plane. This passivity was not a form of a one-sided indifference, he was actively facing all the impressions from his immediate surroundings. His incapacity to be active became particularly evident when he discovered the impossibility of any form of aggression. This extraordinary passivity and helplessness that Rodney Collin found himself in points clearly in one direction, that of infancy: "a new-born state, in which there is nothing to do but accept what comes."

During the flight to Shannon, a stop on the way to New York, he became aware of a change within. It began with the inclination to move and make gestures that Ouspensky had made during an exercise of continuous movements. It included an expression in Ouspensky's face, between the eyebrows, due to concentration of attention. And further:

At the same time there began to enter his mind thoughts and plans about the future, which were O.'s thoughts and plans. These thoughts seemed to him even at the time to be of different levels. Some referred to long-term plans of work on a large scale; others to his conduct in relation to individual people. He saw quite clearly how he had to establish contact with certain people, how and where he would speak to them, exactly what he would tell or ask them, in what words and voice, and so on. In this way he was shown the starting-point for a quite new and intentional relationship with them.

When he had first got on the plane in a state of new-born innocence, he was without thoughts and unable to make plans. Now, a few hours later, he was flooded with details of both and was not in the least doubt that this originated from Ouspensky. That there was no possibility of his old self returning was also clear, as he knew without question that he was not the old Rodney Collin-Smith. The following passage seems instructive relative to further understanding of the phenomena:

... the period immediately after the destruction of personality, when the learner is empty and stripped of all familiar means of communication and self-defence, may be a very dangerous one. At this time he is very vulnerable, and the possibility exists of his being attacked or acted upon by undesirable influences. It may therefore be necessary for the teacher literally to possess him, in order to prevent possession by other forces. At the same time this possession provides an opportunity for him to learn many things directly about the teacher's nature which could not be communicated in any other way. Many of the otherwise inexplicable things that had been done had evidently served to create a sufficiently intimate relation between teacher and pupil to make such 'possession' possible.

In particular he could now, by also accessing O.'s imagination, see a wider relation between the human O. and O. as an esoteric teacher.

When he landed at the airport, he walked with Ouspensky's gestures. He had a meal and found himself eating with traces of O.'s motions. These various manifestations of possession created a new and different relation to his body, as if it was out of adjustment. Being aware of the importance of not losing what had been passed on to him, he kept a strong concentration on a certain point between the eyebrows, knowing that this effort must not be relaxed. It also helped him to stay impartial and untouched by people around him. Although he could see that the possession had gradually started to fade after landing, he felt a complete confidence due to 'something' he felt to be present and which had to be preserved by an unflagging effort to keep his attention.

Walking down the waiting hall approaching the gate, he became aware of a female clerk whom he saw was about to involuntarily wake up. At the same time, he was completely aware that no others noticed anything.

Collin boarded the plane once more. Something delicate was attached to three points in Collin's body. For a while he was afraid that this connection could be interrupted by the frequency of the vibrations from the engines. He tried to make adjustments by changing his position, but when the pitch of the engines changed his fear subsided. Throughout the whole flight, O.'s possession continued.

After passing through Customs, he took a taxi to town, where he had breakfast. Around ten o'clock he finally took a taxi to Franklin Farms. An hour and a half later he rang the bell at the front door. When it was opened by a smiling woman who obviously recognized him, he ignored her and said:

"Will you please tell Madame that someone came to see her."

With this he by-passed her and went into Ouspensky's study in full accordance with what he had visualised in advance on the plane. When Miss E. and F. came to see him, he did not greet them because they obviously related to his former identity. Knowing that he was no longer Rodney Collin-Smith, it was of great importance to him that he did not respond to any references to Collin-Smith so that he could not return.

"I only came to see her: I will wait," he said, when F. started to make excuses for Madame.

The resulting silence had obviously aroused a strong emotional state in Miss E. When she asked about Ouspensky, Collin simply said:

"You must ask him. You should go to that man in England."

He could again see how all this was exactly in accordance with what he had preconceived on the plane.

Then Miss E. said to F.: "Something very extraordinary is happening at Lyne. I must go at once. Can you arrange it?"

When she asked Rodney Collin if they could travel together, he told her: "I have nothing to do with you. You go one way, I go another."

Again, all preconceived, as seen on the plane.

After sitting in silence for a long time, lunch was served. Then he told them that he wanted to be left alone. When F. eventually came to tell him that Madame was ready to see him, he had been walking with his arms stretched out in order to prepare himself, knowing that what would come would be challenging and very difficult. As he went into Madame's room, he closed the door in front of F.

When Rodney Collin entered the room, Madame was in bed. He went straight to her and kissed her hand.

"Don't come near me with those big eyes," she said with an expression of fear on her face.

"Mr. O. killed a man," he said as he sat down beside her.

Questioningly, Madame repeated what he had just said, to which he added: "You know what that means."

"What do you want of me?" she asked him.

He said: "He needs your help. You must come."

Madame told him: "You see me lying here. I am very ill. How can I come?"

Collin replied: "Not like that – next time, in recurrence."

She told him clearly: "Nobody can come between me and Mr. O. to speak of these things."

There was a pause before she added: "Why should I go back to all that? You don't know what I had to suffer all that time in my amour propre. Why should I bear that cross again? No."

Again she paused before saying: "You don't understand that Mr. G. is my teacher. Mr. O. was never my teacher – just a comrade in the work."

Regretting having spoken so freely, she attacked Collin for interfering and said it was typical of him to think that he could judge.

He simply said: "C-S doesn't exist. I don't know what you are talking about."

With uncertainty she kept speaking, but stopped a few minutes later. Then she said:

"I don't know what you want of me – an old woman, very near death. I count my life in days, not in weeks."

Collin replied: "He also."

Then she spoke about herself, before Collin said: "He is a very humble man," to which Madame replied:

"Very good that he became so at last," before she started to speak about him in critical terms.

Rodney Collin now felt that he was losing the grip of his mission to come to her.

"Why do you act?" said Collin, distressed and intent on getting the conversation back on track, as she was showing clear signs of some old patterns in relation to him. He was staring at her intensely.

Astonished she said: "I ... act ... ?"

When her bewilderment had subsided, she continued to point at what she regarded to be typical of him, going on about this for a while. This brought about a turmoil of emotions; Collin returned to gestures of O.'s nature like spreading his hands and he suddenly interrupted her by bursting out:

"Then it is all for nothing, everything that he has done on his deathbed?"

They remained in silence for a while. Then Madame, changing the subject, said:

"I had a letter from someone you know," as she reached to open the drawer in her bedside table.

Collin, realizing that the possibility of a common understanding was coming to an end, suddenly stood up saying: "I didn't come for that."

He crossed the floor and kissed her hand.

Loud and clear, she said: "What, aren't you ...?"

Approaching the door, he looked at her and told her: "Well, bless you, anyway."

With a strong desire to get away, he hurried out and ran to the front gate, where he approached a car that took him to Morristown, where he got a train to New York. On the train he was astonished that he could not remember anything and that what he had received from Ouspensky was gone. Feeling empty and strongly remorseful, he took a taxi to the airport where he got ticket for a flight in the evening, wishing to return to Ouspensky as quickly as possible. Where and when he had lost the contact he did not know, but knew that it was there when he was about to enter Madame's room. He questioned whether he was responsible for the failure of the whole experiment. In apparent contradiction, he did not feel seriously guilty, as he had done what was possible within the range of his understanding. It seemed to him that what had happened was due to forces outside him and he therefore could not control:

The thought then came that his soul had been 'stolen' from him. He remembered a story which O. used to tell about the devil and the sly man: how the devil had been starving for lack of souls, and how the sly man had wheedled the secret of making souls out of him, on the expectation that thus the devil would ultimately get more food. He had a terrible fear that his soul had been stolen or 'eaten' in this way. For a time it seemed to him that Madame had deliberately done this. He strove to put the thought aside, but was unable to so. Such feelings no doubt sound utterly fantastic. It is quite impossible to convey the absolutely real knowledge that he had been in possession of a definite vehicle of consciousness, which was now gone. He was as sure of this as if he had lost an arm or a foot. In this extremity he could think of nothing but to pray with all his strength for the return of his soul.

One hour after midnight the plane took off and Ouspensky's thoughts and movements gradually returned after about an hour and a half. Because of weather conditions, the plane had to return and again he experienced a gradual fading of the impulses. An hour or two later he was air-born again, this time in a larger plane, and after an hour the possession was full and unrestricted:

During these first hours in the air, he seemed also to become aware of a great struggle or battle on some superhuman level. This 'war in heaven' was being fought for the results of O.'s experiment. Everything that had been created by O., whether in himself, in C-S, or in any of the others, seemed now in the balance – the prize of battle, as it were. This struggle was definitely not on the level of any human 'temptation', or misuse of power in a familiar sense. It seemed to lie between light and dark forces on some very high level: and the idea of the devil, and the devil's host, as a cosmic power, seemed very real. This, however, did not frighten him in the same way, and had none of the unutterable terror of his previous 'loss'. He knew that he could do nothing, but endeavour to hold with all his force to what had now returned to him.

Early in the morning, as they were passing Newfoundland, and Ouspensky's influence became renewed, he saw new implications and aspects of new beginnings. This included the role of his wife and many others. He could also now see long term consequences of what had already happened, not in terms of figuring them out, but as if unfolding, originating from somewhere other than his own mind. Both Ouspensky's gestures and movements reappeared in greater range and more subtlety during the flight, together with the curious feeling of safety, accompanied by a powerful way of viewing life around him from inside.

Due to fog in London, the plane had to go to Shannon airport, where they had to stay overnight in Limerick. When he landed in London the next morning, waiting in the arrival-hall, he maintained the determination not to respond to any approaches made to Rodney Collin. He was Ouspensky and was content to be him even for the rest of his life.

When his wife came looking for him, accompanied by H., he recognized them but remained completely still until they finally found him. After the first fearful look had faded from her face, she welcomed him quietly. Collin ignored H., who wore a grimace on his face. When they all were seated in the car and he asked where they were going, Janet told him Lyne Place. He said, being Ouspensky: "Quite right."

When they finally arrived at Lyne, he refused to leave the car parked at the back door. "It is not quite right," he said.

Then H. suggested that the car be driven to the front porch. Once there Collin left the car and entered the house.

Janet Collin, acting tirelessly in support of her husband, had for a long time, in a number of ways, found herself outside the small circle of the four that surrounded Ouspensky. She was also often indirectly supporting the roles of the three others in the unfolding drama at Lyne. She knew that what Ouspensky had staged was of a great scale and that it would have significant consequences for the future. But what was her role in this play, if any? She had tried to put this question aside, thinking it arose from selfishness, but it grew until she realized that it was a real question. Thirty minutes after this realisation Miss R. said:

"I have a message for you from Mr O. He says he is sorry he spoilt your husband's face."

By this signal she knew that he had been aware of her question and that there was an actual relationship to him. It was only later that she understood that this relationship was through the changed Rodney Collin, not her old husband, and that any regrets to this change would break her connection to what Ouspensky constructed for what was to come. In these remarkable circumstances she felt that her husband disappeared each time he went to Ouspensky's room, as if that room was another planet. After his arrival at Lyne, Collin went straight up to Ouspensky's room and, to Janet, 'disappeared'.

Ouspensky was sitting on his bed when Rodney Collin came in and sat himself beside him and asked: "Is it right?"

Ouspensky turned away from him and said: "Quite wrong."

His voice had an unmistakably laconic tone. Collin continued after a pause: "Madame did not wish to understand anything."

"Evidently," Ouspensky replied.

Although Collin understood that something was wrong, he could not clearly see what. Was it the experiment with himself, or was it the attempt to receive help from Madame? Ouspensky seemed to him to know that there was a danger involved in the trip to Madame, and had therefore hoped it could be avoided, but had also known that it was inevitable.

When Miss R., before the journey, had asked why the trip to Madame was necessary, Ouspensky had replied: "Because we are brave."

After Collin had left for the airport, he had instructed Miss P.: "Tell Mr C-S that he is excused from going to Madame."

When she phoned the airport, she was informed that he had already passed through Customs and that she could not speak to him, only leave a message. Remembering Ouspensky's bidding that everything should be verified, she turned to him and asked: "What message for Mr C-S?"

Ouspensky's reply was simply: "No message."

She then told the clerk waiting on the phone that there had been a mistake and that there was no message. These remarkable synchronisations of external and inner events create perfect shapes for an ephemeral puzzle. Another aspect of this same incident is equally inexplicable and strange: others present heard something very different. Miss R., for example, who had been in the same room, understood Ouspensky's same words as the instructions to apologise to Rodney Collin's wife for the bruising of the face of her husband.

Another curious incident that happened after Collin had left for America, was when Dr. Roles, relative to the 'killing' – a phrase that came up with a certain regularity – had asked Ouspensky if Collin would return. He had answered "No," before adding "Your turn tomorrow."

In terms of transformation, Ouspensky appeared to have known that Collin had by now passed beyond a certain point of no return. As there was nothing about Dr. Roles' behaviour in this period that indicated that an immediate dramatic change would occur to him, Ouspensky's 'tomorrow' might refer to a potential, an indirect encouragement, or even serve as a warning.

The short exchanges between Collin and Ouspensky following his return, which turned out to be their last conversation, initiated a new phase. From then on he did not participate in any of the practical elements of the nursing and care of Ouspensky. He gave no opportunity for his old self to manifest, or react to any form of suggestions from outside. Without any compromise, even in regard to the most trivial thing, he followed his new will. When Miss P., while nursing Ouspensky, handed him a pillow, he dropped it intentionally. His new inner relation to Ouspensky prohibited any external relation. One door had opened and another closed. He once again saw that what he had experienced when accessing O.'s thoughts on the plane was unfolding in front of him again, as on several occasions. On one occasion, when he was sitting in Ouspensky's customary place in the Green Room, he called for H. and the following conversation took place exactly in accordance with what he had formerly seen on the plane:

R.C.: "You saw something, but not quite enough. What do you think?"

H.: "I don't know."

R.C.: "You like libraries, reading, don't you?"

H.: (guardedly) "In the ordinary way, yes."

R.C.: "Well, some Tibetans write about it ... how they make some funny body – tulpa, tulku, or something. Then how they put some body into another person. Perhaps you may like to read about it. Tell me sometime."

H.: "You mean the finding of the Tashi Lama?"

R.C.: "Perhaps. Something like that ... though that may be a little different."

A little later, still sitting in the Green Room, now together with Dr. Roles and H., he called for his wife. When she came, he asked the others to leave and the second suggested conversation took place:

R.C.: "Your husband wrote some book."

J.C.: "Yes, I was exactly wondering about that."

R.C.: "You must correct it, get it published. He had quite good ideas about that. This is your responsibility now."

J.C.: "That answers my question."

R.C.: "Who will look after you now?"

J.C.: "The others are looking after me. They are like brothers and sisters."

R.C.: "No, I mean in a more human way."

J.C.: "I don't need that. You made me your wife again."

The Trip To Madame

After these conversations he went directly to Ouspensky's study, which was next to his bedroom where he had installed himself. His wife made his bed and looked after him, brought him food and drinks. On several occasions in the afternoon he was visited by Miss R., who apparently conveyed something from Ouspensky. On the initial occasion she said: "I thought Madame was going to eat you ..."

He replied: "Not quite – I came back."

She went on: "Mr. O gave you a bad feature of his – that you had to go to Madame and be eaten."

And half an hour later: "Maybe we were wrong to blame Madame. She is necessary. If we pray for her, perhaps she will be helped."

To Rodney Collin it seemed that each time Madame was mentioned, regardless of by whom, it was within this same paradox.

In the evening, when his wife had left him, Collin experienced strongly how planetary forces reverberated within him. Recently he had had no more than one or two hours of sleep at night and had therefore decided to go to bed early. But he could not sleep. An impulse, something, impelled him to take a bath and put clean clothes on. When he had done so, he realised that he had not washed his hair. At the time he felt it to be of utmost importance to be meticulously clean. Then, when finished, a sexual force arose in him. Its power was beyond anything he had formerly experienced and it was steered towards Miss P. Its direction did not come from himself but from "some higher control."

When Miss P came to his room a little later, he was not at all surprised, as external circumstances had been synchronised with inner perceptions for quite some time. To Collin it seemed that she was well aware of the whole situation. He asked her to sit down in front of him and these words came to him:

"We have to play all parts. You are a woman, and you must play all the parts of a woman. Do you understand?"

After pretending not to understand and speaking of something else, she left the room. However, it turned out at a later date that she had experienced a similar suggestion, but that she had resisted it because she felt it to be wrong. At the time Collin viewed this incident as a creation that had failed, and that Miss P. had missed an opportunity to gain something for herself that was prepared for her. Later Collin came to see this incident in the perspective of temptation: "... as a temptation above temptation –

that is, a temptation that it was necessary not to resist, but to transcend into some new realm."

During the same evening and night, he was filled with extraordinary creative energy seemingly coming from Ouspensky laying next door. At dawn, after going with his arms stretched out for an hour, he felt that this force had left him and that it all had come to nothing.

Next morning Dr. Roles came to see him because Miss P. had spoken to him about her fears arising from the intense incident she had experienced with Collin last night. Putting his chair very close to Collin he sat down and he said:

"You were quite right when you said, there is something wrong with Madame. You know, when things were fixed in her by G., something was left over from her old personality. This is at the bottom of it. Now, we believe great things are possible. But we want to know which way you are going? Can you discriminate? The old C-S is very clear."

Rodney Collin found Dr. Roles' attitude persuasive, and he said: "You want to make everything ordinary. This is your role."

Without changing his attitude, Dr. Roles replied: "I don't want that role at all …"

Collin started to answer in a compromising and justifying fashion and he felt "something unpleasant and ingratiating" in Dr. Roles' physical closeness.

During this conversation somebody came and said that Collin was wanted by Ouspensky. He went directly to his room where he found him silent, but from his presence he knew right away that Dr. Roles had been stealing 'something' from him. It was not the first time. To Collin it became instantly clear that Ouspensky had been conscious of what took place next door and had therefore asked for him, not only in order to save him, but also to expose the fact that at certain times, a man must "particularly beware of his friends."

Ouspensky remained silent.

At this point Collin felt that everything was going in a right direction, but would later recognise that there was always the danger of self-deception, or rather being besotted with his new powers. As a consequence, one becomes free from former restrictions, such as buffers and considerings when:

> … *freedom is created and at first used by the teacher; but if the pupil comes to believe in it for its own sake, or to feel that everything done in*

this way must be right, then when the teacher's control is withdrawn, he may begin to use his freedom, that is, 'powers', for pleasure or ascendancy over others. This is the way the devil could eat newborn souls. And it is a special aspect of this danger that souls should be made out of the same matter as sex energy. In this danger conscience is the only safeguard.

Miss R., who lately had appeared to him to be Ouspensky's mouthpiece, now revealed her misgivings saying:

"They say the devil is with woman, don't they?"

Collin said: "Not the devil only."

She continued: "It is black magic, isn't it?"

Collin replied: "Can you have the light side of the moon without the dark?"

It was then clear to him that in order to pass the boundaries of good and evil he had to accept all sides of himself. Before Miss R. left, she asked:

"What is it you will not give up? I don't know."

A little later she returned with the earnest request: "You must <u>do</u> something."

Although he knew this was right – he felt the same way – he did not know what to do, though it was clear to him that it had to be something difficult in order to consolidate this new 'something' that he now possessed. It had been given to him and he knew that what comes easily is easily lost.

In the afternoon he went now and then to Ouspensky's room, sitting in silence and watching before returning to his own room, Ouspensky's study. Occasionally Dr. Roles, Miss R. and H. came there simply to sit with him in silence.

After the return from Southampton, Ouspensky's suitcases and boxes had been piled up in that room. A growing concern about the impression of disorder created by the luggage came over him. To him it was absolutely wrong that 'his' room was not in order. He called for Dr. Roles and asked if he could get someone to remove the objects. He agreed, inattentively, then went away and forgot. A little later, when he came back, Collin asked him: "Is it right that the cases should be here?"

Dr. Roles replied: "No, it is not right. They will be moved."

But nothing was done about it.

When H. came, he was also asked: "What do you think, should the cases be here or not?"

H. replied: "It is not right."

But he also did nothing.

Collin now came to see this disorder in profound symbolic perspective. The neglect and indifference in the others characterised and embodied a force that stood against Ouspensky's efforts and intentions. This was not just a test of his own will, but that to: "accept this represented eternal compromise, his dead self, the denial of everything that had been done and given."

On an earlier occasion Ouspensky had said to the others with reference to Rodney Collin: "Do as he says." It now became clear to him that Dr. Roles had forgotten this altogether. Once more he called for him and said: "Will you take the cases, or shall I throw them downstairs?"

With a strange look on his face, probably surprised by Collin's intensity, he left without a word. Right at that moment Collin recognised what he was required to do and that it was inevitable. In minute details, including gestures, he foresaw exactly what was to come. When his wife now went to fetch Dr. Roles it was for the last time. When he eventually came, his face was white. Collin then arose from his chair in the corner of the room, took a cup of tea from the table, dashed it between them on the floor and shouted into his face: "Traitor, disbeliever!"

Dr. Roles backed up and said: "O is dying, and you ask me to carry boxes. O is dying, and you threaten to throw them downstairs."

While all this was taking place, he recognised each word and sentence, as if in a play, and then he finally said: "Traitor and disbeliever, get out of this room! Get out!"

Dr. Roles' last words at the door were: "Remember, I will be with Mr O."

The tone in this last sentence sounded to Collin "curiously unreal."

CHAPTER 13
Locked up – in Search of the Key

The moment Dr. Roles left the room, Rodney Collin saw the next chapter emerge and he knew what he had do: for seven days he must lock himself in. The household at Lyne grew anxious when he sealed himself in and refused to respond to any attempt to communicate.

At five o'clock on the afternoon of Monday, September 29th, 1947, the key was turned, and the door was barricaded with a chest and the unwanted luggage. When he examined the room he was amazed to find tree tomatoes, six glucose sweets, two biscuits, two cups of white coffee, a small pot of tea, some milk, half a bottle of beer and a large jug of water that his wife had brought just a quarter of an hour before. Not only was he surprised that there even was something there, but also that what he found was sufficient for a minimum of a week's supply. He also found two enamel chamber pots that were left from an assortment of bottles and medical instruments that had for some reason been removed shortly before he closed the door, after laying around for several days.

On a bookshelf he found a bottle of ink, together with an almost unused notebook, in which he then understood it all had to be recorded: what has been and that which was to come. It became clear to him that the set-up of the room had an underlying arrangement to it; it was all part of the whole synchronized play. It was only at a later stage he recognised that this whole play started in Southampton, when Ouspensky refused to enter the ship and go to America: "… the sudden 'stop' put to the general flow of mechanical life and activity then, had been exactly to create a vacuum, a crack in time in which the play could be produced."

He now saw it was in all these details that a play was staged, and how it proceeded and was extended through the various characters' roles, their speaking, and how they came and went. And now the stage was set with the exact properties. Being secluded in the room he recognized curiously that the feeling of being Ouspensky was gone and that he was himself and had to stand on his own legs. He felt uncontrolled and safe. The possession had been necessary to supply advice and support in difficult times, when he was unprotected and helpless.

Thoughts and suggestions still came to him from Ouspensky, but the difference was that before he was them, now he received them as an individual.

Feeling alone, neither his former self, nor born anew, he tasted aspects of fear or awe. The certainty of having no alternative was no longer with him, he himself was now responsible. For two hours on this first evening of solitude he walked with his arms stretched out. During this exercise he remembered a former state where there existed nothing except the body and God. He saw the body as a mechanical vehicle, a gift, "complete with all its capacities and experience."

Beside this there existed nothing except the first mover, God. "... this realisation left no place for fear or apprehension of any kind," and it was this realisation that gave him the true answer to the question, "Which are you?"

But this understanding was not a permanent culmination. During the night he woke up, and for a moment didn't know who he was, "or if he were anyone at all." He felt his body to be an empty house where: "some ghost ran through all the corridors and rooms, looking for the inhabitants, but they had all gone. There was no one there." For him this didn't contradict his recent former state, on the contrary, it completed his understanding.

When he woke up the next morning, he felt it right to do yoga exercises that he had previously learned in New York. This would support his body during the testing period. An underlying and central aspect of Rodney Collin's effort at this time was that everything must be made as difficult as possible. Although he could see that this was required of him, he could not fully see why. Later he wrote:

Fixing was then shown to be a definite concluding stage of a much longer process. First came the killing of the learner's old personality: then the implantation of a new principle or soul. Now, the new condition – as yet extremely delicate and fragile – had to be rendered permanent. Without such fixing, the learner would stand in constant danger of losing his guiding-principle, and unprotected by his old shell of personality and common-sense, might lose his direction utterly and fall a prey to every kind of external influence and possession. The two chief fixing agents, [...], are pain and repetition. When intentionally combined with the purifying and sensitising effect of fasting, and used to fix some definite state, attitude and idea, these could act in the same way as a mordant upon a dye. The actual application of these principles, however, depended upon the exercises and methods already acquired by the learner himself. At this fixing stage, it was very doubtful if anything could be required of the learner which he had not independently mastered. While the previous stages were to a very large extent imposed upon him, fixing must be voluntary. Before, he was 'done to': now he must learn to 'do'.

When he was in New York, he had learned some yoga exercises, now he had to use them. Correspondingly, he had now to use the exercise with the outstretched arms that he had learned ten years before, but rarely done. Another exercise, combined with fasting, was running on place. When he was stationed in Bermuda during the war he had tried it, but without great success. Since 1938 he had been doing the Movements. Now in the last days of the week he did the "Big Prayer". This he did, each day, twelve times with the natural stop. Then, in succession, twenty-four times.

One exercise he did during this week – that he came to call 'The Corpse' – was to lay perfectly still on the floor.

So, his days in the locked room were spent as follows:

- Yoga for one hour
- 'The Corpse' for one hour
- Rest
- Writing, the first days of the week
- 'Big Prayer' for an hour, the latter days of the week
- Rest for one to two hours
- Walking with arms outstretched for two hours in the afternoon
- Long rest
- Running on place for two hours
- Short sleep
- Walking with arms outstretched one hour at midnight
- Night sleep.

Whenever he felt strong enough he did 'the continued movements while resting' exercise that Ouspensky had shown him. This varied in length from half an hour to two hours. All these exercises were at his own initiative, except 'The Corpse', that he indicates was suggested to him. Uncontrolled, "he felt O's influence in their arrangement and use; and particularly that O was the source of the mental or inner exercises which seemed to suggest themselves for each individual period."

On the morning of Tuesday 30th, H. came and knocked on his door, asking him to open, telling him that Ouspensky wanted to see him. Determined to adhere to his test, he listened in silence without responding. Some hours later H. approached him again, this time from the garden side, saying: "Mr. O. says unlock the door and come to him when you can."

Collin interpreted this allegorically, and accordingly answered without uttering a word: "I search for the key, and I will come to him when I can."

The answer had formed itself in his heart. Outwardly he refused with a silent gesture. With the distaste for speaking and for the standard of ordinary communication, he shook his head when H. told him that he had a message from Miss P. who wanted to bring him fruit and cool drinks.

Later, when H. asked: "May I come up and speak to you?" before putting a ladder to his window to reach him, Collin simply pushed it down without a word.

He saw these events as temptations. One was breaking the seclusion, another to soften the conditions, and finally, relative to Miss. P.'s message, "to do later for personal motives what once might have been required by higher forces." That all these temptations were mixed with a requirement from Ouspensky, enabled him to see that: "This, in fact, now appeared as the final temptation of all – to obey the teacher's word rather than his meaning: or, in the last resort, to place teacher above conscience."

The recurring thought: "There is nothing but this body and God. What harm can befall?" removed every trace of doubt in him and he knew in his heart that these temptations were to be resisted.

The next day his wife called upon him, asking for a scarf for Ouspensky. He threw it down out of the window, saying nothing. Others were also fruitlessly approaching him that day. They all eventually overcame their temptation and quit knocking on his door. The impulse to begin with the mental exercises or themes of meditation entered him half an hour after he had started either running on place or walking with outstretched arms. After some days, they entered at the beginning of these exercises and could sometimes expand and evolve.

He had once, in a comment made by Ouspensky in regard to St. John's Gospel, come to see that all creatures carry the light of the divinity, an all-pervading flame. Now, within five minutes, his former theoretical understanding of this idea converted into a distinct exercise where this flame not only became recognisable in the body, but where he, through intentional imagination, set fire to his body. During the practice of this exercise it became possible to correct small mistakes in his former intellectual abstraction, which gave great depth to a new emotional understanding.

> *Beginning at the toes it was necessary not only to visualize, but in a certain way to feel, small blue flames first licking round the flesh, then gradually penetrating, charring, consuming it and in the end taking hold of the bone which in turn glowed, grew white-hot, and so on. Slowly, as each part was mentally consumed, but not before, the flames had to be carried upwards, past the ankles, calves, knees, up the thighs and into the trunk, the fire gaining heat and power as it mounted from the increasing intensity of the furnace created below. Reaching the genitals, the solar plexus, the pancreas, and eventually the heart, these were seen to burst into fiercer centres or Catherine wheels of fire within the general conflagration. The fire was then carried up the arms, chest, neck, imaginatively fanned to ever greater intensity by a certain kind of breathing which also came spontaneously. Eventually the fire was imagined as engulfing the whole head, inside and out, even to the flaring up of the hair, so that the whole body was visualised or felt as burning with the heat, brilliance and consuming force of a white-hot furnace. This part of the exercise, conducted very gradually and inch by inch through the whole body, required an hour and a half.*

When this was accomplished, he, for some reason, felt an impulse to bring his attention to seven activated points of fire in his body: genitals, solar plexus, pancreas, heart, throat, and in between the eyebrows, before finally directing these fires to the top of his head. The gathered force of this fire would then enable it to pass through to a potential flame above the head. Collin experienced the various fire-points to have separate colours and qualities and perceived their nature emotionally:

> *... as though each were the 'spirit' or personification of a certain function. Further, the cosmic order of these centres was seen developing like a spiral or a Catherine wheel from the heart. And ultimately a circulation was seen to join them, descending on the right hand side from the crown of the head to the genitals and returning again on the left to its starting-point, in the form of an ellipse of golden rain. Moreover, every spark or drop of this golden rain was a fiery seed or signature of the whole body, and in a kind of vision he saw how a stream of such fiery signatures would rush into the female womb, where one would explode into a new man of fire like himself.*

Within this vision he saw that the ultimate attainment, the liberation, cosmic consciousness, was for the fire within him to gain so much force that it actually penetrated the crown of his head and united with the potential fire above, God. Although he felt that he was on the edge, he confirmed that it did not happen. Within what he experienced in this vision was man's nature, his way, and his goal.

Of all the experiments Rodney Collin went through during these days, the fire exercise was the most comprehensive and it also took place on the last night of Ouspensky's life. Collin came to see his own experience as being a shadow of what Ouspensky went through and achieved. He also thought that his "symbolic awareness of the goal or liberation must have been a dim apprehension of that which O. in fact reached."

It is clear that he saw the whole process in a wider perspective, in which his experience was a reflection of what took place on an immensely higher level, and that it was Ouspensky who carried it through.

The fire exercise had physically eliminated waste matters in his body which caused pain. Some of this pain had provided energy, intensifying his aspiration. Now, when it was reduced, he increasingly, during the rest of the period, came to more clarity in his meditations. This brought deeper insight into the process of fixing. When any imagination of future pleasure or regret was allowed, he saw that it would lead to permanent imperfection.

What was at stake now was the establishment of a fundamental attitude with no backtrack. This included God, his fellow men, his duties, and the course for the rest of his life. When this was assured there would be a "certainty of what he was, what he knew, and what he must do." It was from his growing understanding of where will and requirement blended that he could begin to see what lay ahead.

CHAPTER 14
Outside the Room

At 9.30 a.m. on October 1st, two days after Collin had locked himself up, they found Ouspensky fully dressed on the landing. This was very startling, because his condition was now so much worse since the 25th that it had become necessary to give him morphine. When Dr. Roles saw that he was about to go down the stairs, he protested zealously, but to no avail. Instead of obeying him, Ouspensky pushed him down the stairs, before slowly descending, and sat down with Miss Q. on the couch in the Green Drawing Room.

All the people in the house were called. As they sat there in silence, he regarded them with deep poignancy and benevolence. After a while the silence was broken by Dr. Roles who asked:

"Many want to know how to understand reconstruction."

But Ouspensky did not answer. However, at a later date some expressed that an understanding had arisen internally through this silence. One person "saw that all that was happening must first be understood – then the meaning of reconstruction would grow clear." Another one saw "that it should grow from the unity of those present."

They went on sitting in silence for a very long time. Ouspensky now had folded a handkerchief and held it to his eyes with his left hand as if he was reading. The resounding and loaded silence continued until Dr. Roles once more broke it:

"How are we to make demands upon ourselves?"

Ouspensky just made a gesture in silence but said a little later while making a gesture towards the window: "From time to time you must look."

It may seem striking that Dr. Roles posed this question so close to Ouspensky's death. It is obvious and legitimate to raise the question of what impression Dr. Roles had of all the extensive and almost inhuman efforts that Ouspensky made right in front of them for such a long time. However, for some of the attendees, it was the testimony of precisely these efforts that formed the basis for understanding the answer to Dr. Roles' question, as is clearly evident in the unpublished material. There seemed to be unanimous agreement when Miss Q. warmly and calmly said:

"Perhaps it would be better just to sit and understand, rather than ask questions."

A deep presence and an extraordinary feeling of unity and peace now gradually came over all present, and, as it turned out, this was the last time they sat together like this. Some seemed to have known this there and then.

After approximately an hour and a half, everyone present knew that it was all over and went away in silence, except Mrs. H., who joined him on the sofa. Ouspensky was now in very great pain. After some time, he said, "How beautiful, all people together" before turning to the window and saying: "You see? Beautiful. Tomorrow different, different ..."

Half past two in the afternoon, the pain had increased so much that Dr. Roles found it necessary to give him morphine. The medication did not appear to have a soporific effect and he remained aware. After some time, he was carried upstairs, put to bed and went quickly to sleep. Early in the morning a call came from Franklin Farms to get an update on his condition. They were informed that there were no signs of an imminent death, as Ouspensky was asleep and breathing gently. The last hammering on Collin's door was between five and six on October 2nd, when Miss R. had woken up extremely agitated, but it was of no use. Collin remained silent. The same morning at about seven, Ouspensky drew his last breath.

At five o'clock on Monday, October 4th, Rodney Collin arranged the room to its original order, turned the key and opened the door. Alone, and without being noticed, he left the room where he had for days remained silently secluded and entered Ouspensky's bedroom. It was empty. Ouspensky had died two days earlier. Now, when the bell from his room rang in the kitchen, Janet Collin was the first to attend. It must have been astonishingly strange to meet her husband again after the dramatic conditions of the past few days. Childlike and strange, with an innocent expression, he was sitting cross-legged on the bed. She found it difficult to communicate with him, but told him to shave and wash. He was showing signs of the lack of food and drink and asked his wife for lime juice. When she gave him a comb, he looked at it for a long time from different angles, before saying:

This is the most beautiful comb I have ever seen.[1]

Ouspensky's body was taken to the village church, where there was a simple service, before it was driven to Woking for cremation. Three days later his ashes were interred in Holy Trinity Churchyard at Lyne. Not long

[1] Joyce Collin-Smith, *Call No Man Master* (England: Authors OnLine Ltd, 2004). p42

after, Rodney Collin, Janet, and their daughter Chloe, left Lyne and moved to a rented flat in St. James's Street, London. George Cornelius, a Mid-West American, employed by The Naval Attaché's office and a senior student of J.G. Bennett, had informed Bennett by phone about Ouspensky's death and told him to get in touch with Janet Collin-Smith for further information.

When Bennett eventually discovered her whereabouts and pressed the doorbell in St. James' Street, Janet Collin received him in the doorway, where their whole conversation took place. It must have been an awkward situation. As Bennett was well aware, Ouspensky had forbidden his students to have any contact with him. Another reason for not letting him in to the house could have been to protect her husband from the increasing number of people seeking him out, as the word spread about his significant change. There was, in certain circles, the belief that Rodney Collin's new personal discovery would replace the authority of Ouspensky. Collin was at this time immersed in writing, and his wife saw it as an obligation to protect him from intruders.

CHAPTER 15
The Theory of Eternal Life

Ouspensky's death was pivotal to Rodney Collin's depth of understanding of inner work. It was also to become a backbone and source of inspiration, not only for his book, *The Theory of Eternal Life*, but for the rest of his life.

During the time when he was locked in the chamber beside Ouspensky's bedroom, he felt he gained a greater insight into the universe. Joyce Collin-Smith told me that he referred to this in their conversations as a vision. It was a part of this vision that was now revealed through his writing and would become the manuscript for *The Theory of Eternal Life*. He did not see what he had gained from this vision as a personal achievement, or that he in anyway could claim authorship for it; he simply saw it as a gift or a communication. Therefore, the first edition, published in 1950, did not carry his name, but was published anonymously. It sold extensively, as many people believed it to be written by Ouspensky.

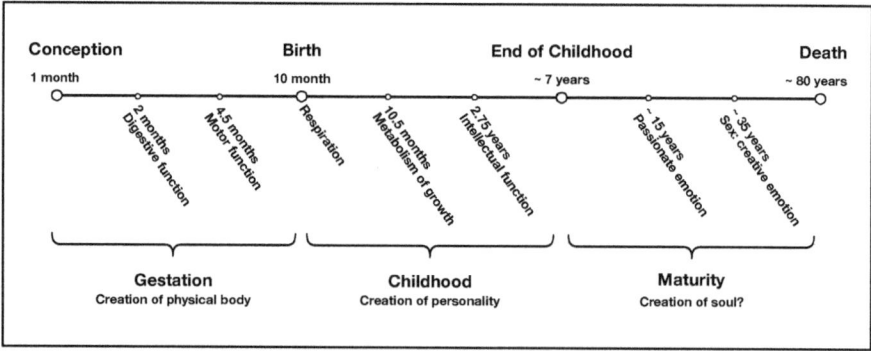

Figure 1. Man's Life in Logarithmic Time

Life, as we know it, begins at birth and ends at death. In the first chapter of *The Theory of Eternal Life*, Collin expands this idea by pointing out that, at the moment of death, man is exposed to an intense energy which is unbearable to the physical body but necessary for a new conception, including the formation of new potentials. Already, here, he challenges our ordinary conception of time, as he claims that this connection of death and

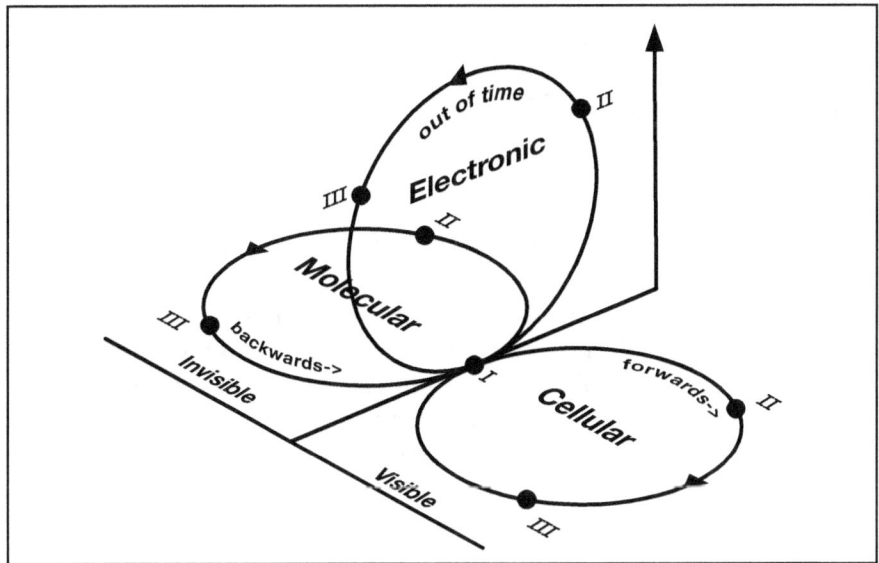

Figure 2. Man's Lifetime in Three Worlds

conception takes place outside time. Less challenging is his division of man's life into eight parts, presented as a logarithmic scale, where each step is characterized by development of various functions, such as growth of the body, gain of personality, and the development of an inner unity.

Considering the religious idea of rebirth from the perspective of the logarithmic scale created a springboard for his visualisation of the course of events between death and birth. By an image consisting of four interlinked circles, Collin demonstrates four different worlds. Our visible world, the cellular world, is placed horizontally along the line of linear time. Next to it, parallel along the same line (of time), is the molecular world, consisting of far more refined matter. The third circle, raised to an upper vertical position, represents an even more refined matter, the electronic world. Finally (not shown in *Figure 2* above) there is the mineral world, which is represented by a circle on the lower part of the vertical plane. This world consists of an almost motionless dense energy.

It is important to note that, in the text, the time periods follow a logarithmic scale for the points *II birth*, *III mature age*, and *I death* in all the three worlds, and that the times in this version are different for the molecular world than those indicated in the diagram in the version of *The Theory of Eternal Life* published by Shambhala Publications Inc., 1984. Hopefully that publication is a one-off.

Here is the chart in the correct version:

Time	Cellular world	Molecular world	Electronic world
II Gestation	10 months	7.3 hours	26.3 secs
III Childhood	8.3 yrs (in total) 7.5 years (age)	3 days	4.4 mins
I Lifetime	83.3 yrs (in total) 82.5 years (age)	1 month	43.8 minutes

When a soul is born at physical death it is the carrier of consciousness in the molecular world. Likewise, the carrier of consciousness in the electronic world is the spirit. When Collin applies his logarithmic scale in accordance with the four worlds, he manages to bring about a proximate duration of the life-span for the different bodies inhabiting the various worlds. Further, the experience of time in these worlds is different; time becomes compressed, as they are worlds in which the same amount is known or experienced in a shorter time. Within what Collin refers to as an intense compression of a soul's own life exists the fact that, whatever man meets during these compressions, it springs from himself. All he then meets and confronts is what he has become and is, and his freedom dwells within that understanding.

A man who has developed a soul before death, while still in the cellular world, will not only be more flexible and enjoy the freedom of the Earth world, but also be more prepared for the entry to other worlds. As the soul is of molecular origin, this would mean that such a man can live in more than one world. But Collin maintains that ordinary man in physical life has no conscious soul and that to create it is the greatest task he can possibly attempt. About the existence of this possibility he writes:

The soul, or body of the molecular world, can only be created artificially by long accumulation of the finest energy which the physical organism produces, and its crystallisation through the continuous attempt to become self-conscious. But ordinary man cannot help spending this energy as fast as it is produced – on fear, anger, envy, longing and his normal state of fascination with himself and the world around him. In order to restrain this wasting of it, he must create will in himself. In order to create will he must have one aim. In order to have one aim he must have learned all sides of himself, and force them to accept the domination of his conscience. Before this he must first awake conscience from sleep. And not one of these stages can he achieve by himself.[1]

Summing up his deductions from the logarithmic scale he writes:

... man's individuality, which inhabits a physical body for seventy-six years, has previously inhabited a soul for one month, and before that a spirit for forty minutes. And birth into that spirit was simultaneous with the death of the previous physical body. In other words, at the instant of death man enters the electronic world or world of the spirit.[2]

Light is given as an example of matter of the electronic world; scent as an illustration of molecular matter. To exemplify the characteristics of the cellular world, he points to the indisputable fact that a body in this world can only occupy one place at the time. The difference of capacity of these matters is identified by their freedom and restrictions relative to their respective dimensions:

Light travels instantaneously in three dimensions, that is, not only along a line like a cellular body, nor over an area, like a smell, but throughout a volume of space.[3]

Collin affirms that light, or matter of an electronic character, not only illuminates whatever it falls on, but also that a consciousness on such a level would embrace within itself whatever is within its range and be experienced as a part of itself.

Human consciousness attached to a body of electronic matter would include all neighbouring beings in itself, and would thus share the nature of God, be joined both to God and to them. This is evidently the significance both of yoga which means 'union', and of religion which means 're-union'.[4]

Within *The Theory of Eternal Life*, Collin explores, with a remarkable certainty and accuracy, a variety of religious and ancient texts that resonate with his elaborated and detailed image of the electronic world relative to consciousness.

---

[1] Rodney Collin, The Theory of Eternal Life (Boulder, Colorado: Shambhala Publication Inc., 1984), p30.
[2] Rodney Collin, The Theory of Eternal Life (Boulder, Colorado: Shambhala Publication Inc., 1984), p33
[3] Rodney Collin, The Theory of Eternal Life (Boulder, Colorado: Shambhala Publication Inc., 1984), p31.
[4] Rodney Collin, Theory of Eternal Life (Boulder, Colorado: Shambhala Publication Inc., 1984), 32-33.

St. John's testimony, "I was in the spirit ... " is taken to imply and demonstrate that it is possible for a man who is physically alive to enter the electronic world and then return to the cellular level to give witness to his experiences. This access must obviously be indirect, as this only becomes possible after acquiring a soul, by using the finest material available within the physical body. About the creation of the spirit he writes:

> The spirit, however, is made of materials which are not available. For man does not ordinarily dispose of free electronic energy. He does not emit light. He cannot normally transmit his thoughts or perform actions at a distance. He enjoys no power characteristic of this state of matter. He may be said to have right to a soul, even though he has not got one; but to a spirit he has no natural right.
>
> His spirit was a free gift from God in the beginning, and remains with Him. To find it man must return whence he came. The achievement of spirit implies transmutation of matter. A man has first to acquire a soul by diverting all his molecular energy to this one end. Then he has to learn how to connect this soul with a still higher level – a level at which it cannot be misused. He must transmute it to an intensity which individual personality cannot survive and where understanding is therefore permanent. Such intensity is found only on the electronic level. This means he must infuse soul with spirit. In himself he has to learn how to convert molecular matter into electronic, that is, to split the atom and release internally a degree of energy which only our own age can begin to measure. It is the release of such energy which alone can carry him up into that divine world attested by these visions. All this means that we cannot imagine the achievement of spirit. We can only say that John's record, even if it conveys little, proves the most important thing of all – that a way does exist from the physical world of living men to the electronic or divine world, and that actual men have both passed there and returned.[1]

Founded on his images of the visible and invisible worlds, Collin examines the concept of time in the invisible worlds in minute detail, including its irregular tempo and how and why it runs in different directions. Through the reversal of time, where cause becomes effect, it becomes possible to envisage that I create the kind of world in which I live, and that the murderer gives birth to the murdered man and is responsible for the latter's life. It is within this realm that one becomes inseparable

---

[1] Rodney Collin, Theory of Eternal Life (Boulder, Colorado: Shambhala Publication Inc., 1984), p36-37.

from the entire level of humanity. Only when mankind as a whole, in the past and future, is regenerated, is it possible to gain a permanent satisfaction on an individual level. Regarding the possibility for this to manifest he writes:

> ... the sufferers must look forward to their saviour, the ignorant must anticipate their enlightenment; they must already be healed by what will happen. This is the inner meaning of faith. Faith is that by which mankind relives the intolerable burden of teachers and saviours in reversed time; that by which the level of the whole is raised.[1]

When we believe that personal and individual salvation is possible, and independent of others and the past, it is, in Collin's perspective, simply because we live in the illusion that time is only moving in one direction. When man at death enters the electronic world it is such a big shock that he cannot maintain consciousness, but can only awaken when entering the successive stage: the world of the soul. After the sojourn in the invisible worlds and the re-entrance into the cellular world, the average man lacks the memory that could provide the information he would need to make changes at critical points in his life. The development of such memory must be done at will and in succession, bit by bit. The most critical to remember is that which we hesitate to recall or discharge.

If we, at death, were to rely solely on a memory created by our ordinary logical mind alone, it seems unthinkable that a confrontation with how and what we have experienced whilst living could be complete or even possible at all. This becomes even clearer when we incorporate Collin's description of the nature of logical mind:

> The characteristic of the ordinary logical mind by whose speed is measured the life of the physical body is that one thing is known or experienced after another. When logical mind passes on to the next experience it is unable to retain the experience or knowledge which went before. This it must leave behind. For the logical mind all proofs are made sequentially or in time. But by the time it reaches the end of its proof, logical mind has already lost sight of the beginning, because things can only pass through it in succession. From this arise all the phenomena of forgetfulness. Relying on the logical mind alone, man must forget.[2]

---

[1] Rodney Collin, The Theory of Eternal Life (Boulder, Colorado: Shambhala Publication Inc., 1984), p52.
[2] Rodney Collin, The Theory of Eternal Life (Boulder, Colorado: Shambhala Publication Inc., 1984), 18.

When man between death and birth enters the molecular and the electronic world, he is, in Collin's perspective, facing the last and most intensive test, where the level of his being will be decisive for his future and that the level of his being is measured by what he wants. He also reminds us about the fundamental idea that a change to a new state or situation is not equivalent to change of being, but rather would reveal a man's true level of being:

> ... the sudden inheritance of a great fortune may bring all kinds of new and interesting possibilities to a thoughtful and self-controlled man, while a weak man will be destroyed by the flood of new temptations which he is unable to master.[1]

A man without any other reference than that of the cellular world will be lost when entering the molecular and electronic world. His various physical appetites cannot be satisfied, simply because he has no physical body. With references to the medieval *Book of the Craft of Dying*, as well as both the Tibetan and the Egyptian *Book of the Dead*, Collin points to the imperative necessity of preparation before death, in order to bear and endure the severe and forceful shock of new states. Such a preparation must take place when still within a physical body, exploring and using its capacity to function as a transformational instrument. By growth of awareness man might discover how his emotional and intellectual inner world could be nourished by impressions coming through the senses of the cellular body. Such growth of awareness could also reveal man's tendencies to live in imagination about the world, himself and others, and eventually enter a more objective state of experience, new knowledge, inner freedom and truth.

When Rodney Collin identifies the one and only factor that separates the level of being of unprepared and prepared man, he points to the difference between craving and longing. As desire and craving constitute such an essential part of our physical life, and the consequences of growth of awareness unfold and unavoidably lead to longing, Collin pinpoints man's two natures. Human constraints and possibilities dwell in his wishes and what he believes and demands of himself. The limitation of identifying with the physical world is that human beings lose their birth-right to inner development, which means that their potential to experience the electronic world will also be lost.

---

[1] Rodney Collin, *The Theory of Eternal Life* (Boulder, Colorado: Shambhala Publication Inc., 1984), p38.

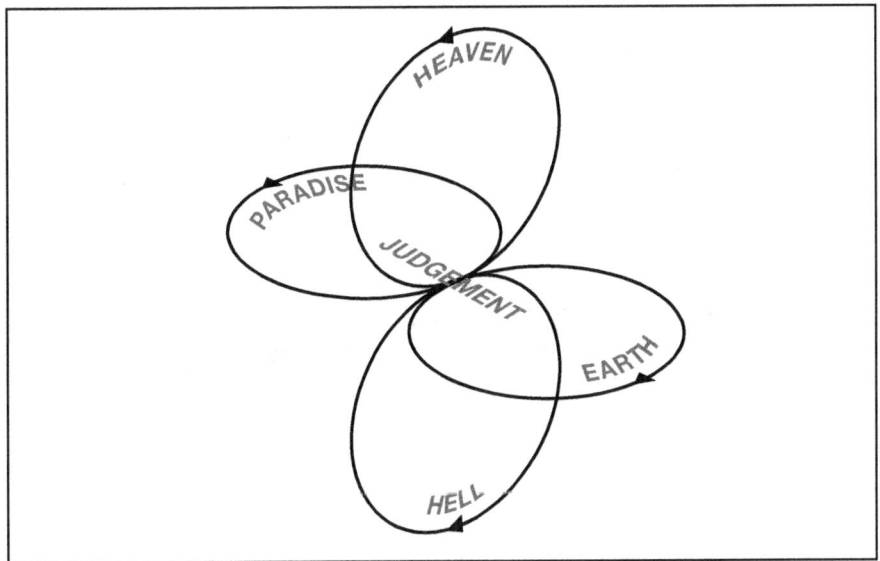

Figure 3. The Cellular, Molecular, Electronic and Mineral World United

Collin stresses the latter and it becomes obvious that this also is a part of his vision: that man, according to universal arrangements, is entitled to experience the life of the spirit. This death-right becomes unachievable due to man's material attachment through an inflexible and rigid experience of identity. It is a general belief that ideas and imagination can easily betray human perception of reality but in Collin's multi-dimensional perspective this treacherous side, under certain assumption, could even become active after death. In Tibet there is a religious tradition of guiding the dead through various phases. In light of Collin's emphasis on imagination, it is not surprising to find that the advice given to the dead in these rituals is clearly addressed to someone who is about to be overtaken by just such imagination. Imagination in the molecular world would thus be the limiting factor that would otherwise form the impressions that would open the door to the electronic world and the realm of the spirit.

> *The man who thought of himself as a millionaire would continue to accumulate imaginary wealth and wield imaginary power, all the while burdened with the cares of preserving what he no longer possessed.*
>
> *... the man who with his whole being believed all to exist in God, and who could completely forget his personal existence in such conviction, might actually experience this truth. And if he did so, it is impossible to*

105

believe that the knowledge and certainty of such an experience would ever again abandon him no matter what the circumstances of his later birth.[1]

In religious terms, Collin's four circled diagram of cellular, molecular, electronic and mineral world correspond to earth, paradise, heaven and hell. '

Hell has historically been the subject of various artists, exposing a mesmerisingly grotesque imagination. Dante's writing, and the description of hell in Christian scriptures, appear to be important sources of inspiration for the hellscapes found in the western world. Often, almost with no exception, The Last Judgement and the actual torments in the underworld are part of the same composition in early European art. Giotto, Jan Van Eyck, Fra Angelico, and Hieronymus Bosch all created vivid infernal examples.

The mineral world in Collin's diagram represents that realm of the cosmos to where a soul descends, backwards through evolution, when it can no longer respond to its own possible evolution. In perspective of the logarithmic scale, also applied to the other worlds in his diagram, time in the mineral world not only moves ten times slower, but also moves in the opposite direction. When he points to the basic causes of a soul's fall from his potential abilities and talent, he indirectly points to the loss of man's original dignity which must, above all, include the lack or loss of contact with conscience.

Collin makes a clear distinction between the suffering and terror caused by man's own merits and subjectively experienced before judgement, and the suffering in the mineral world. The psychological misery and hardship experienced in purgatory, before judgement, can in fact alter and improve his prospect through remorse. The mineral world has the function of receiving waste matter that no longer has the ability to serve evolutionary cosmic functions, but rather would contaminate and violate the whole. From this lower world there is no escape. Here what has become fossilised has the potential to be melted down by the cosmic process, which the Norwegian author, Henrik Ibsen, symbolised by the Button Moulder in *Peer Gynt*. The cosmic function of hell in Collin's perspective is to regenerate nonfunctional psychic products to a state of raw material, which in due time can return to an original position where growth can manifest in form.

---

[1] Rodney Collin, *The Theory of Eternal Life* (Boulder, Colorado: Shambhala Publication Inc., 1984), p47.

Collin's four conjoined circles with its multiple functions (also) forms a holistic image, as it represents the different parts of the universe where the possible fates of man can manifest. Damnation, liberation, human rebirth or recurrence.

According to Collin, the four conjoined circles move towards physical life as it approaches where all the worlds meet and where the journey through the worlds of the soul and spirit come to a final adjudication. What the individual self can gain through this journey, when it meets cosmos as it is, depends on its capacity to consider its own nature relative to it, and repent. This again depends on its preparation before death. Judgement of the individual self, based on the unabbreviated adventure of man's earthly life, claims Collin, takes place when it crystallises into the beginning of a physical body: the moment of conception where chromosomes and genes coalesce.

When he explores the depth of the problem of recurrence into the organic world, he points to the innate capacities that certain people have in various fields, like music, mathematics, and other apparently untraceable predispositions. He writes:

> *Somewhere, in another world, the fundamental chord of a man's life has sounded, and here in this world the physical constituents of his organism have assumed the responding pattern and become tangible to us.*[1]

In Rodney Collin's model, the intense energy released at death, and a sensitivity in parents during the sexual act, is necessary to complete this transition. The energy of both death and conception have the same intensity and subtleness. Vibrations caused by disintegration of the organic body at the moment of death is invisibly transmitted through time to the female ovum. This is the only moment in man's life when an energy that resembles that of the creator comes into existence.

When the sperm and the egg cells merge, the enigmatic development of a new human begins. The genetic code is set from the moment of fertilisation. Not only gender and complexions are determined at this moment, but also a variety of psychological features, characteristics and innate irreversible capacities. By referring to science, he reminds us of well-known established facts, but then goes into detail about a variety of other unknown types of possible influences that chromosomes can be

---

[1] Rodney Collin, *The Theory of Eternal Life* (Boulder, Colorado: Shambhala Publication Inc., 1984), p74.

subjected to. These ideas are based on his eight-point scale, presented in the beginning of this chapter, representing the action of different energy levels in man, each of which has a corresponding system in the body. With reference to these systems and main functions of man he says:

> Suppose three aspects of each function – an 'automatic' or mechanical aspect, an 'artistic' or emotional aspect, and an 'inventive' or intellectual aspect – and further suppose each aspect governed by positive and negative poles. In this way we reach a total of forty-eight main 'controls', which between them might determine the development of every side of the human machine.[1]

Collin maintains that this scale shows how we can expect chromosomes to possibly manifest their influence. When the conjoined circles of the four worlds, gradually moving towards life, has reached the moment of conception, Collin affirms that the process operates so fast that it cannot be contained within cellular matter. As the chromosomes and the genes are of a molecular nature and therefore must comply to molecular laws, they are able to adjust to the fulfilment of the required tempo of the transition at the moment of conception and become the first physically visible sign of life. Collin views the genes and chromosomes to be on the boundary of two worlds, partly in its free molecular state and partly restricted within the aboriginal cell. When he speculates on the possible scientific evidence for a transmission of information in genes and chromosomes across time, he points to the effect of radiation of a certain wavelength and its ability to change human form. These radioactive frequencies have the ability, unlike the radiation of heat, light and sound, to persist in time through long periods. He says:

> This means that the same radiation which can affect the genes of a tulip now, could also produce a similar spore a thousand years hence. Or conversely, the same radioactivity that could produce the monstrous tulip then, can create an identical change today. Has the formative influence travelled backwards or forwards through time? It is the same thing. One can only say that this radiation, which has power over form, is independent of time.[2]

Based on the principle that form on one level is due to influence from a level above, he concludes that only electronic force can modify molecular

---

[1] Rodney Collin, The Theory of Eternal Life (Boulder, Colorado: Shambhala Publication Inc., 1984), p76.
[2] Rodney Collin, The Theory of Eternal Life (Boulder, Colorado: Shambhala Publication Inc., 1984), p78.

arrangements. When, at the moment of conception, the genes are administered and manipulated, it is because the formative influences released at the moment of death reverse through time and re-make the embryo. Collin assumes that psychological characteristics can be transmitted in this process in affiliation with genes responsible for physical features. The psychological features transmitted at death are not identical with those at birth, as they are liable to change during a lifetime. Some psychological character traits, left unattended, will increase, while those confronted and worked upon will diminish. Creative capacities in past life will likewise increase and develop if nourished during life, or dwindle if neglected and overlooked.

Turning to the sexual act of the parents at conception, Collin proposes both a sensational and suggestive perspective of what can become transferable at the moment of death. The advancement and harmonising of the embryo are not only relative to man's former struggles with his weaknesses. The parents' state, purity of emotions, and the intensity of the act also contribute to the new design or field of force. Somehow one would have to increase the level of one's own parents; to teach them and bring consciousness and emotions of such an intensity that it will broadcast itself to them at the moment of conception.

When he raises the question of the number of times man can expect to be reborn, he is reminded of the hundred and eight beads of the necklaces of Buddha. Turning to Plato's Phaedrus myth and the myth of Er, he faces a calculation of hundreds of lives for the mass of mankind. From these sources, he not only utilises the image that man can escape the cycle of rebirth if he can find the right guidance and is willing to make the necessary efforts, but also the assumption that time is counted by a different measure. Being exposed to this new opportunity man must make use of it, or else it will be subject to limitations.

Memory is central in progression through recurrence, but the concept of memory can only apply to a perception characteristic to linear time where past, present and future are perceptible due to the slow movement of time. In the electronic world where there is only NOW and everything is known, Collin not only concludes that there is no memory, but also that it is wrong to view man's different lives in sequence. From this perspective he sees man's recurrence as simultaneous. As we live in a world where our thinking is limited by before and after, Collin sees memory as the nearest approximation to higher perception. In reflecting upon possible memory in the invisible world, he compares man's life to an electric circuit where the circuit is broken at death. However, if the electric tension is sufficiently increased, Collin maintains that a bridge might be expected to appear, completing the circuit and allowing a flow to transit.

Although man can experience extraordinary intensified moments in the span of his life, where an impulse of memory might connect with a moment in another life, it can never be proven. Collin professes that this is due to the nature of memory of ordinary man, which is inextricably rooted in his level of consciousness. For memory to pass death, consciousness must be raised to an exceedingly high level. If not, death will be an impermeable insulation. The wish to remember is a fundamental principle to preserve memory in life and its force is immensely more important to a memory beyond death.

Pointing to an incomplete version of the Greek legend of Lethe and to a degenerated version of the true legend of St. Makary of Alexandria, he illustrates how forgetfulness is presented and justified as something desirable in order to avoid suffering. By detailed references to the more complete versions of these legends, Collin endorses clearly that memory must be preserved at all costs. When he refers to the Russian service for the dead, to highlight once again the importance of memory in a religious perspective, it is undoubtedly in remembrance of the Requiem Service for Ouspensky, held at the Russian Church in Pimlico, London, that took place barely a year earlier:

> Give rest eternal in the blessed falling asleep, O Lord,
> To the soul of thy servant departed this life,
> And make his memory eternal.
> Memory eternal! Memory eternal! Memory eternal![1]

The avoidance of unnecessary suffering is another aspect of forgetfulness in Collin's perspective of the nature of memory. A prerequisite to escape recurrence on an earthly level is consciousness and memory. Unprepared man is, by nature, spared experiences he does not understand, cannot bear or value, and will lose awareness and memory by the formidable shock of death. This, from Collin's viewpoint, is nature's own arrangement to spare unprepared men from suffering.

Collin also proposes the general principle that change of state itself destroys memory. Amongst different examples, such as change of physical sensation, the clearest is how easily we forget our own dreams. The

---

[1] Rodney Collin, *The Theory of Eternal Life* (Boulder, Colorado: Shambhala Publication Inc., 1984), p87.

dynamic concept of transmission of memory from life to various states after the moment of death represents to Collin only half the problem. Not only is the challenge to retain and use such memory in the invisible world, but also to carry further the accumulated memory, including that of the invisible world into the subsequent life.

Bearing in mind the tremendous difficulty of maintaining memory due to change of state, it seems evident that the transition from the invisible world to the world of cellular matter must be more than just challenging. Through a verse taken from Vishnu Purana, a religious text in the Hindu tradition, he presents knowledge that proclaims the latter transition to be the most effective destroyer of memory. The loss of the various forms of memory can also be attributed to the same reason that we forget things in this life: we prefer to engage our mind with an imagined future rather than remembering the past, because we find it too painful to recall. This is how memory atrophies, according to Rodney Collin.

The development of man's memory to such a quality and quantity that it can be conveyed and transmitted to a life beyond the present must start from his current existence. Collin claims that all our experiences are recorded like a collection of films that have been exposed but not developed. Visual impressions, sound and conversations, movements and physical sensations are all collected on separate 'film rolls'. It is intact, but inoperative and reduced to a molecular or electronic scale. With few exceptions, such as when accidentally brought about by resemblance or contrast, ordinary man has no access to this material. To develop these films, or rather, develop these memories, man must provide the developing agent, that is, intentionally apply attention and consciousness to his dormant records. Man must remember himself and ferry and funnel this remembrance through death from one existence to another. This is Rodney Collin's answer and alternative to the otherwise devastating and paralysing confrontation at the moment of death.

Although self-remembering is the central agent in developing memory, Collin recognizes the necessity for an enlarged memory that would include inconsequential and crucial incidents, people and places, all in a sequential progression and made by will. Only such a process will enable man to remain conscious through death. Further, he recognizes man's tendency to evade memory of past events where weaknesses, mistakes and embarrassment not only cause him to repeat the same missteps and errors, but also destroy his ability to be confronted with his own conscience. It is therefore not surprising that he emphasises the necessity of gathering and expanding the memories that we most want to disclaim.

He concludes that to remember oneself in time is the first assignment for anyone who wants to develop memory. In earnest attempts to evoke and remember past events, details can appear to be of little significance, but later appear to have terrible consequences. Rodney Collin emphasizes the necessity of confronting such recollections, as they will reveal a hitherto unrecognized link between what one once was and now is, and thus gain a broader and deeper understanding of oneself. It is through this new understanding that one can discover that one previously only accepted one's past because one did not remember it. Finding dramatic moments in one's past may reveal a pattern where it becomes obvious that former situations were building blocks for a coming summit. Further he continues:

> *It may even seem to him that such 'prefigurations' represent a kind of memory backwards, the invisible echoing of impulses in reversed time, which we already guessed. And he will realise that for the final scene to be played differently, these 'rehearsals' must also be altered, right back to his very infancy.*[1]

It is from this point that Collin sees the beginning of an advancement of a dual memory, where it becomes possible to see, not only what indeed happened, but also what could have taken place if one were more conscious. Man's will to reconstruct his life is inextricably linked to his ability to remember his life, which in turn will lead him to connect the recognized new possibilities to recurrence. Seeing the disparity between what is and what could be is an agonising but necessary process, where the film of memory is developed by consciousness and where conscience acts as a fixative.

Reminding us about the release of the overpowering amount of consciousness and conscience in the electronic state at the moment of death, he stresses the necessity to prepare by gradually and intentionally developing and permanently fixing memory while still alive. Unprepared, memory will be destroyed, because, at that point, consciousness is too strong a developer and conscience too violent a fixative. The fundamental prerequisite for the question of whether man can remind himself of a possible change in the next life is rooted in an increasingly comprehensive

---

[1] Rodney Collin, *The Theory of Eternal Life* (Boulder, Colorado: Shambhala Publication Inc., 1984), p91.

and intense memory. By intentionally creating a relationship to past events through memory, he will, in a future deciding moment, through self-remembering, have the possibility to create a reminding factor for similar moments in the next life. It is such efforts that, according to Rodney Collin, not only give rise to a practical understanding of the principle of how memory can be conveyed across the threshold of death, but also make man realise that to remain conscious through death is the purpose of acquiring consciousness. The important role of human suffering relative to inner transformation is generally recognised as a form of payment.

In *The Theory of Eternal Life* Collin's many perspectives on suffering eventually focus on how man may prepare for a conscious immortality. Turning to art, he points at Shakespeare's capability to illuminate and reveal in his characters all sides of human nature through recognition of one's own identical traits, such as struggles and aspirations, passions and sacrifices, and the broad spectrum of human weaknesses:

> At the same time, by so vividly seeing and expressing all mortal passions, something in Shakespeare, we feel, has gradually separated itself from them, remembering all that and yet remaining aside from it.
>
> In Julius Caesar, Macbeth, Hamlet, we see portrayed with many faces this same man who lives through the greatest suffering and tragedy life can bring, and yet in whom something already begins to exist apart from that and apart from his own human feelings in relation to it. It is this very power which gives to all these characters their curious sense of ineffectiveness, when measured by worldly standards. They are already moving on a different path from the rest of humanity: their lives no longer make sense from the point of view of worldly results. For they are beginning to remember themselves.[1]

This same ability to separate oneself from 'oneself' Collin also found in Rembrandt's self-portraits. According to Collin's view, there is a gradually increasing capacity for inner separation that appears in the line of Rembrandt's self-portraits, where even his earliest images show his desire to see himself without great need for defence. However, it is in his later self-portraits that he can, more completely, see himself from the outside.

After pointing out the basic premise that an escape from constraints requires insight into the inherent possibilities of constraints, Collin concludes that Shakespeare and Rembrandt, unlike most people, are not

---

[1] Rodney Collin, *The Theory of Eternal Life* (Boulder, Colorado: Shambhala Publication Inc., 1984), p93-94.

subject to repetition. In Collin's perspective, repetition is not only a consequence of lack of understanding, but also man's new possibility to understand ever more. To him it becomes an impossible thought that Shakespeare should write Hamlet again, not only because it is perfect in itself and that it is imperfections that repeat, but because it is incompatible with cosmic laws that what is perfect should repeat itself, as it would be a waste. Besides, in both Shakespeare's and Rembrandt's heightened aspiration for objectivity, suffering plays a central part of their development:

> *Over and over again we see, entering the lives of such creative geniuses, some great tragedy or suffering which seems strangely inevitable, which they take no trouble to avoid, and which in some curious way they seem to need. It is as if, at a certain point in their growing objectivity towards themselves, no ordinary experience is strong enough, nothing else but suffering is a sufficient trial of their acquired strength.[1]*

Collin sees the tendency to avoid suffering as something that characterizes man to a tremendous extent. It is when suffering is not avoided, and even at times sought, that an element of intentional suffering can enter, and suffering becomes a test for man's already collected capability to disconnect and divide consciousness from his physical manifestations, where the latter is seen objectively.

It might seem aberrant that Collin does not mention acceptance, or at least some aspects of it, when he deals with the topic of not avoiding suffering. It might be argued that for him it was so obviously fundamental and unavoidable that he found it unnecessary to underline or mention it. However, we know from other sources what importance he attaches to the necessity of acceptance. In one of his notes from Thursday, December 16th, 1948, he described how Ouspensky, by accepting the distortions of his ideas, his weak physical condition and pain and separation from friends, was able to turn it all to his own advantage:

> *It was as though every time the normal reaction would have been to make some demand of the outside world, he instead made an equivalent or greater demand upon himself. In this way he became free.[2]*

Turning to great religious teachers of humanity, Collin brings to mind how Christ did not do anything at all to avoid crucifixion and how Buddha knowingly ate the poison that was served him. Although he points out that

[1] Rodney Collin, The Theory of Eternal Life (Boulder, Colorado: Shambhala Publication Inc., 1984), p95-96.
[2] Rodney Collin, The Theory of Conscious Harmony (London: Robinson & Watkins Books Limited, 1958), p47.

the full meaning of these actions must remain hidden for us, he concludes that it is through withstanding the most terrifying shocks and difficulties that our physical world can provide that we can be tested and prepare for a possible escape from the cycle of human lives. Again we are reminded about the necessity for a full consciousness and memory at the threshold of death and into the split second of entering the electronic world. He states that the mastery of pain generates an intensity of consciousness that empowers it to find its own direction and continue separated from the body. Suffering is to Collin by far the most significant instrument to separate one human structure from another. A consequence of such separation from an intense and fully mastered suffering is also a release of an extraordinary amount of emotional energy. Although he acknowledges the importance of suffering in producing the shock needed, he is not closed to other ways.

> *Perhaps the most ecstatic love and compassion could be used; but in such cases as have been recorded for us, such compassion in fact accepts equivalent suffering, and there appears to be no real difference between the two forces.[1]*

Collin draws a parallel between the release of emotional energy by suffering and energy released by the splitting of electronic shells from the atomic nucleus. In the same way that splitting atoms is an artificial process, the separation between consciousness and the body is artificial. The challenge is, according to Collin, not just to find a sufficiently voluminous and pervasive shock, but one that is at the same time under control. A similar precision as during the splitting of atoms is also required in the process of separation between consciousness and body, with the objective of producing an intentional suffering. Not surprisingly, he points out that the condition for suffering is based on a long and thorough moral and psychological preparation.

The grave dangers involved, where consciousness and the body get inseparably fused together due to premature experiments, makes Collin stress that such intentional suffering, or self-torture, does not belong to man at his ordinary level. Not only does this type of experiment belong to a school of regeneration, but even there only takes place at selected times.

Collin compares suffering with heat as a means to visualise two common traits. They can both be a splitting and fixing agent. It is these qualities that can create the flexibility that allows man, during the ongoing suffering, to

[1] Rodney Collin, The Theory of Eternal Life (Boulder, Colorado: Shambhala Publication Inc., 1984), p98.

become inextricably linked to his fundamental identity by eliminating insignificant aspects. He points out that suffering can both destroy and bring about the man, the crucial point being whether consciousness is attached to or detached from the body. Another parallel he draws with regards to heat and suffering is their ability to eradicate. As the shape of metal can be altered by melting, suffering can eradicate, by consumption, past wrong actions.

In order to clarify his perspective on basic preconditions for suffering intentionally, Collin points to the urgency of having resigned from unnecessary suffering. For those who see the necessity of observing their own unnecessary suffering, it can for a long time seem like an endless task. He only provides a small selection of examples, however, his selection – fear, ordinary worry, apprehension, imagination of disaster and our tendency to be enslaved by the opinion of others – is sufficient to indicate the nature of this kind of suffering and indirectly reveal its lack of necessity. To add suffering to such states is, in Collin's view, not only unhealthy but can also indicate a pathological impulse. To be able to transform suffering it is fundamentally essential to be relieved of these kinds of unnecessary inclinations, because they themselves are an obstacle to the insight that paves the way for the deeper motivation that must be the basis of intentional suffering.

Addressing our ordinary description of suffering, he points to the one-sided perception where nothing else enters and thus fails in its purpose to be an implement for transmutation. In his understanding of suffering as a converting factor, it contains not only an equal amount of joy and suffering, but also a similar balance between physical pain and emotional ecstasy or some similar and intense new emotion. Regarding the body, Collin considers suffering as a constituent of man's organic apparatus, and the fear of suffering as the factor that binds man to mortality. To prepare for a conscious immortality, man must accept suffering intentionally, separate his will from the power of the body and thus become ready for an independent presence in an invisible world.

The last month before Ouspensky died he was very marked by the course of the disease. Despite being physically impaired and experiencing ever-increasing pain, he intensified his activities. Hourly walks, despite the fact that he barely could walk, endless car rides at all hours of the day, and long periods without food and drink serve, in *The Theory of Eternal Life,* as some practical examples of how "a man I knew," obviously Ouspensky, prepared to be able to remember himself through death. Another facet of this cosmic drama, which Collin was undoubtably aware of, was that some in Ouspensky's circle of students would benefit from both his preparations and eventually from his final transition. Ouspensky had more than once stated the principle that, in order to move up on the ladder, one has to put someone in one's place, and consequently is towed up by the cosmic ascent of the one in front. To view the relationship between Ouspensky and Rodney Collin in this perspective seems to make sense in various ways, but particularly relative to many of the ideas Collin presents in *The Theory of Eternal Life,* by which he was personally astonished.

All Rodney Collin's ideas, theories, assumptions and speculations about recurrence and eternal life have their origin and are rooted in his vision of the four-circles chart. He himself describes this diagram as a philosophical machine that makes it possible to reproduce, in a symbolic form, different aspects of the universe. Within the framework of these conjoined circles he identifies, as we have seen, the times of matter in mineral, cellular, molecular and electronic state. The scale of lifetimes of these circles unfolded into a line will vary from 80,000 years to 2.5 seconds. In Collin's attempts to create a picture of his understanding of the universe, he is precisely starting from his four-circle diagram of possible worlds. By envisaging how the three points that comprise the logarithmic scale in the cellular world (10 months, 8 years, and 80 years) form the basis of a triangle in contact with the other three worlds, he reveals a central point. The structure of triangles in the other worlds forms similarly on the basis of the points that define their logarithmic scale. From their point of conjunction these triangles radiate into all worlds. This point, which is common to all worlds, is not only the point of death and conception but also the point of universal judgement.

A more central point than where life begins, ends and then begins again is difficult to imagine, and apparently represents the source of all life from Collin's perspective. It is from this source that all the triangles come to possesses an incessant and circulating energy that represents the first motion in his model of the universe, 'Life'.

Collin's second motion of the universe, 'Form', arises from seeing the six intermediate points on each circle as organs or functions in their respective worlds. From an eternal transmitted circulation of energy between these points arise the variety of forms appropriate and corresponding to the actual world in question. The connection between the corresponding points of the circles of the various worlds by which influence can manifest represents Collin's third universal motion: 'As above, so below'. The motion between these three triangles forms the static solid of the universe in Collin's model. The lives that pass round the various circles are created from the interaction within these three triangles in a tempo applicable to the resistance of the individual worlds. The individual lives with their original inherent amount of energy must thus pass through the different worlds at different speeds.

Collin's fourth motion of the universe, 'Time', refers to the passage of lives within the various circles.

His fifth motion represents the differentiations of worlds constructed by the recurrence of all elements in the universe located in their own place. The electronic and mineral world is separated at the level of interpenetration of paradise and earth, the heaven world is then rendered invisible when seen from the mineral world below, just as the interior of the terrestrial world remains hidden in its own complexity when seen from the electronic world above. In other words, heaven and hell are separated by the plane of the molecular and cellular world representing the surface of the earth.

The sixth and last motion of the universe is the unity obtained through a complete and continuous simultaneous inner and outer movement of all the circles, which must therefore be regarded as one. This does not only mean that they fully interpenetrate each other, but also that their spinning exists at all points. A body that is composed of electronic, molecular, cellular and mineral matter exemplifies the idea that everything is everywhere.

According to Collin, by trying to imagine all six motions simultaneously. we will be facing a figure that is probably the closest representation, for a purely logical mind, of a correct model of the universe.

CHAPTER 16
A New Beginning

On November 19th, 1948, Collin had completed the work on his manuscript for *The Theory of Eternal Life*. He had already left England and all the uncertainty that characterised Ouspensky's students after his death. His inspirational visions during the period when he locked himself up at Lyne had finally been given an expression. It is interesting to note how clear and deliberate he was concerning the necessity of giving understanding a form. In a note written on October 27th, shortly before he finished the manuscript, he points at the necessity for each person to find the right expression for his understanding and that anything with no outward expression is suspect and "awfully like imagination." It becomes clear from this note that his ideas of expression were not limited to writing or talking and indirectly indicate that certain forms of expressions may have their own time. Ouspensky would absolutely refuse to talk about certain things he had formerly written. Another aspect of a person's right expression is its ability to open new doors and complete the potential within their former understanding. To Collin, right expression can have the magical inherent ability to make transient understanding one's own and fuller, which in turn can reveal new and unsuspected connections.

Ouspensky, who for years went into detail about the theory of man's transition to higher levels, spoke less and less and eventually became silent. Then he performed what Collin calls the miracle, the performance of which became an expression so perfect that it transcended any other expression.

It seems unthinkable that Rodney Collin, with his perspective and understanding of understanding, would not give his pervasive experience at Lyne a form to convey a content for others to share. In a note from July 30th, 1948, about four months before completing his manuscript, he declares that understanding cannot be static but must either diminish or increase. He was reflecting on a conversation with Ouspensky at Longchamp's in New York in 1943, where Ouspensky told him that in order to learn more one has to teach.

It is obvious from this note that Collin's perspective of the increase of understanding is inextricably linked to sharing and helping others to understand, and that this not only requires the discarding of elements of self-importance, but also a clear recognition of the difference between understanding and opinion. In this note he stresses the importance of the willingness to share, and explains that even people who have got very far gradually understand less when they become unwilling to take the responsibility to share their own understanding. Supporting, sharing, and inspiring others were Rodney Collin's precepts, and seem to have become refined through a growing sensitivity to other people's own initiative. He would not force his feelings or ideas on others, but rather seek to become aware of their own real, deep purpose and understanding.

Joyce Collin-Smith told me once that, when she was with him in Mexico, people from his groups contacted him at all hours of the day. At one time, when she saw that he was very tired, she asked him if he should not consider withdrawing a little and rest. He replied: "One has to do what one can." Although he knew the necessity of rest and tranquillity, there were periods during which day and night restlessly intertwined and where everything was given up to obligations.

After Ouspensky's death there was uncertainty, confusion and indecision among many of his followers. Essentially they divided into three different groups. Some gathered round either Dr. Roles or Rodney Collin, others turned to Franklin Farms in hope of direction. Madame Ouspensky was severely affected by advanced Parkinson's disease, but still oversaw the work at Franklin Farms through a cluster of selected students led by Ouspensky's former secretary, Dorothy Darlington. When Madame Ouspensky finally gave her advice to those who had approached her two months earlier, she was unambiguous, but the reactions were diverse. At Lyne Place the wait had been almost unbearable for many, and when her telegram finally came in early January 1948 saying, "Get in touch with Mr. Gurdjieff in Paris," it was received with some relief.

Dr. Roles was one of a delegation of three that originally went to America to seek Madame Ouspensky's advice, but he dismissed it. Later he justified this by saying that her advice was against Ouspensky's rules. Undeniably this incident echoes the saying: 'Tell me what I need to know, but it had better be what I want to hear'. One of the most prominent members of the people from Lyne who took the advice was the 66-year-old Dr. Kenneth Walker, who then came to lead those of Ouspensky's followers who accepted Madame's advice. It must have been saddening to see that two of his oldest friends, Dr. Francis Roles and R.J.G. Mayor, had no intention whatsoever of going with him to Paris.

G. Adie was another of Ouspensky's faithful followers who travelled to Paris. It would later become clear, from his personal work and work with others, that his decision was undoubtedly correct. The circle of die-hard Ouspensky loyalists was not limited to England. They were also to be found in Cape town, South Africa, where Fairfax Hall held the reins, and amongst several students at Franklin Farms, including Dr. Ralph Phillips and his wife. Dr. Roles, who seemingly felt that Ouspensky's cape fell on his shoulder, decided to continue to his best ability in what he perceived as Ouspensky's footsteps, with the idea in mind to discover the source of the teaching. Rodney Collin and Dr. Roles obviously had different and contradictory perceptions of the road ahead. The search for the source of the Work was initially given an external aspect by Dr. Roles. Rodney Collin's perception of the abandoning of the system was for him a turning point for an intensified, renewed and ever deeper inner search, based on his own real understanding, pure longing and deep wish. Although he saw reconstruction in a multitude of perspectives, it was for him chiefly an inner search and renewal. To Rodney Collin the road ahead was to work from a real place within himself, from where he believed he would receive whatever was needed. He refused to follow any old mind; he followed his own star.

In light of the unquestionable benefit to people coming under Gurdjieff's influence, one may wonder if Rodney Collin made a mistake in not going to Paris. A categorical 'yes' excludes countless other possibilities and it isn't possible to know for certain. However, Collin's written works and practical deeds are a clear indication of his achievements. The sincerity of both his mental and emotional approaches to the challenges of self-examination and expanded consciousness hold a special position for those who find themselves trapped in a desert of theories, or have in other ways run into dryness – he opened doors through what lay in his heart. In this perspective his effort has the function of a spare wheel. It is impossible to say what the consequences of his contributions for the Work-Community would have been if he had followed Madame Ouspensky's advice, which he did not ask for, and gone to Paris.

Some questions are best left unanswered and this seems to be one of them. In order to remain open and to follow what he experienced as an obligation handed down from Ouspensky, it was virtually a duty for him to recognise that some fundamental issues do not allow any compromise. It is also possible that the road to Paris was not in line with his individual cosmic drama, which of course is also difficult to confirm or deny.

Before Collin left England, Dr. Roles watched some people drift away from him and towards Collin. It is difficult to see how this could not affect Dr. Roles' attitude towards Collin, but they remained on friendly terms.

Dr. Roles' external search for the source put him in contact with many people and led him on many paths. His main concern was to find a simple and natural way to self-remembering, which he believed would lead him to his goal. But wherever he looked and whatever he experimented with, he failed to find what he could regard as authentic. In 1951 he had a following of about a hundred people and at that time he formalised their activities by setting up The Society for the Study of Normal Psychology, where one of the activities was to stay up to date on the latest in neuroscience, psychology, and other relevant scientific fields. In his view, this activity was an essential part of what he perceived as the 'reconstruction'.

In 1960 he met Maharishi Mahesh and through him, a year later, Shantananda Saraswati. Saraswati undoubtably made an indelible impression in respect of self-remembering. From that moment, and until he died in 1982, he seems to have been convinced he had found what he was looking for. But was it the source of Ouspensky's system he had found? Dr. Roles thought so. He was equally convinced that the introduction, in 1963, of the Mevlevi whirling dervish ceremony was consistent with Ouspensky's message of reconstruction. Some would probably argue that this was stretching the elastic too far.

In 1997 The Study Society published a commemorative edition of *The Bridge* to mark the anniversary of Ouspensky's death. The journal contains a wide variety of heartfelt articles and poems that pay tribute to his work as a thinker and teacher. However, many of the texts are marred by the claim that Dr. Roles, by amalgamating the Advaita teaching with that of Ouspensky, had acted somehow on orders from him. In light of the numerous detailed descriptions in the unpublished material about what took place before Ouspensky's death, such a claim becomes problematic. There is no confirmation in this material, nor even a hint of an indication, that Dr. Roles at any time received such instruction from Ouspensky.

There is no reason to doubt that he acted in good faith, but his notions of the meaning of reconstruction do not affect what is at issue here. What I am pointing to is that there seems to be an abyss between what he imagined and what was actually said and done at Lyne Place. In this unpublished material Dr. Roles appears as a bit of an outsider in Ouspensky's closest circle. A perspective possibly obscured by his regular dutiful attendance and unshakable loyalty. Given that he was a faithful friend and organizer and not least Ouspensky's always available physician, it is hard to imagine that he was not quite up to date with what was actually going on while the drama unfolded at Lyne. However, so many events point in that direction that it becomes impossible to ignore them. Dr. Roles' unstoppable urge to recreate the system seems to have been characterised by an idealism, with a propulsion that was not under adequate control, but rather appears to have been self-reinforced through the fact that more people were inaugurated and engaged in 'the search for the source'.

Richard Guyatt was one of a trio that Dr. Roles designated as responsible for further operation of the Study Society before he died. In his article in the commemorative issue on Ouspensky he repeats the idea that Ouspensky gave Dr. Roles specific instruction, as the system lacked a method, and that the missing part of the system was found after 14 years when Dr. Roles met Shankaracharya.

It is a well-known fact that a delusion that is repeated sufficiently can often appear as a truth. But it is also a fact that truth is never a delusion. The article is not unique. Much of this tribute in the journal is permeated by the same lack of historical accuracy. Seekers of esoteric knowledge have met resistance at all times. In various labyrinths, among myriads of elements, they must gradually orient themselves on the road ahead. Sometimes with help, other times without. Historical distortions inherited through generations can become such a labyrinth. More than anything else, Ouspensky's books have been a door opener for people who have sought out The Fourth Way. It is predictable that some find odd and challenging the claim that *In Search of the Miraculous* has a one-sided function of being a literary lock to the Adviata teaching, and consequently obscures various lineages of the Gurdjieff teaching.

However, challenge without difficulties is unthinkable and when any maze's difficulties are not accepted, it turns into a trap.

That Dr. Roles chose to interpret Ouspensky's request for a new beginning in the form of outward quest is not so strange in isolation. More notable, however, are some of the central aspects of what he emphasised when meeting what he personally regarded as the original source. In a letter to students in England during a training camp in Rishikesh in June 1961, under the direction of the Maharishi, he was able to assure them that he had not only found the source of the system but was now reunited with it. The direct prelude to this seems to be related to an evening talk in which the Shankaracharya was addressing self-remembering and the necessity of meditation. Albeit in different terminology, self-remembering can be traced back to different religions and secular traditions that *share the same source*. To claim that one of these directions was the source rather than another and to over-claim that this was Ouspensky's missing link is problematic, and does not exactly provide a key to understand the eternal unity in diversity. If it was Shankaracharya's use of the word 'self-remembering' that evening which supported Dr. Roles conviction, as indicated in his correspondence, it all becomes quite disturbing and incomprehensible because this term's form, regardless of terminology, serves only as a carrier of the substance that constitutes its content.

Dr. Roles' oblique conclusion that he had found the source which he believed Ouspensky lacked has contributed to an effective promotion of his version of the Fourth Way. That his business was a further development and completion of Ouspensky's work is not only questionable but a completely different question. Dr Roles utilised the terminology 'Ouspensky's Fourth Way' in order to enhance the marketing of his findings. That Dr. Roles found something of true value to himself and many others cannot be questioned, but mixing Ouspensky into it all is a flawed and unnecessary tactic.

Whatever one might think of Dr. Roles' dispositions, it is perhaps his own startling words that reveal his point of view, perspectives and insights. As late as the summer of 1982, he let the following words fall about Ouspensky and Gurdjieff in a conversation with Dr. Peter Fenwick in the presence of Professor Richard Guyatt:

> ... *Ouspensky didn't realise that we already had, every human being has, a Divine Self, a spark of the Divine Self within him, whether they know it or not. Ouspensky's teacher denied this.*[1]

In a note from January 25th, 1948, three months after Ouspensky's death, we get an impression of Collin's perspective on the incompatibility between himself and Dr. Roles and how he consciously accepted and steered away from conflict and animosity:

> *Two currents begin to separate – those who see this new beginning, and through it quite new possibilities in a more free and individual way; and those who think that nothing new was shown, and who wish to*

---

[1] The Bridge -P.D. Ouspensky Commemorative Issue (London: The Study Society, 1997), p240.

perpetuate the old way and old attitudes. It must be like that. One has only to read the New Testament to see it was always so. And the only important thing, I believe, is that people of the two views should not fight or obstruct each other, but each go on with what they have to do.[1]

When, after some hesitation, Collin finally decided to go to Mexico, he was leaning heavily on his understanding of Ouspensky's abandonment of the system and not least on his strong recommendation to start anew. For Collin the idea of reconstruction was endless. He seems, at the time of leaving England, to have some mild acceptance for those who did not see Ouspensky's death as a beginning of a new age. Five years later, either his patience with the custodians of the inherited tradition was close to zero, or he was intentionally creating a shock to draw attention to what to him was a living fact. Anyhow, July 24th, 1953, he wrote:

It was put into our hands to be the agents of miracles. And we tell people to control the expression of their negative emotions, not to push, and to form an orderly queue for an unknown bus, which may one day take them to a twopenny stage nearer heaven! I wonder that a great voice doesn't come out of heaven thundering: 'O ye of little faith!' When will people understand that a new age has really dawned? When will they stop sealing up the terrible crack into heaven which Ouspensky has made, with precautions and good behaviour? We must allow divine madness to take possession of us now, before hell freezes!

To Rodney Collin it was unquestionable that Ouspensky's quest for the miraculous had succeeded and was fully accomplished by his death. The drama that played out in the closed circle of his most intimate students at Lyne in September 1948, where telepathy was commonplace, not only made them witness to the miraculous, but they also took part in it. Through these experiences, he saw how Ouspensky, in silence, showed:

… what it means for a man to pass consciously into the realm of the spirit.[2]

This was a turning point and it created in him a key attitude to life. To break down the resistance to the miraculous, in himself and others, became a major task for him. His own experiences of higher realms became a source of inspiration for his determination to be an instrument

---

[1] Rodney Collin, The Theory of Conscious Harmony (London: Robinson & Watkins Books Limited, 1958), p179.
[2] Rodney Collin, The Theory of Conscious Harmony (London: Robinson & Watkins Books Limited, 1958), p179.

to encourage others. He firmly believed that the energy released at Ouspensky's death gave him direction and further understanding. Later, his perspective of Ouspensky's influence expanded beyond those few who were with him at the end, to include people on a wider scale. Collin understood this to be possible because Ouspensky, by mastering death, made a way open.

The prerequisite for taking advantage of this new opportunity is to have a positive attitude. In Collin's recognition of how the dawn of a new age necessitates the abandoning and reconstruction of the system, one is reminded of the attitude of Ibsen's Peer Gynt when he finally meets the button-moulder. It was far from positive; Peer did not want to be melted down.

It was not always surprising to Collin that people found his convictions too fantastic or morbid and even questioned his sanity, but he tried to make them understand:

> All that Ouspensky did and said at that time seemed to me to have exactly this purpose and effect – to sort out the people who could respond to the miraculous from those who could not [...] It was very clear that if a man in a higher state of consciousness acts directly from the perceptions of that state, [...] he will seem mad to men in an ordinary state.[1]

Robert de Ropp, Rodney Collin's old friend, from the time in Dick Sheppard's Peace Pledge Union, later became very sceptical of the role Collin perceived he had after Ouspensky's death. Although he never failed to regard both Janet and Rodney as devoted to Ouspensky, he saw Rodney Collin as having contracted a virulent form of False Messiah disease. De Ropp claims that this syndrome occurs among people with the natural characteristics of being less scattered and less divided than the usual population. In addition, he believed that they also lack less in will and unity than the average man. He identified the cause of the syndrome as an error in the emotional brain, where a powerful emotion that could lead to self-transformation instead becomes a source for an ever more tight connection with that which one should free oneself from.

That Rodney Collin was less scattered, stronger in will and more together than the average man, seems undeniable. However, there is a significant gap between the other fundamental criteria in de Ropp's diagnosis and Rodney Collin's character and actions. To imply that he, in

---

[1] Rodney Collin, *The Theory of Conscious Harmony* (London: Robinson & Watkins Books Limited, 1958), p39.

lack of conscience, used attributes he had acquired through inner discipline to demand absolute obedience and thus dominate others is a delusion that does not conform to the impressions of those who knew him well. Such claims are obviously incompatible with Collin's actions. When de Ropp sought out Collin at the Rockefeller centre during the war to join him at Franklin Farms, he obviously had another image of him as both large and genial. His diagnosis of Collin comes later and supplements the range of critical characteristics connected with inner work that he awards generously to a number of people, something that is a feature of his later writing.

When he criticises himself, it is characterised as the consequence of his confidence-inspiring self-examination. It is highly questionable that his subsequent analytical search of others was equally objective simply because it was critical. After a closer examination of our own negative characterisation of others, most of us have to admit that we are often moving in a landscape where our subjectivity hangs like a fog, so low and impenetrable that we do not even see our own hand. As it is not within the scope of this book to speculate as to the causes of de Ropp's recurring disapproval of others, we will leave this and simply conclude that there must be a reason.

CHAPTER 17
Mexico

When the Collins went to Mexico it was after some hesitation. To break away from England was not so easy for them. It was the same for several of their companions, however, in addition to an unshakable trust in Rodney, they were motivated by the social climate which included rationing and other aftermaths of the war. In addition, the Labour Party's policies and post-war measures put some pressure on wealthy people like Janet Collin. One way or another, there was a lot of uncertainty in England at that time.

It's also conceivable that there was a certain amount of tension between the various factions of Ouspensky's followers which Collin wanted to distance himself from and help to neutralise by leaving. However, what was crucial to Collin was his rock-solid faith that rested on Ouspensky's call for reconstruction and the need to start over and he seemed now, more than ever, to be a man of action and not reaction.

They first settled in Guadalajara, a large city in the eastern highlands of Mexico, where Collin made the final touches to the manuscript of *The Theory of Eternal Life* on November 19th, 1948. They had been traveling with a group of followers, who must have been overwhelmed by the unfamiliar surroundings. Guadalajara, with its wide brimmed sombrero-dressed figures and distinctive mariachi-music, was the most Mexican of all cities. There must have been little in the external circumstances that did not indicate that something new was about to happen. Collin, on the other hand, had been familiarized with Mexico during his wartime service and had already developed a passionate relationship with both the country and the people.

After November they all moved to Tlalpan and installed themselves in an old hacienda outside Mexico City. More of Ouspensky's followers arrived from England and the community at Tlalpan grew. In Mexico City they rented a flat where meetings were held regularly. They attracted new people, mostly Mexicans, but also foreigners who had been stranded in the city for various reasons, and the community grew. Due to Janet's financial independence, there were no economic constraints to implementation of the projects that they thought may benefit their work.

Mexico

In 1949 they bought a property outside Mexico City with a panoramic view of the valley and the city. Here, at 9000 feet above sea level and 2000 feet above the city, Rodney Collin decided to raise what would be known as the Planetarium of Tetecala. By digging and carving out two areas in the eruptive ground they created two chambers and prepared the ground level for the rest of the construction. The lower part consisted of two chambers linked together: the Chamber of the Sun and the Chamber of the moon. In a circular space between the chambers rested an upturned shell on a stand capturing the sun at summer solstice. A curving narrow passage surrounded the chambers. Above ground there were to be two halls. One for Movements and folklore dancing and one to house a library.

It became clear early on that the order of magnitude of the project was so extensive that the effort the group itself could make was insufficient. Labour was therefore hired from nearby areas. Hard physical work in a hot climate at 9000 feet elevation was demanding. With management lacking experience of similar projects, it was easy to lose track. The progress was late – very late – and it was not due to climatic conditions alone. Both the work team chairman and several of the employees were exploiting the situation, to the point of it becoming a major scam.

Although the Collins led a frugal way of life, it was obvious that someone in the neighbourhood smelled money. Collin was not devoid of critical sense, but he was apparently too trusting and naïve at times. Having, as Joyce Collin-Smith put it, 'charity at the tips of his fingers' and excessive trust in others is a curious classical human combination. On the other hand, it was not in his nature to meet people with a closed scepticism, which can be another trap. However, the challenges for people with such different starting points are the same, although the road may be different: reaching a kind of a balanced centre in a pendulum. In perspective of inner growth there is always something to learn and what is to be learned always takes a shape and form.

Collin's confidence, exaggerated at times, would later prove to be the shape of his challenge. To draw attention to Collin's at times unfounded trust in others is not intended to point to an excessive character trait, but only an aspect among many. Among those who knew him well, he was regarded as gentle and amiable with a quality of dignity and authority around him. In light of many of his writings, these qualities were obviously developed through conscious self-examination. One of and possibly the best quality that enables one to understand others is self-understanding, echoing Gurdjieff's advice: "judge others by yourself and you will rarely be mistaken." In this perspective, Collin's self-insight did not erase his naive inclination, but placed it in a more holistic context.

As the work proceeded at the site of the planetarium, Rodney Collin could focus more on the details of the project. While the peons continued the construction above ground, Collin was daily labouring at the curving passage around the two chambers below. His manual skills were well developed and daily he tirelessly carved out pieces for the mosaic and applied them to the walls of the underground passage. Bit by bit a picture took form that showed human evolution from the most primary level to the perfect man.

Beside the work on the Planetarium, plans were made to build houses for the community on the site. Although the work on the Planetarium dominated their activities at times, a multitude of chores was initiated. Following Janet's initiative and leadership, a health care clinic was established, where a doctor from the city came twice a week on a regular basis as a service for the poor workers and peons in the area. Woman and children, literally dressed in rags, were given full skirts and blouses by another work team, also led by Janet, including their now teenage daughter Chloe.

As a contribution to self-aid, they purchased an old hacienda, where local women produced blankets and serapes in Aztec designs that were aimed at American tourists. Rodney, who wanted to expand the business, applied for an export permit, but had to give up due to bureaucratic reluctance. With a seemingly invincible courage, he kept starting new projects. A mine for the extraction of silver, salt and various nitrates was explored, but the combination of lack of roads, lazy workers and an endless bureaucracy put an end to it all. In Mexico City he established the first English bookstore, Library Britannica. To publish Mexican versions of Ouspensky's and Maurice Nicoll's books, in addition to his own, he founded the publishing firm, Ediciones Sol. In a note from February 22nd, 1950, he expresses his unconditional optimism and confidence:

> It is very difficult to convey the strange springtime feeling of beginning from the beginning, of a new unspoiled start, which one gets in Mexico just now. Everything is growing, expanding, developing; everywhere building – houses, roads, factories, schools – and among all kinds of people an enormous enthusiasm, a sort of optimistic certainty in something, in some possibility. Only in exactly what, nobody knows.[1]

---

[1] Rodney Collin, The Theory of Conscious Harmony (London: Robinson & Watkins Books Limited, 1958), p182.

Mexico

In the first months of 1950, an extraordinary number of people from different walks of life applied to the group. Collin seems pleasantly surprised at how strikingly easy and natural it was to achieve a mutual understanding and sympathy amongst miners, ballet dancers and politicians, etc. The key for further development of these relations was to meet people on their own level, speak with them individually in their own language, and relate to their actual life. That these new relations could not be based on any presentation of an intellectual framework was clear and obvious to him. The possibilities, as he saw it, were within the framework of actual life, like in cultivating, building, dancing, educating and improving. This attitude, which opened up an unlimited amount of new meanings of the term reconstruction, came to influence and nourish his work. And so he came to practice the difference between thinking, talking and actually doing the work. To him work was not a one-sided question of effort, energy and will, but a sincere recognition of seemingly right motivations. On June 20th, 1951 he wrote:

> *Some people are like men laboriously digging an enormous well to reach water, when a clear stream is flowing past two yards away. In some, pride in effort has to melt, and they have to sit back quietly and let good things gently soak into them, certainty gently spring up in them.*[1]

The unfortunately widespread idea that insight is only gained through some sort of self-mortification, restriction, shame and going against oneself was not something he trusted. After Ouspensky's death it became clearer than ever that what can bring you back to your own path could be both good and pleasant. This new and simplified approach with gravity in a sincere wish seems to reveal his reconstruction in action.

When Joyce Collin-Smith joined him in Mexico, she had not seen him for a couple of years, but had read his books and corresponded with him extensively. She was taken by surprise when she, after one hour in his company, realised that he was completely different from her recollection of him. The group of people that had come with him when he left England was in minority, outgrown by Mexicans. His lectures and the group meetings were mainly held in Spanish, which she did not understand. She quickly felt left out. Although she, as she expressed it herself,

> *... talked my head off, asking questions and expressing my opinion on everything.*[2]

---

[1] Rodney Collin, The Theory of Conscious Harmony (London: Robinson & Watkins Books Limited, 1958), p4.
[2] Joyce Collin-Smith, Call No Man Master (Authors Online Book, 2004), p59.

She felt isolated and feared that she would struggle to learn much. The constant pressure of inquiries that Collin was subject to made it difficult for her to find an opportunity to talk to him. One day, in the Collins' new home in Rio Naza, she was finally able to catch up with him:

> I sat on a long sofa and tried with increasing urgency and exasperation to question him about the basis of his present day thought. 'I don't understand anything! I am waiting to get some sort of revelation of what your work is actually all about', I burst out finally. The blue eyes regarded me benignly. 'Joyce, nothing can happen until you are quiet', he said. Until that moment I had not realized the depth and extent of my inner agitation.[1]

Our ordinary ideas of effort, understanding and change is generally coloured by some sort of doing. Collin had himself for years struggled 'to do' and wrote in a note from November 5th, 1949 how impossible that was, however much he tried. His advice to Joyce is ancient, but contrary to most of our ordinary thinking. It also indirectly reveals another conception of a more demanding effort where we, potentially, can become actively passive.

Doing nothing is not easy, we are too concerned with fulfilling desires that maintain a self-image. To step outside formerly known footprints and into a virgin landscape without paths, and where our own sincerity becomes the wizard, seems to be the vital part of the nature of the new beginning Rodney Collin is pointing to. A pure wish to be oneself has no compromises.

Joyce took his advice and tried to relax and be present to the best of her ability and, as recommended, in silence:

> Suddenly the room began to swim in a rather alarming way. I thought the slatted light and shadow might be about to give me a migraine headache, to which I have always been slightly subject. I said shakily: 'Could you close the blind, Rodney?'
>
> He reached behind him and pulled the cord. The lines of black and white disappeared and the room became marginally dimmer. Still we looked at one another and nothing was said.
>
> Then slowly Rodney's face began to change in shape and type. I couldn't understand what was happening.
>
> 'You look like an old man', I blurted out. 'There's a growth of a bit of a beard'

---

[1] Joyce Collin-Smith, Call No Man Master (Authors Online Book, 2004), p2.

'It's only because I haven't shaved for a few days', came a voice out of Rodney's mouth that was not Rodney's voice at all.

Frightened, I glanced about the room in confusion. Then I looked back again. The face of the man cross-legged in the chair was the square, heavy-jawed, bespectacled visage of Piotr Damianovitch Ouspensky, Rodney's beloved master, always known in the household now simply as O.

'You are Mr. Ouspensky!'

'I was called that', answered a different guttural voice.

In a few moments, the O face faded completely, and like a television program in which one picture is panned in over another, an oriental face appeared.

'You're Chinese now'.

'Tibetan', he answered.

Then with great rapidity, a series of different faces superimposed themselves one on another – dark-skinned, middle eastern, Mediterranean and northern European, of several different apparent ages and types, some wearing headgear of one kind or another. My heart thumped as I watched.

'Who are you?' I asked at last.

'All these and many others too', answered the voice of Rodney Collin, and his sunburned, grey-haired, blue-eyed twentieth century face appeared as normal as if it had been there all the time.

'Your other lives?'

'The curtain of time grows thin', he answered me.[1]

Shortly after this incident Joyce experienced an intensified period where impressions were reaching her with an unknown rapidity, she seemed to be braided in and out of time and she saw herself and people around her shifting roles that seemed so familiar to her. Talking to Rodney about it, he told her that he thought such a thing as a group soul may exist, where people incarnate within reach of each other, though their relationships shift. To try to make sense of such phenomena, within the limits of our ordinary conception of time as only linear, would be absurd and impossible. As our conception of time is linked to our psychic function, a change, like expanded consciousness, would consequently change our relation to time. Our actual experience of it would be different. However,

---

[1] Joyce Collin-Smith, *Call No Man Master* (Authors Online Book, 2004), p62-63.

in order to think differently about time we need to allow for a fifth dimension, as in the example of Evremov.

Joyce and I spoke of her experience of the transfigurations of Rodney several times over the years, as we found it so remarkable. I can only state that I knew her very well for many years and found her to be a serious, intelligent and sound person. The way she spoke about her experience made it impossible for me not to trust her.

Rodney Collin was well versed in Mexican culture and familiar with culture-historical places that he would sneak away to at various times of the year. Sometimes these excursions were expeditions of several days, other times more like extended picnics. One of these trips, when Joyce was with him, went through what is known as the Road of the Dead and to Teotihuacan to visit areas of Aztec and Toltec origin. When they finally arrived and stood in front of The Pyramid of the Sun, Rodney asked Joyce what she wanted. Looking at the pyramid she told him, gritting her teeth, that she wanted to go to the top. There was only one problem, Joyce could hardly walk. She had sprained her ankle a little earlier and it was now so swollen she could hardly let it touch the ground. Rodney's wife, Janet, who knew her condition, looked at her and said: "Oh Joyce don't be tiresome."

I looked at Rodney. He held out his hand, ignoring Janet. 'Come along then,' he said, 'if that's what you want.'[1]

After immense struggles they made it to the top.

Sitting under the sun they remained in silence watching the rest of the group appear as tiny figures as they had all assembled at the top of the Pyramid of the Moon.

Joyce seems to have had a revelation where she recognized Rodney Collin as her brother. Collin did not directly confirm this but admitted the possibility and pointed to a karmic link.

Group trips were regular at times, but Collin also went alone into deserted areas and could be gone for several days in a row. In our countless conversations, Joyce told me that on those occasions he left without any luggage and little food, often just with water and a bag of nuts and raisins. No matter what he did, he didn't seem to restrict himself in any way. He always found time for private conversations with guests or group members when they requested it in between practising movements, authorship or leading group meetings. It is easy to imagine that such a high level of

---

[1] Joyce Collin-Smith, *Call No Man Master* (Authors Online Book, 2004), p68.

activity consumed a lot of energy, but it was precisely through these activities that he generated energy.

Practical activities created a platform for interpersonal relationships, which again gave rise to his understanding of possible new beginnings. It would have been a significant challenge to find the right balance between initiative and restraint. What was clear to him, however, was that a new beginning was incompatible with an intellectual approach, where new people would only be met with theories.

He saw that practical approaches not only opened the door to experiences of harmony in interpersonal relationships, but also clarified the thresholds that needed to be recognised, understood and overcome. In other words, for Collin, it was of utmost importance to approach people at their existing level of daily life, being and understanding.

By giving harmony a central aspect in inner and outer work, it seems he found a factor that had the potential to relieve polarisation, isolation, animosity and other subjective psychological constraints, such as fixed and repetitive attitudes of both mental and emotional character. A perspective that seeks to build on the idea of harmony requires a kind of openness that presupposes apparent contradictions are part of a larger and more holistic picture. Such perspective can give rise to a new mindset and meanings. The viewpoint on Ouspensky's separation from Gurdjieff has, more often than not, been based on, and concluded with, incompatible contradictions. However, Collin's view on their roles and interrelationships is an example of an expanded and more holistic view than what has traditionally emerged.

On July 18th, 1955 he wrote:

> *In my understanding the whole field of higher influences which was transmitted to us through Gurdjieff and Ouspensky forms a single whole, a world if you like. Those two strange and great men are the opposite poles of that world. That is why they had to separate. That is why, during their lives, one had to work with one or the other of them, just as one has to live either in the northern or southern hemisphere. If one thinks of them as individuals, they will always seem contradictory and antagonistic. If one thinks of what lies behind them, one will see that both they and their work were complementary, and that they were being used to launch into the world a great new esoteric experiment. What is the final meaning of that experiment nobody knows yet. Perhaps it is to prepare the way for something that is yet to come. In any case it was to*

demonstrate the harmonious development of man, as Gurdjieff once called it.[1]

Ostensible contradictions and rivalries between Gurdjieff and Ouspensky are, in Collin's opinion, nothing more than a manifestation of an objective lawfulness in which two different roles clash together to give rise to something new and greater. He regarded this type of conflict as an inherent pattern that a school receives when it manifests on Earth. He perceived the relationship between Plato and Socrates and Jellal al-Din Rumi and Shems-edin as possible parallels. Nevertheless, this objective lawfulness on which he based his understanding, was to him an adequate explanation of the distinction between Gurdjieff and Ouspensky.

When he, in January 1951, unequivocally emphasised that he regarded the Work as one whole, it was because he had experienced a level of understanding where apparent inequalities were reconcilable.

Collin believed that the total effect of Gurdjieff's and Ouspensky's work in the world, being an example of harmony, was beyond what could be imagined and that the influence of both groups and individuals on the modern society and in the world were significant.

According to the Gurdjieff and Ouspensky teaching, no phenomena can arise unless there is an interaction between three forces. Active, passive and a neutralising force, where the latter is the formative force.

Collin's emphasis on harmony must not be confused with an attempt to achieve direct access to a neutralising force, but must rather be understood as an expression of an active positive attitude or force that gradually develops will, which indirectly helps to give neutralising force room to manifest. In a note written April 30th, 1949, he is clear that neutralising force, in itself, is a gift and not something that one can directly calculate.

Ever since Ouspensky's death, it became clear that Collin and Dr. Roles had divergent visions of the future. It became important for Collin that this divergent vision wouldn't give rise to strife and dissatisfaction between them. From this period, we can see an undercurrent of his passion and longing for harmony, which eventually came to the surface early in 1952 and became a central theme at various levels and in different contexts. It became a recurring theme in both his letters and notes and he came to regard harmony as the key for our time and the future. Simultaneously, he pointed out how demanding it is to develop the ability to project harmony.

---

[1] Rodney Collin, *The Theory of Conscious Harmony* (London: Robinson & Watkins Books Limited, 1958), p121.

He did not regard harmony as a sentiment, but as a science and an art to be developed; a task which neither religion, psychology or science had fulfilled. The only exception was in the realm of sound, where, in Collins' perspective, harmony had been fully developed.

To elucidate the necessity that and the scale at which all levels of Work must embrace harmony, he writes:

> *In individual man, harmony among functions; harmony between body, soul and spirit; harmony among its different members, harmony between its leader and its origin; in the great esoteric impulse launched through Gurdjieff and Ouspensky, harmony among all lines and groups; harmony between them, their founders and God; in the world, harmony among all branches of knowledge, all peoples, all esoteric lines. [...] Was the new beginning for Gurdjieff and Ouspensky all part of the same great plan? The transfer of the two poles of the Work from earth to a level where they could operate in an immensely more complete and penetrating way? I believe it is something like that. I believe that Great School, having an enormous new esoteric impulse to launch in the world, marked out two men who would act as opposite poles of this impulse and whose life work would be preparation for it. The real beginning, the conception of this new influence, I believe began with their deaths. Began when their polarity was translated to what we have come to call the electronic world. That was the conception. But when and what is the birth? Would not the whole effort be to create harmony, into which it could enter?[1]*

The 1950's would in many ways prove to be fruitful years in Mexico. The country's economy, which had been struggling since the 1930's, had a spectacular economic take off in 1950, followed by a rapid economic growth that was to last for 30 years. The outlook for the population suddenly turned out to be bright, very bright. The entire social structure was given a boost through industrialisation, healthcare and education. Unemployment dropped dramatically. On the other hand, there was a strain exerted on communities by the ever-increasing urbanisation.

At the turn of the year, the influx of members to Collin's group was significant and the original English colony was still more in a minority as some of them had drifted off.

---

[1] Rodney Collin, *The Theory of Conscious Harmony* (London: Robinson & Watkins Books Limited, 1958). p184-185.

The group's activities had not gone unnoticed since its initiation in 1948 but had created a curious enthusiasm among many at different social levels. Rodney Collin, with his central position in the activities and with his radiance of friendly calm and natural authority, became the subject of special interest. Rumours about him easily spread and led to exaggerations, especially when mixed with imaginary notions and speculations. Anyway, he became a featured, reputed and legendary figure in a variety of different environments. That he was aware of having achieved a certain notoriety in this period seems obvious. Just as obvious, he was not deceived into believing that this was an advantage. On the contrary, he clearly believed that becoming visible limits future possibilities, and that if one used one's name, regardless of whether it was for good or bad intentions, it would weigh down, limit and be a burden on one's fate.

Among Collin's many concepts, ideas and opinions, which he expresses in his correspondence and notes from 1950, he is particularly keen to convey that there is a unity behind all apparent inequalities. One of the most important tasks in the Work is reaching an understanding of unity and then to melt down the suspicion and resistance that exists between different groups. The fear and condemnation and blaming of other lines of Work have their origin in an inadequate perspective. However, the elimination of previously impenetrable barriers did not mean that groups should compromise or mix, but only that with a more holistic understanding they could make their own Work more fruitful. He was still of the conviction that it was necessary for groups not to be mixed so that a larger plan, where different groups had different tasks, could develop without interruption.

After coming to Mexico, he felt that many doors had opened for him. Not only more doors than he could have hoped for, but also more doors than he could attribute to only one teacher. It became increasingly apparent to him that there were some underlying forces that, through tremendous efforts, tried to unite people on a certain level through understanding.

Cooperation and harmony, when seen from a holistic perspective, becomes self-evident. In Collin's holistic thinking, there is no limit to where one might seek harmony. The natural consequence of Collin's experience and understanding of the meaning of wholeness/unity was undoubtedly his gradually growing commitment to harmony.

By giving harmony such a central and all-encompassing meaning, Collin achieves not only a diverse practical approach, but an approach that paves the way for ever new experiences. This key concept of unlimited harmony challenges the ordinary thinking that often springs from fixed and subjective ideas of good and evil and almost uses it as a regenerating springboard to reach a new and higher state of mind.

In a passage from a letter written on February 15th, 1951, Collin exemplifies such a transition from one state of mind to another. He writes:

> *In the chapter on 'Experimental Mysticism' in A New Model it is described how in certain mystical states 'what is ordinarily objective becomes subjective, and what is ordinarily subjective becomes objective'. In self-remembering, one takes the first step towards this, and it may happen that inner voices, arguments, thoughts, emotions, hopes, fears, aspirations, which in the ordinary way are felt as subjective, as 'I' and 'mine', suddenly becomes objective, becomes 'he' and 'his'. In this way one begins to find different people within one. One's own inner life becomes the object of observation, gives one new and important impressions. And one comes to perhaps the deepest question of all, 'Who am I?'*[1]

Collin points to something absolutely crucial here: That an expanded and objective understanding is conditioned by a new consciousness. In other words, it is not conditioned by abstract thinking, reasoning and formation of concepts.

Collin's new level of consciousness was the premise of his holistic view. This view became the source of his attraction to and understanding of the necessity for an all-encompassing harmony.

It is essential to keep in mind that when we refer to 'Collin's holistic thinking', it refers to an expression of thoughts, wishes and actions that are formed in an expanded consciousness. Such expressions may be a signal from, but never a bridge to, the understanding Collin himself had. That such experience is ineffable and cannot be fully reduced to mental concepts, is a known historical phenomena in all esoteric teachings.

Not long before Joyce had arrived in Mexico, a strange character nicknamed 'Mema' had joined the group. Her real name was Guillerma Dickins. She was born in 1916 in the outskirts of Puchuca, at the time a small mountain town on the Mexican high plateau, where she lived her childhood years in a semi-feudal society among great haciendas. Her strong interest in Mexican folklore had eventually led her to extensive

---

[1] Rodney Collin, *The Theory of Conscious Harmony* (London: Robinson & Watkins Books Limited, 1958), p3.

travels, visiting the country's most remote areas where she studied the country's infinite variety of traditions, but especially its dances and music.

This interest later led her, in 1954, to write the book Dances of Mexico. Using illustrations by the Mexican artist, Mireya Iturbe, and step notations, she recreated three of Mexico's most famous and colourful dances.

Mexican religious practice was essentially Catholic, with the addition of some superstition and elements of ancient knowledge. As a devoted Catholic, Mema made her confessions regularly. She claimed that during a confession she had told her confessor about a receiving a clairvoyant message to seek out Rodney Collin and was advised to pursue the impetus.

The confessor, who supposedly recognised Collin's name, later gave her his address. When she later visited Collin and was shown into his study where a portrait painting of Ouspensky hung centrally, she exclaimed:

That's the man who sent me![1]

During my countless conversations over the years with Joyce Collin-Smith, we regularly talked about Mema. I wanted to understand but could not help being sceptical of most of what Joyce had told me about her, so it was most often I who raised the topic. Joyce, who undoubtedly shared much of my scepticism, nevertheless kept an open mind and did not completely reject Mema's merits. Although this was beyond me at the time, I later learned to endure my lack of understanding of what I perceived as Collin's trust in Mema. Joyce would smile knowingly as I stubbornly tried to explain my doubts, possibly as an attempt to open cracks in my inflexible attitude. However, on a number of other occasions she challenged my rigidity directly.

The original housing community at Tlalpam had been dissolved and the Collin's had moved to Rio Naza 5. Other members of the community had also established themselves individually in the surrounding area. Joyce believed that Mema's arrival and influence caused the cessation of the group's common household. Many were critical of her almost unstoppable propensity to communicate 'messages' of varying content. Among several of Collin's older followers there was a strong suspicion and a marked dissatisfaction with her behaviour. Others were uncertain and did not know what to believe. However, a third group, mainly associated with Collin's wife Janet, was thrilled and intrigued by Mema's role as a medium.

An example of a message from Mema, that many would consider absurd, can be found in the following passage where Joyce writes:

---

[1] Joyce Collin-Smith, Call No Man Master (Authors Online Book, 2004), p73.

MEXICO

Her comment at an art exhibition that she found Turner pallid and incomprehensible became: 'Mr. Ouspensky did not approve of Turner's style.'[1]

It is easy to imagine that there were some who did not need too many 'messages' of this calibre before certain misgivings and impatience inevitably came to the surface. Despite internal turmoil in the group and the cessation of cohabitation, the construction project in Tlalpam continued.

Several of the original members had drifted off after Mema's entry. However, a narrow circle, primarily Mexicans who were obviously under the influence of Mema, seem to have intensified their activities during this troubled period. They met regularly in Rodney Collin's study in the rented apartment in Rio Naza 5. What their activities were is uncertain, except that Joyce, who didn't speak the language and wasn't invited to participate, knew that a tape recorder was being used. Nevertheless, Joyce felt that these meetings were a direct reason for several of the group members to withdraw.

Joyce, who lived with the Collin family, could not help but notice that Mema's frequent visits eventually became a daily occurrence. This despite the fact that she had her own household. Mema was married to Toby Dickins, an Englishman originally from Brighton, who worked in Mexico City for the international company, Kodak.

Collin had long been preoccupied with the idea that it would be possible to explore traces of schools of The Fourth Way from ancient times. One day he told Joyce that this was possibly imminent, with the help of Mema. He had over a period of time gathered the basic material for further research and planned a trip to Europe and the Middle East to verify his assumptions. The idea was to gather material in a written form which he considered important for the future.

Joyce was intrigued by the idea of this project and wanted to participate, but it was not practical. At home in England her husband and daughter awaited her. The departure for the expedition and Joyce's return home were coincidental and together they flew from the Central Airport of Mexico City to New York where they parted. Mema, Janet and Rodney Collin, and their 17 year old daughter, Chloe, travelled to Paris, while Joyce proceeded home alone.

---

[1] Joyce Collin-Smith, *Call No Man Master* (Authors Online Book, 2004), p74.

After returning home, she contacted Dr. Roles and asked if she could rejoin the London group, but he was hesitant. He eventually gave in, but placed a strict condition: she should not under any circumstances talk to anyone in the group about her perceptions of or experience with Rodney Collin.

After Janet and Rodney Collin, Chloe and Mema had arrived in Paris, Chloe was accepted as a student in a convent school in Paris, where she was to be taught Greek and Latin. It was believed that with such knowledge she would be able to help her father in the future. Mema and the Collins travelled to Athens, then Rome and on to England, where they had planned to meet friends. These extensive journeys were only possible because of Janet's fortune. Although she had for many years contributed significant sums to Lyne Place and Franklin Farms, in addition to a number of projects in Mexico, she was obviously not short of money. Nor was there any immediate danger that she would be, because consumption was confined to the income from investments and the capital remained untouched. All the money was held for her in a trust. This was an arrangement provided by her father, Wilfred Buckley, who, with his Victorian mindset, initially did not have much faith in women's ability to handle money.

Joyce recalled incorrectly that Mema and the Collins returned to England in late 1955, after various trips in Europe and the Middle East. However, letters from Collin to Joyce dated August 25th, November 1st and December 27th are all written in Mexico in 1955. Another letter to Derry and Joyce with a letterhead from The Ritz Hotel, Teheran, is dated June 2nd in the same year. This indicates that the return to England must have taken place sometime between June and August. In addition, this indirectly confirms that the trio made not only one but two trips from Mexico in their search for traces of esoteric schools. In a letter from August 1955, Collin refers to what must have been the second trip:

> There was a tremendous amount to arrange after being away so long, and it took some time for us to get our feet firmly on the ground after being in the air for three and a half months. Now things are sorting themselves out, and the line of work for the next year begins to emerge. As yet we have hardly begun to put together what was collected on the trip.

After Paris, Mema and the Collins went to Seville, where they witnessed Seneca de Seville, better known as The Holy Week, which is celebrated during the week leading up to Easter. It features an up to twelve-hour long procession where massive floats carrying lifelike religious figures and objects are eventually brought to the Cathedral. Various images of a sorrow-full Virgin Mary are central. Collin came to regard the ceremony as an expression of how man tries to re-live the history for himself. Impulses from this week contributed to a perspective before setting out on this expedition. In a note from July, 20th, 1955 he wrote:

> ... it is now clear that this last trip was a journey in search of the Passion.[1]

The Passion of Christ and the Gospel Drama gradually gained a central position in his consciousness. Not only did he see them as the most significant and perfect expression of a school on Earth, but that all schoolwork, at all times, was an attempt in various ways to reflect that.

What largely occupied him in Rome were the many traces of various circles that set in motion constructive undercurrents in the 19th century that later impacted European culture. In 1952 Collin was already aware of the vital influence of these circles.

Collin considered Alessandro Cagliostro to be their fundamental inspiration. His real name was Giuseppe Balsamo and he was born in 1743. With his close connections to a number of the Royal courts in Europe and eventually a dubious reputation as a magician, healer and alchemist, he was perceived as a glamorous but contentious figure. As a young man, he became a novice in the Catholic Order of St. John of God, where he was taught chemistry and spiritual rites. After a meandering existence, he came to London where he became acquainted with Comte de Saint Germain, an adventurer with prominence in European high society. Cagliostro's fame grew, even leading, among other things, to him being recommended as Benjamin Franklin's physician during his stay in Paris. Later he became a Freemason at Esperance lodge in London, before he visited various branches of the 'Rite of Strict Observance' in search of converts to his own 'Egyptian Freemasonry'. He was expelled from France in the wake of prosecution and eventual acquittal for having participated in a crime. Together with Marie Antoinette, he was falsely alleged to have defrauded the Crown's jewellers in the acquisition of a diamond necklace.

Cagliostro was tried by the Inquisition in Rome for heresy. His original death sentence was commuted to life imprisonment and he died in prison

---

[1] Rodney Collin, *The Theory of Conscious Harmony* (London: Robinson & Watkins Books Limited, 1958), p113.

in 1795 at the age of 52. We have barely touched the surface of all that could be said about him.

It is difficult to determine the specific reason why Collin points to Cagliostro, a character whose life seems as doubtful as it was diverse, as a founder and source. Another interesting but also unanswered question is what caused Collin to say specifically that Cagliostro founded these circles in Rome just before he was imprisoned in 1789. Collin may have been aware of something that was not widely known, or the explanation may simply be that Cagliostro's inspiration was of a more general character, yet strong enough to somehow contribute to a renewed interest in vital and fundamental issues of life. His ability to inspire is undeniable. The writings of Tolstoy, Dumas and Catherine the Great all contain characters that can be inferred to be him.

The influences of the circles of Rome spread rapidly in ever-broadening spheres in Europe and elsewhere in the first 30 years. With a few exceptions, Collin identifies known and unknown persons involved only by surname. In order to contribute to a greater understanding of why he mentions these in this context, I have added some relevant factual characteristics to some of them.

In Paris, many gifted and influential people were involved in this period. Juliette Récamier, who was known for her salon where Parisians from leading literary and political circles met, was one. Others he mentioned from the French section were the painters Ingres and Chateaubriand, in addition to the Orientalist and founder of Egyptology, Jean Francois Champollion.

Through his studies, Collin also discovered that a number of prominent German people were involved: The chemist, Baron Bunsen, who throughout his life sought to be a bridge-builder between Protestants and Catholics, the composer, Mendelssohn, and the historian, Niebuhr. The latter, Barthold Georg Niebuhr, was a leading historian of Ancient Rome and the founder of modern scholarly historiography. He was deeply rooted in the classical spirit of the Age of Enlightenment, also known as the Age of Reason. From the 17th to the 19th century this philosophical movement came to dominate European thinking.

Collin also mentioned a painter called "Shadow." This must be Friedrich Wilhelm Schadow, who not only was a friend of another painter Collin mentioned, Peter Cornelius, but also belonged to the same brotherhood of German painters in Rome, The Nazarene. As an author, Schadow is best known for his lecture, *The Influence of Christianity on The Visual Arts.*[1] Schadow held that that an artist must believe in and live out the truths his essays paint. He was originally Lutheran, but like Overbeck, the third German painter Collin mentioned, he turned to the Roman Catholic Church. Overbeck felt that European contemporary culture had become corrupted and that it had escalated by discharging its Christian orientation. He came to Rome in 1810 and it became the centre of his labours for 59 years.

Schadow, Cornelius and Overbeck all lived in the old Franciscan monastery of San Isidoro, sharing the precept of hard and honest work and holy living.

Since it is beyond this book's intended scope to give a detailed overview of all the 26 people Collin maintains are important to 19th century culture, we will, for the sake of order, only list the others, along with their nationality and profession: Bertel Torvaldsen, the Danish sculptor; Georg Zoega, the Danish archaeologist; Frans Liszt, the Hungarian musician; Percy Shelley, the English poet; and Gioachino Rossini, the Italian composer.

Before we move on, however, there is reason to dwell a little on the difference between Collin's view and that of the Nazarenes.

In light of the significance Collin gave the Nazarenes, with their fervent desire to revive the honesty and religious spirit of art, the lack of legacy must be disappointing, despite the fact that they must undoubtedly be considered successors of Durer, Michelangelo, Perugino and the young Rafael.

Often considered to be drawing on German romanticism, critics described an excessive tendency to let emotions control the image expression as sentimental, sweet, cheesy, and stencil-like. Being sceptical of academic models and mechanical competence, the Nazarenes rejected the late Baroque Classicism. They were inspired by the early German and Italian Renaissance, which they re-generated into an energetic linear style, suited to their innocent, albeit impassioned and rarely understood, commitment to nature.

Among some art theorists, there is even the idea that the cradle of kitsch was to be found among the Nazarene's painterly expression of their aesthetic and ethical ideals. The conception of art and, not least, the perception of what can be considered art or not, seems to mainly relate to an institutional context, which owes a great deal to Immanuel Kant. The

---

[1] Schadow, Johan Gottfried, *The Influence of Christianity on The Visual Arts*. Dusseldorf, 1854.

presentation of his aesthetic thinking, to be found in his work, *Critique of Pure Reason,* has proved easy to use as leverage to justify both anti-art and institutional power. On close inspection, we find the use of this 'crowbar' to be the very source of alienation to the object of art itself.

There is little disagreement in the philosophical academic community that Kant's aesthetic does not relate to the assessment of individual works of art as such, but rather to the formal function of judgement. Consequently it is not an appropriate means to determine whether the Nazarenes succeed in conveying the ferocity of their message. What Kant's influence has contributed to, however, is the obvious fact that objects that were initially intended as a protest to the traditionally elevated role of art, are not only approved by institutional concentrations of power as artistic objects, but also occasionally given an elevated central position in the history of modern art. One such example is Duchamp's famous 'pissoir.'

This illustration can help to shed light on how it is possible that a direction within art that Rodney Collin perceived as an important impulse was later portrayed by some as a religiously overheated image-rhetoric. In the same way that one would expect a leading art connoisseur, such as Bernard Berenson, to assess a work of art primarily based on its aesthetic expression, it is impossible to imagine that much of what one today calls conceptual art could be legitimised without relying on Kant's aesthetic thinking as presented in his main work.

With regard to a later generation, Collin mentioned the following: the Norwegian writer, Henrik Ibsen, the English poet, Robert Browning and the Scottish writer, Robert Stevenson. He emphasized that the list was not complete, but that many more were involved. According to Collin, the Rome groups were located in the areas around Via Gregoriana and Via Sistina. Another of their haunts was the French Academy at the Villa Medici. He further mentions that members of these circles contributed in the restoration work of the churches of Sant'Andrea delle Fratte and Santissima Trinità dei Monte.

It was in the wake of the frequent movements from one ancient site to another that Collin gained an overall historical perspective and

> ... *began to see history as a tremendous play of school influence, buildings, teaching, creating, disappearing from one place and appearing in another.*[1]

---

[1] Rodney Collin, The Theory of Conscious Harmony (London: Robinson & Watkins Books Limited, 1958), p114.

Mexico

In their search for traces of former schools, history and art were always the starting point, whether it was the investigation of early Christian schools in Rome, or a school connected to Gothic cathedrals in France. As Mema and the Collins travelled on to Muslim-oriented areas like Damascus, Bagdad, Teheran, and Isfahan, Collin was surprised by the growing and strange impression that something was missing. This he saw in light of the fact that they had left a world in which Christian-oriented values are often taken for granted. On July 20th, 1955 he wrote:

> It is something to do with individual hope, recognition of the value of each individual soul. In the East, of course, there are wise men and good men and religious men, but I have never felt in the West this strange apathy and hopelessness among poor people, as though they have nothing to expect but death. Evidently the coming of Christ changed the whole nature and possibility of all levels of beings on the earth. Where this is not recognised, there is a curious stagnation. From this I understood in a new way what the 'conversion' of a country meant to the Apostles or to medieval missionaries. However imperfectly it might be done from a human point of view it meant an actual transmutation of human possibilities in that area. It was really a miraculous process.[1]

As they travelled to Egypt, Syria and Lebanon, where they sought dervishes and Sufis, they came to regard their activities and influences as a hidden form of Christianity. Collin assumed that the reason they needed to operate under the radar was that these countries simply had not been ready to receive Christianity more openly. He also assumed that their function and role were linked to the rectification of certain erroneous steps committed by Mohamed.

Before they returned to Mexico through Rome, Paris and London, they also visited Jordan, Iraq, Persia, Turkey and Greece where, once again, they found historic traces of former schools and their influence.

Previously, when they were in Italy, they had seen the variety of creativity and understanding that sprang from the Renaissance that originated from the Medici household. Collin considered that the Medici family's banking business was a shining illustration of the relationship between business and esoteric influence. As contributors they not only helped to build churches, establish libraries and founded the Platonic Academy, but they also supported Donatello, Fra Angelico and Michelangelo, all of whom proved to be invaluable in a larger cultural historical perspective.

[1] Rodney Collin, *The Theory of Conscious Harmony* (London: Robinson & Watkins Books Limited, 1958), p113-114.

Later, when in Luxor, Egypt, the three travel-companions saw the chapel of Nativity, the Mammisi, among the Ptolemaic temples that Collin came to regard as a proclamation of what was to come, the birth of Christ. The original ancient Egyptian meaning of the word Mammisi, which is really a modern form, was 'house of birth'. The term is derived from the core of the temple's decoration, which constitutes its essential theological theme: the birth of a divine child.

Wherever they went, everything they encountered appeared to support their ever-growing notion that the drama of the birth of Christ is central to human history.

Collin believed that there had been, at all times, an indivisible and unified influence that guided man and that it was the lack of such an understanding which made life and living unnecessarily difficult. He saw persecution, fear, fanaticism and contradictions as consequences of the lack of such insight, and that it was consequence of ordinary man not challenging his own ignorance. Rodney Collin frequently noted that understanding is not wrapped up like a gift but is a result of deep and honest self-examination and hard work under qualified guidance.

During these journeys, but also later, a more holistic picture gradually emerged for Collin, in which the birth of Christ had a uniquely central role. Ouspensky's abandonment of the system and his subsequent necessity to reconstruct everything now appeared to Collin as a part of a plan put forward by higher powers and substantively of the same importance as the coming of Christ.

In his perspective, he saw the work of former schools as contribution and preparation for the arrival of Christ, while he regarded the work of the later schools as a confirmation of what Christ brought. The concepts 'before' and 'after' transcend ordinary meaning and gain a higher overall significance when Collin points out that these schools were all participants in one and the same project. As a 'Herald of Harmony', Collin could not afford to regard the possible mistakes of ancient schools as anything other than part of a process. This illustrates how a conscious attitude cannot only free itself from both aspects of linear time and psychological constraints, but also indirectly change the past.

To understand the extent of what Rodney Collin was trying to embrace, one must consider the meaning of Christ's esoteric message. Anchored in this directive, on July 20th, 1955 he wrote the following:

This is our work also, in fact it is the only Work. But it is so big, so strange, and so many-sided that we had to come to it through a teaching where the name of Christ was hardly mentioned, lest it be taken on too low a level. Evidently our work will be measured, not by what we say or write, but by the degree in which we can manifest charity. When it is present, there is happiness, understanding and harmony. When vanity and sleep take its place, everything becomes confused again. If things go wrong, as they certainly do, one knows that it is because one has failed to project conscious harmony. In so far as things go right, one realizes that one has been helped to do so.[1]

Not unexpectedly, Collin found the most exquisite and perfect example of a school in human history in both the Gospel Drama and the Passion of Christ, which he believed later experiments echo in various ways. One feature of the gospels that he found particularly rewarding was their ability to store different types of patterns. On December 10th, 1954 he wrote:

If one understands the way different types and levels reacted then, one will recognise those reactions always and everywhere.[2]

In the story of the road to Emmaus, Collin found features that reminded him of his own way. Christ had appeared to two of the disciples who were on their way in the world, unaware of his resurrection. After waking up and recognising him, they went back to the other disciples, who did not believe what the two had to say, before Christ himself arose among them all.

I think the way to Emmaus is the Fourth Way. In the Fourth Way people have to be disillusioned at home, to go out bravely into the world to find truth, to be illumined there, and then bring light home again.[3]

Sharing one's experiences and understanding was something Collin constantly emphasised in group contexts. An essential aspect of this was that what is not shared is dissolved and lost. Around the beginning of February 1955 he briefed his group, at four group meetings, about a number of the findings from their journeys. Although at this time he had obviously not collected, edited or digested the material, he still chose to share his preliminary results. As late as August 25th that same year he had

---

[1] Rodney Collin, The Theory of Conscious Harmony (London: Robinson & Watkins Books Limited, 1958), p114.
[2] Rodney Collin, The Theory of Conscious Harmony (London: Robinson & Watkins Books Limited, 1958), p112.
[3] Rodney Collin, The Theory of Conscious Harmony (London: Robinson & Watkins Books Limited, 1958), p112.

clearly stated, in a letter to Joyce Collin-Smith, that he had not yet assembled this material.

However, he must have formed some structure from this material, because the content of all the meetings had clear and independent themes. At the first meeting they dealt with the Egyptian gods, architecture and their hieroglyphs. The second meeting dealt with the Phoenicians and the Jews, including the meaning of the alphabet, form and content of dances, and information about Solomon's Temple. The Greeks' discovery of the inherent freedom of individual human conscience was the theme of the third meeting, where it was also pointed out how the Greeks felt that the laws of rhythm and harmony were all-encompassing in their lives. The last meeting of this series was based on the conditions of the century before Christ and various indications of his arrival and also the corrupt aspects of the teachings of ancient times. The contrast between the unlimited transparency Christ showed to people interested in his message, and the closed, narrow and selective practices of the past priesthood, which sought to render form immortal by the construction of tombs, temples and mummification, was also pointed out.

Collin knew that what appeared to be contradictory in history could lose its contradiction if it was seen through an understanding, love and will that were unified by consciousness.

He adopted the attitude of a harmoniser who knew that nothing in history should be left out, but everything should be deliberately included in order to see through contradictions and into new opportunities. It is hard to imagine that these meetings did not make an indelible impression on sensitive participants.

The itinerary, as presented so far, provides an overview of various countries and findings related to these. However, if we look closer at the order of destinations, we will find that the traveling companions repeatedly returned to the previous stop. This was frequently at the request of Mema to visit new or previous destinations, in expectation of new sources or discoveries.

Not only were Mema's oracular prophesies considerably costly for the travel budget, but time and time again they traveled without finding any of what she had indicated. A classic example of how Mema's voices led them astray are the visits to various libraries. She would claim that by finding a specified book and looking up a given page, they would, say, find information not only on how the Fourth Way had come to Florence, but also which people had brought it to the Medici family.

MEXICO

We have previously mentioned Rodney Collin's at times excessive trust in individuals. Although it fluctuated in the context of several of Mema Dickins' 'messages', they were often followed up. Many have wondered how both Janet and Rodney Collin could be so easily be led. The English historian James Webb's description of her may give an indication of why it was not so easy to categorically reject her:

> Mrs. D was an impressive personality and a powerful medium. Her renderings from Gurdjieff and Ouspensky were accompanied by the appropriate manifestations; she would walk like a man, her face would seem to contort into the outline of Gurdjieff's or Ouspensky's, and her voice grew harsh and guttural, even rendering Ouspensky's famous chuckle. She had been known to exhibit the stigmata and, according to some reports, could open the wounds 'at will'. She had been brought up in the intense atmosphere of the Mexican Catholicism, and it was to be expected that her messages would contain the flavour of authoritarian Christianity.[1]

Whether it was Mema's compelling and detailed manifestations of Ouspensky's character traits, which the Collins knew better than anyone, that led them to trust her is uncertain. Likewise, it is unclear to what extent her directions contributed in their search for the traces of schools, or if they contributed at all.

Everything was not as before when they returned to Mexico. Once again Collin discovered that several of the original English contingent, well versed in the Work-ideas, had left the group. According to him, they:

> ... had not agreed with the way the Work was developing.[2]

Already before this period, several people had actively expressed their scepticism about Mema Dickins' direct influence on the Collins and some of the content of the group's activities. This seems to have escalated after the trio's return home in 1955. Many blamed Collin for being willing to rely blindly on Mema without proper or adequate evidence. Others who criticised him emphasized his increasingly religious representations of the Work. In 1954, while in Rome, Rodney Collin had converted to Roman Catholicism. He himself saw no contradictions between the Work and the esoteric aspects of any religion.

In October 1954 he wrote:

---

[1] James Webb, The Harmonious Circle (Boulder, Colorado: Shambhala Publications Inc., 1987), p490.
[2] Joyce Collin-Smith, Call No Man Master (Authors Online Book, 2004), p74.

I realized over many years that our work is not a substitute for religion. It is a key to religion, as it is a key to art, science and all other sides of human life. Only one must put this key in a lock and use it to open a door. Every man needs a religion, but our work enables him to find esoteric religion. [...] By temperament, inclination, study, and by the country in which I have to work, I became Roman Catholic. I had already anticipated this several years ago. It only needed the right moment and opportunity. For this time is a crossroads.

Other people, at the same crossroads, might join different religions, though it seems to me that Roman Catholicism has the greatest reserve of esoteric truth. In any case, whatever religion they chose, it would be the esoteric part which they joined. So there would be no contradiction between them. For the esoteric parts of all religions are connected, as our tradition shows. The forms of religion are inside time – those living in time can chose what form they like. Beyond time, in the place from which our direction comes, there are no forms, there is only truth and understanding.[1]

Despite some internal turbulence in the group, there was, in the main, a momentum and a basic belief and confidence in the opportunities for internal growth.

Such persistent optimism is not created by a caring and insightful leadership style alone but is largely based on the individual student's sincerity and ability to persist in self-observation to cultivate his search for his true nature.

However, for some, such a search can develop into fanaticism. It seems unlikely that fanatics and the energy they generate would not be corrected quickly and effectively. Collin was very clear that fanaticism is not only due to one-sided certainty, but that the security fanatics experience is based on the ignorance of the landscape between the goal he sees and his own point of departure.

Much was still unchanged though. The work on the planetarium proceeded and the publishing business at Ediciones Sol was active. During Collin's life, this publishing house would translate and publish 14 titles, in addition to a number of pamphlets he wrote himself.

Theatre activities had been established as a part of the group's artistic development. This project also continued after the return to Mexico. Jean

---

[1] Rodney Collin, The Theory of Conscious Harmony (London: Robinson & Watkins Books Limited, 1958), p125.

Anouílh's play, *The Lark,* about Joan of Arc, was produced and performed in the autumn of 1955, with Rodney Collin playing Bishop Caucheon. However, the theatre-group, which called themselves the Unicorn Players, had already, in the spring of the previous year, performed *Peer Gynt,* by the Norwegian author Henrik Ibsen, where Collin took the role of the button-moulder.

The show, which was mainly attended by residents from Tlalpam and surrounding areas, must have been a public success with its total of 12 performances. The members of the Unicorn Players themselves provided scenery, costumes and other props, as well as instruction.

The successful set up of Ibsen's play had been a source of inspiration when they began the preparation for *The Lark* the following year, but the results turned out to be different and more challenging than with *Peer Gynt.*

In a private letter from late December 1955 Rodney Collin wrote:

> *The Lark meant a tremendous six weeks' burst. Every night unbroken for three or four. The costumes, designed by Jean Joy-Smith, and the presentation were gorgeous. The surface of the play we came to feel was tedious and ill-constructed, but underneath there are such powerful ideas and vivid characters that all that time came to life astonishingly. Poor Joan – how she must have suffered! 'Nobody understands, nobody will ever understand!'*
>
> *One can hear her voice, and it is a cry that goes right through one's heart.*

The strain and the intrusions of organizing the play left the group involved somewhat disorganised for a short period. However, they were soon assembled again.

At the end of the first week of January 1956, ten days after he wrote this letter, a group of friends from Peru, with whom he had established a working relationship, were expected. As a part of the preparation for their arrival, he created a presentation of parts of the material they had collected on their last expedition to the East.

The work of translating Ouspensky's *In Search of the Miraculous* in 1952, Maurice Nicoll's and not least Collin's own book, *The Theory of Celestial Influence,* and his own pamphlets had borne fruits. Increasingly he received inquiries from a number of people in South America where he had a widespread influence. In addition to establishing a group in Peru, groups were founded in Argentina, Uruguay and Chile. In addition, he nurtured contact with people across much of the American continent.

Among his own writings, there can be little doubt that it was the series of his paper pamphlets that had the greatest impact among most people. The pamphlets were affordable, easy to read and published in relatively large numbers. These writings became, for many, the gateway to his main work, *The Theory of Celestial Influence,* which was published in Spanish in 1953.

The first of these publications in English was *The Herald of Harmony* and was printed on May 20th, 1954. Rooted in the perception of the birth of an imminent new age and a time of decline, Collin takes us through humanity's contradictory history. In a wealth of examples, he points out how duality is maintained, with the consequence that man remains in an amputated world where suffering, perversions and atrocities become inevitable. Further he shows how religious dualism is forced to its knees by its own ignorance:

> *If love universal were the new revelation, then love erotic was the new sin. If heart were blessed, then liver and lights were damned. If God were one and Christ his only-begotten son, then Osiris, Astarte, Baal, Zeus, Vishnu and Tao were false; and all their servants, priests, sages, philosophers, magicians demon-driven.[1]*

Even fourteen hundred years after Christ there were few who raised a finger in protest without endangering life and health:

> *From Elymas' blinding springs the Inquisition: ten thousand human bonfires of Jew, Arab, Aztec, making heaven hideous from Toledo to the mounts of Mexico.[2]*

It was not due to the absence of a vision that man lacked a foothold for a dignified life in coexistence with their fellow men and life as a whole. With Christ, according to Collin, the vision was shown, but how to realise it was not. The journey through time continues at dizzying speed; Collin points out new contexts as we pass plants, animals, man, metals, scientists, artists, music and warriors, before slowing down and dwelling in reverence in front of two figures, *The Russian* and *The Greek.*

Rodney Collin was open about his understanding of Gurdjieff and Ouspensky as two opposites that were absolutely legally necessary to launch a teaching into the world that could contribute to an objective

---

[1] Rodney Collin, The Herald of Harmony (Tlalpam: Ediciones Sol, 1954), p8.
[2] Rodney Collin, The Herald of Harmony (Tlalpam: Ediciones Sol, 1954), p8.

understanding of existence, including Christianity. The preparation had, as in previous times, followed the legalities that had been enshrined in time:

> *Mankind needs half-a-thousand years to prepare itself. The Renaissance prefigured the Newcomer, as the age of Buddha, Pythagoras, Lao-Tse prefigured Christ.[1]*

For Collin it was inconceivable that a real manifestation could take place without a triad. Just as inconceivable as if a child could be born without a man and a woman. Collin perceived the third factor as the invisible 'Great School' that sent these two messengers:

> *The Greek destroyer of men's complacency, trickster, magician, hypnotist, juggler of light and dark, new Orpheus, charming his slaves with music nostalgic of beyond. Compassionate sorcerer, diabolic saint; djinn from alchemic bottle, compounding of laws and frailty, Arabian Night's delight.*
>
> *The Russian – firm and invisible. Compiler of wisdom; master of silent experiment, unrecognised effect; new scientist, himself his laboratory, his pupils retorts and their contents, the work transmutation. Stern guide, most loving friend; austere in the sacrifice of lesser prize, in power perfected jovial. Planter of seeds, the gardener of the soul.[2]*

Bearing in mind that Gurdjieff referred to himself as a teacher of dancing, the comparison becomes too obvious to be misunderstood:

> *The Greek as masterwork turned cosmic laws to dance – a tide of harmonious movement, bewitching as Maya itself, subtle and difficult as very dance of worlds. By dance broke down men's obstinate separateness; made pigmy passions echo to universal ones; evoked in the world of men a shimmering image of universal harmony.*
>
> *Soberly, year on year, the Russian thought:*
>
> *'Find what you want:*
>
> *Be simple and sincere:*
>
> *By understanding be freed from illusion and from fear:*
>
> *Remember yourself – always and everywhere'*
>
> *'Change destructive emotions into harmony:*
>
> *Study the laws:*

---

[1] Rodney Collin, The Herald of Harmony (Tialpam: Ediciones Sol, 1954), p19.
[2] Rodney Collin, The The Herald of Harmony (Tlalpam: Ediciones Sol, 1954), p19-20.

Serve faithfully the work:
Remember yourself – always and everywhere'.[1]

Embedded in musical imagery, Collin highlights four basic prerequisites for participating in the universal harmony:

First, let each note sound clear and full.

1. Being oneself, starting from one's innate essential attributes:

"Let each type be himself, know his own nature, ring to the vibrations God has given him."

2. Being open to oneself and others:

"... let each note – remembering itself – listen for the chord. Hear its own sound, ringing with other sounds struck simultaneously. [...] taste chord from chord, know the nature of those in which he sounds and why."

3. Acknowledgement:

"Let each note accept the key to come, follow the new tonic now revealed to it. Let each type yield to him who unites them all: all craft to the greater truth."

4. Faith:

"If note has not faith in the music to be played, in Composer, Conductor and Holy Symphony, what use? Without faith, each note's a pointless tedium. With faith, each note shall know that it is not, has no existence but in the infinite music which evokes it. And knowing this, knows all, to the ultimate inspiration of the work."[2]

The Herald of Harmony can be seen as a poetic, psycho-historical description of the relationship between Gurdjieff and Ouspensky, both the various religious approaches through earlier times, and the historical aspects. By invariably viewing their interactions in the context of the legality of a triad, Collin sheds light over a shadowy landscape full of misunderstandings that has created much unnecessary interpersonal disharmony. But first and foremost *The Herald of Harmony* is an encouragement to the underlying longing for an affiliation with existence that many experience – where all permeates all.

Another pamphlet that Collin published on Ediciones Sol was *The Whirling Ecstasy.* Here we find a selection from *The Lives of the Gnostics,* written between 1318 and 1335 by Aflaki, a disciple of Jelal ad-Din Rumi's

---

[1] Rodney Collin, The Herald of Harmony (Tlalpam: Ediciones Sol, 1954), p20.
[2] Rodney Collin, The Herald of Harmony (Tlalpam: Ediciones Sol, 1954), p25-26.

grandson. The lyrics reflect Aflaki's devotion to Rumi. The same devotion can be seen in Rodney Collin's pamphlet. Rumi's teaching focuses on the roots of the roots of the Quran and, not being constrained by a theological formalism or juridical hairsplitting, go to the Quran's deepest message.

Rodney Collin's selection provides a concrete example of his conviction that esoteric aspects of the various religions are equal, that their practice is associated with a continual movement and that the metaphor can be a bridge to reality. Although several of the 25 verses that make up this collection appear in a subsequent order, they can also be read as free-standing sections. One of these verses goes as follows:

> *One day Shems-ed-din said:*
>
> *"I will tell you a secret, so that our Master Jelal-ed-din shall not hear. A single farthing of his is worth a hundred thousand dinars to me. Whoever comes to me, is submitted to him, for a door was shut and he has opened it. To know our master, I am imperfect. I know him imperfectly, for each day I observe in him some state, action or quality which was not there before. Understand our master a little better than hitherto, if you wish to gain peace. He is the very form of truth. He pronounces fine words: don't be satisfied with them, for behind each is something you should ask him.*[1]

Perhaps the most curious publication on Ediciones Sol, is *Notes on The Gospel of Saint John*. In full conviction that the texts were written by Ouspensky, it was published in 1949 in a two-language edition, English and Spanish. However it was later withdrawn, as Collin was no longer sure that Ouspensky was the originator. However, the release was far from accidental. Not only was the text found among Ouspensky's surviving papers, but the manuscript also dealt with one of the four Gospels that Collin knew Ouspensky considered outstanding. Unlike the other three, which, in Ouspensky's opinion, could be understood primarily by the intellect, Saint John's Gospel requires an emotional approach:

> *St. John's Gospel cannot be understood by the mind at all.*[2]

There is reason to believe that, according to Collin's perception, the design of the text corresponded with Ouspensky's approach to St. John's message.

---

[1] Rodney Collin, The Whirling Ecstasy (Tlalpam: Ediciones Sol, 1954), paragraph p10.
[2] P.D. Ouspensky, A New Model of the Universe (London: Kegan Paul, Trench, Trubner Co., Ltd, 1938), p153.

Probably the least distributed booklet published by Ediciones Sol is La Pirámide de Fuego. It was originally published in Spanish but has since been translated into English, titled The Pyramid of Fire. Based on ancient Mexican esoteric doctrine that could not rely on a written language but bases its transmission on an oral tradition supported by images, Collin has drawn parallels to concepts from *The Fourth Way*.

With the exception of the first chapter, most of his illustrations are taken from the Codex Borbonicus, which was written by Aztec priests just prior to the Spanish conquest of Mexico (1519-21). The exception applies to the illustration taken from Fejervary-Mayer, a marginally revised version of the Codex, which Collin believed originated from the Codex Vaticanus B, also known as Codice Vaticano Rituale.

Collin's text contributes insights into the perennial philosophy through perspectives that reveal that Gurdjieff's ray of creation is consistent with the Codex. Regardless of whether his reference points are rooted in the eight musical notes of nature or man, it becomes apparent not only that what is created springs from a higher level, but also how what is below reflects what is above. In the triune constellation Lord of the Death, Lady of the Death and the neutralising Lord of The Dead Warriors, he shows how this ancient doctrine was originally in possession of knowledge of the triads and the six processes. He wrote:

> Each world is the toy and arena of the three gods, three forces. And depending on which of them leads, which of them follows, and which one concludes, six different kinds of games may emerge, six processes that create all that occurs or that can occur. And the six kinds of Divine Game decide the growth, digestion, purification, disease, healing, or regeneration of this world.[1]

On the limitations of man and how his potential possibilities relate to a holistic view and the mutual maintenance of all elements, he pointed to how the calendar of their culture specified how human life was subject to laws related to celestial influence. The rhythm of such influences are diverse and range from growth and fertility to clashes and war.

> Man cannot do. Whether he wages war, loves or harvests, it is the rhythms of the great gods, the planets, that act upon him and make him do. When man understands that he can do nothing for himself, he may

---

[1] Rodney Collin, The Pyramid of Fire (Privately printed, 2007), p10.

Illustration 1. Tecciztecal and Tonatiuh, The Moon and the Sun, shine in the sky and over the Earth and all its creatures.

learn to serve the gods. Thus, he has to become conscious of the rhythm of the gods.[1]

In the Codex's illustration of the play under eternal celestial influences between Tecciztecal, the Moon, and Tonatiuh, the Sun, Collin recognised the double nature of man and that the soul is not given, but is an opportunity related to consciousness.

Over the surface of the Earth exist the kingdom of Nature, the formless life of the waters, trees, insects, animals and two kinds of men. One kind is the ordinary man, naked, unarmed, always threatened by the darts of death. The other kind is the superior man. Under the altar's shadow the

---

[1] Rodney Collin, The Pyramid of Fire (Privately printed, 2007), p14.

maguey thorns of repentance transform into the soul's wings and in his hands he keeps the four states of matter in equilibrium.

He has attained consciousness: HE IS. He has attained will and he can do. The dying animal, tied up to the tree that feeds it, gives its vital energy to the Moon, Tecciztecal, whereas its body, then a corpse, is eaten by the Earth, Tlaltecuhtli. Thus, in the cosmic hierarchy, everything eats and is eaten, devours and is devoured. Plants get nourished by minerals and then provide nourishment for animals. Animals feed on plants and, in turn, become food for the earth. And man too, as an animal organism, devours plants and, in turn, the Earth devours his body. And if he is no more than just a body, he has no other fate.[1]

Although Rodney Collin had a suitable background to enable him to examine the esoteric fragments in this material, there can be little doubt that he received some help in understanding the illustrations themselves. In a brief but insightful preface to a later English translation, Rolando Altamirano suggests that such help was given, although not by whom. In this material, as in the basis of ideas of The Fourth Way, the double nature of man and the prerequisites for internal transformation and the formation of the soul are inextricably linked to the question of consciousness.

In between Mother Earth and the Herald of Heaven we see the symbol of the dual nature of man, the earthly centipede of his spinal cord, entwined with the celestial serpent of consciousness that can inhabit it. And again, below and to he left lies what remains when the wings and the serpent have flown away: the dead warrior's heart. His head lies over the altar. The skull of the dead prisoner lies upon a rack of skulls; because life will return to its source, and the soul to its origin.[2]

Among the diversity that makes up this unique and valuable material from two ancient Mexican Codexes, it is the 'blood' of all necessary sacrifices that unites everything and everyone.

What is this blood that stones share with the soul and men share with the planets? It is nothing but universal unity, the unique creative force that freezes in a myriad of forms and that, once liberated by sacrifice, returns to unity. Because to sacrifice means to act intentionally, to do consciously. When we sacrifice that which we will loose anyway we trick the destiny that takes it.[3]

---

[1] Rodney Collin, The Pyramid of Fire (Privately printed, 2007), p17.
[2] Rodney Collin, The Pyramid of Fire (Privately printed, 2007), p19.
[3] Rodney Collin, The Pyramid of Fire (Privately printed, 2007), p28.

CHAPTER 18
Janet Collin Answering Gods

In Rodney Collin's earlier writings, there were few hints, if any, of poetic language. However his linguistic representations were characterized by his emotional nature which is evident, especially in his personal correspondence. This often present emotional aspect never dominated, but was balanced with a bridled mental clarity. It is therefore likely that the consistent poetic thread we find in the Herald of Harmony was chosen to penetrate deep into the reader and that Janet Collin inspired that choice. Collin's wife had a lively relationship with poetry and periodically wrote very actively herself. A little known fact is that during April 1951 Ediciones Sol published a book with her poems entitled Answering Gods.

All the poems were printed in both English and Spanish, which explains why the book became a full 291 pages. All poems referred to personal processes related to inner work, without inclinations to daydreaming. *Answering Gods,* or as it is also called in Spanish, *Dioses Que Responden,* was published under the pseudonym Anna Logan, borrowed from Rodney Collin's mother's maiden name. Impressions from these poems most likely aroused and contributed to Collin's choice of expression in his *Herald of Harmony.*

The total of one hundred poems were divided into five chapters which clearly pointed to a progression related to the life-task the poems refer to: *Before the Gate, Bitter Welcome, The Death of Venus, Interlude* and *Answering Gods.*

The book was dedicated to her husband, showing how interwoven and inseparable their lives were.

> *I write for others, but I live for you.*
> *And as I need you, so do you need me;*
> *You need me to give others what you may.*
> *I need you to live; give me other life.*[1]

The humility that emerges in her dedication must not be confused with submissiveness. Janet Collin was a strong woman and, as can be witnessed

---

[1] Janet Collin, Answering Gods (Tlalpam: Ediciones Sol, 1951), Dedication to R.

in many of the poems, full of courage and an indispensable sense of direction. She always looked for a door in a wall, as all really unusual woman do.

In order to give her the room that rightly belongs to her in a book about her husband, and in order for the poems to speak for themselves, we let her take us on a journey among some of her own experiences. We shall save our comments for later, when they can hopefully serve a purpose.

From the chapter *Before the Gate*:

> *I have come a long way; the usual way.*
>
> *I travelled through pleasant places, through places that were hard,*
>
> *Through places where I became dirty and others that made me clean again.*
>
> *Then I reached the gate; it was as far as I could go, the road led me no further, it ended there.*
>
> *Most people turn back at the gate; they suppose it to be a wall in which there is no opening; But I knew better, because, by good fortune and the grace of God, I had met a man who told me that the gate existed, and not to waste time looking for it till I came to the end of the road.*
>
> *And I know it is a gate because I saw it open when he passed through.*
>
> *So now I am standing before the gate; how can I make it open for me?[1]*

From the chapter *Bitter Welcome*:

> *I tried to find stillness*
> *Sought it in churches and in nature,*
> *Tried to refrain from conversations,*
> *And stop the thoughts running round in my head.*
> *Sometimes I caught a glimpse of stillness,*
> *Then it was gone.*
>
>
> *Now stillness has taken me.*
> *I wished to possess it;*
> *Now it possesses me*
> *Because I am empty.*
> *Pain has mastered me*
> *So that I can no longer be active;*

[1] Janet Collin, Answering Gods (Tlalpam: Ediciones Sol, 1951), p2.

162

Janet Collin Answering Gods

I fought till I was so tired
I could no longer struggle.
My body, exhausted by weeping,
Lies still.
My mind, tired out of thinking, thinking, thinking.
No longer turns upon itself.
I can no longer feel,
For emotion has blazed itself to ashes,
Quiet, cool, soft ashes
Into which I sink down and down
And deeper down to stillness.
Stillness is not to be prized lightly,
And you have to pay if you really want it.
I paid unknowingly,
But evidently I paid enough,
For now I have stillness
No; stillness possesses me.[1]

From the chapter *The Death of Venus*:

"Shall I never be myself?
For now I am nothing
But the embodiment of a dream.
*I ask myself: '**Who am I?**'*
But rather the question seems to be:
*'**Do I exist at all?**'*

If there is someone who asks,
There is someone who is.

The someone who is does not dream.
Who then is the dreamer?
A puppet moved by dreams?

---

[1] Janet Collin, Answering Gods (Tlalpam: Ediciones Sol, 1951), p114.

Rodney Collin

Confront each other now,
Dreamer and I;
'Who am I?'[1]

From the chapter *Interlude*:

How quiet the night has fallen
After the rain.
There were the usual street noises;
Men talking, two dogs arguing,
The clanking of a tram.
Then a little sighing wind
Swept out of the darkness
And everything seemed to grow quiet
As the rain began to fall
In a sudden soft rush of gentle drops;
And there was no sound
Except the whisper of the rain.

Now the rain is over,
But the quiet is still here.[2]

And finally four poems from the last chapter called *Answering Gods*:

Who sees only good
Betrays the good that he sees,
And will become blinded
By the evil that he contemplates.

Who does not fear evil
Has no faith in the good,
And will be destroyed
By the evil that intimates him.
Who knows the taste of evil

[1] Janet Collin, Answering Gods (Tlalpam: Ediciones Sol, 1951), p174.
[2] Janet Collin, Answering Gods (Tlalpam: Ediciones Sol, 1951), p182.

Janet Collin Answering Gods

Knows the taste of good,
And will be saved
By swallowing the evil.[1]

*

Grief is contained by time;
If time is opened,
Grief flies to the world's end.

Grief is the fear of time;
See time whole
And grief is gone.[2]

*

One moving pattern binds
Planets and men.
Each one has meaning
In his relation to the rest
But none alone.
Men go mad when they do not see
Their connection with each other;
When they understand
Their true relation to the whole
They become more than men.[3]

*

He who would believe
In miracle
Must first disbelieve
In the impossible.[4]

[1] Janet Collin, Answering Gods (Tlalpam: Ediciones Sol, 1951), p242.
[2] Janet Collin, Answering Gods (Tlalpam: Ediciones Sol, 1951), p212.
[3] Janet Collin, Answering Gods (Tlalpam: Ediciones Sol, 1951), p224.
[4] Janet Collin, Answering Gods (Tlalpam: Ediciones Sol, 1951), p240.

Rodney Collin

Via sharp psychological details Janet Collin establishes a relationship between her inner and outer world. Progress is created by an increasingly well-founded yearning that is based on sincerity. From a literary standpoint, one can assert a certain kinship with romanticism through her use of symbols to point out that man and the universe are inscribed in each other. Janet Collin, however, was not primarily a writer but a seeker with a remarkable flair and this is precisely why the content emerges so forcefully.

The poems had been written over a period of many years and no doubt many had been written long before she arrived in Mexico. The spectrum of experiences that the collection echoes testifies to a longstanding maturity in which endurance was only one of many qualities that had to be cultivated.

CHAPTER 19
Further Life in Mexico

Rodney Collin wrote his only theatre play, *Hellas* in Mexico in 1949. Given the ease with which he, at the age of eighteen, had written Palms and Patios, one should not be surprised by how effortlessly he employed the basic characteristics of classical Greek literature in this four-act play. In the preface of November 7th, 1949, one can already sense that this play is one of his contributions to forming the reconstruction which Ouspensky, at the end of his life, had stressed was necessary. In addition to traditional acting, the play also includes singing and dancing. The dances referred to here are undoubtedly from the repertoire of Movements that Gurdjieff taught his students while he was still in Russia and which are often referred to as 'the old Movements'. The characteristic 'The Weaver' is easily recognised.

The ideas expressed in this play are not original. They have been expressed many times in history in various ways – now philosophically, now as poetry, and again in painting or even in architecture. I and others learned them as a system of psychology. But psychological language already has a fin de siècle flavour: as the author of that form well knew, when he declared before he died: 'I abandon this system. Try to reconstruct it all'.

So much was put into the fashionable jargon of our day – in scientific terms, with electronic matter for divinity, and nuclear fission for its attainment. But not everyone is at home with molecules, and those that are grow tired of them at times. So now we return to legend, striving to reanimate a more attractive form. For myths defy fashion, and no matter how recast, like gold, will never spoil.

The choreography, however, is described from actual dances (once a true expression of ideas), brought from the East, and reconstructed some years since in Europe and America. These dances have not only a symbolic, but practical effect both on performers and on audience. Unfortunately the knowledge of them, always precarious, may entirely disappear with the few who mastered them. Should these dances, and

167

particularly what lies behind them, be lost, then our play will certainly become – as, barring a miracle, it may be in any case – unplayable.[1]

This preface is in many ways a journey through parts of the Fourth Way history, but also a description of his own history in relation to his own journey on the path. The transition from fashionable scientific terms to myths was clearly an expression of an ongoing purer quest and testifies to insight, flexibility, and a willingness to pay.

In terms of the vulnerability of these dances, it is understandable that some have recently expressed concern over the commercialisation of the Movements, in some cases detached from their original context and sold like any other commodity as weekend courses.

An underlying theme in *Hellas* is the eternal recurrence of planets, civilizations, gods and men, forming a backdrop against which Plato, Homer, Plotinus and Apollonius complete the circle of their lives.

... the same life, and yet different – accompanied always by the same elusive Hellas, personification of pre-Christian Greece.

It is questionable whether Janet devoted much of her time to poetry around the time the Collins moved to Rio Naza, while still living in Tlalpam. In addition to her practical contribution to the medical Clinique for the poor that she had initiated, she also had an administrative position in the project, as well as her leading role in the daily household at Tlalpam.

Her longstanding participation in the household at Lyne Place and Franklin Farms, where Madame Ouspensky had ruled firmly, had provided her with invaluable experience. Unlike Franklin Farms and Lyne place, there was a general ban on smoking, the meals were kept simple and frugal and the daily rhythm was regulated with a punctuality to meals, lectures, movement-classes, meetings, and a clear request that the lights go out at ten o'clock. There was no avoiding the fact that some people found the form to be challenging.

One of them was the artist, Leonora Carrington, who at the age of eighteen left a safe and prosperous life in Lancaster to study arts in London where she met the painter Max Ernst. Together they travelled to France where Ernst was interned at the outbreak of World War II. Unaccompanied and lonely, she decided to leave France. After an exceptionally problematic escape route through Spain via New York, she ended up in Mexico in 1942.

---

[1] Rodney Collin, *Hellas* (Cape Town: The Stourton Press, 1951), Preface.

FURTHER LIFE IN MEXICO

While in Paris, Carrington and the female Mexican painter, Ramino Varo, were introduced by Andre Breton, surrealism's foremost advocate and founder. At the time Ouspensky's books were widely read in artistic and intellectual circles and many felt attracted to this mindset. One of them was the writer René Daumal, who in 1930, at the age of 20, met Alexandre de Salzmann and established a life-long relationship with the Gurdjieff work.

The fact that Roberto Matta and Gordon Onslow-Ford spent the summer of 1938 in Brittany studying Ouspensky's *Tertium Organum*[1] also says something about the extent of interest in these ideas in the Parisian artistic circles at the time.

It was in Paris that both Varo and Carrington became acquainted with the ideas of the Fourth Way. Varo had personal contact with key followers of Gurdjieff who lived in Paris at that time, and she was part of the same social circle as Daumal. Three years after their first meeting, Carrington and Varo met again in Mexico where they continued to explore their interest in Gurdjieff's ideas of expanding consciousness and Ouspensky's multidimensional concepts. Several years later, in 1948, Carrington became aware through the British Embassy that Rodney Collin had arrived in Mexico and was told by Elsie Escobedo:

He is one of the illuminati, and just the person you were looking for.[2]

Escobedo, turned out to be well informed about Collin's whereabouts but misinformed about Ouspensky's last days as well as Collin's intentions, due to rumours that were circulating. She told Carrington:

He was Ouspensky's constant companion when he was a broken man, buried in a mine of self-pity. Seeing him die in a drunken stupor brought him to the decision that he should himself become a spiritual guide.

It was not long before Carrington got in touch with Collin and took part in a number of activities at Peña Pobre in Tlalpam. When she arrived, Rodney Collin came to greet her and said:

Here we are separated from the outside world, in the midst of a desert, we may only traverse alone and in silence. Do not be afraid if you come up against your inner fears, for I shall always be there for you.[3]

---

[1] O'Rawe, Ricki. "The Re-enchantment of Surrealism: Remedios Varo's Visionary Artists." *Bulletin of Spanish Studies* 95.5 (2018): p533-561.
[2] E. Poniatowska, *Leonora* (Serpents Tale Profile Books Ltd, 2015), Chapter The Weight of Exile.
[3] E. Poniatowska, *Leonora* (Serpents Tale Profile Books Ltd, 2015), Chapter The Weight of Exile.

Within the old hacienda was a large garden, lavished with dog roses, geraniums and trees, and the whole area was surrounded by a wall. In the old large main house the Collins lived with their three employees, while the students lived in smaller buildings on the plot.

Leonora perceived Rodney Collin as both innocent and gullible and as a person that others could easily exploit. As previously mentioned, Joyce Collin-Smith believed that he was too much at the disposal of others, a viewpoint obviously shared by Carrington. Whenever he had helped, Carrington noticed, he always asked:

"Do you require anything more?"

During lunch and dinner, Collin would sit at the head of the table reading. One day, after reading from Gurdjieff's text about The Sheep and the Wolf, he turned to Carrington and asked:

"What do you understand by a sheep and by a wolf?"

She answered: "According to Gurdjieff, the wolf and the sheep must live together in harmony. The wolf represents the body and the sheep the emotions. Have I understood this correctly? The truth is that I find it quite impossible to believe that the wolf and the lamb will lie down together, and even more impossible that you refuse to permit me to smoke here."

Collin told her: "If you succeed in giving up cigarettes your victory will be your salvation."

But Carrington would not give up easily: "And who told you that I wish to be saved?"

In her frustration, she wrote to Remedios Varo and complained, and among other things criticized and ridiculed the Collins. It probably puzzled her when Collin mildly told her:

"If only, rather than sarcastically mock everyone else, you would follow your meditation exercises, this retreat could be of great benefit for you."

She replied: "I have the feeling that, wherever it is I am going, I'm still carrying a sack of rocks on my back."

Collin told her: "These are the rocks made by your own curse, they belong to your false personality, one that you have yet to renounce."

Again she reacts: "What do you mean? There is nothing in the least false about my personality!"

Then Collin told her: "That's what you think. You need to look more deeply inside yourself, recall your past history, tear off the mask to reveal your true self. Gurdjieff said: 'You must make every effort to ensure that your past does not become your future.'"

Leonora was self-determined, suspicious and critical. The power relationship between teacher and student seems to have been somewhat combative and may have been rooted in her political radicalism. Collin's religious approach to the work ideas may also have been problematic for Carrington, who had rebelled against her religious upbringing at an early age. In any case, she maintained an interest in the Gurdjieff work and worked later under the guidance of Christopher Fremantle, who she met during one of his visits to Rodney Collin at Tlalpam. Her relationship with the Work through Rodney Collin was also a source of inspiration for other female artists because later, not only R. Varo, but also the Hungarian photographer, Kati Horna, and the Swiss photographer, Eva Salzer, came to Tlalpam before the Collins decided to leave the house in spring 1954.

Leaving Peña Pobre must have meant a big change for the Collins and the group. Collin must have understood that the time for this project had come to an end and that it was time to move this experiment to a new phase. With Janet Collin's resources in hand, there was no reason to believe that this change was due to financial conditions.

Collin was convinced that Ouspensky's death had provided new opportunities and that his breakthrough through the process of dying had opened a door that, until then, had been closed. This conviction of his seems to have grown in spring 1954. He believed that these new opportunities could be available to many. However, the availability of these required that each realise that it was actually possible to work on oneself in more circumstances than hitherto thought, and that it was possible to free oneself from doubts and fears and thus come to a conviction that real work is actually realisable.

Collin believed that if one went back to the old material, e.g. *In Search of the Miraculous* and Nicoll's commentaries, with such an attitude, work could be absorbed differently and become an integrated part of oneself. Collin had no doubt that such conviction is accompanied by a new sensitivity and a new understanding that would itself help man to carry a living memory of these qualities in his ordinary daily life.

Collin took Ouspensky's brusque answer at a meeting in spring 1947, in which he categorically rejected a participant who had pointed out his own mechanicality and inability to do, as a supporting argument for his own view of the need to believe in the possibility of working in all circumstances and everywhere.

Rodney Collin

Collin's attitude to change is evident in a note he wrote the same spring that they moved, and can be seen from both an external and internal perspective:

> *When one takes one big new intentional step in life, many other things, which seemed difficult and ominous before, begin to smooth themselves out. The main step may be very difficult, but this in itself may make secondary things easier.*[1]

Intentional change is inextricably bound to direction made available with insight and wish. Thus wish can affect the conditions of a person's life. A wish can put an individual in touch with limitations in such a way that their potential becomes available. A deep wish can open doors that are closed by subjective desires and has the inherent ability to lead one across the threshold into a future. Without a future one moves in a recurrent circle in an enclosed space, separated from everything and everyone, often in the illusion of 'belonging'. Subjective desires always seem to be an echo of a self-image, while a deeper wish is in harmony with what a more objective order wants for the individual.

Collin saw aims in perspective of voluntary and involuntary suffering and that if a person's goal was to avoid suffering, they would be unable to associate suffering with anything positive.

> *Suffering is a fixative [...] It tends to fix whatever part of man's nature is uppermost while the suffering is being endured. Naturally, if it is involuntary it tends to bring with it resentment, self-pity and so on, and fixes them. On the other hand, if a man refuses to suffer except when he is making efforts for a definite aim and knows what he wants, then he tends to fix aim and determination.*[2]

Rodney Collin, whose aim was to live in the miraculous atmosphere of reality and participate in the exchange of energies coming in from higher levels and passing to various aspects of inner and outer life, seemed to be more and more sensitive to the need for change, and was prepared and able to deal with it. For him, a decisive aspect for this exchange to take place was that there were no blockages, and it is precisely in Collin's insight and understanding in this context that we can find examples and reasons for his sensitivity and flexible forward-looking ability to act.

[1] Rodney Collin, The Theory of Conscious Harmony (London: Robinson & Watkins Books Limited, 1958), p159.
[2] Rodney Collin, The Theory of Conscious Harmony (London: Robinson & Watkins Books Limited, 1958), p169.

As one searches his written sources for material that illustrates and supports this side of his insight, it becomes obvious how extensive it is, and his underlining of the need to clean the emotional side of man stands out clearly. When he points out that this side is basically clean, it must be seen in light of the fact that the emotional aspect of man does not have an original negative half, as opposed to man's intellectual, moving and instinctive sides where many negative aspects have a natural function. A prerequisite for negative aspects of emotional center to 'exist' is that there are sufficient imaginary notions. Such notions are formed through deafening associations to what were originally pure impressions. The consequence is that the inner voice of the heart drowns before it has been able to give advice and direction:

> If one learns to listen to heart, it will tell one things so clearly – what must be done, what must not be done, the real nature of people and places and things. Only it speaks so quietly, so subtly, and immediately a flood of reactions, explanations, excuses, theories have swamped it, and we do not even recognise it speak. Only listening carefully to what it wants to say, and remaining still until it has spoken, one cannot really do the wrong thing.[1]

Another, but related, aspect of dealing with necessary change and new opportunities is through acting as a pure and understanding instrument for a larger plan and realizing that it is connected with urgency. November 15th, 1951, Collin writes:

> To me this means scrupulously right action in relation to every individual and every situation concerned, firmness when firmness is required, gentleness when gentleness, and so on. It means right action in relation to individuals, to groups, to whole lines of work. Collin-Smith simply does not enter into it. He is not of sufficient interest. But if what is then understood as necessary to the plan is scrupulously carried out, that provides all the work Collin-Smith needs or requires. This is what I mean by less and less importance attached to personal work. The focus has to shift elsewhere, and the rest will take care of itself.[2]

An important aspect of the guidelines Collin found in interpersonal relationships was the handling of pressure from others involved in the group's work. One can realise the necessity for not wanting to minimise

[1] Rodney Collin, The Theory of Conscious Harmony (London: Robinson & Watkins Books Limited, 1958), p95.
[2] Rodney Collin, The Theory of Conscious Harmony (London: Robinson & Watkins Books Limited, 1958), p150.

such pressure by remembering that this pressure occurs among a group of people who have already passed a test that one could not have initiated oneself. *This* would be an expression of the desire for growth.

Here we see a clear indication of a confidence that a higher meaning can unfold if man through self-insight makes his illusory personal identity passive. It is easy to overlook the efforts that underlie Collin's inner position here, where choices have become a reality and constraints new steps on a ladder. Anyone who has tried to find his way in the maze of life can have some appreciation of such efforts and how demanding they can be, provided that one has understood that the only enemy in the game is oneself.

A well-known expression in the work is the term 'man cannot do', which not only reflects all the basic aspects of man's lack of freedom, but is also, by implication, a significant reminder of the need for effort to be able to do. Collin did not accept the unilateral and lopsided emphasis on man's lack of freedom.

The manifestation of this one-sided view can have many different causes. Just to mention two: It can be a tool for controlling others, a type of 'power feature', or it can be 'inherited' through imitation of someone one is fascinated by and/or afraid of. Unfortunately, these two examples can unite in the opposite sequence, creating an obvious vicious circle. Whatever the reason may be, the underlying cause is based on immaturity and lack of insight. Collin considered the negative attitude to this expression as both perverted and blasphemous and felt that it was necessary to counter it with the idea: 'it can be done by three'.[1]

Because Collin saw the solution to the human dilemma of limitation through the perspective of the law of three and a need for a right combination of active, passive and neutralising factors, he could argue that the aphorism 'man cannot do' was only half of the aphorism and that the whole should be: 'one cannot do, but it can be done by three'.[2] Later, when we look more closely at the various triads, it will not only be evident that Collin refers here to the triad of regeneration, but it will also provide an explanation as to why such an aphorism may appear to be a half-truth.

It is difficult to pinpoint a certain incident or specific reason for the shutting down of the house at Peña Pobre, where activities had been flourishing and varied. However, instead of thinking in these terms, the answer must be sought within a larger context. Collin expresses in his

[1] Rodney Collin, *The Theory of Conscious Harmony* (London: Robinson & Watkins Books Limited, 1958), p72.
[2] Rodney Collin, *The Theory of Conscious Harmony* (London: Robinson & Watkins Books Limited, 1958), p72.

correspondence in 1953 that, in addition to doubt, he had found reservations and clever carefulness to be limiting factors for the growth of what Ouspensky had made available. Combined with his feeling of urgency, these factors may have very well been of significant importance when the experiment of Peña Pobre came to an end.

For years Collin had put stone upon stone in the process of accumulating knowledge and especially understanding. In 1953 and 1954 he seems more willing than ever to not be limited by clever carefulness but encounters challenges and difficulties in a more active and ongoing way. He understood that the combination of freedom achieved through inner work and courage was a prerequisite for being able to work in all circumstances and that this would secure the anchorage to the place in oneself where one could always find help. In a letter from September 2nd, 1954, he asked the rhetorical question:

> *But how few of us want to be free or brave! This is why warnings about keeping away from harmful circumstances makes me rather uneasy. They sound so reasonable, so right. But to avoid danger is so often to avoid opportunity, and he who successfully hides from the devil very often hides from God too. Men are naturally timid, and my experience is that they will eagerly snatch up such good advice to make their timidity decent.*
>
> *The only answer I would wish to be able to give to: 'Quo Vadis?' is, 'Up!' That means constantly leaving more behind, constantly embracing a larger view. But how much help, how many kicks and cajolings we need to leave anything behind at all! Really I think it is the panorama alone that persuades us. And that is available for all to see – if they look round and up.[1]*

The planned travels to Europe and the Middle East in 1954 and 1955 may also have been a contributing factor for the closure of the house, but there is no reason to assume that the travels alone formed the basis for such a decision.

However, the many different possible explanations for the Collins' decision seem to rest on a fundamental desire for change in order for new opportunities to take place and the avoidance of repetition. About a year before the closure of Peña Pobre, we find the following in his correspondence:

---

[1] Rodney Collin, The The Theory of Conscious Harmony (London: Watkins Publishing, 1977), p173.

Sometimes I feel that we are all being hurried along by some higher power as fast as we can manage, and that many of the things which look to us difficult are more like a sharp kick in the rear administered to those who want to hang behind. Something seems to be saying: 'Hurry, hurry!' 'Very difficult times', we say. If we saw a little more, we would probably thank Heaven.

I see one thing interesting in connection with this hurrying on. The new lessons and moves are not difficult. What does make difficulty are the lessons we were supposed to learn way back, and failed to do so. They come back at us each round with renewed kick, until they are understood.[1]

It was in the midst of all the changes in the Collins' life in the spring of 1954 that Rodney Collin would see the result of his efforts to reach out to more people with his writings. On Thursday, May 20th, the printing house in Callejon de San Antonio Abad 39 completed work on several pamphlets, including the aforementioned *Herald of Harmony*. The second and the third in this series are respectively *The Christian Mystery* and *The Mysteries of the Seed*. The prospective audience for these pamphlets was primarily Roman Catholic. They were not intended as a substitute for religion but as an inspiration for inner work. Collin had for a long time seen the Work as key to religion, as well as art and other aspects of life.

In the *Herald of Harmony* Collin proclaims Gurdjieff and Ouspensky as representatives, for our age, sent by a higher Hierarchy or Great School. Jesus, the former messenger from above, could not fulfill his message of love due to the age's lack of harmony. The recurring dispute among groups springing from Gurdjieff and Ouspensky was in Collin's perspective a negligence of the complementary qualities that formed the base and united their work, namely polarity. Seen in such light, Collin's tireless struggle for harmony has a clearer prospect; few figures in the history of the Gurdjieff-Ouspensky work have seen more unity in plurality than Rodney Collin.

The pamphlet, *The Christian Mystery,* written during Lent in 1952, gives a compressed image of the universe and universal laws and points to man's position, nature, role and potential. Here Collin also underlines the necessity of consciousness to enable the soul and spirit to develop and manifest in an image of God.

In drawing clear lines through the history of civilizations from Atlantis to Rome via Egypt, India, Chaldea and Greece, all parts of a cosmos, he revealed their destiny and how the world waited and suffered:

[1] Rodney Collin, The Theory of Conscious Harmony (London: Watkins Publishing, 1977), p155.

Each was generated by the hierarchy. Each reached for understanding, prayed, failed, struggled, left monuments, grew old and died.[1]

In the personification of historical figures he illustrates how a gift fulfills its purpose only through reception:

First brute mankind was cherished by the sons of God made sons of men. Later, these were aided by sons of men made sons of God. Together they formed the hierarchy. Hercules, Krishna, Buddha, Socrates.

The messengers were multiplied. Many men rose. Yet the masses remained sheep – with or without a shepherd, yet still sheep. Far off, on the heights of the stairway, a door remained closed. There was traffic on the lower flights, yet the door remained closed. What next?[2]

In a condensed form of language, rooted in the laws of the enneagram, he takes us through central biblical aspects and opens doors to esoteric interpretations. He clarifies how different cosmoses have body, soul and spirit. Through various epochs and events in the history of nature and human beings, he points at the consequences of an underlying force that enables, sustains and is existence. This is how he points to the unspeakable but makes visible a universal force. His vision of *The Christian Mystery* breaks the boundaries of a one-sided religious perspective, as exemplified by his description of how the spirit of the Christian mystery manifests in time:

Monuments of the return to the mystery of God. Monuments of the inner penetration. Words, books, paintings. Of Luther and Laud, but Blake also and Goethe and Ibsen. No religious words but still the same. All these are magnetic centers in the body of Christendom. Inns upon the Way of Glory. They evoke the original glory, store it, gather and give it. And every traveler who passes is judged thereby.[3]

Collin's intricate enneagramatic expositions appear towards the end of the pamphlet as a cosmic monogram, in which the price of the entrance ticket to regeneration is clearly conveyed with practical examples:

And the soul of the Christian mystery?

Ah, the soul!

That is your business.

---

[1] Rodney Collin, The Christian Mystery (Mexico: Ediciones Sol, 1954), p10.
[2] Rodney Collin, The Christian Mystery (Mexico: Ediciones Sol, 1954), p11.
[3] Rodney Collin, The Christian Mystery (Mexico: Ediciones Sol, 1954), p23.

For the soul of the Christian mystery is made by the passage of Christians along the Way of Sacrifice. Not otherwise can it be made.

How shall we go? How shall we move from the place we are?

In this wise shall you move from the place where you are.

When you are born, say: 'God bears me'.

When you are at your mother's breast, say: 'Oh Moon, let me depend and know'.

When you come the first time to the temptation in the wilderness, know that it is the means of Growth.

When you meet others who belong to the Christian mystery, say: 'I recognise God'.

When you receive the bounty of nature, say: 'God recognizes me'.

When you feel the warm flesh upon you, say: 'O Venus, let me love and give!'

When you see the suffering multitude, see God in them, say: 'I love God'.

When your sins are forgiven, say: 'God loves me'.

When you feel song in your throat, movement in your limbs, say: 'O Mercury, let me praise and serve'.

When you come a second time to the temptation in the wilderness, know that it is the means of Purification.

When you receive the water of understanding, say: 'I serve God'.

When you are reviled, cheated, abandoned, sick, know that it is the means of Crucifixion.

When you go down into hell, say: 'God serves me'.

When the mind turns, the will stirs, say: 'O Saturn, let me understand and do'.

When you come to the agony in the garden, know that it is the battle with Corruption.

When you are revealed to yourself, say: 'I understand God'.

When others reveal themselves to you in judgement, say: 'God understands me'.

When passion turns blood to fire, makes limbs like air, say: 'O Mars, let me dare and destroy!'

When you unwittingly wound, carelessly break, say: 'I destroy God'.

When illness overtakes you, say: 'God destroys me'.

When others turn to you, you turn to others, say: 'O Jupiter, let me support and bear'.

When you come a second time to the agony in the garden, know that it is the means of Healing.

When you suffer pain, say: 'I bear God'.

When you die, know that it is the means of Ascension.

In the name of Christ, in the name of our Teacher, Amen.[1]

The subsequent pamphlet in the series, *The Mysteries of the Seed*, demonstrates an approach that can provide concrete examples of what and how esoteric knowledge manifested in some of the earlier civilizations described in *The Christian Mystery*.

The material in *The Mysteries of the Seed* is based on the Lesser and Greater Eleusinian Mysteries. The origin is often thought to be Orpheus and his circle but according to some sources the origin is significantly older. Collin refers to a potential source in which the Danaids, an initiated Egyptian group, delivered the mysteries to a Pelasgian woman, before they were invaded and destroyed by Dorians. The mysteries were later reformed by Orpheus.

The opening text, following a Homeric hymn from sixth century, is the myth of Demeter and Kore (Persephone) which gives man hope in this life of an afterlife. The Eleusinian Mysteries represented an ancient Greek myth about Demeter and her daughter Persephone. Based in the ancient city Eleusis, the secret initiation rites were celebrated every year in antiquity. The dialogue and the scenes, following the myth of Demeter and Kore, takes place 800 B.C. when Eleusis was incorporated into the Attic state and Athens was no longer a kingdom but an aristocratic republic. Collin's careful selection of texts in *The Mysteries of the Seed* reflects not only values that are in tune with the Fourth Way, but also the timelessness of questions and answers about the human situation and potential:

This world of multiplicity, these myriad forms.

Like a deep-scented flower of death burst into many blooms.

It roused desire, Psyche, lured you from heavenly life.

From being one, your self is broken in the prism of time.

[...] Arise, offset the water of forgetfulness. Drink. Of the water of remembrance. Drink![2]

---

[1] Rodney Collin, The Christian Mystery (Mexico: Ediciones Sol, 1954), p23-24.
[2] Rodney Collin, The Mysteries of the Seed (Mexico: Ediciones Sol, 1954), p31.

Face the dread apparitions born of your own mind;
Empusa of the triple face; dog, ass, and woman,
Your own multiplicity. Know her for what she is.
A creature of the low imagination.
Distrust, believe her not, be mindful.[1]

Give up your suffering, lend it no force.
Remember who you were from the beginning,
A child of starry heaven, pure, unspoilt,
Freed from obsession with past wrong and old desire[2]

Divest yourself of wishing, willing and imagining,
Know that nothing is yours, nothing is needed[3]

Before you could be born, you had to die
Before you died, you had to be awakened.
This is the mystery of Eleusis.[4]

Collin's conversion to Roman Catholicism created distrust in some circles of orthodox followers of Ouspensky and Gurdjieff. They believed that he had lost his way. Collin, who believed that the esoteric parts of all religions were connected and who had found the greatest reserve of esoteric truth in Roman Catholicism, now was met with scepticism and lack of tolerance.

In 1955 in an attempt to reassure a correspondent that he was still on the Fourth Way he wrote that "no one either in or out of the Church"[5]could convince him of any contradiction.

One important link between Ouspensky, Gurdjieff and the Catholic Church that he kept returning to in his correspondence in 1955 was the Hierarchy. For him, Ouspensky's 'Inner Circle of Humanity' and the 'Church Triumphant' of the Catholic Church were identical:

---

[1] Rodney Collin, *The Mysteries of the Seed* (Mexico: Ediciones Sol, 1954), p31.
[2] Rodney Collin, *The Mysteries of the Seed* (Mexico: Ediciones Sol, 1954), p32.
[3] Rodney Collin, *The Mysteries of the Seed* (Mexico: Ediciones Sol, 1954), p33.
[4] Rodney Collin, *The Mysteries of the Seed* (Mexico: Ediciones Sol, 1954), p37.
[5] James Webb, *The Harmonious Circle* (Boston: Shambhala, 1987), 492.

FURTHER LIFE IN MEXICO

The Hierarchy consists in Our Lord Jesus Christ, the spirit and the redeemer of our universe, and all his conscious helpers, great and small.[1]

As we saw in *The Herald of Harmony* Collin was convinced that it was exactly the Hierarchy who had sent Gurdjieff and Ouspensky to earth.

At the same time as he experienced a certain hostility in some circles, he experienced an ever-growing interest for his work in South America where all the groups expanded. The Mexico groups' local welfare schemes also received increasing public attention and Collin was eventually regarded as an Albert Schweitzer figure by many. On the other hand, others came to see him as more and more suggestible in a negative sense. By nature he appeared to be increasingly simple and open, almost like a child. This was an appearance that created both wonder and trust, but also confusion and a fertile ground for misinterpretations and condemnations.

People well versed in Gurdjieff's teaching will remember how he warned against suggestibility, but also was clear about a stick having two ends. In order to understand Collin's perception of one of the forms of suggestibility and not to confuse it with negative aspects, it is informative to see what assumptions Collin viewed as necessary. In his correspondence from February 7th, 1956 we find:

> *As to all suggestions and possibilities, we must always remain very open to what people suggest and to what life brings. We have to learn to respond continually to what comes to us in a living and true way. The rest will come by itself.[2]*

Now, as for the key to this openness, he wrote on January 11th the same year:

> *We must try to be kind and sincere and truthful. It is no good to be kind without being sincere. It is no good to be sincere without being kind. And neither are any good unless we try to connect them with truth. It means one has to be much more simple and open, remembering oneself and forgetting oneself in one.[3]*

The key here is that Collin's frame of reference is based on response, which is an active action, while the negative aspects of suggestibility are a consequence of an inability to act, in other words a reaction.

Of course we cannot rule out basic human traits such as envy and jealousy as the source for the critical expression among some more or less

---

[1] James Webb, *The Harmonious Circle* (Boston: Shambhala, 1987), 493.
[2] Rodney Collin, *The Theory of Conscious Harmony* (London: Watkins Publishing, 1977), p13.
[3] Rodney Collin, *The Theory of Conscious Harmony* (London: Watkins Publishing, 1977), p79.

prominent figures in the Gurdjieff-Ouspensky tradition, both in Europe and America. The limit for subjective interpretations is almost limitless because the limits are as subjective as the interpretation.

From the middle of the 50's we notice some striking behaviour in Collin. His already high level of activity with group meetings, personal meetings and movement classes, was constantly increasing in scope. Day-long expeditions in the Mexican wilderness and mountain-landscapes became an increasingly frequent occurrence, equipped, as before, with very little food, preferably just a bag of nuts and raisins. In addition to these trips, which he often took alone, he began to participate in traditional Mexican Pilgrimages.

After one such nocturnal pilgrimage in January 1956, from the Planetarium in Tlalpam to the shrine of Our Lady of Guadalupe, he fell over during mass in the Basilica. What was thought to be exhaustion, later turned out to be one of a series of consecutive heart attacks.

Collin, who never spared himself physically, went about two months later to Buenos Aires and Lima to visit the groups there. Although he was clearly exhausted, he continued at a pace that was obviously extreme. In Lima he led daily group meetings for a week, in addition to hour-long movement classes. He also found time for a vast number of private conversations with people that wanted help and advice.

One month before leaving for Lima, Rodney Collin was intensely concerned about settling all his business affairs and before the travel left nothing unresolved. He told his wife:

> All debts must be paid before moving on to something new. And I know that something new has to begin. The trouble is that I don't know what it is. I can't see clearly how to begin anything.

About the journey he told her:

> This journey to Peru is tremendously important. There, something very big is going to begin.

CHAPTER 20
The Journey to Cuzco

On Tuesday, April 24th, the Collins, accompanied by John Grepe and Mrs. Dickins, left Mexico for Peru. John Grepe was one of the original members of the group and was responsible, on a daily basis, for the bookstore, Libraria Britannica, that the Collins had set up in Mexico City. After the week with the group in Lima they left for Cuzco on Wednesday, May 2nd.

The aircraft, which was without a pressurized cabin, took them to an altitude of 19,000 feet. It was equipped with rubber hoses to ensure that the passengers received sufficient oxygen. Janet, who was sitting in front of her husband, discovered along the way that he had fallen asleep and that the nozzle for the air supply had fallen out of his mouth. After she had placed the mouthpiece in his mouth and he again received oxygen, he woke up.

When they had landed they went straight to the hotel and unpacked. Collin decided to take a walk, but he was back after half an hour. He mentioned that he had been to the Cathedral and that he had seen a disabled boy.

It is not uncommon for newcomers to Cuzco to experience discomfort due to its 11,500 foot-high location. They had been advised to take Coramine to alleviate discomfort caused by the altitude. To Janet's great surprise, Collin had actually bought Coramine drops. Usually, Collin did not touch any form of medicine other than Aspirin, that he would rarely take. In the following twenty-four hours he was to take several doses. After lunch in the hotel, they felt so unwell and tired from the altitude that they lay down on the beds to rest. After a short while, however, Collin got up and said that he wanted to go for a walk but would be back at 3:30 p.m.

Collin, who had previously been to Cuzco to study Native American cultures, had agreed to meet two friends from that time for a sightseeing tour of the ruins.

At 3:30 p.m. Janet left the room and went down to the hotel reception where they had agreed to meet. Collin was not there, but she met the person who was to guide them to the ruins, Sr. Espinosa. He told her:

"Your husband has got a lame boy and is buying him clothes."

They left the hotel reception and, standing in front of the hotel entrance, Espinosa pointed to a small shop across the street where there was an eager gathering of people peering curiously in through the shop's door and window. Janet crossed the street and went into what turned out to be a general drapers. She found Collin between piles of clothes in the crowded store. He was kneeling in front of a Native American boy, around 12 years of age, and was helping him to put on a pair of dungarees and a new shirt. Janet, who had not made her presence known but stood still looking at it all, was stunned by Collin's facial expression, which she experienced as unusual and different. When Collin first noticed Janet he exclaimed:

"Look, we are buying new clothes. We have been up the mountain to pray to Christ that this boy may be healed."

Collin was obviously referring to the imposing 26 feet high white sculpture on the hillside that towers over the colonial center of Cuzco. He continued:

"Then we bathed, so as to be quite, quite clean."

A young news-vendor, that Janet talked to a little later, told her that he had been so impressed with Collin's attitude to the boy when he saw them walking in the street that he had decided to follow them and see what was to happen. He told her that they had gone to the public baths where they both bathed and Collin had washed him before drying him with his own shirt.

Once the boy had been dressed in the shop, Collin took him by the hand and led him to Janet who recognised signs made towards her by the boy and said:

"He is saying that he is hungry."

Before leading the boy out of the shop, Collin told her:

"First we must buy him his shoes, then he can eat."

The boy, who was called Modesto, had great difficulty walking. His right leg, locked at a deformed angle, forced him to walk on his right toes, helped by a rod. The crowd of people outside the store grew and they followed Collin and the boy closely after they came out of the store and went further up the street. After a short while, Collin stopped and turned to the crowd that stood still and said:

"This boy is your responsibility. He is yourselves. You must pray to Our Lord to make him well. If you pray enough, he will be healed. You must learn to give, to give. You must learn to look after each other. You must learn what is harmony."

A voice in the crowd said:

"That is all very well for you, you are rich."

Collin answered:

"Everyone can give something. Everyone can give a prayer. Even if you can't give anything else you can always give a smile. That doesn't cost you anything!"

Collin and the boy then continued up the street.

One hour later Collin brought the boy to Janet at the hotel where he was given some chocolates before they went downstairs to the lobby were Sr. Spinoza sat waiting. They called a taxi and they all went to the Church of Santo Domingo. When they got out of the cab, Collin noticed a little girl outside the church crying. He went straight up to her but gave her no attention when he discovered that she was only crying out of temper. Then the four of them went into the church where Collin led them to the side altar where they all knelt and he recited the following prayer:

"In the name of the Father and of the Son and of the Holy Ghost we pray that this boy may be healed."

They returned to the hotel after passing the Cathedral, where they let Modesto off. Shortly after their return Collin told his wife that he was going out again but would be back in 20 minutes. When she asked him if he was going to confession, he said: "Yes." During the evening several people came to their room to ask Collin about his work before they went to bed at about eleven.

During the night Collin woke his wife up and told her:

"I am afraid. I think I have done wrong. It seemed so important that the boy should be healed that I offered my own body in exchange for his. Now I realise that I was prepared for other work."

She asked him:

"If God has other work for you, do you think that some words you said will make Him change His plans?"

Collin then said:

"If you invoke the name of the Holy Trinity, as I did, what you ask will be done."

Collin went right to Communion in the morning. After breakfast John Grepe, Mrs. Dickins and the Collins had decided to go outside town to see some ruins. They were just about to get into the cab when Modesto suddenly showed up. This homeless and orphaned boy who originally came from one of the mountain villages had found a special place in the church tower that he insisted on showing Collin. Modesto got into the car and they all drove off to the Cathedral. Collin and John Grepe followed Modesto up the staircase in one of the Cathedral's towers while the others remained in the car.

When they returned, the company continued their trip to some Inca ruins outside town before returning to the hotel for Lunch. After lunch the Collins went to their room to rest where Janet fell asleep. She was half asleep and only vaguely aware of her husband as he stood up and went out before she fell asleep again. She was woken abruptly by the sound of the cathedral bells. She checked her watch and discovered that it was 3:15 p.m. Soon after, the phone rang from the reception. It was the driver they had booked for a new excursion who announced that the car was ready. Janet went downstairs and outside the entrance of the hotel to look for Collin. John Grepe and Mrs. Dickins joined her almost at once.

Immediately after, a man appeared and asked if they were with Señor Collin. After receiving confirmation, he asked that they go immediately to the hospital as there had been an accident.

They got into the car that was originally ordered for the second trip to the ruins and drove straight to the hospital. They were shown into a small room full of talking people, including a number of nurses dressed in white overalls. On a stretcher against a wall, Rodney Collin lay on his back. His right leg was broken and pulled up in a position that was exactly the same as the shape of Modesto's invalid leg.

A young man was the first at the scene of the accident. He said he was driving across the square in front of the Cathedral when he had seen Collin fall. To verify the time on his wristwatch, he had looked up at the Cathedral's clock. It was 3:15 p.m. when Collin came crashing to the ground. He had immediately parked his car and got out to help but could not detect Collin's pulse when he lifted his arm. However, someone else who came to check his breath against a looking glass had registered that there was still a weak breath. When the ambulance arrived after fifteen minutes, there was no longer any sign of life.

A lady who had also seen Collin fall said he had fallen in an upright position with both arms out in the shape of a cross while his head was leaning back. He had hit the ground with his feet first and fell backwards and then remained in a full length position. The impact was later confirmed in an autopsy which showed that the spine had penetrated the brain. People who had gathered in the minutes before the ambulance arrived saw him lying with his eyes open and his arms outstretched in the shape of a cross, smiling.

A local resident who had studied Ouspensky's books for several years organised a 'chapelle ardente' in his drawing room. His black wooden coffin was surrounded by two burning candles on each side and a large crucifix at the head end.

A Franciscan priest came, and they all prayed the rosary. Throughout the evening and the night they kept watch. Every now and then Janet looked into the small glass window in the coffin lid, she could see that he was still smiling.

At five in the morning a man came in and sat down in front of the coffin. He was crying and exclaiming loudly. This man had had a conversation with Collin the day before and was now obviously drunk. After a while Janet took action and got him out of the room where he said:

"I did not mean to cry but the sense of my own personal loss was too much for me".

She suggested to him that other people might feel the same. Then he said:

"The loss of Señor Collin's great intellect is a loss for the whole world".

Janet said: "That is no reason why you should disturb other people. At least consider the children who are asleep."

To this he commented: "In the face of such a tragedy that is of no importance whatsoever."

She shook him hard by the arm in an effort to get his attention.

"Don't you shake me!" he said.

Janet replied: "Then stop trying to shake other people."

He said: "If I could do harm to someone, I would."

"Well in any case," Janet told him, "please don't smoke here."

With a bewildered expression he put out his cigarette and left.

A Mexican priest, an English Salesian brother, and three Franciscan monks, dressed in their traditional brown robes, arrived at 10:00 a.m. Three members of the Lima group, who had arrived by plane in the morning, also attended the Mass held at the foot of the coffin. The monks sang the penitential psalm.

When the clock approached three in the afternoon, there were about 40 people present and the priest began the prayer for the dead. A man who had been severely affected after seeing Collin with Modesto in the street of Cuzco and a floor waiter from the hotel had both begged to be allowed to carry the coffin. The other bearers were John Grepe and the three group members from Lima.

The story of Modesto and Collin's death was on everyone's lips in Cuzco. The population was greatly affected by Collin's care for the poor orphaned Native American boy. About 200 hundred people attended the funeral where the coffin was put in a temporary niche. The following day Janet bought a plot of ground surrounded by rosebushes in an angle of a wall of the old church. The place is located apart from the other graves but has a beautiful location that is bathed by the afternoon sun. In the pavement where Collin fell Janet had a stone inscribed with the words:

Here Rodney Collin gave his life to project harmony. May 3rd, 1956.

Although Janet and her friends did everything they could to track down Modesto after Collin's death, he was gone. Janet assumed that the police interrogation had frightened him so much that he had fled. According to Janet, Modesto recounted during police interrogation that Collin had suddenly stood up with a gasp and then hit his head on a beam before falling forward.

In the evening on the same day as the fall, Modesto told the bell ringer at the Cathedral that he was going out to find his 'godfather'. Due to his immaturity and naivety, he failed to understand that Collin's fall had killed him. The boy was well-known among the locals and they promised Janet they would find him and take care of him.

During a previous visit to Cuzco, Rodney Collin had had conversations with a local priest, Padre Lira, and suggested setting up a home for orphaned Native American children, as there were many in the area. This was obviously what Janet had in mind when, on May 17th, 1956, she wrote in a letter to Collin's brother, Derry:

"We are opening a memorial fund for this purpose, and hope that Modesto will be the first boy to live there."

On May 4th, the day after the death, Joyce and Derry received a telegram from Janet briefly explaining the course of events. Moreover, she asked Joyce to travel to see Cloé in France to give her the terrible news. For Joyce herself, Collin's death came as a shock that left her in an almost hysterical state. Derry, however, who had lost his only and much-loved brother, remained calm and appeared as an unshakable rock to the great comfort of his wife. While Joyce packed what she needed, Derry called to book airline tickets and arrange hotels.

The next day, on May 5th, Joyce left Heathrow and landed in Paris in the afternoon. Waves of grief and despair overwhelmed her from time to time. She had cried so uncontrollably on the flight that one of the flight attendants asked her if she was ill.

Arriving at the hotel in Rue des Saint Peres, she walked back and forth in her room. Now and then she knelt by the bed in a fervent desire to find the peace and strength to convey the tragic news of her father's death to her young niece, Cloé.

Early in the morning of May 6th, as she knelt with her head resting on her arms, exhausted from crying, she heard a voice that seemed to come from outside herself:

"It is quite all right. Tell her it's quite all right."[1]

The voice made an indelible impression and gave her an inner peace that accompanied her when she later that morning went to the convent school to see Cloé.

The news of the death created shock, bewilderment and grief in the young girl, but through her religious roots she gradually came to a form of acceptance that it was all in God's hands and his will. When her mother, in a long letter, gave her the impression that the death was a happy one and that her father "now would be able to help everyone and reach all those he loved," she must have found further reassurance. Under the circumstances Cloé thought she should go home, however her mother made it clear she expected her to stay at school to complete the exams, which were only a few weeks ahead.

In the four days they spent together before she returned to England, Joyce lived in the guest wing of the convent. During the days they walked around the monastery. They often sat on a stone bench by a stone table under a flowering lilac tree, either talking or in silence. The nuns, who were very gracious and accommodating, arranged a requiem for Rodney Collin.

In previous years, Collin had been in regular contact with a bookseller in Paris named Albert Rouhier, a connection that eventually developed into a friendship. Rouhier had provided Collin with books of an esoteric nature. On one occasion he had sold Collin a unique and very valuable collection of books from the Dr. Cabrera collection, which were sent to Mexico, where they were to be installed in the library at the Planetarium. Before Joyce left Cloé to go home, they decided to visit Albert Rouhier and bring him the news of Rodney Collin's death. When they arrived at the bookstore, they were warmly received. Joyce had never met him before, but he recognized Cloé immediately and embraced her. After they had told him about Collin's death, he became very serious, and said repeatedly, while shaking his head:

---

[1] Joyce Collin-Smith, *Call No Man Master* (Authors Online Book, 2004), p87-88.

"Je n'avais aucun préssentiment."[1]

He was completely dismissive when Cloé told him that her mother had assured her in her letter that it was a happy death:

"No. He will have to pay a high price," he told them.[2]

Addressing Joyce, who suggested the possibility that other's love for Collin could help erase debt, he was equally categorical:

"No. He himself will have to pay. You can't pay for him."[3]

Albert Rouhier's attitude undoubtedly reflected a belief that Rodney Collin had taken his own life, a speculation which later found fertile ground in certain circles in the Gurdjieff-Ouspensky tradition, which had initially been critical of Collin's work, in particular his attitude in his literary contributions.

The spread of rumours surrounding Collin's passing started immediately after his death and escalated across several continents. In England it was Dr. Roles who was showered with letters from all sides containing a myriad of stories about why and how Rodney Collin died.

The rumours were not only numerous, but also bore little relation to the course of events that Janet had conveyed to Joyce and Collin's brother, Derry. Dr. Roles had called while Joyce was away and Derry could only confirm his brother's passing. Dr. Roles told him Joyce could call him if she 'needed' to. She told me later that when she called he had said:

"I knew he was going to die a violent death, he was a violent man."

When she visited him in his office, he showed her a pile of letters regarding Collin's death. He wanted her to read through them, but after reading some, she saw that they were largely permeated by gossip, subjective attitudes and premature judgements and that they were incompatible with the facts Janet had given her. The basic theme was that Collin had gradually lost his grip on his own existence and simply gone mad. Joyce was surprised that the sharpest disdain came from some of Collin's former friends. His association with Mrs. Dickins was central to the general criticism.

However, after a detailed review of some of his correspondence and notes from January 5th to April 12th, across a total of 29 different dates in the same year as he died, there is no suggestion that we are dealing with a human being who is about to or has already lost his mind. On the contrary, he advocates, with the same calmness and collectedness, the necessity of

[1] Joyce Collin-Smith, Call No Man Master (Authors Online Book, 2004), p89.
[2] Joyce Collin-Smith, Call No Man Master (Authors Online Book, 2004), p89.
[3] Joyce Collin-Smith, Call No Man Master (Authors Online Book, 2004), p89.

penetrating the depth of human spiritual potential through the pacification of ego and egoism in order to experience life, conscience and the unity of existence.

No matter how strange one might have thought Collin's various ideas to be in the first place, there was no significant difference in his thinking towards the end of his life. He handled ideas and language with persistent rationality. Additionally, there appear to be no reports from Rodney Collin's closest followers at the time of his death, including his wife, to indicate that he was insane.

An interesting aspect of the problem of how to understand others was evident in one of Collin's descriptions of Ouspensky and might be relevant here. Collin wrote:

> It was very clear that if a man in a higher state of consciousness acts directly from the perceptions of that state, without bothering to consider the fashions and weaknesses of ordinary life, he will seem mad to men in an ordinary state. Evidently great teachers have to soften their truth to the understanding of their hearers, to be 'gentle' with them – but for a short time their work may exactly consist in not compromising with ordinary life at all. This will be the real test of those who have studied with them, and will show whether they have really understood or have heard only words. 'From that time many of his disciples went back, and walked no more with him.'[1]

It seems likely that some of Collin's students at times adopted aspects of Collin's way of being that is compatible with such a perspective.

For those who did not necessarily consider him mad, but who regarded entry into Catholicism as evidence that he had lost his original path, an excerpt from his correspondence of March 12th, the year before his death, would perhaps have provided some perspective:

> Religion means the art of becoming consciously re-joined to God. But with the aid of the Work a man can go straight to the esoteric side of the religion he chooses. The religion he chooses is his own business, of course. I myself became a Catholic last year. I had been moving towards the Catholic Church ever since I went to France at the age of sixteen and made a bee-line for the cathedral in every city. But it is the esoteric side of Catholicism which interests me, and the esoteric sides of all religions are in harmony.
>
> There are no contradictions, for the Hierarchy is one, and the esoteric sides of all religions were launched by it, as was the great experiment

[1] Rodney Collin, The Theory of Conscious Harmony (London: Watkins Publishing, 1977), p39.

191

started through Ouspensky and Gurdjieff for our own time. I belong to the Fourth Way, and always will. It is a very special way, much more different from the other ways than most people realize. But it can enter everywhere, harmonise with the real side of everything. The creation of harmony is its task. I want to learn more, participate in harmony on a bigger and deeper scale.[1]

Rodney Collin's death at the age of 47 years was a shock to many. In the wake of a dramatic event, there is often a peculiar tendency to re-frame the truth. Rodney Collin's approach to inner work could be controversial and there were rumours that he had committed suicide. For those who truly knew him and knew what he stood for, they could only meet this vile and monstrous claim with silence. Thus, an event that is only dramatic because of its destructive nature can become a scandal. The underlying urge to create a scandal is due to psychological malnutrition or perhaps more precisely, emotional deficiency.

The rumours that circulated inevitably coloured Collin's reputation and may affect attitudes to his literary contributions. This is most likely to pose a problem to those who are young or new in the Work. However, the impact has been significantly neutralised by continued reference to various aspects of his ideas by several prominent representatives of the Gurdjieff and Ouspensky doctrine, such as Dr. Maurice Nicoll and Beryl Pogson.

Much changed after the return to Mexico. Janet clearly did not see it as her role to take her husband's place, however, three individuals were inclined to believe that Collin's mantle fell on their shoulders and tried their luck in turn. Others realised that an era was over. Mema Dickins, with her customary dominance, had a go at leading the remnants of Collin's group. The original idea of the Planetarium was scrapped. What was originally intended to be The Chamber of the Sun was converted into The Chapel of Christ. Likewise, the Chamber of the Moon became a Madonna Chapel.

Rodney Collin's original idea of an integrated library was also ignored. The unique book collection from Dr. Cabrera was deemed by Mema Dickins to be inappropriate in a Catholic environment. The books not only received an indefensible lack of care, stored where moisture and microorganisms could damage them, but some were even destroyed outright. In Paris, the news of the collection's tragic fate reached Albert Rouhier. In a letter sent via Joyce, he expressed his concern and strongly

---

[1] Rodney Collin, *The Theory of Conscious Harmony* (London: Watkins Publishing, 1977), p127-128.

requested that what might be left of the collection be preserved for the future. This appeal appears to have been futile.

For quite some time, Mema Dickins, now surrounded by a group of young priest apprentices, continued to convey 'messages' and appeared regularly as stigmatists with bleeding palms. Later, as her role gradually waned, and two other leadership figures slipped away, John Grepe was given a central role among the remnants of the group.

It isn't clear how Mrs. Dickins ceased to play a prominent role in the group, but it is probable that people came to see her as a little hysterical and simply got bored. Later in life, according to one of her four children, she absolutely refused to talk about her past.

For Janet the landscape had shifted. She lost not only the love of her life but also her spiritual mentor. She had not yet completed the journey from the comfortless paralysing turning point in Cuzco to an inner position where the challenges themselves became the way forward. Janet Collin was a strong woman. She had learned that acceptance is a remedy for every burden and that what presents us with requirements and demands is not Work. Supporting those around her who took Collin's death heavily became her comfort.

After her husband's death, Janet Collin took charge of his surviving papers and his published works. From his extensive correspondence and notes between August 4th, 1944 and April 12th, 1956, she conjured up the manuscript for *The Theory of Conscious Harmony.*

The way in which she has categorised the excerpts and compiled the texts exemplify the span of Rodney Collin's work. As she indicates in the preface to *The Mirror of Light,* another book she published, there is some uncertainty about whether all material can be attributed to Collin, although it was found in his notebooks. However, she had the selection published because she knew Collin would have fully agreed with the content. The following excerpt from the introduction sheds light on the problematic position of man with a simplicity and clarity that was so characteristic of him when dealing with crucial questions:

> "We live our life in a mirror; everything is reversed. When we see a scene it is received in the brain reversed. The rays go out, cross and are received in reverse. Reality exists in the place where the two lines cross. If we can find it. The same takes place in our thoughts; we think that cause is effect and effect, cause. For us, the physical is more real than the spiritual. That which our senses perceive we call objective, while all that

is imperceptible to our physical senses we call unreal or imaginary. We think sowing and reaping are essentially different and fail to understand that they are the same. We regard birth and death as antitheses and have altogether forgotten that to die is to be born. The life we live, the world we live in, is a mirage. If we understand a mirage we understand a miracle. We should study more about the mirror.[1]

For a number of years, Janet Collin, despite her arthritis, engaged in social work, in particular the teaching of Mexican children. Regardless of her fortune, she chose a thrifty and frugal way of life. On Sunday, September 5th, 1971, at 11:30 a.m. the circle was closed; Janet Collin died at her home in Monterrey 12, Acapulco.

According to Gurdjieff:

The highest aim and sense of human life is the striving to attain the welfare of one's neighbour.

Rodney Collin became a human being; a receptor and reflector of impressions from different levels and scales, always ready to respond to the true needs of himself and others.

Four weeks before he died, he wrote:

I was in the presence of God;
He sent me to earth;
I lost my wings;
My body entered matter;
My soul was fascinated;
Earth drew me down.
I reached the depth;
I am inert;
Longing arises,
I gather my strength;
Will is created;
I receive and meditate;
I adore the Trinity;
I am in the presence of God.

---

[1] Rodney Collin, The Mirror of Light (London: Watkins Publishing, 1977), p7.

PART 2

Rodney Collin's Celestial Theories

CHAPTER 21
The Theory of Celestial Influence

On one of the first occasions Collin met Ouspensky at his home at Gwendwr Road in London in 1936, he introduced himself as a writer and asked how he could contribute.

Ouspensky simply said:

"Better not to get too involved. Later we may find something for you to write."[1]

Collin was relieved at Ouspensky's response. He felt insecure and was concerned about how his writing could be useful. For the next ten years he wrote virtually nothing about the Work.

However, in 1947, two months before Ouspensky's death, he began to outline the basic main features and structure of the manuscript for *The Theory of Celestial Influence* and experienced this as a fulfilment of Ouspensky's original promise.

In order to trace the impetus and source of the manuscript we must return to a group-meeting held in New York in 1944. The members were assigned the task of classifying the sciences according to the principles of the Work and the different worlds that the Work embodies. Ouspensky's rationale for the thesis was that the existing classifications could not be considered satisfactory, either in light of Work-ideas, or from the viewpoint of the current era.

At this meeting he pointed out how the work of English philosopher Herbert Spencer, who transferred Darwin's theory of development to areas such as art, science and social life, was interesting but far from satisfactory. Although Spencer gained recognition in several disciplines, primarily in pedagogy, sociology, anthroposophy and religious history, he is probably best known as the man behind the term 'survival of the fittest'.

Collin's objective in *The Theory of Celestial Influence* was to shed light on the human position in the universe. Rather than unilaterally emphasising a scientific approach based on the accumulation of measurable facts, or an approach where universal laws and principles are rediscovered by an

---

[1] Rodney Collin, *The Theory of Celestial Influence* (London: Vincent Stuart Publishers Ltd, 1958), XIX.

individual in a moment of higher consciousness, he seeks a broader representation where these are seen in context.

He uses analogy to reflect the experiences of a higher consciousness down and into the world of phenomena (that are available to us in our daily life). At the same time he tries to achieve, through a classification and coordination of facts from our world of phenomena, a movement up and in the direction of the abstract legalities that are moving downwards.

Accepting the inherent nature of the two methods and the distance between them, he acknowledges that the task of uniting them may prove impossible. Although he emphasizes that there will always be an invisible territory between the two directions where evidence is unthinkable, he argues that it is precisely in this border area that they can and must unite. He accepted unconditionally that a mutual and consensual understanding must remain inaccessible to the purely logical mind. However, he was willing to take the risk of trying to reconcile the two approaches because he saw so clearly the future limitations that lay in separating them.

On one hand he saw science, with an increasingly materialistic and narrow specialisation, and on the other hand he saw how religious and philosophical principles constantly distanced themselves from scientific knowledge.

Rodney Collin chooses to begin his thesis on man and cosmos with nothing less than all possible dimensions of both time and space – the Absolute. Early on, in exploring how this includes all aspects of the universe, beyond those imaginable by human beings, including the present, past, and future in all universes, he realises the impossibility of coming to anything other than a philosophical view. Our minds are simply too limited to be able to handle such comprehensive material. When, in addition to the above factors, he includes not only everything that has manifested in all such universes, but also everything that has been proposed as possible in existing and potential new universes, one can get a taste of how formidable these ideas are to the mind.

Collin's starting point for an approximation of this all-encompassing material is through a modification that builds upon and takes into account the limitations of the human mind.

The three basic factors of his modification are:

- Body
- Quality
- Laws.

As a basis for examining the relationships between a unity and its components he sets out the following three principles:

1. Affectability/the effect of radiation of something greater.
2. The passive attraction of something bigger upon that which is smaller.
3. The delay of the impact of emission from something bigger upon something smaller.

Collin illustrates his three mental images: radiation, attraction and time, in the form of a ball, in which the ball's weight, size temperature and radiance as a whole form a unity. It will, through these three factors, affect its surroundings with heat and light respectively and an attraction proportional to mass. The delayed effect of these influences will accord with and be proportional to the intermediate distance.

With this basis for illustrating the interaction between a unit and external elements, he follows with a description of how the same relationships behave within one and the same unity. In this example, the ball has a warm south pole and a cold north pole. Assuming that the form, size and shape of the ball remains permanent, Collin writes:

> ... the greater the heat of the south pole, the greater the rarefaction of matter in its neighbourhood, and in consequence the greater the condensation of matter in the neighbourhood of the cold pole. If this process is carried to infinity, radiation and mass become entirely separated, the south pole representing as it were pure radiation, and the north pole pure mass.[1]

The infinite number of relations and physical conditions within the unity, the sphere itself, is thus created by radiations, attraction and time. Collectively, these three factors produce the formula that underlies a perfect definition of any part of the sphere and can therefore indicate its essence, limitations and possibilities. Collin concludes, making his remarkable model the center of gravity of a world view, that if we call the South Pole heaven and the North Pole hell, we have formed a representative figure of the Absolute of religion.

Collin points out how his cosmological model, the universal sphere, evades human logic and measurability and at the same time he reminds us that this sphere includes all imaginable and unimaginable possibilities.

Based on his two-poled model, in which all the worlds move from the pole of radiation to an equator of maximum expansion and then gradually

---

[1] Rodney Collin, *The Theory of Celestial Influence* (London: Vincent Stuart Publishers Ltd, 1958), p52.

fade to the pole of mass, he shows how this model is capable of including new ideas and recent research. The new idea of the universe expanding he sees in light of the radiation of a pole to an equator of maximum expansion. Those who assume that the origin of the universe is due to a dead density, which keeps getting warmer before it ceases in a total and final fire, is focused on the pole of the mass and in a movement in the direction of the radiating pool. However, those who imagine that the total fire was the cradle of origin, and where a constant cooling down takes place, take the opposite starting point.

Collin considers Einstein's 'cosmic repulsion' as an attempt to meet a third and necessary factor where both pole properties meet in time or delay.

Collin points out that all these explanatory models are both correct and wrong, and at the same time he reminds us of the story of the three blind men who, after touching an elephant, came to different conclusions.

The only thing that can be said, Collin claims, is that the Absolute is one and that within this unity there are three forces: radiance, attraction and time, and that the interaction between them creates infinity.

The visual representation of celestial bodies for human beings is, for Collin, a key to a more objective understanding of the limitations of human comprehension.

When the Milky way, the Sun and the Earth appear to us as a bow, disc and ball respectively, this is a perception that is fixed and bounded by our position.

Seen in the perspective of dimensions, a curved solid, a curved plane and a curved line are, respectively, three, two and one dimensional.

Therefore, the Earth appears as three-dimensional, the Solar System as two-dimensional, the Milky Way as one-dimensional, however, the Absolute remains invisible because we cannot perceive it in any dimension.

For a further demonstration of human limitation in terms of perception, and to indirectly point to the need for a new and different approach, Collin explains how dimensions become invisible. The Earth, for example, does not appear as three-dimensional in relation to the Solar System but as a line in motion, while the Solar System in relation to the Milky Way no longer appears as a plane, but a point. In this way, he shows that for every ascending progression on the celestial scale – the Earth, the Solar System, the Milky Way, the totality of galaxies – in each case, a lower dimension becomes invisible.

Because each cosmos in itself is three-dimensional, this progression must be two-sided. That is, at each expansion of the scale, a 'higher' dimension will be added, which will then be invisible to the smaller entity.

A human being, as he moves on Earth, who is himself a three-dimensional solid, will be able to move in two of the Earth's three dimensions. In his three-dimensional world, where he moves on the Earth's surface, which is a two-dimensional plane, the Earth's thickness will supply a third dimension that is higher and disproportionate to the third dimension of man.

In other words, in Collin's celestial hierarchy, each superior world would seem to exclude the lowest dimension in, for it, the underlying world but at the same time add a dimension to the world above. Each world will thus possess an additional dimension to a lower world and a smaller dimension to the world above. The consequences are that each world becomes partially invisible to both the world that is larger or smaller than itself.

In Collin's model, this means that the lowest dimensions in the smallest world become invisible as the highest dimension in the greater world becomes visible.

With this study, Collin manages to demonstrate how and why celestial bodies, such as the Milky Way, are largely invisible to man, because man cannot see enough dimensions.

Exactly what astronomical phenomena such as the Milky Way are and what relationships they have to other galaxies is to impossible to determine through ordinary study. Collin's proposal for solving this problem is based on the idea that the relationship between interpenetrating worlds is itself a constant.

By detailed analogy, he demonstrates parallels between celestial bodies and the inferior worlds of electrons, molecules and cells, and that the same additions and subtractions of dimensions that we find in the relationships between celestial bodies also apply to microcosmoses. However, he also presents a parallel problem:

> If [...] we compare the human body to some great body of the Milky Way, and one cell of it to our Solar System, and we wish to find a viewpoint comparable to that of a human astronomer on earth, we should have to try to imagine the perception of something like a single electron of a molecule of this cell. What could such an electron know about the human body? What indeed could it know about its cell, or even its molecule? Such organisms would be so vast, subtle, eternal and

omnipotent in relation to it, that their true meaning would be utterly beyond its comprehension. Yet no doubt the electron could perceive something of its surrounding universe; and though this impression would be very far from reality, it is interesting for us to imagine it.[1]

The key to overcoming obstacles often resides in man himself. Collin claims that because man himself is the superior world in relation to the lower worlds inside, it becomes possible, to study and know these worlds.

When Collin raises the fundamental question of what a cosmos is, he recalls that order and harmony are the Greek meaning, while in the Pythagorean view it also meant a self-evolving or self-transcending whole. Turning to the phrase from the book of Genesis, "God created man in his own image," he concludes that the hallmark of a cosmos is a divine image and that its characteristics can be found on all levels.

Exploring the structure of the universe, Collin not only demonstrates man's limited perception relative to the heavens, but also establishes the existence of a hierarchy of cosmoses.

When he explores the time of the universe, he is obviously concerned with the question of whether it is possible to measure the duration of the Milky Way and the Solar System, for example, and also the question of whether there is a relation between space and time. Collin delves into a question that emerged from his own reflections on what constitutes the current world of an electron, a molecule or a cell. What an electron could perceive from its immediate surroundings is just:

… a stationary cross-section of the human body, at right angles to the artery in which their cell was destined to move.[2]

According to Collin, it is this that constitutes its universe or its present for an electron, molecule, or cell.

Other cross-sections further up the artery, that a cell will reach later, represent its future, lower cross-sections its past. A cell travelling along the artery of man travels along man's third dimension, that is his length. It is this dimension that represents the cell's fourth dimension, time. Likewise, it is the cell's third dimension that would represent the dimension of time for the moving molecule. Man's third dimension, the cell's time, is outside the time of the molecule and is regarded by Collin to be the molecule's fifth dimension and somehow associated with existence after death.

[1] Rodney Collin, *The Theory of Celestial Influence* (London: Vincent Stuart Publishers Ltd, 1958), p7.
[2] Rodney Collin, *The Theory of Celestial Influence* (London: Vincent Stuart Publishers Ltd, 1958), p8..

The time of the electron, deriving from the third dimension of the molecule, cannot extend or repeat its individual life and is thus unable to enter the third dimension of man. This is the sixth dimension, the unknown, the dimension where all imaginable and unimaginable possibilities are realised.

From this, Collin deduces that all cosmoses can be seen in the perspective of six dimensions where the three first represent its space, the fourth its time, the fifth its eternity, and finally the sixth, its absolute.

Collin elaborates further:

> ...we have to suppose that with each change from one cosmos to another, this whole period of dimensions shifts, one being abandoned, one gained, and the rest changing, each into the next. Thus the length of one cosmos will appear as time to a lesser cosmos, as eternity to the next smaller, as absolute to the lesser still, while to the fifth cosmos it can bear no relation at all.[1]

Based on his six-dimensional thesis, Collin produces orderly tables that illustrate how different worlds such as cells, man, nature, the Earth and the Sun are woven together into a whole.

Early in this chapter we pointed out that, to understand man and cosmos, Collin took the greatest possible perspective – the Absolute, which must therefore be able to include all possible dimensions in both time and space. Through his six-dimensional perspective, he laid the foundation for further development of precisely such an understanding.

No matter how tempting it is to embody all details of Collin's ideas and theories, it is beyond the intent of this book to give anything but a relatively brief summary of some key features of *The Theory of Celestial Influence*, not only to shed light on his ideas and their foundation, but also on the man behind them.

Through one of his early psychological reflections on the six-dimensional model, we glimpse a new aspect of how man is limited.

He observes that the more one perceives a living being and compares it to another in the first three dimensions, the more diverse it appears, while their mutual design and striking similarities gradually become more apparent when considered in four and five dimensions. And further:

> ... when we perceive things in three dimensions, we see them at their maximum of differentiation. Living in a world of three-dimensional

---

[1] Rodney Collin, *The Theory of Celestial Influence* (London: Vincent Stuart Publishers Ltd, 1958), p20.

objects, we are experiencing creation in its most cold, separate and exclusive aspect. This indeed is one explanation of the curious loneliness and desolation of men with their present three-dimensional perception.[1]

After establishing the model that embraced all the cosmoses and having shown that time was an implicit factor, Collin was concerned with the individual time of each cosmos. With the idea 'as above so below' as a starting point, it was his belief that if he found a way of calculating time for one cosmos, it would be the key to identifying time in the others.

In his work on the temporal aspect, he concludes that in every cosmos, including man, time, and space, we are continuously connected to a pattern, although:

... form multiplied by its time yields its very self, its own unique signature, by which it differs from all other beings in the universe.[2]

In the intimate relations between form and time, where time leaves traces in form, and the form's origin is revealed by time, one finds the destiny, capacity and character of man. In other words, man's lifetime is himself. It is this link that, according to Collin, puts man in a constant and very definite relationship to cosmoses, regardless of whether they are larger or smaller than man himself.

This leads us to Collin's further deduction:

If each cosmos has its own time, which – along with its form – constitutes an inalienable and unique property of its being, what shall we make of the fact that each cosmos either includes or forms part of every other? For instance, every single man contains within himself the cosmoses of electron, molecule and cell, and he forms part, – however small – of the cosmoses of Nature, Earth, the Solar System and the Milky Way. That is to say, somehow hidden within him or pervading him, work the times of all other cosmoses of the universe.[3]

That man, apart from his own time, participates or can participate in the time and being of all other cosmoses was to Collin one of man's greatest mysteries and the clue to some of his unrealised possibilities.

From former calculations, based on human breath, calculated to be 28,000 breaths in a full circle of day and night, Collin revealed a close

[1] Rodney Collin, The Theory of Celestial Influence (London: Vincent Stuart Publishers Ltd, 1958), p22.
[2] Rodney Collin, The Theory of Celestial Influence (London: Vincent Stuart Publishers Ltd, 1958), p30.
[3] Rodney Collin, The Theory of Celestial Influence (London: Vincent Stuart Publishers Ltd, 1958), p31.

relationship to other worlds through their 'breathing'. A blood cell, whose day of work lasts between 8 to 18 seconds before it returns to its starting point, the heart, after depositing oxygen to distant parts of the body and returning with carbon dioxide, corresponds to a day of work and sleep of man, if one takes into account that it takes six seconds for a blood cell to be restored – that is to return to the heart after passing through the lungs.

Collin writes:

> *If we take for convenience 12 seconds work and 6 seconds rest for the blood-cell, we get a 'day' of 18 seconds; and thus a 'life' of six days.*[1]

To verify his blood cell lifetime calculations, Collin applied a completely different method of a cubic scale formula which gave almost exactly the same result.

Through his calculations, Collin came to see life, day and breath as cosmic divisions of time for each individual cosmos. These calculations, spanning from electrons to the Milky Way, included the day and lifetime of molecule, blood cell, man, world of nature, Earth and the Sun.

When he calculated the average life expectancy of a human, he concluded that it was 28,000 days. In a remarkable way, this number corresponds to man's breaths per day. The figure 28,000 turns out to be consistent with many facets in his table of time of the various cosmoses, for example, the time of a blood cell is 28,000 times that of its constituent molecules. He found similar relationships between man and the world of nature, and between the Milky Way and the Earth. Using the same calculation model, but based on breath, he concluded that a molecule's day equals a blood cell's breath and that a human's day is equivalent to a breath of nature.

On the basis of these various calculations, he concluded not only that breath, day, and life were true cosmic time-divisions, but that minutes, hours, weeks, and months appear to constitute a significant proportion of a whole, where experience on one level is somehow connected with those on several others.

Turning to digestion of impressions, he introduces a possible further shortening of human time. Unlike food and air, whose time of digestion can be calculated respectively within a day and seconds, digestion of impressions is significantly quicker.

---

[1] Rodney Collin, *The Theory of Celestial Influence* (London: Vincent Stuart Publishers Ltd, 1958), p26.

Through computation, Collin develops different but parallel time-aspects, such as a moment of self-awareness corresponds to 80 years at the level of the Solar System, which in turn corresponds to the approximate average life expectancy of man.

A prominent feature of Collin was his openness regarding the accuracy of his theories and assumptions. This may seem almost contradictory, as many of his calculations appear to be not only well-weighted and often precise, but also coincidental. When he portrayed his method as analogical, it was among other things to emphasise that he himself did not regard the representations as scientific. It is therefore not surprising when, in his investigations of the times of the universe, he emphasises the necessity of perceiving the representation as orders of time rather than exact measurements.

One of the results of his efforts and the consequences of sharing them was to support a broader view of time and to challenge our ordinary and narrow perception of time as a linear phenomenon. This is an area where our minds tend to become sloppy and feeble and where the sense of proportion is lost. To help individuals break down fixed notions that prevent them bridging everyday experiences with a world of higher laws was undoubtedly among his deeper intentions and desires.

Collin writes:

> ... *if our deductions are correct, we may suppose that all living organisms have similar divisions of their time. This means that between its birth and death a cell breathes as many times as does a man in his lifetime. And a man receives within his life as many perceptions as the Sun. Once rid of our accustomed belief in one time, we come to the strange conclusion that all lives are the same length.*[1]

The Sun and the Solar System were not only a central theme for Collin, but fundamental to a more comprehensive understanding of the universe and human position and potential. He imagined that the various planets, including asteroids, were originally projected from a central point, the Sun. The size of the Solar System, and its vast field of influence, he considered, relatively speaking, to correspond to the distance between the human ovum and the life that can sprout from it.

By exploring the relation between time and space he attempted to establish what changes take place in the third dimension, length, as it

---

[1] Rodney Collin, *The Theory of Celestial Influence* (London: Vincent Stuart Publishers Ltd, 1958), p34.

moves through the body of the solar system. A challenge that Collin was well aware of was that man conceives only a cross section of a higher dimension just as a blood cell only a sees a cross section of the human body because it exists in fewer dimensions than the body.

Just as a cell's time coexists with human time, Collin believed that the Solar System's time coexists with human time. His challenge then was how to understand what was the past and future of the Solar System as coexisting and solid. He concluded that for man to imagine how the Solar System perceives itself would be similar to how a cell would imagine how man perceives himself, or is perceived by others.

Because his earlier calculations had shown that a moment of perception for the Solar System lasted for 80 years, roughly equivalent to a human lifetime, he considered his previous model of calculation as unsuitable, because any attempt at an exact material analogy would sooner or later produce material that would appear inconceivable to man.

Since the Sun's significance and brilliance already blinds us when viewed from our ordinary three-dimensional perspective, Collin deemed it impossible for man to imagine a four-dimensional sun, and that the only thing we could suppose from our impressions of the Sun is that it represents the fundamental life-force of that Solar System.

He also came to surmise that the Solar System is expanding and that the Sun is gradually warming. He considered the possibility that the degree of radiance of the central sun in different solar systems could determine their development. And, just as a human being has to possess a complete system of organs and functions, a solar system has to possess planets and elements to be able to evolve.

Intensity and penetration were properties Collin associated with the development-potential of both a solar system and a human, in terms of the central light of a solar system and a human's central consciousness. What therefore distinguishes one solar system from another, or a human being from others, is the degree of intensity and penetration.

Not only did Collin come to see that light and consciousness follow the same laws, but he came to regard them as identical phenomena, albeit on different scales.

Central to this perspective, despite the fact that neither man nor the Sun can change its constitution, the Sun, like man, must utilise the self-generating ability inherent in its nature in order to fulfill the purpose of the universe: to become conscious.

Collin writes:

For a man to be fully conscious, all his parts must become fully conscious. For a sun to become fully radiant, all its planets must become radiant. For the Absolute to remember itself, all beings must remember themselves.[1]

To demonstrate basic characteristics of the Sun and causal relationships between the Sun and the Solar System, in addition to their external influence, Collin provides the analogy of the behaviour of the electric coil. This kind of inductor is a passive electric component that creates a magnetic field when electric current flows through it. It consists of an insulated wire wound into a coil around a core, with the strength of the field varying according to the number of turns and the voltage and amperage.

In Collin's analogy, the Sun is surrounded by eight coils – its planets in their orbits – which are acting as transformers of solar energy. However, he proposes a prerequisite: that they can act as such only if they differ in their conductivity as metal does. Because he could not verify the attribution of metals to the planets, he admits that these calculations are suggestive speculations.

In respect of the production of a magnetic field created by the electric current, he observes that it rotates clockwise in concentric lines. He writes:

If we now try to translate this from the world of spirals seen in the sun's time to the world of spinning balls seen in man's time, we shall understand how it is that all rotating bodies in the universe create and are surrounded by a magnetic field.[2]

It was in their rotation that Collin found the indication that they are sections of a line carrying tremendous currents that are moving into another dimension.

Based on the original central energy of the Sun, which determines the speed of the current, he saw the speed of a planet's movement around its orbit as an effect of the intensity of the available sunlight. And he regarded the individual planets to be surrounded by magnetic fields that both overlapped and interacted with others.

---

[1] Rodney Collin, *The Theory of Celestial Influence* (London: Vincent Stuart Publishers Ltd, 1958), p40.
[2] Rodney Collin, *The Theory of Celestial Influence* (London: Vincent Stuart Publishers Ltd, 1958), p42-43.

THE THEORY OF CELESTIAL INFLUENCE

Collin makes an intriguing point about magnetic influence. Pure light, which in itself is invisible, is given form in the manifestation of the Northern Lights. The Aurora Borealis becomes visible only when magnetism acts on free hydrogen ions. This led Collin to the general principle that the rise of visible form is due to magnetism acting on matter.

Although the influence of the Sun's light by far exceeds the tempo of magnetic influence, it is the latter which is the underlying source of emanation of planets, including the Moon, simply because the light they emit is not their own, but the Sun's. Collin then concludes that the combined and assembled magnetic influences of the planets and the moon is the source for creation of forms on Earth, just as the Earth plays the same role in regard to other planets.

When he refers more directly to how different types of energy affect man, he references this light, magnetism and sound. Because they have different origins and operate at different speeds they generate and shape different phenomena.

The Sun's light, the source of life, the planet's magnetism, the premise of form, and sound, with its origin in nature, indicated to Collin a clear hierarchy of energies in cooperation.

> *From first cosmos to last electron, the whole universe is a complex of coils within coils, spirals within spirals, magnetic fields within magnetic fields. In this aspect each creature transforms a single force to the exact tension required to drive a galaxy, a man or a mote. And when its resistance decreases with the span of age, by this very tension it is fused, the form of its magnetic field is dissipated, and it dies.*[1]

As planets do not emit light of their own, but only reflect light from the Sun, Collin considered them to be transformers, performing functions in the Solar System similar to those in the world of man, such as respiration. Fulfilling their role in the Solar System, Collin regarded them as units comprising a complete unity and as such possessing all possibilities. In light of the idea that higher cosmos functions are sources for lower cosmos functions, he examined the possibility that man is influenced by the Solar System and that human endocrine glands are the recipients of such transfer. By looking at functions in the opposite direction, he found that all respiratory functions, from man to plants, constitute one single standing function in nature.

---

[1] Rodney Collin, *The Theory of Celestial Influence* (London: Vincent Stuart Publishers Ltd, 1958), p45.

In a seemingly tireless emergence of constructive reflections, he writes as he moves beyond the limits of our own solar system:

> ... *taking Mercury, Venus, Earth, Mars, Jupiter and Saturn as functions of the Solar System, and remembering the millions of suns and systems which compose the Milky Way, we have to think of all possible Mercurys together as constituting one organ for our galaxy, all possible Earths together as a second galactic organ, and so for the rest.*[1]

Collin painstakingly lays stone upon stone and produces a progressively more holistic picture of the universe that was undoubtedly rooted in a vision linked to and driven by a deep emotional understanding .

To regard his theories on celestial influences as an expression of some sort of definite truth and a final understanding would be a misconception.

He insisted his method of analogy must be regarded as incomplete. Even at its most precise it could only reveal a partial truth. New discoveries seem to have led Collin to new questions, as will be the case for anyone exploring universal truths in a dynamic world where the only constant is change.

On Monday, September 20th, seventeen months after he had laid down his pen and finalised the manuscript to *The Theory of Celestial Influence*, he wrote in a note:

> *It is only recently that I have begun to realise the sublime importance of the relation of the Sun to the Fixed Stars. Evidently man's great hope and great salvation lie beyond the Sun. It is a wonderful vision.*[2]

It is difficult not to interpret this as Collin's vision of a God in which all beings move and live, are penetrated and embraced, and where distance is non-existent.

When Collin seeks to highlight aspects of the interrelationship between the Sun, planets and Earth, he begins with three fundamental and universal causal factors. Referring to several ancient philosophical systems, he shows how these factors represent active, passive and formative characteristics. Whether it is the Hindu's Shiva, Parvati and Vishnu, the trinity of Christianity with Father, Son and the Holy Ghost, or the Indian Sankhya's three gunas, Rajas, Tamas and Satva, they all have similar features that manifest on any scale. When he clarifies this, he refers to

---

[1] Rodney Collin, *The Theory of Celestial Influence* (London: Vincent Stuart Publishers Ltd, 1958), p48.
[2] Rodney Collin, *The Theory of Conscious Harmony* (London: Robinson & Watkins Books Limited, 1958), p132.

beings from the animal kingdom to the world of stars, but also includes the realm of thoughts and aspiration.

Through compelling practical examples, he reveals that it is the interconnected relationships of the three forces and not the phenomena through which they manifest that are essential for a triad's content. In a specific example related to trading he reveals how the law of three has invisible characteristics. In this triad, man is active and the goods being traded are passive. Only through the introduction of money can an exchange occur between the first two.

Although a coin or a banknote has a physical and visual appearance, the property of money as power is invisible. Considering that today we mostly use a card and a code, Collin's portrayal becomes all the more clear. In choosing an example that clearly shows the three principles, representing the unknown, undetected but decisive factor in any situation, Collin demonstrates how the third factor always remains invisible to man at his usual level of perception. Turning to chemistry and physiology in regards to the third force he writes:

> In some cases it may be merely physically invisible – as many chemical processes involving the interaction of active acid and passive alkali are made possible only by the invisible presence of moisture. Or again its method of action may be invisible, as the method of action of catalysts in chemistry and enzymes in physiology remain invisible.[1]

In a given example where man's desire is to raise his consciousness, we see that will is active force, passive force is the inertia in his physical constitution, while the knowledge and aid of an esoteric school is the neutralising force. As we will see later, when Collin explores human psychology, triads exist whereby humans can navigate in, for example, their quest for a higher consciousness.

Collin notes that a significant aspect of the third force is its ability to remain untouched by the results it produces through contact with the active and passive forces. One of the consequences of this is that it remains undiminished:

> They cannot lose their virtue or be used up. Thus it is a characteristic of the third principle that it is always unchanging, invisible and unrecognized, and it can be neither commanded nor manipulated by

---

[1] Rodney Collin, The Theory of Celestial Influence (London: Vincent Stuart Publishers Ltd, 1958), p50.

the other two factors. In relation to them its role will always be mysterious.[1]

According to Collin, the third force's various forms of invisibility are not random, because they place the things they refer to in a responsive relationship with man and can thus act as a third force in his transactions and interactions. Therefore, a man who wants to achieve what he desires must be able to reckon with this force, which in turn requires taking invisibility into account.

When Collin explores the creation and maintenance of life on Earth, it is in the perspective of a triad. In this triad the life-giving trait of the Sun is active, the receptive nature of Earth is passive, while the planets, standing between the previous two, act as a third force. In this example, Collin introduces a significant extension of the cosmic concepts regarding the various forces in which the Sun represents Life, Earth Matter (materials), and the Planets represent Form.

Collin clarifies the different aspects of importance as follows:

By the Sun is meant all its emanations, including those received as heat, light, ultra-violet rays and other radiations as yet unrecognized, as well as its function in sustaining the whole Earth in its proper place and orbit. By the planets is meant the combined effect of the movements, magnetism and reflections of the main planetary bodies, taken as a whole. By the Earth is meant the basic material commonly available on the surface of our world, taken devoid of life and form – that is to say, the chemical elements from hydrogen to lead, in their unorganized state.[2]

As for the invisibility of the third force, Collin reminds us that the essential and deciding function of the planets have been unstudied and unseen for a long time.

The Sun being the source of life and energy, Collin proposed the hypothesis that the world of nature is a consequence of the planets being the creator of form and function, while the Earth is the supplier of matter, the raw material. Collin has here outlined the general conditions of life on Earth. But in order to understand different and often contradictory or complementary aspects of existence, it is crucial to understand the importance of the patterns of combinations in a triad.

---

[1] Rodney Collin, *The Theory of Celestial Influence* (London: Vincent Stuart Publishers Ltd, 1958), p51.
[2] Rodney Collin, *The Theory of Celestial Influence* (London: Vincent Stuart Publishers Ltd, 1958), p52.

To clarify the significance of these possible combinations, he points out how the triad of trade can have different consequences depending on the order of the triad. Not only can money serve men and men serve money, but goods can come to dominate men and money may lose its value, etc. These variations, which are due to interactions of a triad, can have consequences for both individuals and society on a larger scale. Based on this way of thinking, Collin makes an approach to understanding the different combinations of the triad that include Sun, planets and Earth.

The Sun, planets and Earth are combined in six ways in Collin's model, representing the core of the fundamental and universal processes to which there is no alternative. Any phenomena on Earth resides within one or another.

1)   Sun, Earth, Planets (Life - Matter - Form)
       Incarnation, Growth, Multiplication, Elaboration.

2)   Sun, Planets, Earth (Life - Form - Matter)
       Decay, Disintegration, Destruction, Elimination.

3)   Earth, Sun, Planets (Matter - Life - Form)
       Transformation, Refinement, Purification, digestion.

4)   Planets, Sun, Earth (Form - Life - Matter)
       Disease, Rebellion, Corruption, Crime.

5)   Earth, Planets, Sun (Matter - Form - Life)
       Adaption, Invention, Healing, Renewal.

6)   Planets, Earth, Sun (Form – Matter - Life)
       Regeneration, Re-Creation, Change of Nature, Art.

In the first triad, Life acts upon Matter and coordinates the dormant and unorganised chemical components needed in the production of a living entity marked with its discriminative Form.

Collin writes:

> *All men are alive: this they owe to the Sun. All men are composed of carbon, oxygen, nitrogen, hydrogen and small quantities of calcium, iodine, phosphorus, etc.: this they owe to the Earth. All men have a distinctive shape, colour, size, speed of reaction, and other outer and inner qualities... The same may be said about animals, birds, fish, insects, plants and all other living beings.*[1]

---

[1] Rodney Collin, The Theory of Celestial Influence (London: Vincent Stuart Publishers Ltd, 1958), p54.

Later, when we look at the anatomical systems and their regulators, where Collin addresses the importance of the glands relative to the design or Form of an organism, the actual mechanism behind the influence of the planets will be described.

In the second triad, where the life-giving factor dissolves Form, the constituents of an organism return to nature.

Collin says:

> Pull up a living plant, and expose it to the rays of the Sun: in a comparatively short time its carbon and oxygen will have been released into the air, and its nitrogen and mineral salts into the Earth. All processes of burning, rusting, rotting, decay and elimination in general proceed by the same order of forces.[1]

Referring to agriculture, where the release of nitrogen from one crop is necessary for the next, Collin concludes that, generally speaking, the balance between growth and decay is necessary.

In the third triad, where Matter on Earth is refined through influences over time from the life-giving Sun, new forms of life are created. Again, Collin points to the planets as the organiser of Form:

> Take rock as the sample of Earth. Solar heat and cooling crumble it; planetary-produced weather and metrological cycles lay down its dust in soil-beds of particular size and disposition. These soil-beds, in the next stage of transformation, themselves may be taken as inert matter or earth; the Sun, acting by photosynthesis, transforms soil into plant-tissues; while the action of planets determines the form into which the plant-tissue grows and the colour it assumes.[2]

Although this triad and the foregoing are very different, Collin considers them both complementary to the triad of growth. A distinctive feature of these triads, as he highlights, is that they all move in an order where one thing naturally leads to another.

In the fourth triad the Form fails its role as a carrier of content, but instead begins to operate without considering its original task, and thus corruption arises. Here Form acts upon Life, and the consequence is Matter.

---

[1] Rodney Collin, The Theory of Celestial Influence (London: Vincent Stuart Publishers Ltd, 1958), p54.
[2] Rodney Collin, The Theory of Celestial Influence (London: Vincent Stuart Publishers Ltd, 1958), p55.

In the human body, the renewal of cells is a necessity of Life. Collin points out that when cancer cells renew, the renewal happens at the expense of the body as a whole. From a global perspective, Collin sees the man-made shift of the balance in nature as an example of this triad. Today, 73 years after his depiction of the causal condition, when this problem is more topical than ever before, few see it from Collin's planetary perspective:

> *Mankind, stimulated to pathological activity by planetary influence, periodically makes war on the animal and vegetable kingdoms, and reduces this or that area of the Earth to desert.*[1]

Regardless of whether this legality manifests itself in a global, bodily or interpersonal context, it has a persistent and self-perpetuating character, originally established by a disproportionate reaction to planetary influence.

The fifth triad is an expression of how Matter, using the right Form, can detect spirit. Regardless of the scale in which this process manifests, it is always a counterpart to disease, crime or other degrading forces, while paving the way for various forms of regeneration.

Desert sand, that over time acquires organic properties and provides growth-conditions for cactus, which in turn provides conditions for insects, that in turn lay the foundation for bird-life, is an example for Collin of this triad's manifestation at the level of organic life on Earth. On the scale of human affairs, he writes:

> *... this process means the creation by man of a new form in which natural laws can operate, that is, invention or discovery. But each invention stands alone, each healing is an end in itself. Every operation of this process represents a self-contained and separate effort.*[2]

Later, when we take a closer look at Collin's views on the six processes in man, it will be clear that without the fifth triad, not only man but the entire universe would be doomed.

In the last and sixth process where 'the creature emulates the creator, and itself creates,'[3] we see how Form itself becomes Life through its organisation of Matter.

---

[1] Rodney Collin, *The Theory of Celestial Influence* (London: Vincent Stuart Publishers Ltd, 1958), p55.
[2] Rodney Collin, *The Theory of Celestial Influence* (London: Vincent Stuart Publishers Ltd, 1958), p56
[3] Rodney Collin, *The Theory of Celestial Influence* (London: Vincent Stuart Publishers Ltd, 1958), p56.

In Collin's planetary perspective, the planets, which initially only reflect the Sun's light, acquire the function of the Sun relative to their own system of satellites. Through the planets' imitation of the Sun, they are able to influence the Matter that is within their scope. When this process manifests in art, it is because the artist reflects a cosmic order through the organisation of the material he has chosen as a medium. In a spiritual context, Collin says:

> Saints and great teachers, disseminating the light of truth in the darkness of ignorance, and supporting, according to cosmic laws, the disciples who revolve about and depend upon them, emulate the solar source of light and themselves achieve it.[1]

Collin stresses that, unlike all the aforementioned triads, this stands out as significant, as the Form here possesses a separate initiative that by surpassing the Matter lifts it to a higher level. It is this process that, in Collin's understanding, changes the nature of a being and makes the impossible possible.

As we saw in our earlier review of Collin's *Theory of Eternal Life*, he considered Matter in four different categories which in religious terminology correspond to Earth, paradise, heaven and hell. These correspond respectively with Matter in cellular, molecular, electronic and mineral form. In *The Theory of Celestial Influence* he refers to the different forms of materials to point out how the different forces of the six triads combine.

The Sun, that is the source and premise of life, emits matter in electronic state, while the other celestial bodies only either reflect or emit accumulated energy. Based on the assumption that these celestial bodies have a form of atmosphere that is of gas, Collin infers that the planets, in their outermost and atmospheric form, possess matter in a molecular form. Therefore their trait as a Sun-reflector operates at a molecular level, that in turn affects and controls the Earth's atmosphere. Based on the speed of sound, he concludes that molecular speed, unlike the speed of light, which is of electronic nature, is significantly slower.

Collin attributes matter in mineral form to the Earth, which is in his perspective a raw material warehouse without its own natural movement.

In a unified representation of the previous details, the following may shed light on a greater context:

---

[1] Rodney Collin, *The Theory of Celestial Influence* (London: Vincent Stuart Publishers Ltd, 1958), p57.

The Theory of Celestial Influence

...the Sun, planets and Earth combine to produce Nature or organic life. It means that matter in electronic state, matter in molecular state, and matter in mineral state combine to produce matter in cellular state. All organic life on Earth, all cellular matter consists, from one aspect, of electrons or matter in electronic state, from another aspect of molecules or matter in molecular state, and from a third aspect of minerals, or matter in mineral state. In men, animals, plants, these three states of matter are superimposed upon each other, so to speak, to create the fourth or 'natural' state of matter.[1]

Not surprisingly, therefore, Collin argues that all living beings possess characteristics that can be attributed to the nature of the Sun, planets and Earth. Different forms of life carry different amounts of the different forms of matter. In one example he refers to the distinction between a turtle and a dog, where the dog has a higher element of molecular matter. The turtle on the other hand has, due to its shell, a higher proportion of mineral matter.

Because human potential is so linked to the reception and interpretation of impressions made by light, Collin concludes that the proportion of electronic matter in humans is higher than in both dogs and turtles.

Based on the connection between the different types of matter and speed, Collin thought that the orbital movement of the celestial bodies was an indication of each planet's degree of development. Small planets with high degree of density, that have few or no moons, move at the slowest pace, while large planets, that support the most moons and emit their own radiance, have the fastest orbital rotation.

Collin suggests that it is the planets' rotation that makes the separation of matter possible and indicates two properties of rotation, an outward centrifugal force and an inward centripetal force. His assertion that neither Mercury nor the Moon rotates is not accurate. The moon orbits the Earth once every 27,322 days and its synchronous rotation is so slow that, as seen from Earth, it may not appear to be moving. Because the movement is so slow, Collin's reasoning as to why the Moon is a homogenous and solid sphere with no organic life or atmosphere is still relevant. Interestingly, newer science has concluded that, in the extremely thin layers of gases on the lunar surface, there are only 100 molecules per cubic centimeter.

In the process of separation through rotation, molecular matter will first be separated from mineral matter and lay the foundation for an

[1] Rodney Collin, *The Theory of Celestial Influence* (London: Vincent Stuart Publishers Ltd, 1958), p58.

atmosphere. In the next step through time, he says matter in cellular form will appear.

He reveals a holistic view in the parallel of this process to man, in which the boundaries between matter and psychology unite, or perhaps better put, cease:

> ... for man, the separation out of his different sides – physical, mental and emotional – and his consequent recognition of them and their relation to each other, is a sign of increased consciousness and control, so for the Planets the increased separation of matters which results from rotation must also be regarded as a criterion of development.[1]

In order to substantiate the claim of a link between the speed of a celestial body's rotation and the possibilities and limitations of cellular life, Collin examines life conditions in various places on Earth. The speed of the Earth's rotation depends on where on the planet one is located. At the Arctic Circle, where the torque is low and the matter is mainly in mineral state, Collin points to the limitations of cellular life. Similarly, the conditions for life present in the atmosphere at the equator, where one finds matter in the molecular state, is equally challenging. Collin seeks to prove the connection between speed and the assumptions of life by demonstrating that the most favorable setting for cellular life is found in the areas between the extremes of the lowest and highest torque.

Based on the model of rotational speed, Collin draws the conclusion that prerequisites for cellular life are non-existent on the surface of Jupiter, but on the other hand it possesses matter in molecular form. He considers the same to be likely for Saturn, Uranus, and Neptune. Further, he envisioned that planets possess all four forms of matter in a certain order, all a product of rotational speed. Mineral state is at the centre, followed in order by cellular, molecular and electronic.

He imagined the possibility of identifying the planets' level of 'development' based on the combination of the different types of matter and rotational speeds:

> ... we may say – in searching for organic life elsewhere in the Solar System – that certain planets appear not yet to have progressed to the point where cellular life is possible; while others on the contrary have developed to a stage where such forms of life have been transcended altogether. All are at different stages of development, yet all are equally

---

[1] Rodney Collin, The Theory of Celestial Influence (London: Vincent Stuart Publishers Ltd, 1958), p60.

necessary to the whole system – as bones, blood and brain may be said
to be at different stages of development, while equally essential to the
existence of the whole man.[1]

Inspired by the idea of the characteristic of planetary development, Collin turns to what may be considered essential to human development. Having noted that the life-giving factor of life on Earth has its origin in solar matter, he points out that it is locked up by the planets through influence in molecular form. Then molecules, through the nature of Earth, are locked up into mineral form.

Returning again to man, he draws our attention to the fact that any advancement or regeneration of human form relies on an ongoing process where the mineral matter of the body is unlocked first into cellular and secondly to an electronic state.

About this reversal he writes:

Such unlocking will inevitably be accompanied by an increase in the
speed of the organism – a process, taking the regeneration of nature in
its largest sense, which is theoretically only limited when all the matter
of this organism is unlocked into electronic state. In such a condition, it
could supposedly travel at 300,000 kilometers a second, and thus, like
light, exist in all parts of the Solar System simultaneously.[2]

Referring to how any kind of natural growth and the manifestation of the conglomerate of diversity of life is associated with the retention of solar energy, Collin shows how contradictory the relationship between growth and regeneration is, despite the fact that regeneration opens the door to not only the fastest, but also the highest and most sacred form of matter.

Rodney Collin's studies of scientific material in connection with the work on *The Theory of Celestial Influence* were extensive. It shows that his assumptions and conclusions were not unilaterally confirmatory considerations that presented themselves as a consequence of his spiritual nature and religious experiences. His fact-based foundation, however, was never a limiting factor, but rather a springboard for his constructive creativity. This is evident in his scrutiny of the various characteristics of the Sun.

He claims that the size of the Sun is a by-product of its heat, on the basis that material becomes enlarged when heated. It acquires another state of

[1] Rodney Collin, *The Theory of Celestial Influence* (London: Vincent Stuart Publishers Ltd, 1958), p62.
[2] Rodney Collin, *The Theory of Celestial Influence* (London: Vincent Stuart Publishers Ltd, 1958), p62.

being that is independent of its material origin. He draws a parallel to man by referring to the fact that consciousness has a similar independent relationship with the elements that form the body. Addressing 'being' in this context he writes:

> ... the Sun and its planets appear not to differ greatly in their composition, but only in this state of being – which for lack of better measure – we attempt to calculate as heat.[1]

An aspect of the Sun's impact on the Earth's atmosphere is the effect of magnetic fields. Sunspots, which have their own magnetic fields, are part of this influence, in conjunction with the Sun's other magnetic fields. They follow, in Collin's view, the same rules as the influences of the planets. A strange phenomenon is that these sunspots follow an 11-year cycle in which they move towards the Sun's equator and return to a higher latitude.

Something that Collin discovered, based on this 11-year rhythm, was the remarkable fact that the rhythm matched the table of times and cosmoses that underpinned his multi-dimensional calculations of time in *The Theory of Eternal Life*.

Collin writes:

> This eleven-year pulsation, according to the time-relation already established, exactly corresponds on the Sun's time-scale to magnetic frequencies on the scale of man. So that some intimate relation seems to exist between the range of vibrations felt as magnetism by different cosmoses, and we may even say that the sunspot period is our human way of registering 'the personal magnetism' of the Sun. It is thus hardly surprising that this period should so profoundly affect all life deriving from that source.[2]

As we have seen, it is Collin's conviction that the Sun's light is the source of all life. However, it is the Sun's magnetism that, according to Collin, transmits form in such order and quantity that it is sufficient for the life span of the Earth. Further he believes that similar distribution of form, through magnetism, also applies to the planets and their longevity. This means that the Sun is the origin of Life, Form and Matter.

Regarding the question of the source of the Sun's constant energy and its nature, Rodney Collin found the theories of the nuclear physicist Hans

---

[1] Rodney Collin, *The Theory of Celestial Influence* (London: Vincent Stuart Publishers Ltd, 1958), p67.
[2] Rodney Collin, *The Theory of Celestial Influence* (London: Vincent Stuart Publishers Ltd, 1958), p67-68.

Bethe particularly interesting. Bethe took the basis of the idea that atoms of various elements on the Sun were not immutable but could emit energy through degradation and recombination. He assumed that due to the fierce power and tension on the Sun, hydrogen atoms, with their simple electrons, would continuously attack 6-electron carbon atoms with such force that they would be able to form 7-electron nitrogen atoms. Because these atoms are light and unstable, some of them will radiate into space and leave behind a heavy carbon atom. Then, when a hydrogen atom is united with this, a stable nitrogen atom is established. When a new collision occurs with a hydrogen atom, the nitrogen atom will be lifted to a light oxygen atom that will emit a free electron. At this stage of the process there remains a heavy nitrogen atom that is attacked by hydrogen. The result of this is the following: when the hydrogen atom captures a nitrogen electron, a 2-electron atom of helium is formed, while the 7-electron nitrogen atom is converted into what it all started with, a 6-electron carbon atom.

When Rodney Collin considered this process, in which four hydrogen atoms are transformed into a helium atom and two sun-rays, in the perspective of triads, he discovered that it was consistent with the triad of growth: *Sun/active, Earth/passive, Planets/mediating.*

Collin writes:

> *Hydrogen, the active element, plunges into the passive element carbon, to produce an intermediate element helium and a certain radiation of life which is the very signature of this order. The production of energy by the Sun is of the nature of growth. It is the growth of the Solar System.*[1]

Another thing he noticed in the study of Bethe's Carbon cycle was how matter in the molecular state turned into matter in electronic state: transformation of hydrogen into light rays. Here he draws a parallel to human respiration, where air-molecules are eventually converted into nerve-impulses that form thoughts and emotions: if one communicates expressions of thought or feelings to others, for example over a phone, these expressions can affect them over a long distance.

In respect of the transformation of hydrogen to light, Hans Bethe characterised it as change of matter into a state in which it can be transmitted over a long distance.

When Collin attempts to measure the sum of energy expended by a free electron during its lifetime, he leans on a fundamental feature of Max

---

[1] Rodney Collin, *The Theory of Celestial Influence* (London: Vincent Stuart Publishers Ltd, 1958), p70.

Planck's quantum theory. According to Planck, solar radiation is not passed on regularly, but in pulses, with a certain amount of energy and a fixed relationship to the wavelength of light. From this Collin suggests that one light wave embodies a day for an electron, while the quanta or pulse represents its whole life. Regarding the amount of energy contained within a quantum, which is dependent on the frequency of the radiation, Collin again draws a parallel to man, by pointing out that a man's emotional impulses are more intense than those of man transmitting impulses of thoughts.

When Collin focuses on the idea that light is undiminishable and eternal, he acknowledges the fact that the intensity of light diminishes proportionally with distance, but reminds us that this refers to a given point of observation. He writes:

> *If we remember that as distance grows greater, the imaginary sphere which receives the light increases in area in the same proportion, then we realise that the total amount of light received from a given source is exactly the same at a distance of a million miles as at a distance of ten yards. No fraction of the light of a single candle is lost even when it reaches the outskirts of the Solar System: it is only diffused around that prodigious circumference.*[1]

Bearing in mind the dizzying notion that light that originated half-a-billion years back still exists, it is hard to imagine that even the most dedicated sceptic wouldn't nod in acknowledgement when Collin says he thinks light can live forever. However, it is not as likely that the sceptic would be as accommodating when Collin, on the basis that he regarded the light as undiminishable, eternal and omnipresent, not only saw it as a vehicle for divinity, but as the consciousness of God.

We have seen how suns are formed through a condensation of electronic radiation and that the process of locking up form does not imply any loss of electronic matter. According to Collin, the original hydrogen atom, in that it breaks up into electrons, will find its way back to the Solar System and again become light when, after death, it is no longer encapsulated in our physical bodies. The reason this is beyond our comprehension is due to our ordinary consciousness being linked to our sensory apparatus.

Collin believed that only a consciousness that has a level of matter in an electronic state will be able to have a satisfactory relationship to this

---

[1] Rodney Collin, *The Theory of Celestial Influence* (London: Vincent Stuart Publishers Ltd, 1958), p72.

process. Out of this he raises two fundamental questions that are almost like an echo from his book *The Theory of Eternal Life*: Is individuality involved in this process? And if so, whose consciousness is of such a caliber that it can exploit this expansion of its own means of transport? In other words, the transport that takes place as man moves from one level of consciousness towards a consciousness of an electronic nature.

We will return to the answers to these questions later and especially in connection with the processing of Collin's views on how the six different cosmic processes operate in man. But before we leave atoms and hydrogens for now, we will look into how one of these processes manifests in the outer world of man. In Collin's view, the atomic bomb was an introduction of a process that was unnatural, in the sense that it belonged not on Earth, but on the Sun. The potential consequences, as is known, are the extermination of all life:

Man prostitutes solar energy to produce dead matter.[1]

In a triad perspective, the form reduces spirit to matter. Spirit or matter is, in other words, reduced to a passive position, while form has the active role, with the consequence that matter manifests as death. This is the triad of crime and corruption.

When he looks into the planets' more specific influence on humans and nature in *The Theory of Celestial Influence*, one of his fundamental models for understanding this is to consider movement and changes, for example in the form of fusion, re-combining and separation. As we have seen before, Collin argues that the formation of various forms on Earth has its origin in the influence of the planets. In a strikingly detailed way, he refers to calculations that not only provide relevant information about periodic levers such as war and famine, but also refer to how this is due to the nature of a planet and the relationships of the planets. Collin assumes their influence is magnetic in nature and that these influences follow a clear legality, similar to the one embodied in the musical octave that the Pythagoreans created to echo the music of the spheres. To Rodney Collin this was not a legend but a fact:

The octave or musical scale is a notation, adapted to man's hearing, of this harmony of the planetary cycles, which in turn is an echo of a great law which controls the development of all processes in the universe.[2]

[1] Rodney Collin, The Theory of Celestial Influence (London: Vincent Stuart Publishers Ltd, 1958), p77.
[2] Rodney Collin, The Theory of Celestial Influence (London: Vincent Stuart Publishers Ltd, 1958), p81.

However, this legality, which is not rigid but controls the overall structure, allows sufficient flexibility to enable change. Collin considered the law of octaves as a fundamental part of the structure of the universe that was inextricably linked to any part and process. According to him, whether it was nature's different variations, such as content, form and colour, or the human ability to discover and find a new understanding, they were related to this structure.

Referring to the Moon's obvious periodic influence on Earth, Collin proposed that the planet's influence on humans also has a similar periodic character that corresponds to cycles in us. His hypothesis that women's menstrual cycle is connected with planetary influence focuses on two points. One is that planetary influence occurs through matching rhythms in man, the other is that it occurs through man's internal organs. In a broader context, he saw how such influences could have decisive implications for everything from periodic increasing and declining birth rates, economic recovery and recessions, to cycles of war. Referring to Professor Ellsworth Huntington's book, *Mainsprings of Civilization*, Collin wrote:

> *Much interesting work has been done recently on the cyclical character of many biological and human phenomena – a 92/3-year rhythm for the fecundity of animals, an 18-year rhythm in building activity, a 54-year cycle in man's harnessing of natural energy and in the form of this society.*[1]

Collin believed that these rhythms could not only be recognised individually, but also in complex patterns:

> *... separate 3-year and 4-year rhythms, acting together, produce a 12-year repeating pattern. 8-year, 9-year, 12-year, 15-year and 30-year cycles, superimposed one on the other, will create a pattern of behavior recurring every 360 years, and so on.*[2]

By identifying the planetary origin and the legal development of the forms, including cyclic rhythms, Collin believed he had found the archetype for the development of all progression. He also believed that even if history repeated itself, in repetition it would always contain the possibility of new opportunities that a human being can exploit and make use of in the development of himself. To regard planetary influences as

[1] Rodney Collin, *The Theory of Celestial Influence* (London: Vincent Stuart Publishers Ltd, 1958), 84.
[2] Rodney Collin, *The Theory of Celestial Influence* (London: Vincent Stuart Publishers Ltd, 1958), p84-85.

something that unilaterally contradicts human internal development, Collin argues, is wrong. Shifting influences can not only lead to a man being robbed of something that he wants to keep, but also to rid him of something he does not want. However, it is important to point out that that Collin did not have a deterministic view but believed that certain influences could awaken aspects of man from where he can himself address unimaginable new possibilities.

As we have seen before, man's perception of larger and smaller cosmoses and their times stands in a certain and irrevocable relationship. Because the time-relationship between both the Solar System and the cosmos of nature is so different from the human cosmos, perception of movements in organic growth and movements of celestial bodies becomes invisible to him. With this as a starting point, Collin indicates the way forward for the person who wants to develop his potential:

> ... to discover his actual place and possibilities in the universe man must return to a critical study of his own unaided perception. This will show him what he is, and from where he can start. For telescopes, microscopes, spectroscopes, radio, radar, the cinema and so on, are in fact mechanical imitations of higher human faculties which he does not yet enjoy. Their danger is that they may hypnotise him into believing that he already possesses these higher functions, and thus persuade him that he is in a different position from that which is his in reality. From such imagination about himself, he can never proceed further.[1]

Taking into account the influence of various sources, it is easy to perceive these as distant and independent spheres. However, by illustrating how light circulates in the Solar System, Collin shows how not only the different parts are linked to a whole, but also how all possibilities become available to the different parts. In this context, he draws a parallel to how human blood circulation unites all the organs of the body and produces a whole.

Just as the heart provides the supply of blood to the different body parts, the Sun surely radiates light to the different parts of the Solar System. Using an enneagramatic representation, Collin is able to illustrate how the light moves from maximum strength to become invisible and then return to a new maximum. About the order in the enneagram itself he says:

> ... this strange figure – 142857 – can explain to us an infinity of things, because in it we have stumbled on a mathematical enigma which in fact

---

[1] Rodney Collin, The Theory of Celestial Influence (London: Vincent Stuart Publishers Ltd, 1958), p88.

hides one of the fundamental laws of the universe. When unity is divided by seven, this recurring decimal – .142857 – results. And when a complete cosmos is divided into its life-principle and six functions, it is precisely the sequence of this figure which represents the relation between them.[1]

It is on the basis of the latter sequence that Collin believed he found an indication of a representation of the relative mass of the various organs that control the functions within a cosmos. Likewise, he believes that the same sequence explains the disparity of mass among the body's controlling glands, even though they appear to play approximately equal roles.

When we later look into Collin's portrayal of various essential body-types, which, by the way, must not be confused with what is presented in the 'new age market' as personality types, we will get closer to the relationship between types and the human gland system.

After an analysis of the formative planetary forces, the next natural step for Collin was to look into the raw material these forces have created. In the chapter *The Elements of the Earth* in *The Theory of Celestial Influence*, he reminds us how all growth in the universe can basically be attributed to a descent of spirit into matter, and that such matter has different degrees of density. In this regard, he proposed that matter with least density is the most intelligent, as it has the most powerful and penetrating properties in addition to being the most far-reaching.

By directing the spotlight on the Earth's elements, he sought to investigate whether it was possible to establish a scale through which we can understand their density. Based on any material's smallest particle, the atom, Collin gradually approaches a scale. Previously, he had found it possible to find conformity between atomic structures and planetary electrons by ranking the elements according to their number of electrons. However, this method of atomic numbers, based on Mendeleev's periodic table, would prove to be too simple to embrace the scale Collin sought. It was only when he began to regard atoms as shells or solids that a scale of density of elements began to appear:

Atoms of different elements have any number of shells from one to seven. The top shell in turn may have any number of electrons from one to its maximum complement, with resulting variations in surface rigidity; so that if a shell with a full set of electrons be regarded as made of steel, those with less might be as if made of oil, rubber or plastic. This

[1] Rodney Collin, The Theory of Celestial Influence (London: Vincent Stuart Publishers Ltd, 1958), p90.

picture gives a good idea of the relative densities of different elements. The greater the number of shells, the more dense will the element be; while among the group of elements with the same number of shells, that will be more dense whose topmost shell is more rigid.[1]

However, variations in density are not limited only to these seven categories or periods. Within each period there are activities that correspond to the number of electrons found in the topmost shell. This means that each element is drawn to another that has a complementary number of electrons. As a concrete example, Collin refers to how sodium, that has an outstanding electron, seeks chlorine, which lacks an electron, to form salt. With the exception of certain gases, such as helium, neon, argon, krypton and xenon, whose electronic compliment is entire, Collin argues that all other elements are incomplete and naturally seek perfection, as Plato claimed that the soul of man sought his complementary half.

The span of the general scale that he eventually found begins with hydrogen and helium and extends to radioactive substances, such as radium, actinium, thorium, protactinium and uranium.

Leaning on science, his elaborations are often so detailed and mathematical that it might be easy to forget that his aim was the understanding of intelligence and to explore man's perceptions. However, in order to form a picture of Rodney Collin's investigations, it is necessary to shed light on a number of details. At the same time, it is important to remember that, in terms of the breadth and depth of his work, here we only touch the tip of the iceberg.

In his further exploration of the scale of density, he made connections with the law of octaves in six of the foregoing seven periods. About the first of these he notes that hydrogen stands alone and is in that way comparable to solar energy. After delving into his various approaches, he wrote:

... we do indeed begin to glimpse at last that general scale of all matters and energies in the universe, for which we have been seeking. For this table of atomic weights, extending upwards into the realm of radiant matter, is there continued by measurement of the quanta of energy which such free electrons carry. While downward it continues again through the molecular weights of all organic and inorganic substances compounded from these elements. The table of quanta of

---

[1] Rodney Collin, *The Theory of Celestial Influence* (London: Vincent Stuart Publishers Ltd, 1958), p94.

radiant energy, the table of atomic weights of elements, and the table of molecular weights of compounds, do in fact form one single scale.[1]

From this Collin concludes that everything is not only physical and comparable, but that everything from light to excreta is measurable.

To make available a holistic view that would be approachable in daily life conditions, Collin sought to find simple, objective and measurable classifications of phenomena within human studies. He noted, for example, that geology and psychology actually studied matter and motions, but in different forms. Likewise, he saw how the approach to light, sound and heat varied among different human studies. Collin believed that this contributed to alienation:

> *... a well-educated man who has mastered the different series of names for things provided by religion, science, art, poetry, fashion, politics, finds himself in a world so complicated that he is constantly losing his way in it. For everything he meets has at least half-a-dozen different labels, depending whether he is looking at it as a devotee, a scientist, an artist, a poet, a man of the world, or a politician.*[2]

Collin's desire to ease this kind of confusion was his motivation for arranging a table of speeds of diffusion. Within the framework of ten categories, where each phase is separated by a factor of one hundred, he produces an objective and clear classification. Let us take a look at the extremes of this table:

> *In category 1 we find light, originating either from the Sun, from multitudes of suns (galaxies), from solar reflections (planets), or from stored accumulations of solar energy (coal, oil). Such energy, characteristic of suns, is not confined to the Solar System, but judging from what we perceive of distant galaxies, can travel through the universe indefinitely. Within the same category falls the movement of individual electrons – 30,000 kilometers a second rising nearly to the speed of light for some electrons shot from exploding atoms. The continual atomic disintegration which is the nature of a sun yields free electronic motion of that kind and speed which we call light.*[3]

---

[1] Rodney Collin, The Theory of Celestial Influence (London: Vincent Stuart Publishers Ltd, 1958), p99-100.
[2] Rodney Collin, The Theory of Celestial Influence (London: Vincent Stuart Publishers Ltd, 1958), p100.
[3] Rodney Collin, The Theory of Celestial Influence (London: Vincent Stuart Publishers Ltd, 1958), p102.

In category ten, where we find man's slowest form of common measurability, we find chemical change in stone and metal, in addition to sedimentation and wear. A movement lower than this category must be perceived as Absolute Zero, claims Collin, and reminds us at the same time that molecular movement ceases, theoretically, at -273° Centigrade. The implication of such a cessation of movement in mass is, Collin believes, beyond the comprehension of man.

Table of Speeds of Diffusion

Category	Speed	Description
1	?	Solar or luminous
2	3000 km a second	Planetary or magnetic
3	30 km a second	Planetary or magnetic
4	300 m a second	Atmospheric or nervous
5	3 m a second	Animal or warm blooded
6	3 cm a second	Vertebrate or muscular
7	1 m an hour	Invertebrate or liquid
8	1 m a year	Vegetable or cellular
9	1 cm a year	Bony or accretive
10	1 cm a century	Mineral or crystalline

Central to Collin's investigations of the elements of the Earth is the question of how these elements interact to provide the material necessary for the diversity of life that exists on Earth. Once again, he takes the basis of the potency of the triads and the legality associated with the octave. Collin's point of departure for his probing was the simple elements of the atom. In his perspective, the atom is the raw material that through steps and stages gradually produced complex and intricate forms of cellular life.

By showing how combinations of atoms of different atomic weights are the prerequisite for the formation of water, for example, Collin shows how organic components, which are absolutely crucial factors in the formation of life, constitute the first step in what will turn out to be the formation of a general scale of density for all organic substances.

The next step in this scale is amino acids, because they are bridge builders between molecular compounds and proteins. Amino acids are half alkali and half acid, therefore they can form an intricate and virtually unlimited number of varied structures. About the formation of proteins and comparisons with some of his previous calculations, Collin writes:

To make even the simplest kind of protein molecule, several hundred amino-acid units must be built up into a definite form called cyclol. Whereas the molecular weight of most amino-acids is about 130, an elementary protein – the albumen of egg-white – has a molecular weight of about 34,000. Indeed, the molecular weight of many if not most proteins seems to run in multiples of 17,000 or more probably of 16,384, which is exactly seven octaves up from the group of amino-acids mentioned, and ten from the basic element oxygen. We are, it is clear, following a quite definite line of development, that knife-edge between acid and alkali upon which the whole realm of organic life is built.[1]

Knowing that the production of molecular structure on this scale of density may appear to be considering developments from the bottom up, Collin reminds us that these structures are the results of a higher cosmos, the cell. Genes, sections of chromosomes and chromosomes themselves are the natural subsequent steps in Collin's model. About the interval between *mi* and *fa* on his scale he says:

The sudden large factor of multiplication between the amino-acid molecule and the protein molecule indeed represents that natural interval between the notes mi and fa, which on another scale we saw filled by the whole realm of organic life on earth. Below this point the notes of our present octave belong clearly to the molecular world. Above it they already owe allegiance to the cellular one. At this interval, to bridge the gap between two worlds, something invisible and intangible has entered. This factor we call – in our narrow human understanding of the word – life.[2]

It is a well-known phenomenon that the effect of the gravity of the Moon on the side of the Earth facing it contributes to a tidal wave on both sides of the planet twice a day. However, as Collin points out, what is not as widely known is that this shift is a movement to maintain a cosmic balance.

Through his customary analogue presentation, he concludes that at various levels there is a cosmic arrangement for maintaining a balance that is measurable in terms of responsibility:

One man's work can support two dependents, another man's two hundred; the nucleus of a carbon atom carries six electrons, that of copper 29. Earth sustains one moon, Jupiter eleven. Such satellites can

[1] Rodney Collin, The Theory of Celestial Influence (London: Vincent Stuart Publishers Ltd, 1958), p107.
[2] Rodney Collin, The Theory of Celestial Influence (London: Vincent Stuart Publishers Ltd, 1958), p108.

be imagined in many different ways – as offspring, as pupils, as dependents, or even as functions of their 'sun'. Studying the Solar System and the planets, it becomes clear that each of these similes contains a certain element of truth. In any case, this cosmic arrangement appears to imply in some sense a sun's 'responsibility' for its satellites, their 'service' to the sun; and again a passage of energy or knowledge from the sun to the satellites, and a reciprocal aspiration by the latter to acquire such energy and ultimately to emulate their luminary.[1]

Against this background, he believes that the Sun and its satellites exist in a mutually responsible relationship. In this context, however, Collin believes that the Earth's contributions are of an extraordinary character:

... in relation to its satellites the Earth bears a responsibility which seems unique in the Solar System. It has only one moon, but the latter's size compared with that of its parent is such that not even the Sun itself seems to have shouldered such a task. The total mass of all the planets in the Solar System is but one 800th of the Sun's own mass. But the mass of the moon is no less than one 80th that of the Earth. The Earth seems to be carrying ten times more weight, size for size, than does the Sun.[2]

The short version of the consequences for the Earth of this load can be compared to the balance-weight of a pendulum, or the load on an anchor point in a mechanically moving apparatus. When Collin highlights this strain, it seems primarily because it points to the great and inevitable forces the Earth is exposed to. Earth is, in his perspective, not only the most pressed planet in the entire Solar System, but also the least free.

The myths about the Moon's influence on human shadow sides are many and have a long history. You don't have to believe in werewolves to have a perception that humans are affected by the Moon. Collin references Swedish chemist Svante Arrenhius, who found it statistically detectable that human ovulation follows the moon-cycle. Recent Danish research[3] has shown a clear link between activity, sleep length and metabolic health. After examining 795 children aged 8-11 through 9 lunar phases, they found changes consistent with Moon cycles. The study was comprehensive and included measurement of insulin sensitivity, appetite hormones and

---

[1] Rodney Collin, The Theory of Celestial Influence (London: Vincent Stuart Publishers Ltd, 1958), p109.
[2] Rodney Collin, The Theory of Celestial Influence (London: Vincent Stuart Publishers Ltd, 1958), p109-110.
[3] Sjödin, A., et al. "Physical activity, sleep duration and metabolic health in children fluctuate with the lunar cycle: science behind the myth." Clinical obesity 5.2 (2015): p60-66.

blood pressure. The survey included 13,000 24-hour accelerometer records of both sleep and activity. Despite demonstrable correlation with lunar cycles, they did not come up with an understanding of the potential underlying mechanism that could explain the connections.

Collin argues that much of human movement and tensions are subject to the pull of the Earth's great balance-weight, due to the high fluid content of the human body. For one of man's two circuits of fluids, the heart acts like a pump. However, the second, the lymphatic system, maintains fluid movement through physical action. Because the discomfort of not moving over time is not just unbearable, but causes an irresistible impulse, Collin considers that the Moon induces movement in man. A significant and decisive aspect of these necessary movements for Collin is whether they are intentional and targeted, in the sense that they serve a man's aim, or whether they are involuntary and purposeless.

The result of the infinite amount of involuntary and unnecessary movements such as grimaces, gesticulation, bodily postures, restless fidgeting, etc., is a bottomless loss of energy that could be used intentionally. Collin points out that a consequence of the maintenance of these types of movements is that a number of them turn into habits that imperceptibly penetrate aspects of a man's life:

> A characteristic habit, gradually spreading into all sides of a man's life, in time becomes his chief weakness. For instance, a man has on the one hand a tendency to be shy, and on the other a tendency to be meticulous in the performance of small tasks. While still a boy he acquires the habit of wanting to finish what he is doing rather than meet other people. Gradually, it begins to seem right and inevitable to him to complete even the most trivial task before fulfilling an engagement...
>
> Such a chief weakness may spoil a man's life, get him into endless trouble, prevent him from accomplishing everything that he attempts. And the curious thing is that to the man himself the weakness may remain quite unknown and invisible. For to him each instance will seem separate and inevitable, and it will never occur to him that he could act in any other way. Chief weakness is thus built on habit, habit on involuntary action, and involuntary action on pointless movement. And the primary cause of this whole sequence is the apparently innocent influence of the Moon upon liquid matter. It is for this reason that the

path of conscious development is sometimes described as 'escape from the power of the Moon'.[1]

When Beryl Pogson wanted to convey the content and significance of the following excerpts from Gurdjieff's *Beelzebub's Tales to his Grandson* in a group meeting on 15th June, 1966 in London, she employed excerpts from Rodney Collin's text regarding the Moon's significance for the functioning of the lymphatic system and all the habitual and unnecessary consequences associated with the necessity of physical movements in order for this system to function:

> *And so, when thanks to the change of tempo of their blood circulation, there is obtained the temporary removal of the action of the localisation of that false consciousness which has already inevitably become the 'absolute ruler' of their common presence; thus giving the sacred data of their genuine consciousness the possibility of unrestricted blending with the total functioning of the planetary body during the period of their waking state; then indeed if in a corresponding manner the crystallisation of data is assisted for engendering in that localisation an idea of something opposite to that which has already arisen in them, and is, as it were, fixed, and if moreover the actions evoked by this idea are directed upon the disharmonised part of the planetary body, an accelerated change in it is made possible.*[2]

Like Collin, when he links this theme to the development of chief weakness, Pogson also expands what could initially look like a purely physical matter to include how thoughts and feelings can become habitual.

> *It is said the Moon governs tendencies, potentialities derived from the past, past lives – these can easily become habitual. Here is the first important work on our psychology, to see mechanicalness. You see why Gurdjieff stressed it so much. First of all, all kinds of habit belong to this influence. What the Moon really governs here is one's response to life, the habitual way that one receives life. Can you see what the transformation has to be? There must be a different response to life.*[3]

Another central theme in Collin's investigation about the Moon is its function as a magnet. When the Moon covers the Sun on certain

---

[1] Rodney Collin, The Theory of Celestial Influence (London: Vincent Stuart Publishers Ltd, 1958), p113-114.
[2] Beryl Pogson, More Work Talks (York: Quacks Books, 1993), p47. This seems to be from the very first version of Beelzebub's tales.
[3] Beryl Pogson, More Work Talks (York: Quacks Books, 1993), p49-50.

occasions, this is related to combinations of size and distance that Collin did not think was random but represents an unseen force. The persistent influence of the Sun is interrupted in such circumstances. Collin, who regarded the Solar System as a series of transformers, therefore came, in his electrical analogy, to regard such events as an interrupted current. He compares this interruption to a ring-bell circuit where a magnet and a spring break a circuit and produce a mechanical oscillation.

Based on 28 total eclipses of the Sun within a sequence that repeats itself after 18 years and 11 days, he arrives at the Moon interrupting solar radiation at a frequency of 120 cycles in 80 years. When he calculates this according to his earlier depiction of different times in the universe, where 80 years for the Sun corresponds to one thirtieth of a second in the time of man, he concludes that it will correspond to a frequency of four kilocycles.

An adjacent phenomenon that Collin found impossible to regard as random was that the Moon's turn around the Earth was identical to the Sun's rotation around its own axis, taking into account the Earth's own movement. From this perspective, he came to assume that, although the Moon is attached to the Earth's field, it is still a part of the solar facility for the production of a required force. Since the Sun's radiations must be significantly greater than the four kilocycle interrupting frequency of the Moon, Collin concludes that the latter's role must be to deliver pulses of ongoing high frequency current. He leans on ordinary electrical theory when, in this context, he writes:

> ... this would give rise to an alternating current in any adjacent circuit tuned to the frequency at which the pulses occur.[1]

However, he relies on his own perspectives when he argues that the Earth itself can be considered to be such a circuit.

Collin is clear that the full significance of a high-frequency current in the Earth's field is beyond our comprehension, but points to an effect of this type of current that he believes is relevant and is widely known among electricians: the skin effect. This is a phenomenon that occurs when a direct low-frequency current is sent through a wire. The higher the frequency is, the closer to the wire surface it will travel. Collin assumes that the consequence of the skin effect will be that the Moon-created high-frequency effect will be able to pass on the transformed solar energy to the Earth's surface, more specifically to Earth's organic belt. Just as the Moon,

---

[1] Rodney Collin, *The Theory of Celestial Influence* (London: Vincent Stuart Publishers Ltd, 1958), p116.

by balancing Earth's gravity, helps keep all organic liquids in suspension and prevents them from falling to Earth, the skin effect contributes with a corresponding lifting feature. Thus, they both help to sustain organic life on Earth.

Based on his own theories, but primarily relying on Faraday's discovery of electromagnetism, Collin believed that he could bring to life the theories of planetary influence of the past. Mesmer's theory of animal magnetism from 1766 was among those that had previously been rejected or simply ignored. Drawing a parallel between the planet's function as wiring charged with a Sun-induced current and the subsequent magnetic field around the Earth, and the ability of nerves to produce electrical impulses to generate magnetism in animal physiology, he saw, in principle, no difference between planetary and animal magnetism.

For Collin, the natural attraction and repulsion between genders and types was a concrete example of experience of animal magnetism:

> Every time two people's eyes meet, they can feel and study the closing of a magnetic circuit.[1]

It is not surprising that Collin believed that the Moon was the great magnet of all nature, or that man has a magnetic and not just a physical body.

The immediate sensitivity of another person's physical condition a human being may experience is, in his view, linked to magnetism. However, he stresses that when such sensitivity includes the experience of a person's needs for well-being or their suffering, it must not be confused with an emotional understanding that is not only faster, but also more profound. All phenomena that can be associated with the magnetic body are considered mechanical and they therefore cannot in any way be associated with consciousness or psychic progress.

In Collin's view, the Moon is a lifeless planet, but with a potential. Through intricate calculations based on the assumption that the distance between a planet and its origin is essential to its ability to rotate and thus life, he draws the inference that the Moon is midway between fertilisation and birth. Collin seeks to clarify Earth's relationship with the Moon in terms of its future as an independent planet.

In Collin's model of how life-giving energy is transmitted, the centrifugal current that occurs between the Earth and the Moon, through the Moon's

---

[1] Rodney Collin, *The Theory of Celestial Influence* (London: Vincent Stuart Publishers Ltd, 1958), p117.

sucking, pulling and lifting effect, serves as the umbilical cord. His view was that every living organism has an individual and outstanding magnetic field that is withdrawn when it dies. Because the Earth does not recycle this liberated tension, and all new life is based on new solar energy, Collin presumes this energy is deposited elsewhere.

> ... the magnetic current released by the death of living creatures flies to the lowest level of the ionosphere, which is now recognized as the level where lunar magnetism takes effect.[1] There it joins the general magnetic current connecting the Earth and the moon. Calculations based on the delay between magnetic disturbances on the surface of the sun and the repercussions in the atmosphere have shown that the magnetic influences travel at about 400 miles a second.[2] In ten minutes that which made the difference between a living and a dead body has flown to the moon which sustained it during life. This magnetic current is the moon's lifeline, the umbilical cord which connects it with its mother Earth.[3]

When Rodney Collin explores the world of nature, he considers the different forms of life according to levels and density, and not separate classes of creatures. For Collin, it is primarily the number of different natural kingdoms possessed by a being that identifies it. This is clarified in his depiction of the different levels, where he initially states that a stone belongs only to the mineral realm. However, a rose belongs to the plant kingdom and, in addition, to the mineral realm it grows on. A butterfly, nourishing itself by the rose, is also an invertebrate animal and thus possesses even more of nature's kingdoms. About dogs, he says:

> A dog is mineral by its bone structure, vegetable by its connective tissue, worm-like by its system of digestion, but beyond these vertebrate by its spine and the dependent nervous system which bring powers of motion, sensation, coordination of perceptions and logical action impossible for the invertebrate.[4]

Before we look in more detail at how Collin regarded man in this context, it is appropriate to return to the basis of his depiction of nature's different levels, or what he describes as the six realms of nature.

---

[1] Sydney Chapman, The Earth's Magnetism, p77.
[2] Sydney Chapman, The Earth's Magnetism, p77.
[3] Rodney Collin, The Theory of Celestial Influence (London: Vincent Stuart Publishers Ltd, 1958), p22
[4] Rodney Collin, The Theory of Celestial Influence (London: Vincent Stuart Publishers Ltd, 1958), p123.

Barysphere, the realm of metals, that surrounds the inner core of the earth, constitutes the first of these. It is not only particularly resistant to pressure, but also similarly insensitive to vibrations, qualities that caused Collin to characterise it as dense and 'dead'.

Lithosphere, the realm of minerals, is significantly thinner and consists of volcanic stone material in the crystalline forms of silica, magnesium, iron and titanium.

It is in the top layer of the lithosphere we find the soil that forms the basis of the realm of plants, the third of the six realms of nature.

The realm of plants finds nutritional basis in mineral salts. Because plants are living tissue in cellular form, they are able transform the life-giving Sun radiation into growth energy using photosynthesis. It is precisely here, in the realm of plants, that we find the catchment area for what we have previously dealt with: the formative influence of the planets that manifest in the myriad of different life forms we have on our Earth.

The fourth realm of nature is invertebrates. These countless creatures not only find their nutrient base in the plant kingdom but help maintain viable soil.

Collin points out that in the fifth realm of nature the difference between invertebrates and vertebrates is as significant as the difference between plants and minerals. The introduction of the spine, nervous system and brain sets vertebrates in an unprecedented light and forms the basis of potential abilities and properties. They can utilise the primary properties of solar radiation and also use light to receive influences individually, in addition to influences received through other parts of the sensory apparatus.

The realm of man is the sixth and final realm of nature on the globe. Collin suggests that because man possesses so many common denominators with the forgoing and underlying worlds of nature, the question of what is unprecedented about man may seem difficult to answer at first glance. In considering what man is in this context, he identifies obvious traps which may also serve as a warning to anyone who desires to answer this question.

Collin believes we should be especially cautious in applying human concepts to this world. Man's ability to adapt should not be confused with animal conditioning, nor should we confuse the animals' herd instinct with human cultural memory. Referring to termites and bees, he suggests that not only humans live in cities. In describing man's number of feet, he makes the humourous comment:

Men stand on two legs; but so do ostriches, while storks stand even on one.[1]

When he summarises specific human characteristics, the list is not long. As pure peculiarities, besides the use of clothes and tools, he mentions heat treatment of food. Man's ability to conceptualise, with the subsequent possibility of developing a sense of what is right and wrong, is undoubtedly the most outstanding of human features in Collin's eyes, because it aids in the formation of some of the prerequisites for consciousness and thereby the development of a soul. Collin never fails to point out that what remains is only a potential and he identifies the human refined nervous system as the basic organic contributor to the possibility of developing new capacities.

The idea that man is not born with a soul but only with a budding potential is unknown to most people. Throughout history, Christian writers have almost explicitly claimed the opposite, which has not only come to anchor this doctrine, but to a significant extent also influence Western thinking. Later, when we deal with inner transformation, we will return to this.

During Collin's explorations of the realm of nature, a broader picture emerges, showing how the different realms mutually sustain each other:

Plants eat metal-salts, invertebrates eat mineral matter, vertebrates eat whole plants. Man's food differs from that of other vertebrates in being cooked and hot while theirs is cold and raw. Thus man – whether by nature or artifice – may be said to eat food of the nature of warm invertebrate flesh. Only one creature we know eats whole vertebrates, the complete carcasses of horses, elephants and donkeys, with spines and bones – and that is the Earth.[2]

Because man is vertebrate, it may seem obvious that they are eaten by the Earth, like other vertebrates. However, Collin saw that the dead human being participates in several different food chains. As a complete vertebrate it is eaten by the Earth, but in the form of the deposit of mineral salts by invertebrates, it's eaten by worms. As we have seen before, man nourishes

---

[1] Rodney Collin, *The Theory of Celestial Influence* (London: Vincent Stuart Publishers Ltd, 1958), p125.
[2] Rodney Collin, *The Theory of Celestial Influence* (London: Vincent Stuart Publishers Ltd, 1958), p126.

the Moon through its magnetic field, while human consciousness, which distinguishes him from all other vertebrates, nourishes that which is higher than both the Earth and the planets: the Sun.

In his initial investigations into the world of nature and Earth, we find that Collin occasionally regards them as separate cosmoses. However, he experienced some natural uncertainty in this distribution because nature plays a two-sided role. On the one hand it is an integral part of the planet Earth and on the other hand it has a separate relationship with the Solar System, in a life-giving development role.

In the perspective of nature in space, he not only concludes that nature has a key role as a bridge-builder between the Sun, Earth and Moon, but also points to how the whole Earth, without exception, is involved in the realm of nature and came to regard them as one cosmos. Based on this united being's creative qualities, he suggests it possesses an emotional nature. By way of illustration, he references Mozart and Beethoven:

> … *it is not their bones and muscles we think of, but their creative or artistic role.*[1]

For Collin, nature's myriad of shapes and colours that make up the Earth's poetic aspects were crucial impressions for the understanding of our world. One-sided scientific knowledge without this aspect was for him an uninspiring and lifeless matter.

The aforementioned order of matter from metal to human, via mineral, plant, invertebrate and vertebrate, which can be considered layers of matter in a natural order of decreasing density, all interpenetrate. Collin points to the law of diffusion to illustrate how subtle this interpenetration is. Particles in a fluid that do not follow the law of gravity, but are subjected to attack from molecules, still form an accurate geometric order:

> *This law of diffusion, which we can very well watch as we pour milk into a glass of iced coffee, is not in fact confined to minute particles. The apparently aimless settling of mayflies upon the ceiling above a lamp is found to produce a perfect gradation of density from light to darkness. The erratic colonisation of a new country by the whim of individual immigrants results in a perfectly graded diffusion of population from the centres of communication and wealth towards the wilderness. In fact, the whole habitation of the Earth by man follows this law. Individual particles spread from a more favorable medium into a less favorable one*

---

[1] Rodney Collin, The Theory of Celestial Influence (London: Vincent Stuart Publishers Ltd, 1958), p127.

in perfect geometrically decreasing gradation. In just this way do the lower realms of Nature diffuse or penetrate into the higher, and the higher into the lower.[1]

Regardless of the theme and model of manufacture, Collin's divisions into levels are always characterised by a span between the extremes of the density of mass.

Collin believed that the different natural realms correspond with different periods of the table of elements, and can thus show where their gravity is. He refers to how radioactive elements in period seven, which in his view are native to the earth's interior, also found in smaller amounts in the lithosphere, but not on the earth's surface, indicate how substances diffuse upwards. He also assumes that the dense metals of period six are native in the barysphere. Although they wander closer to the earth's surface than radioactive elements, they have no natural space there.

In period five where we find elements that relate to the lithosphere, we find diffusion of particles that move both up and down. In this world of minerals, we find not only silica, magnesium, and iron, but also oxygen, that contributes to metals oxidising. Elements which belong to this period rarely penetrate into the top organic realms. However, there is one exception, iodine. The incidence of iodine is significant in marine environments and acts as a stabiliser in man's biological apparatus.

In the realm of plants, we find substances belonging to period four, which contribute to the enrichment of the soil and promote cellular growth. Potassium, calcium, iron and copper, but also carbon, nitrogen and oxygen, where all the latter are substances that penetrate downwards.

In the realm of invertebrates, period three, we find substances that are present in both insects and vertebrates in water, namely chlorine, sodium and not least phosphorus. When many of these substances, albeit in small quantities, are useful for the human organism, we can say that they move upwards.

In period two, where we find nitrogen and oxygen, we also find carbon, all fundamental elements of the vertebrate world.

Collin identifies the inherent potential of man with hydrogen and period one. He writes:

The very tension, vitality and awareness of a human being depends, as we know, upon the hydrogen ion concentration of his blood. Hydrogen

---

[1] Rodney Collin, The Theory of Celestial Influence (London: Vincent Stuart Publishers Ltd, 1958), p128.

appears to play something like the same role with regard to man's higher functions and to his power of transmuting solar radiation into the highest forms of energy, as it does in relation to the Earth. For it is the ionosphere or sphere of hydrogen sixty miles and more above the Earth's surface – the 'heaven' of the ancients – which receives and transforms the electronic energy of the sun in its purest form.[1]

It is tempting to view Collin's inclination and ability to create a holistic picture of the myriad elements of existence in the light of aspects of Erich Fromm's analysis of different types of religious experiences. Fromm argues that the disharmonious in man creates needs that go far beyond the needs of his animal origins, and that these needs lead to an irresistible urge to restore balance and unity between himself and nature. When man, by right thinking, seeks to restore this unity and balance, it is to create a mental image that can serve as a coordinate system that can provide answers to where he stands and what he should do. Because man is not merely an intellect, however, such a system of thought will be inadequate. Fromm further argues that a pursuit of unity and harmony must include the entire human life-process. An all-encompassing and satisfying orientation-system must therefore also include sensory and emotional elements.

Collin's investigations of the different realms of nature where the various realms correspond with elements from different periods and from which it draws its structure, is just one of his many expressions of a quest for wholeness. By pointing out how the different layers are not sharply separated from each other, but rather interwoven, he highlights some of nature's basic harmonic aspects. In the latter model, which ranges from barysphere via lithosphere, the realm of plants in the soil, invertebrates in the sea, to vertebrates in air, to an atmosphere steeped in elements from the Sun, we find exactly that which can help satisfy the higher nature and deepest urges of man. In *The Theory of Celestial Influence* he reminds us not only that these considerations reveal themselves and become available in the perspective of octaves, but that a broader and more all-encompassing insight only becomes available if one takes into account that every phenomena in nature participates in octaves running in all dimensions:

The structure of the table of elements only became clear when it was seen as an octave squared. In the same way, although the medium of air seems characteristic of the horizontal period 2, it in fact includes in its composition all the inert gases – helium, neon, argon, krypton, and

[1] Rodney Collin, The Theory of Celestial Influence (London: Vincent Stuart Publishers Ltd, 1958), p129.

xenon – of the vertical note do. Although the medium of ocean seems characteristic of period 3, it includes traces of all the halogens – fluorine, chlorine, bromine, and iodine – of the vertical note re. Although the medium of soil seems characteristic of period 4, it comprises all the alkalis of the vertical note si. And similarly for the lithosphere and barysphere. It is this squaring of octaves which produces the incredibly subtle upward and downward diffusion which we remarked on earlier. It explains certain anomalies of matter found in unexpected places, that would remain incomprehensible if we tried to understand them on the basis of horizontal octaves only. It means that every realm of Nature permeates every other, constituting the headquarters as it were of a form of life which exists everywhere.[1]

Collin concluded that when an octave could appear as squared, it must also be able to appear as a cube. When an octave of the realms of nature could be detected both with a vertical span, stretching from the Earth's middle and up to the ionosphere, and horizontally within these strata, he believed that one should also be able to find the same octave in the dimension of time.

By extending through the aeons of geologic times he did find it. Starting with Precambrian rocks, he could trace a wholly mineral world, free of any fossil life. Similarly, by going through the various periods of his model, he could compare nature's historical experiments to man as he appears today. In this perspective, it is clear that each period is based on the next, but also that it is a two-sided movement that confirms Collin's idea that mutual maintenance is not a one-sided process:

In each era the first crude experiments are made to prepare the type of being to which the world will next belong. The lonely trilobites of the primary foreshadow the invertebrate world of the secondary; the unwieldly diplodocus of the secondary, doomed in his own time, is the forerunner of the slender horse and tiger of the next age; the manlike monkey of the tertiary supposes a world of true men in the present. This experiment of later forms in earlier times corresponds to the downward diffusion of higher elements which we noted earlier. The mollusc in the age of tree-ferns is like silica from the period of invertebrates imbedded in the realm of minerals. And in the reverse sense, the primitive forms of life which still exist in the era of man play, like the element iodine in his

---

[1] Rodney Collin, The Theory of Celestial Influence (London: Vincent Stuart Publishers Ltd, 1958), p130.

body, a stabilizing role in the higher world into which they have penetrated.[1]

Another interesting aspect of the geological octave is how it clearly shows how each note's duration matches its density. As barysphere, lithosphere, and biosphere vary in size, Collin found that the sequence of geological periods show a corresponding logarithmic diminishment. This observation led indirectly to his conclusion that vibrations of the notes of a raising octave are ever more compressed because their duration decreases progressively.

Referring to his previous study on the lives of beings of different scales and the work of English physicist, astronomer and mathematician, James Jeans, who wrote: "Human life has changed more in the last 50 years than reptile life did in 50 million years in the Jurassic and Permian Eras,"[2] Collin concluded that all geological eras are in reality equally long. These two seemingly contradictory beliefs, which Collin expressed in the same breath, describe how reality extends beyond any individual perspective and can thus create a continuity for reality-contingent precepts about phenomena in the world. Collin, however, hoped that James Jeans' assumption of the acceleration of the timescale was exaggerated, because such a speed of change would limit dramatically the time man has to realise his potential.

To understand the nature and potential of impressions is and has been a challenging area. When Collin approaches this problem he begins with the perception of animals. When Ouspensky raised the question of the relationship of the nature of perception relative to animal intelligence in *Tertium Organum*, it bore the hallmark of a philosophical approach. When Collin took a similar starting point, he chose a physical angle of attack. For both Ouspensky and Collin the fundamental difference between human and animal perception was time.

Rooted in his principled understanding that all life is equally long, Collin's calculus determines that a gnat lives 30,000 times faster than a human being. As a consequence, all forms of energy, measured by vibrations per man's second, to which a gnat was exposed, would be reduced 3,000 times, when measured by gnat's time. Although Collin acknowledges that one initially knows little about a gnat's perceptive organs, he nevertheless believed that it should be possible to form a general

---

[1] Rodney Collin, *The Theory of Celestial Influence* (London: Vincent Stuart Publishers Ltd, 1958), p131.
[2] Sir James Jeans, *Through Space and Time* (Cambridge University Press, 1934), p47.

picture of a gnat's time versus human time and in that way gain new insights:

> For the gnat, human 'sound' (4th to 15th octaves) will disappear altogether or become a slow rhythmic pulsation. Radio waves and the lower electrical frequencies (25th to 30th octaves) will acquire the nature of magnetism, heat and light that of electricity, and x-rays that of heat. Light in turn would be represented by gamma rays, and the fact that these rays do not exist in nature may have a certain cosmic meaning. It may mean that for certain reasons Nature, in relegating creatures to the scale of insects, has banished them to a region where there is no light, and thus no possibility of the perversion of divine energy."[1]

Among the many and unforeseen consequences of calculations based on a gnat's time, it is only possible in this context to look at some fundamental examples related to time, space and density. Collin thought that when the perception of radiation changes, then the perception of linear space has to change accordingly, since the ability to measure space is mainly related to the distance different energies move in a given time. As a consequence, this would mean that a sound moving 1100 feet per second for man would only be able to move one third of an inch per second for a gnat. With regards to density, water will be experienced by gnats as solid and air as liquid. He believed that this was possible to observe directly through simple experiments:

> ... gnats walk on water as though it were solid, and swim, float, and hang sideways or upside down in air as though it were liquid. We see them, too, irresistibly attracted to sources of light, not as light, but in the same way that bird migration follows certain invisible fields of terrestrial magnetism. And again, we can quickly prove that sound vibration is beyond the gnat's range of perception by the futility of any attempt to frighten it away by shouting.[2]

Because such characteristics reminded Collin more about the world of cells than that of animals, he believed that we would understand insects better by considering them as free cells and beings without an individual opinion. Their meaning, in other words, is inextricably linked to their belonging to a beehive, ant-hill, etc., of which they form a part. Even for

---

[1] Rodney Collin, The Theory of Celestial Influence (London: Vincent Stuart Publishers Ltd, 1958), p132-133.
[2] Rodney Collin, The Theory of Celestial Influence (London: Vincent Stuart Publishers Ltd, 1958), p133.

small fish and birds, he believed that the concept of individuality was of marginal importance:

> *A flock of starlings or a shoal of mackerel weaves, turns, wheels, and migrates immense distances in the air or sea with the same unity and coordination as a hive of bees or a human body. Direct relation to the cosmos of Earth, which is characteristic of large mammals and is expressed by the sense of up, down, and sideways, is still very vague in a single bird or fish.[1]*

He saw the ability of birds to orient themselves during their annual migration in the context of seasonal changes in the Earth's magnetic fields with which their physical organs were interacting. By his calculations, creatures of this scale of time have lost only four of the lower octaves of sound. In return, they have another four that are inaudible to man. He imagined that the five wavebands, which different creatures can receive through their five senses, both move up and down the electromagnetic scale, according to their different timescales. Various phenomena in nature, which are usually perceived as a manifestation of a sixth sense, could consequently be explained by the fact that one of the five senses is positioned such that a shift in the band of radiation can occur.

Referring to an article in Scientific America, Collin points to a Hummingbird as a striking example of the living rate of an animal matching its size:

> *Each gram of (its) tissue metabolises 15 times as fast as a gram of pigeon and more than 100 times as fast as a gram of elephant.[2]*

According to Collin's time calculation, the life of this bird is a hundred times faster than that of man.

In addition to Collin's belief that insects, birds and fish are free cells, he likened domestic animals to free organs. As before, he believed that this way of thinking could lead to better understanding. Because their reactions and perceptions are both somewhat comparable with that of man, he choose to view them in perspective of mechanism rather than time. When comparing different animal's anatomical functions with the equivalent in humans, he saw that certain of the animal's functions were greatly exaggerated, while others only satisfied the most necessary requirements.

---

[1] Rodney Collin, The Theory of Celestial Influence (London: Vincent Stuart Publishers Ltd, 1958), p134.
[2] Pearson, Oliver P. "The metabolism of hummingbirds." Scientific American (January 1953).

Thus a horse is a walking muscular system, a cow is a walking mammary gland, a pig is a walking stomach, a hen is a walking ovary, and a dog is a walking nose. A very true understanding of animal psychology can indeed be obtained by learning to concentrate attention in a single such function in oneself, and directly 'feeling' there the nature of its particular perceptions, interests, and needs.[1]

By considering the mechanical structure of animals, Collin believed that one could not only get a clear picture of what they represented purely symbolically, but also gain an insight into their deeper being. About the pig, which loses its flexibility in the neck region and therefore cannot look higher than its own eye-level, he writes almost in a telegram style:

The pig lives in a plane world; the sky does not exist for it. For the stomach there can be no astronomy.[2]

One of the characteristics that limits the ability of animals to focus their attention compared to man is the location of their eyes. By having eyes on either side of the head, their horizontal view is particularly effective, but at the same time it limits their ability to focus the way humans can. Collin highlights this being-difference between humans and animals in order to emphasise the importance of the psychological consequence of this ability:

It makes possible the sensation: 'I am here, and that object is there.' This sensation is the beginning of self-consciousness.[3]

Collin proposes that animals are not capable of this form of intelligent self-consciousness and thus lack the possibility of regeneration. He argues that this is due to the structure of their nervous system, of which the location of the eyes is only an outward sign.

Although he categorically rejects the possibility of psychological regeneration for animals, he allows that there are variations and degrees of ability to focus among them. The cat, which for Collin stands in a special position, partly because it always seems to have a body awareness, is such an exception. However, it is not the eyes but the ears that give the cat this advantage. He writes:

Nature appears to have played a very curious trick upon the cat. If a dog is an experiment in the function of smell, a cat is an experiment in

[1] Rodney Collin, The Theory of Celestial Influence (London: Vincent Stuart Publishers Ltd, 1958), p136.
[2] Rodney Collin, The Theory of Celestial Influence (London: Vincent Stuart Publishers Ltd, 1958), p136.
[3] Rodney Collin, The Theory of Celestial Influence (London: Vincent Stuart Publishers Ltd, 1958), p136.

the function of consciousness. But it is consciousness unrelated to mind, without meaning, and without the possibility of development. Comparing cat and man we begin to understand how consciousness can exist without intelligence, and intelligence without consciousness.[1]

What originally began with the structures of the universe and passed through, among other things, the harmonic movements of the planets, the realms of nature and animal perception, eventually arrives at Collin's main concern: man's possible evolution. It is obviously no coincidence that the chapter on animal perception ends with a focus on the potential of human regeneration, or that it is exactly this chapter that forms the bridge to the chapter of man as a microcosmos.

Against the backdrop of Collin's previous analytical analogue models, it is not surprising that he draws parallels between human anatomical systems and the long body of the Solar System. He viewed human systems, based on the central position of the heart, that collaborate and exchange energies in a harmonious network, as reminiscent of the Solar System. Each of these systems is regulated by the respective glands through finely tuned secretions.

A coherent picture begins to form in this context when Collin considers the sevenfold order of human functions in light of interacting nervous controls manifesting through the universal law of three, where a third force is fundamentally necessary to relate two opposing forces:

> *... the cerebro-spinal, which serves conscious functions; the sympathetic, which stimulates unconscious or instinctive functions; and the parasympathetic and vagus, which are explained as slowing down these instinctive functions, and thus acting as complement to the last. This suggests to us one control for relaying active nervous impulses, another for relaying passive nervous impulses, and a third for relaying the mediating impulses of thought, reason or consciousness.*[2]

Collin also explores the law of seven in this context of the human organism: a fundamental and universal law that refers to a legality in any manifestation or order. For Collin, this law seems to be reflected in the manifestation of the glands and their outputs. However, because these legalities intervene in countless ways, he is clear that there is no one-sided division, but rather that both these laws provide an opportunity to

[1] Rodney Collin, *The Theory of Celestial Influence* (London: Vincent Stuart Publishers Ltd, 1958), p137.
[2] Rodney Collin, *The Theory of Celestial Influence* (London: Vincent Stuart Publishers Ltd, 1958), p138.

consider the same phenomena in different ways. Being able to see these two laws in action simultaneously would mean that we should be able to fully comprehend the Solar System or the human organism. Because this is beyond the capacity of our ordinary brain, he compares it to the impossibility of seeing a mirror's surface while seeing what it reflects. He writes:

> We can not mentally simplify the interaction of these two laws, for a living cosmos is the simplest model of their union.[1]

The following systems that Collin focused on, and which collectively constitute the realm of nature within man are: skeleton system, lymphatic and pulmonary system, arterial and cerebral system, and finally a system he does not define more closely, but which he associates with feelings and conscience. An interesting approach to the understanding of aspects of these systems is his electrical analogy, which he links directly to the variations of the pressure and rate of flow of energies within their respective circuits.

The following example, in which the underlying energies that produce emotions are in action, can serve as an illustration. He writes:

> The flow here is so small that weeks, months or even years may pass without a man being aware of anything more than an occasional ineffective trickle. On the other hand, when energy transformed in this way does become available, its power is enormous. It may make him found a monastic order, or commit a murder. The amperage is low, but the voltage extraordinarily high.[2]

When Collin lay out a schematic diagram of the human body, similar to his previous diagram of the Solar System, in which the Solar System appeared as an expanding spiral of planets, he got an unexpected hint of the possible order of the glands and their interrelationship. The source of the spiral in this chart was the heart. The subsequent points of the spiral became thymus, pancreas, thyroid, parathyroid, solar plexus, where adrenals are located, then on to the post-pituitary, anterior pituitary, then sex glands, before ending in the pineal body.

When Collin considered his new findings in the light of a human embryo's first fortnight, where the first multiplication of cells develop the

---

[1] Rodney Collin, The Theory of Celestial Influence (London: Vincent Stuart Publishers Ltd, 1958), p139
[2] Rodney Collin, The Theory of Celestial Influence (London: Vincent Stuart Publishers Ltd, 1958), p140.

three germ-layers that form the original impulse to the first three glands in the spiral, he believed he had discovered the newfound spiral's original form. By combining this information with what he already knew about glands, he was able to create an overview image in the form of a table.[1]

Table of the Endocrine Glands

Gland	Function	System
Thymus	Growth	?
Pancreas	Digestion, Assimilation of food	Lymphatic
Thyroid	Respiration, Combustion of air	Pulmonary
Parathyroids	Blood-circulation, Tissue building	Arterial and Connective Tissue
Adrenals	External Motion, Fight and Flight	Cerebro-Spinal and Voluntary Muscle
Posterior Pituitary	Inner Reflexes, Physical Sensation	Sympathetic and Involuntary muscle
Anterior Pituitary	Mind and Reason, Bone Structure	Cerebral Cortex and Skeletal
Gonads	Reproduction, Creation, Higher Emotion	Genital
Pineal	?	?

With regards to the thymus gland, where the function is related to growth, Collin questions which system may be applicable. If we assume that the prerequisites for optimal growth are related to a well-functioning cooperation between all the glands, then it is tempting to ask whether it is possible that this cooperation itself can be regarded as the missing system. Can this 'system' coincide with the fundamental features of growth that are characterised by multiplication and differentiation in a continuous, chain-like progression? Either way, there are two other question marks Collin puts in his newfound table, related to the function and the system regarding the pineal gland. This gland has long been surrounded by uncertainty and speculative notions and it was not until 1958, two years after Collin's death, that Professor Lerner was able to link it to the production of melatonin and its main function: the regulation of sleep patterns. Collin was obviously aware of pre-Cartesian views on the pineal gland, and Descartes' theses about the gland's attachment to animal spirits

---

[1] Rodney Collin, The Theory of Celestial Influence (London: Vincent Stuart Publishers Ltd, 1958), p141.

and the idea of it being the principle seat of the soul. Although it might have made an impression on him, it was not sufficient to contribute to a final understanding of its function and to which system this mythical gland belonged.

Because the table of glands clearly demonstrated a movement from physical to psychic, from coarse to fine, Collin, in the form of his electrified analogous representation, could argue that the order of movements showed an increasing voltage and a decreasing amperage.

By considering the table of glands in the perspective of the categories of speed of diffusion, he made the remarkable discovery that they all corresponded. It was this finding that made it possible not only to calculate the speed of the processes of each function, but also clarify their mathematical relation to each other:

> *If, as we scientifically know, the blood-stream, influenced by the parathyroids, courses through man's veins at one metre a second, and cerebro-spinal impulses, influenced by the adrenals, flash through his nerves at 100 metres a second, then we have to imagine the two pituitary lobes carrying out their communication at 10 and 1000 kilometres a second, whatever this may mean. All we can corroborate by experience is that the mind, powered by the anterior pituitary, can 'be present' anywhere, in any imaginable place or time, instantaneously, that is, without measurable interval. Yet according to his idea, true sex, its peculiar understanding and experience, should be a hundred times faster than the mind. And the perception of the unknown pineal function a hundred times faster still.[1]*

Collin was astonished when he realised that the gland-spiral of transforming energies mirrors the order of planets in the Solar System, in reverse. In the Solar System, what is smaller, finer and under greater pressure is nearer the center. Close to the center of the human system, however, we find what is under less pressure and is larger and grosser. For the Solar System, this means that the amperage increases towards the circumference, while it is the voltage that increases for the human system. Initially he thought this was strange, until he remembered that the power of a radio receiver is in inverse proportion to the power of the station that sends the signal.

---

[1] Rodney Collin, *The Theory of Celestial Influence* (London: Vincent Stuart Publishers Lta, 1958), p142.

It is at this point in Rodney Collin's research that it crystallises an understanding of the importance of the many corresponding implications between celestial bodies and the human organism.

This insight was not a consequence of a one-sided intuition, but the result of years of work. For years, in addition to many conversations, Collin had spent days in libraries in London and New York in search of scientific material that he found relevant to Ouspensky's ideas published in *A New Model of The Universe* and *Tertium Organum*. As Ouspensky's closest student, it is natural to assume that Collin presented and discussed aspects of his relevant investigations and findings. It is unthinkable that, in addition to his "theory of eternal life", the experience he had in the time he was locked up while Ouspensky was dying should not have had an impact on the development of his new ideas. To what extent and in what way seems impossible to say, but we know that the disturbing experience of that time changed him as a human being and came to characterise his later work.

In Collin's further work on the understanding of the exchange and transformation of celestial influence, it becomes clear that the glands themselves were not recipients, but rather mechanisms that made visible, through physical motion and action, invisible impulses:

> ... *the intricate antennae of the great nervous plexuses – the cervical, the cardiac, the solar, lumbar and sacral – constitute the apparatus sensitive to such planetary transmission.*[1]

In Collin's depiction, the heart and the Sun have a parallel and equal pattern, in which glands and planets respond in relation to a cosmic plane that they are both guided by and faithfully follow.

It was on this foundation that he could begin the preparation of what was later presented as the essence-types. Traditions and beliefs built on the notion that human fates and events can be interpreted or influenced by celestial bodies and their positions have existed since ancient times, and yet have not established any foothold in the scientific environment. For example, empirical tests in controlled studies have not been able to substantiate the truth of astrology. It is difficult to say to what extent Collin was uncomfortable considering his ideas in light of the general proposals of astrology. What we can establish, however, is that he firmly believed that astrology's objective studies of correspondences and tendencies were prompted by prognostications and fortune-telling. Despite this he saw it as

[1] Rodney Collin, *The Theory of Celestial Influence* (London: Vincent Stuart Publishers Ltd, 1958), p142.

a necessity to investigate whether there could be any comparable perspectives.

In the Greek, Arab and medieval traditions, it was believed that various creatures contained matter similar to celestial spheres and thus were influenced. It was considered that man stood in a special position in that he contained within himself all affinities. The various affinities were embodied in different parts of the body. Consequently, what then determined which type a man was depended on which of these parts was most developed. An obvious problem was the variation in which parts represented what in different periods and traditions.

In exploring possible connections between body types and celestial influences, Collin sought to consider new ideas in the context of scientific research. Here, as in all contexts affecting inner work, Ouspensky's mantra 'verify' was an imminent and fundamental principle.

In Collin's view, it was only in the Middle Ages that interesting attempts were made to approximate an understanding of the interaction between planets and body types, but that this material has largely been lost. He also believed that astrology never figured out how and with what medium these transfers took place. Despite the obvious flaws and limitations of astrology, he thought that the words lunatic, mercurial, venereal, martial, jovial and saturnine could be used with certain modifications.

With an attitude freed from superstitions and associations related to astrology, but with a certain anchoring in its main theses and not least in the light of modern ideas, Collin came up with the following proposition:

> *Each endocrine gland or its associated nerve-plexus is sensitive to the magnetism of a particular planet. This particular magnetism will naturally be strongest when the planet is in the zenith and shining vertically through the minimum thickness of atmosphere, exactly as the Sun's light and warmth are strongest at midday. The lower in the sky it sinks, and the acuter the angle at which its influence must thus pass through the blanket of air, the feebler its effect, as with the sun at morning and evening. When below the horizon altogether this effect will be felt only in a diffused form, much modified by the peculiar magnetism of the Earth. The height of a given planet in the sky will thus be an exact measure of the degree of stimulation imparted to the corresponding gland at a given moment*[1]

---

[1] Rodney Collin, The Theory of Celestial Influence (London: Vincent Stuart Publishers Ltd, 1958), p145.

One of three basic aspects that Collin attaches to the glands, relative to the influence of the planets, is the moment of conception, in which the disposition of chromosomes interacts with planetary influences and forms a human hereditary essence.

The second aspect is the moment of birth where man is exposed not only to air, but also solar and planetary radiations that affect what we normally recognise as an individual essence.

Quintessence,

the hidden and the potential principle of unity,[1]

is the third aspect and is associated with the future and a potential growth of a soul.

Based on the second aspect, Collin begins to explore details of his ideas about glandular types. This work does not follow a straight line but considers a number of challenges. Because all the glands are equal and necessary for a harmonious whole and cannot individually be isolated, one can also not talk about pure types.

In his approach to identifying types, Collin was restrictive and restrained and believed that his descriptions of the different types had to be seen as glandular caricatures. He writes:

> *If we study so-called 'types' it thus only means that we try to find extreme or even pathological cases of the dominance of one or another gland, in order to determine its special nature. Even so, there is something distasteful and unreal about such descriptions, as there is about the 'average man' of statistical investigation. They both remind us of those we know, and at the same time omit all that is alive and interesting about them.*[2]

For Collin, the ideal human represented a being in which not only all the glands were in balance, but which appeared to be a synthesis of all different types. He emphasises that such a human being cannot arise randomly, so it follows that such a being would be a product of an esoteric direction.

Without going into minute details, we will look at which glands Collin attaches to the different types. Later we will return to more elaborate descriptions. At the beginning of the outgoing spiral, we find the thymus, long known for its importance for growth in childhood, and which Collin

---

[1] Rodney Collin, *The Theory of Celestial Influence* (London: Vincent Stuart Publishers Ltd, 1958), p146.
[2] Rodney Collin, *The Theory of Celestial Influence* (London: Vincent Stuart Publishers Ltd, 1958), p147.

links to solar type. With a touch of beautiful frailty, transparent milk and roses skin, delicate bone building, well-formed teeth, long legs, long neck and, incidentally, a look reminiscent of Peter Pan, they often appear as adult children with expressive eyes and an incision of elegance.

The pancreas is involved in digestion and control of blood sugar levels and is associated with the lymphatic system. According to Collin, this gland contributes to a lesser extent than others to define one type, yet can influence formation of characteristics such as moody, passive and introspective. As a result of the abundance of lymph, they will appear round and shape-full. The face is similar, round and moonlike.

Next comes the thyroid gland, situated in the front of the neck and consisting of two connected lobes.

> *This gland controls the combustion of air in breathing, and like the damper of a locomotive furnace, regulates the heat produced and consequently the speed of the whole mechanism. The more intensely the thyroid works the quicker and more nervous will the appearance become. The heavy element, iodine, which is often mentioned in connection with this gland, is like the weight hung upon the damper-door, to prevent it springing open and burning out the furnace.*[1]

Reminiscent of the classical sculptures that have shaped this ancient and airy figure, mercurial individuals are charterised as quick, restless, inexhaustible, lean and clear cut. Adjectives used to describe the mercurial nature, such as fickle, flighty and erratic, also provide clues, as do descriptions such as quick-witted, sprightly and lively.

Parathyroids are four small glands located near the thyroid gland on the front of the neck. The glands produce a hormone that regulates calcium levels in the body. About these glands Collin writes:

> *... they work against the thyroid (which produces movement and volatility), by promoting the metabolism of the stabilizing element lime, and the mediating element phosphorus. With parathyroids under-developed, the individual becomes pathologically nervous, jumpy and oversensitive to the mildest stimulus, even of light. The parathyroids accentuate the passive, vegetative life; they produce steadiness and tone of muscle and nerve – as it were a sensitive calm and warm passivity.*

---

[1] Rodney Collin, *The Theory of Celestial Influence* (London: Vincent Stuart Publishers Ltd, 1958), p148.

THE THEORY OF CELESTIAL INFLUENCE

Their field is that of 'flesh and blood', of tissue-building and increase in bulk.[1]

Rooted in the historical depiction of Venus, this type is inextricably linked to a feminine role, characterized by growth and inactivity. The remarkable sculpture known as 'Venus of Willendorf', dating to 24,000 – 22,000 B.C., is almost a caricature of Collin's description and testifies to how clearly and almost infinitely this character trait has been part of human history.

The adrenal glands lie on top of each kidney and produce more than thirty vital hormones that have implications for metabolism for the body's overall resilience. Secretions from these hormones are behind phenomena such as fear and flight, and manifestations such as rage and pugnacity. Collin describes them as 'glands of passion' because they express fundamental impulses for self-preservation. The visual features of a martial body type are characterized by a relatively small but densely built body with abundant hair growth, freckled skin, sharp teeth and a low hair line. A classical expression of a warrior.

Among the characteristics of the posterior pituitary that Collin highlights are how it controls the involuntary muscles of the inner instinctive parts of the body such as intestines, bladder and uterus, and that sodium plays a key role in this gland's business. Because it regulates the production of breastmilk, he regarded this gland as the gland of maternal qualities. The physical traits of the body type Jovial, which he associates with this gland, are stout, short, a large head, tendencies for a voluminous midsection and a sparse hair growth on the body. In general, Jovial is cheerful, gay, optimistic and tolerant. Their tendency to periodicity can characterise their activities, moods and temperament.

As the aforementioned gland advocates feminine features, so the anterior pituitary advocates masculine traits. This body type has a long bone structure and a musculature that is firm and large. The long head has protrusive jawbones, square jaw and over the mouth, where we find large teeth, sits a notable nose. This seemingly abnormal growth, which by the way is particularly visible in the hands, feet and joints, Collin links to the excessive secretion of the gland. Another aspect of Saturn that Collin highlights is the ability for abstract thinking and reason, a comprehending mind with a distinct learning ability. With a capacity for self-control and

---

[1] Rodney Collin, *The Theory of Celestial Influence* (London: Vincent Stuart Publishers Ltd, 1958), p149.

an inherent ability to control their surroundings, we sense the outline of a leader.

Collin does not connect the next gland on the outgoing spiral directly to any type. This gland that represents sex has the same position in the spiral that Uranus has in the Solar System. To avoid misunderstandings and to understand its role, sex must be viewed from a wider perspective:

> ... *every other gland affects sex, lends sex its colour, and tries to pass itself off as sex. In order to be understood in its purity, sex must be separated from the Venusian sensuality of the parathyroids, from the martial passion of the adrenals, from the maternal affection of the posterior pituitary, and from the saturnine masterfulness of the anterior lobe. Sex must be something different from all these and more fundamental. It must be connected with the ultimate principle of two sexes, and their joint power of creation. And it will include all the deepest emotions which arise from this interaction, and which, besides children of the body, give rise to music, poetry, the arts, and the whole aspiration of man to create in emulation of his Maker.*[1]

This resonates with Beryl Pogson's portrayal of the necessity for a balance between the pineal gland and the sex glands, which is a prerequisite for the doors of the higher mental and higher emotional centers to be opened. From her perspective, the three wise men represented these two centers plus the sex center. In view of the central role they had at the birth of Jesus, if one views the sex function in the form of an octave, re-birth, procreation, becomes the obvious lowest note.

When Collin considers human blood circulation in the context of the glands and their functions, he draws parallels to the Solar System. Just like the body's sun, the heart, pumping hydrogen, carbon, nitrogen and oxygen to the outermost nooks and crannies of the body, the Sun's life-giving light unites all planets, either by direct lighting or indirectly through the glow of individual planets. When the blood passes from one organ to another, secretions from all glands are brought to new destinations. Released hormones in various quantities are essential for the human condition. Collin points out that man himself, through attention and interests, influences this process from moment to moment.

A particularly interesting aspect of his analogy is revealed when Collin claims that secretions from the glands follow a sequence similar to the planets when they sound their note in time:

[1] Rodney Collin, *The Theory of Celestial Influence* (London: Vincent Stuart Publishers Ltd, 1958), p150.

... the digested products of the pancreas go to serve the parathyroids in the building of tissue; this tissue-building demands the aeration made possible by the thyroid; the speed of respiration in turn affects the vigour of thought and determination arising from the anterior pituitary; thought and determination translate themselves into the passionate activity of the adrenals; such activity requires corresponding work of the inner organs from the posterior lobe; and this instinctive work in turn calls for more products of digestion from the pancreas.[1]

Collin sees life at the level of blood circulation as a coherent and circular chain of action and reaction in which the identification of cause and effect is not necessary for a deeper and more holistic understanding. One detail that he emphasizes, however, is that man's three nervous systems contribute to a more refined distribution of the secretions of the glands. In other words, this distribution is a continuation of the crude output of the glands distributed by the bloodstream.

As an example of the consequences of a higher degree of refining, he refers to the contribution of the thyroid gland to the storing of memory regarding music and words, something which is generally not recognised. He further argues that aspects of the pineal gland are also not known because its potential is only activated in higher states of consciousness.

Common to the blood circulation and the three nervous systems is that they are spread out throughout the body and that they both, according to Collin, connect all the glands, but through different routes.

In fact, recent research shows that sympathetic nerve fibers send impulses to not all but almost all glands, while the parasympathetic nerve fibers only extend to a limited number of glands. What impact, if any, this may have on Rodney Collin's theories is a complex medical question that concerns the issue of which glands are affected or not in a given context within his various theses. The importance of the glands to the immune system was only known five years after Collin's death.

Without dwelling on Collin's meticulous and detailed investigations of the various nervous systems, we can still form a simplified, general and relevant picture of their essential characteristics and importance.

The cerebrospinal system relates to sensation and control. The sympathetic system relates to involuntary organs and contributes to necessary adjustments in bodily functions, while the parasympathetic system's nerve fibres mainly go to the body's internal organs. For this

---

[1] Rodney Collin, *The Theory of Celestial Influence* (London: Vincent Stuart Publishers Ltd, 1958), 152.

reason, this system has the greatest impact on the internal environment of the body. It is mainly activated when we are relaxed and has an important function in, among other things, the regulation of digestion and urination.

According to Collin's table regarding speed of diffusion, all systems work at different speeds, and also, according to his calculations, with different energies. Cerebrospinal can't work faster than we think. The sympathetic system can work faster than our attention can follow, while parasympathetic, which is related to sex, intuition and self-preservation, works with unimaginably fast impulses.

When Collin assesses the cooperation of the nervous systems under the law of three, it becomes apparent that interactions can be considered in six different combinations. Some are triggered when thoughts or instinct are dominant, others when the whole organism is under the influence of the highest kind of emotions. Because their individual energies are adapted to the task of the systems, they work mostly independently. Attempts to think about a deep emotion, or thinking when one is instinctively excited, he regards as the expression of leakage between centers.

In addition to the six possible combinations for cooperation between the nervous systems, Collin reveals a seventh solution, albeit so inconceivable in our ordinary situations that he presents it only as a theoretical possibility. However, there can be no doubt that it is precisely this kind of theoretical possibility that he not only believes and hopes for, but which he puts his whole life energy into to realising. In this perspective, his terminology, his use of the word theoretical, becomes an indirect metaphor for how far away from his potential man ordinarily is. In the seventh context, where all forces are active at the same time, the cosmos in which the forces arise unites with a cosmos of a higher order:

> ... these three systems are arranged so that, in certain circumstances and at one particular point in the brain, a connection could be created between them. In this case all three energies would run freely through all three systems. With what result? By the general circulation of intellectual energy, a man would become conscious in all his functions. By the general circulation of instinctive energy, all his functions would act to his best advantage and in harmony. By the general circulation of emotional energy, all his functions would work at the intensity of fear or love. Such a condition, in which instinctive processes were as conscious as thinking, in which thinking was as fast as attraction, and in which reason, emotion, and action combined as harmoniously as breathing

and sleeping, is at present unimaginable. We can only say that the
human machine is in fact designed to make it possible.[1]

Many questions arise when one stands before such statements. How theoretical or factual was this mindset for him personally? Careful as he was in distinguishing between vague assumptions and what he considered likely and probable, how could he so purposefully sum up a composition of distinct details that concluded so indisputably that the human organism was designed for such a holistic experience? Does this throw new and augmented light on his experiences from the time around the final phase of Ouspensky's life, which was so groundbreaking for him?

When Collin examines the strange phenomenon of the slowing down of time, he argues that time is not the same in different phases of a human life. Just as a falling object gains momentum and increased speed, as human life progresses the pace changes, with fewer and fewer events taking place in every hour:

> *He thinks to tame time by measuring its passage in years, but time*
> *cheats him by putting less and less into them. So that when he looks back*
> *over his life and tries to calculate it by the scale of birthdays, he is in a*
> *strange way foreshortening his existence, like a man looking at a picture*
> *which elusively curves away from him.[2]*

When we previously reviewed the basic features of *The Theory of Eternal Life*, we noted his division of man's life into eight parts, represented as a logarithmic scale, where each step is characterised by development of various functions, such as growth of the body, gain of personality, and the development of unity.

As he approaches the problems of significant time, relative to the resonance of the glands to the planets, he also adopts a circular logarithm that represents the long body of man's life. In this model the real vital processes are absolutely central and of crucial importance for an understanding of the true scale of organic time – quite different from the time provided by a calendar of years.

Beginning two months after conception and indicated in months until the age of 76 years, the milestones in a human life will have the following sequence: 2-4.5-10-20-44-100-200-440 and 1000. In this scale, the distances between the points are of equal duration. The points in time

[1] Rodney Collin, *The Theory of Celestial Influence* (London: Vincent Stuart Publishers Ltd, 1958), p154-155.
[2] Rodney Collin, *The Theory of Celestial Influence* (London: Vincent Stuart Publishers Ltd, 1958), p156.

correspond mainly to the clear stages of development in a person's life, but also to the time for the development of potential.

Two months into pregnancy the foetus has received a human form and structure. After four and a half months, it has developed its own blood circulation and acquired involuntary movement. After ten months, a child manifests voluntary movements, whereas after two and a half years there is a simple intellectual process underway where it refers to itself as 'I', often in sentences that are more or less complete. At the age of seven, the child has acquired the ability to mentally digest impressions. At the age of fifteen, puberty and sex function are marked, while thirty-five years marks the period in which a man, traditionally speaking, is at his height in terms of abilities and powers. That seventy-six years represents the normal end of man's term in Collin's depiction, must be seen in light of what was considered as life expectancy in the fifties.

By comparing these times with the cycles of the planets, Collin discovered a strange conformity. He found that a lunar cycle was equivalent to the first milestone. The completion of a minor cycle of Mercury corresponded with point two. The moment of birth, which is marked by man's first breath and breathability, occurs at ten lunar cycles, etc. In short, Collin found consistency between all the time-points and other planets' cycles. The only point that did not exactly match his comparative calculations was the last milestone, where the completion of the cycle of Uranus was only somewhat consistent with average life expectancy. It is almost strange that Collin does not mention that it is this fluctuation that allows his calculations to remain relevant, given that average life expectancy varies within one and the same period of time, due to many factors, including geographic location and the result of the development of prosperity.

On the basis of the importance of this correlation between the planets and the true time of man, he writes:

> It seems literally as though for the new organism time begins at conception. More correctly still, all times begin, that is to say, the organism counts the time of each planet from that critical moment when time begins for it, the moment of conception. Here it begins, not as the individual type … but simply as a new representative of mankind. Where the planets then stood, how they then shone, represent its normality, the starting-point of the race of life. And as each planet in turn and according to its own cycle returns to that starting-point, it

springs the mechanism of a responding function. The clock-hands after different intervals return to zero; as each does so, an alarm rings, and yet another aspect of the mechanism is set in motion.[1]

Collin explains the exchange of powers, in this context, with the law behind the concept of resonance. Any physical structure has its own frequency, and any system that can vary will absorb energy and fluctuate when affected by a periodic force with the same frequency as its own.

The fundamental premise of resonance is that the parts involved are attuned. Collin's idea is that the basic tone is set from the positions of the planets at the moment of birth while the glands are still dormant. As a planet continues in its orbit, the prerequisites for impact change, until it gradually returns to its original position. In his perspective, man is not only a representation of a microcosmos, with his organs arranged in an ascending order from the heart, but also a dynamic being in time, and as such a living model of the Solar System.

Another strikingly synchronised order Collin discovered was how both the Moon and Mercury, representing a foetus of two and four and a half months respectively, lack atmosphere, in the same way that a foetus lacks air. As milestone one has shape and structure and milestone two involuntary movement, the Moon and Mercury possess the same limitations. In other words, they have as yet, in this perspective, neither individual atmosphere nor individual movement. As an unborn child, they are both dependent, but looked after. The Moon in that it is embraced by Earth's magnetic field, and Mercury in that it is enveloped by zodiacal light.

Without going into all of Collin's elucidatory nuances, we can generally state that the other planets' relationships correspond to the logarithmic timescale. They clearly bear the mark, as a child after birth, not only of being able to breathe, but also possessing a separate atmosphere and of being able to practice voluntary movements.

Only the very outermost planets can be said to possess a similar capacity for self-awareness as that of a mature human being that reaches the sixth milestone. Jupiter and Saturn in particular possess a family of satellites and approach the physical state whereby they can sufficiently absorb solar light and begin to radiate independently, something which is impossible for the Earth and Mercury without going through a complete physical transformation. Collin saw parallels in the context of assimilation of nutrition: what for the human organism constitutes nourishment in the

---

[1] Rodney Collin, *The Theory of Celestial Influence* (London: Vincent Stuart Publishers Ltd, 1958), p158-159.

form of food, air and impressions, he saw for the Solar System as solid spheres, atmospheric spheres and spheres of light.

After a detailed unfolding of man's life with a focus on his milestones, and a summary of the number of days and planetary cycles at the ninth and last milestone, Collin writes:

> We find to our awe that the whole company of planets have returned again to that same disposition which governed at the outset.
>
> Throughout man's life their various tempi have ruled this or that function and aspect of his existence. The quick lunar pulse of lymph, the tempo vivace of his mercurial nature, the moderate beat of flesh and blood, the andante of intellectual striving, the slow largo of instinct, and the majestic grave of man's deepest emotion – all these have risen and fallen in him according to the quicker or slower rhythms of the Planets. By their perpetual harmony they have woven the intricate counterpoint of his life. In unison at last, they strike together the one great cord which sounds his death-knell.[1]

From early childhood, Rodney Collin had tried to satiate his almost all-encompassing thirst for knowledge, as if it were the most natural thing in the world. The time with Ouspensky had opened the door to an inner and outer universe, while the time after Ouspensky's death opened the door from his own inner world into a universe that was constantly expanding. It was when he crossed the threshold of the latter doorway, that concepts such as outside and inside seemed to lose their last remnants of the one-sidedness to which all thinking that is inextricably linked to sensory experiences necessarily leads, and which Maurice Nicoll aptly characterised as sensuous thinking.

What until then had been a unifying vision became, through further inner work and ever new discoveries in his research, not only a vision but increasingly a reality. There is every reason to assume that he was less surprised by what he found than that he found what he did. What appeared to be coherent, synchronous, parallel, and consistent analogues must have emerged as pieces in an unprecedented cosmic puzzle. One of the consequences of removing the boundaries set by sensuous thinking is that the concept of time is freed from its linear captivity. It is impossible to appreciate the full impact this had on Collin but it clearly provided access to completely new ways of perceiving existence, of which we have already seen many examples.

[1] Rodney Collin, The Theory of Celestial Influence (London: Vincent Stuart Publishers Ltd, 1958), p166.

THE THEORY OF CELESTIAL INFLUENCE

A consequence of individual time differing from time measured in the form of a calendar is that different people move at different speeds throughout one and the same year. One of the features of the calendar year is that it conveniently unites common interests. Collin did not consider a year to be a unit of individual time but as a background that personal time moved against. Therefore, a human's experience material for a year is not a one-sided affair but an extensive network of trans-temporal echoes.

Although a human life is measured from fertilisation to the termination of the organic body, Collin is clear on the difference between the chemical biological being and what he strictly sees as human. In his definition the degree of consciousness or awareness is essential. When what is perceived as normal human consciousness is confined to an organic form, it is because its potential is not considered.

He considers the question of the possibility of awareness to penetrate into other times in light of the connection with the Sun's creative transfers of energy. As previously noted, electrons are sealed within molecules and molecules sealed within cells. Collin considers the latter cells as part of the human organic body and simultaneously an extension of their original origin. This means that electrons, molecules and cells continue to work in the organic body in their own time.

Collin does not draw any final conclusions regarding these matters but points to the obvious fact that, were such an expanded consciousness to take place, it would involve a complete reorganisation and re-routing of the nerve impulses between the cerebrospinal and sympathetic system. These theoretical investigations may have been prompted by a desire to understand some of the mechanisms underlying Ouspensky's strange manifestations shortly before he died, where he apparently went in and out of various time periods. A number of his own experiences from the same period, where linear time appeared to be halted, may also have been a source of inspiration to try to better understand these events.

One thing he was sure of, however, and as his investigations had incontrovertibly shown, was that the basic questions of any investigations about time were:

Whose time, time of what?[1]

The first time Collin drew on the idea of the six processes in *The Theory of Celestial Influence* was, as we have seen, in connection with their

---

[1] Rodney Collin, *The Theory of Celestial Influence* (London: Vincent Stuart Publishers Ltd, 1958), p169.

function in the Solar System. When he later returns to them it is in the context of the microcosmos of man.

Before we go on to see how Collin explores growth, elimination, digestion, corruption, healing, and regeneration, it seems necessary to say something generally about these processes and what the different numbers represent. This is the sole reason for the following personal commentaries. The ancient idea of the six processes is a part of esoteric teaching and contains and embraces any component, part, substance, constituent, or ingredient that continues, proceeds or advances. The interrelations of these six triads as a whole, in their succession, is represented by the six groups of numbered triads below and the sequence of the elements within the individual triads themselves are as follows:

$$123 - 213 - 132 - 312 - 231 - 321$$

The most mystical of all of them is number 1, which represents life. How are we going to define this? Well, I don't think we can. The ability to define is a function of the intellect. Our intellect is but a tiny fragment of the organic structure of man and, even though it is necessary and helpful, it can neither go beyond itself and fully define man as a whole, nor comprehend the vastness that man finds himself in. This is the reason why this function cannot define life.

Number 2 represents matter, the material of the collected content. Number 3 represents form. The form of a product is a carrier of what it contains. The function of the form is to carry something, and this makes the manifestation of the content possible. It can also intensify and strengthen the expression, often through restrictions. Essential for the understanding of a triad's function is that where the different number ranks always remains the same in terms of what represents the active, passive and neutralising factor. In other words, active, passive and neutralising factors always retain their position and order.

By presenting the processes in the light of human as a microcosmos, Collin highlights the fundamental features of human nature and how these form the basis for both limitations and possibilities. Furthermore, he clarifies how resistance and obstacles are necessary factors for innovation, maintenance and progress. By choosing the human organism as the example of the first triad, growth, he makes available new knowledge against a familiar background.

Everything that can grow must have been born. And everything that grows does that through multiplication and differentiation in a continuous, chain-like progression. Within the nature of continuation, one element comes to its end in order to give rise to another. In this triad, where life is thrown into matter, and where the consequence, the form, manifests as a living phenomenon, we see the technical mechanism upon which any form of manifested life relies.

Because Collin himself emphasised that the impulse of life is a mystery, there is room to add that in this triad we face the ultimate imaginable task form, as a function, can have: the actualisation and the appearance of the hidden source of life.

Collin delineates the scope of this triad by saying that it only begins after the instance of conception is accomplished. This not only removes the basis for possible obscurities and confusion but also opens the door to the fact that conception belongs to another triad, namely re-generation. By seeing this in the context of what he said about death and conception in *The Theory of Eternal Life*, a holistic picture emerges that at the same time expands the meaning of the elements of this image.

> *Where previously were two elements, male and female, is now but one*
> *– the fertilized or impregnated ovum. In this single cell two poles form,*
> *an active and a passive, and the genes becoming polarized between*
> *them, the cell splits into two, then four, eight, sixteen, thirty-two and so*
> *on. It is an exact living model of that Absolute sphere, infinitely*
> *propagating galaxies, ...The radiation of life acting upon matter, yields*
> *infinite multiplicity of form.[1]*

He compares the different stages of pregnancy with other cosmic phenomena, showing that, for each new step, the triad retains its order, whereby the active life impulse constantly penetrates deeper into matter and form.

Multiplication, differentiation, organisation, and function and form in combination are what he regards as the general phenomenon of growth. Here the thymus gland is associated with cellular multiplication and the thyroid with form and function. About growth, seen in a broader, psychological and emotional perspective, he wrote:

> *... in man's psychic life it stands for eternal compromise, impulse*
> *encountering resistance, need meeting obstacles, to come to rest at the*
> *halfway solution, the point of equilibrium. It is the way everything*
> *happens in the life of mankind – the manners, customs, habits, the*

---

[1] Rodney Collin, *The Theory of Celestial Influence* (London: Vincent Stuart Publishers Ltd, 1958), p172.

endless complication and diversity that spring from the adjustment of ambition to circumstances, of one desire to other desires. It is the resultant of forces.[1]

Moreover, he states that when all this is happening unconsciously and involuntarily, then it can admittedly lead to accumulation of experiences, but not to a digestion of the impressions, in the same way that the accumulation of knowledge will not develop being. Collin's approach directly challenges Darwin, or at least popularised Darwinism, which he considered both deceptive and perverted. This can be summarised by Collin's notion that development is incompatible with a lack of consciousness and will. Darwin's model of how the physical Earth matured and how species were added, was, in his view, a parallel to how physical man matures, which does not address the potential ability of a given species to transcend itself. He expresses his opinion on how contemporary discourse demonstrated a poor grasp of the concept of growth in this satirical comment:

It is even distorted into a kind of manufacturer's guarantee that every individual octopus shall one day develop into a Buddha, and that without any effort or intention on their part all men shall inevitably become wise.[2]

In the next process, digestion, it is obvious that one thing becomes another, but what is not so obvious is that within this process of refinement the coarser elements are acted upon by something from a higher, more intelligent level. This succession is always initiated when one substance comes in contact with another that is more refined. The action of enzymes upon an edible substance in one part of the process of digestion is an example. Whenever a more intelligent entity acts on a coarser one, the coarser one that began the process in the active position is raised out of its former place.

As an example of processes belonging to this triad, Collin mentions cooking, distillation, refinement, and purification. When the digestive process refines what was basic food, it simultaneously provides fuels for the various functions of the human organism. One can get an indication of how intricate these processes are when Collin reminds us that the

---

[1] Rodney Collin, *The Theory of Celestial Influence* (London: Vincent Stuart Publishers Ltd, 1958), p175.
[2] Rodney Collin, *The Theory of Celestial Influence* (London: Vincent Stuart Publishers Ltd, 1958), p176.

aforementioned functions, such as respiration, arterial and nervous systems, all work with different fuels.

Also, because his examples for this triad are rooted in the human organism, this helps to clarify, among other things, the active and passive elements of the triad. The food we eat is passive matter, enzymes will, through the liquifying action of salvia and digestive fluids, release and refine coarser food-molecules. In this process Collin identifies Life in an active position, while the product of that process, which becomes available to the lymphatic system, becomes the neutralising factor of Form. In a chain-like propulsion, the digested product then becomes passive matter in an ongoing sophistication where, for example, secretions from liver (Life) contribute to further refinement in the digestive process.

By considering the digestive process in the perspective of an octave, Collin is able to show how nature helps to counteract the inherent limitations found in an interval. In this octave, the original and passive food is *do, re* is the chyme, while the refined nutrition brought to the blood by osmosis is *mi*:

> ... *passive matter of the venous blood meets an activating principle not, this time, from within the body, but from without. The bloodstream, exposed over the enormous surface of the lungs to the air, is suddenly vitalized by the addition of external oxygen (life), and emerges as refined or arterial blood (form).*[1]

To understand digestion from a wider point of view, one must include subjective bodily sensations. Already at the level of the process in which the circulation of arterial blood takes place, the attempts to explain digestion in purely physiological terms begin to show their clear limitations, in Collin's view:

> ... *we know that blood-circulation brings with it certain subjective sensations of warmth and well-being; a deficient one with sensations of chill and depression.*[2]

Many will probably be able to acknowledge that such sensations can not only characterise a person's emotional life but can also have implications for their general attitude toward their own life and the

---

[1] Rodney Collin, *The Theory of Celestial Influence* (London: Vincent Stuart Publishers Ltd, 1958), p177-178.
[2] Rodney Collin, *The Theory of Celestial Influence* (London: Vincent Stuart Publishers Ltd, 1958), p178.

world. Arterial blood passing through the brain activates electrical nerve-signals, so that what we generally call thought-activity can manifest. When energies are further refined, they form fuels that man needs to move and act, but also for the body's inner working. Collin links the last and most refined to the physiological side of the sex function, but also to the inherent potential ability to develop higher and creative emotions.

While human digestion of food is an automatic process, digestion of impressions is related to consciousness, understanding and choice. Digestion of air is initially a mechanical process, but as we will see later, when looking into Collin's views on regeneration, we will be able to understand that a further digestion of air is associated with consciousness.

The third triad is elimination. The main function of this process is to maintain health and avoid imbalance. This function is not meant to take part in the process of regeneration, but to avoid destructive elements overtaking and outweighing the effects of normal growth. When destruction is out of proportion with growth, or occurs to a significant extent before its time, then it is corruption. Whenever this natural cycle is interrupted, the normal release of waste products comes to a halt and these matters then acquire the capacity to cause disorder – namely to corrupt a living organism, an individual or a social structure. Waste matter in the body that isn't expelled causes sickness or mental and/or emotional blockages. It also creates physiological disturbance and further psychological malfunctioning.

The triad has the subsequent order: Life, Form Matter. Here active Life breaks down the passive Form with Matter of a specific character as a consequence. Collin explains the nature of elimination in the context of the previous triads, also describing how these different processes form an organic whole:

> ... in the process of digestion, incoming food (matter) met with active digestive juices in the body (life), and was transformed into chyme, a form in which it could be assimilated into the lymphatic system. In the present process, the same active principle (still life) enters first, and attacking the food (now form), by the same splitting separates off its indigestible part (matter), which is eliminated into the intestines. The product of this triad, excreta, stands midway between its original form as food and completely fossilized organic matter, such as wood, and while no longer of any use to the human organism, may nevertheless serve as nourishment for a different level of creation represented by the

vegetable realm. What is interesting here, however, is to see how the two processes of digestion and elimination are indissolubly locked at every stage, and that the same active element acts in both, but in a different place, a different role.[1]

In this triad, as in the previous one, Collin found that a purely physiological illustration was insufficient to provide a comprehensible picture. Collin seems to have reached the limit of such a model in this triad in the conditions around sweat as excretion, where the active force, through heat, increases metabolism and breaks down waste matter in cells and tissue. When elimination reaches the level of brain activity, it is the by-products of previous perceptions, in the form of imagination, that, according to Collin, characterise excretion. He doesn't explore this further at this point because, to tame this kind of imagination by will and skill, as we shall see later, belongs to another triad.

Talk is a form of elimination related to the mind and is characterised by the lack of visible cause or specific purpose. In other words, it is the kind of talk that neither has nor requires attention. Collin emphasises that talk can have a healthful effect, but at the same time he cautions that this type of talk doesn't only discard waste matter of the mind, but also risks discarding large amounts of impressions and thoughts.

It is natural to associate this type of talk with the external and superficial sides, but Collin also sees a connection with more essential features. For the quiet Saturn type, more talk can be cleansing of their constipated mind; for the Jovial type's mental health, on the other hand, choosing a more restrictive line may speed up digestion and bring about understanding.

Tears, which are obviously attached to instinctive functions, through the sympathetic system, spring, in Collin's opinion, from a psychological level, as do posture, gesture, and tone of voice. Singing and dancing can also, in certain contexts, be excretion of a psycho-emotional character, which can contribute to increased purification and well-being.

We can view popular culture through Collin's interpretations of elimination. Music belonging to this triad is often coloured by sentimentality. Sometimes intense rhythms are predominant, and we also find a tendency toward melodic and lyrical repetition that can further intensify the effect of the music. Hit songs and what we call popular music or evergreens play an important role in the process of elimination for an individual or society as a whole. It is interesting that, within different

[1] Rodney Collin, *The Theory of Celestial Influence* (London: Vincent Stuart Publishers Ltd, 1958), p181.

genres, certain songs are considered 'standards' – what standards are they living up to? We don't listen to standards to increase tension, quite the opposite. What makes them function so well within their standard? What are their characteristics? The answer is found within their function, not in their form.

Sentimentality can have the effect of dissolving tension between people and leading them to a frictionless unity. Strangely, music that arouses aggression allows a feeling of individuality to remain when a person is within a mob, mass, or crowd, such as a rock concert. Repetitiveness sustains and supports any of these actions already in motion, either the sentimental or the aggressive. The grand gestures of Wladziu Liberace, Elton John, and Frank Sinatra are at their ultimate laxative peak when used to accentuate the sentimentality within a piece of music as tools for activating the process of elimination.

These performers may look hollow and insignificant. But nothing which is something, that is, has a function, can be called nothing. Not even sometimes.

Relative to sexual and emotional functions, Rodney Collin writes:

> ... we are reminded, not so much of physiological excretions, as of the indefinable communication of pathos, anguish or joy, and the whole play of higher human expression. It is misleading to try to associate the waste products on this level with tangible substances, for they evidently take the form of emanations too subtle for physical measurement and analysis. Certain kinds of laughter, which are a means of rejecting impressions too contradictory or difficult for the recipient to understand, may also belong here. But in general, we can say that what is 'given off as waste', that is, what is passed out into the world, must be proportional to what is refined within. A man can only expel the by-product of what he has digested, refined and understood – but this he must do.[1]

Before we delve into Collin's investigations of the next triad, corruption, let's first try to formulate an easy-to-understand but precise characteristic of this criminal lawfulness. When one part of a whole starts to live its own life, separate from the original pattern set out for an organism, an activity, an ecosystem, social structure, or any other interrelated system, then it is the process of corruption. As we will see,

---

[1] Rodney Collin, *The Theory of Celestial Influence* (London: Vincent Stuart Publishers Ltd, 1958), p183.

the Life principle is found in the passive position. Form is in charge, obviously having forgotten its role as a servant, a medium, a herald, or more specifically, a carrier of a substance beyond Form. When a form is not carrying any substance other than its own form, it is ridiculously out of touch with its objective role, which is to contain a substance. When the form of a sermon, rite or ritual is the active element in this triad, a sacred meeting ground where initiation could take place is turned into a circus.

Collin's first example of corruption relates to basic body functioning, where waste matters are prevented from leaving the body in a natural way, as in the case of constipation, where it begins to decay in the organism. He also points out how rheumatism, in some contexts, can be linked to inadequate elimination of urine. Furthermore, he reiterates how cellular waste matter can be deposited in muscle mass in the absence of an adequate sweating function. Thus it is apparent how the natural and healthful process of elimination is corrupted by the abnormal and degenerative.

In the latter process, he aptly uses the term poison. He also uses the terms disease and rebellion. It is worth noting, however, that he makes a clear distinction between corruption and destruction. Destruction stays within the framework of what is necessary and proportional to what is refined by digestion, whereas the corruptive process violates such limits. He paints a picture of corruption as boundless and brutal ruthlessness.

Mental toxins, as a result of unexpressed thoughts, can lead to both physical and moral degradation when morbid notions, fixed ideas and dreaming are allowed to proceed freely.

When laughter, singing, tears and other physico-emotional languages associated with the sympathetic system are not allowed a natural outlet, daydreaming, regrets and unfounded fears can arise.

Collin seemed particularly keen to clarify the way this process expands. Attention at various levels is necessary in order to understand, protect, stop or limit the scope of this triad:

> *... in this process inert matters on a higher level serve as infectors or poisoners of inert matters on a lower level; and conversely how inert matters on a lower level serve as passive material for the infection of those above. As we can soon see by observation, physical tension leads to morbid thoughts, which lead to groundless fears and apprehensions, which lead in turn to violent or self-destructive emotions. And similarly in reverse. The process of disease has the particular characteristic of*

*'spreading' or infecting all the raw material, both higher and lower, with
which it comes in contact and which it immediately corrupts.*[1]

As an example of real crime in the world of men, Collin shows how
knowledge, skill and understanding (Form) can be used to destroy a higher
potential (Life) and where the victims' situation is reduced to a lower level
than it was originally.

Rodney Collin was, as we have seen, an unconventional thinker and his
attitude to various issues could be surprising. An example is his openness
to the possibility that large-scale crime, according to some cosmic
requirement, would announce its intentions in advance.

Referring to Hitler's book *Mein Kampf*, Ibsen's play *Peer Gynt* and Josef
Stalin's laconic commentary: "You can no more expect sincere diplomacy
than wooden iron or dry water," Collin concludes that, although the
declarations are made in a justified manner, it is man's inability and lack of
wish to see things in the light of reality that is essentially the reason why
warnings about corruption are overlooked.

Collin's perspectives of the fifth and penultimate triad indicate that the
process of healing involves additional substances or actions applied to an
entity that has lost its original balance and function. For example, the
healing effect of music can allow us to experience grief and sorrow as they
really are and to remain in touch with what caused them without escaping
into self-pity, self-indulgence, or any other kinds of unnecessary suffering.
In such a case, the healing effect of music can help us to open up and accept
the truth of our situation. It is interesting that the word 'truth' in Sanskrit
is the present participle of the verb 'to be'. Whilst corruption fights the Life
principle, in healing, Life plays the role of neutralising unorganised Matter
with the necessary Form, as it once again flows through a system or an
organ from which it has been shut out.

The basic importance of the triad of healing can hardly be made clearer
than when Collin emphasises its purpose and ability. The universe would
be damned, he argues, if unhindered corruption could spread without
being corrected by a healing triad. He uses the inherent abilities of the
body to illustrate how the form in this triad regains its life-giving
properties when abnormalities are corrected.

In a fascinating short version of the history of medicine, he gives an
insight into how the triads' principles have at various times found new

---

[1] Rodney Collin, *The Theory of Celestial Influence* (London: Vincent Stuart Publishers Ltd,
1958), p191.

forms of expressions through the ingenuity of man, and that the body's natural physiological ability to heal is no different from the art of medicine. They are only different in terms of scale and medium.

The medieval medical basics were to create balance in organs and organisms according to the form of four humours (or qualities), hot, cold, wet and dry, by adding the counterpart to what emerged from a diagnosis. Lowering fever with cold covers is a typical example of this kind of treatment. The affinity of the various human organs to the planets and herbal medicine also constituted a fundamental part of the medieval medical business, where the goal was to achieve balance in what Collin refers to as 'the world of organs'. The usual notion that the medieval medicine system was flawed and built on superstition was, in Collin's view, a misinterpretation. In his opinion, while it was the case that the forms of treatment gradually had to give way to new discoveries, another significant reason was that the knowledge of the underlying principles of treatment had simply been lost.

In the 1830s medical renewal the organs were no longer at the center, and the focus moved to organic compounds, where cells and molecules gained a central importance:

> Such treatment applied directly to lower cosmoses, and utilizing the times of those cosmoses, could of course yield results very much faster than the old-fashioned treatment of organs. And its speed and exactness seemed literally miraculous in comparison, as intervention of the laws of another cosmos must always seem miraculous from the point of view of our own. Study of the life of cells brought to light the role of bacteria, the accomplices of corruption on a cellular level. And very much of the of the enormous progress of medicine under Pasteur and Lister in the second half of the nineteenth century was based on asepsis or antisepsis, that is, the elimination or destruction of these agents of disease in the cellular world.[1]

Somewhat later, Ehrlich combined germicides with dye and managed to produce close to one thousand molecular combinations, which paved the way for the discovery of a plethora of sulfa drugs that proved to be able to regain balance in what Collin characterises as the molecular world. Not only did these medications have great and unprecedented accuracy, but they worked immensely faster than any former drugs.

---

[1] Rodney Collin, The Theory of Celestial Influence (London: Vincent Stuart Publishers Ltd, 1958), p195.

Collin objected to what was modern medicine in his day, on the basis that it didn't adequately consider the body's own ability to heal.

> *… it is quite clear that medicine can not go back on its own discoveries, can not retreat from the world of molecules into which its healing has now penetrated. In fact, there is only one way out. For healing to be complete, that is, for it to achieve the real benefit of the whole man, rather than the killing of a particular germ or the stimulation of a particular hormone, the patient must himself make acquaintance with the intelligence of his own instinctive function. He must first listen within himself for its voice, and when he recognizes and distinguishes this voice, he must trust in its wishes and obey its commands.*[1]

According to Collin, humans can develop the ability to put themselves in touch with their own instinctive intelligence and thereby place in a cellular organ a precise electronic image of health to which it can conform. This is his description of the characteristics and abilities of faith-healing. However, the prerequisites for this ability, building a bridge between intellectual invention and instinctive intelligence, are very demanding. They not only assume a significant control of mind, but also an attitude that is free from any kind of negativity and doubt. In other words, only a completely positive attitude can lead to a direct communication with an organ in the organ's own language, where Matter organizes Form and thereby produces Life.

As a concise overview for the sixth and final triad, where Form is active, Matter passive and Life is a neutralising force, the following can be said. Intentionally applying one's skill or mental ability – Form – to convert one's experiences – Matter – in imitation of Life, or in other words to re-create it, belongs in principle to the process of regeneration. The original impulse initiating the process of re-creation is so vivid that no word or concept can describe or replace it. It can only be recognised and received by one who has, to a certain degree, cultivated an ability to be present to his or her own existence.

In order for something to be re-created, something else has to die. Before we can combine with an external situation, there has to be some kind of inner work to prepare us. What does it take for us to view an event in front of us a little more objectively? It comes down to valuation and the gradual process of inner separation of the valuable from the valueless, through an awakening conscience. What is valuable in this connection is that which

[1] Rodney Collin, *The Theory of Celestial Influence* (London: Vincent Stuart Publishers Ltd, 1958), p196.

supports an expansion of consciousness and life, and allows them to flow, not that which restricts them. This is one of the distinguishing features of regeneration.

Initially Collin highlights various forms of regeneration. For instance, how some animals can mysteriously regenerate body parts, where Form regenerates Form. Although the human organism, in the renewal of its skin, can be said to possess this form of regeneration, to understand the full significance of the process for man, one must realise its psychological nature. The starting point is man's inherent ability to become conscious. In other words, human regeneration is man's ability to re-create himself as a conscious being.

On the question of how such a process can be carried out, Collin is very clear:

> *The order of the process of regeneration is that form organizes matter in imitation of life. Man himself is this form: in this process everything depends upon his initiative, his will, his persistence. For this reason, this process does not happen by itself. It is, as it were, a freak of being, of which only very few men are capable and then only in connection with a certain very definite aim and concerted efforts.*[1]

To shed light on what Matter is in this context, Collin reminds us of different aspects of man's mental activity. As we have already seen, Collin considered man's meaningless imaginings and the endless stream of idly turning thoughts as the excreta of the mind. On the other hand, registration, ordered comparison, and storage of perceptions are mental characteristics that can become part of the regenerating process, in that the functions of *these* characteristics work with the waste matter of the mind. The mind is thus divided in two, where one part watches and witnesses the other.

For those who are familiar with intentionally splitting the attention, it will come as no surprise that Collin emphasises how extremely difficult it is and what considerable effort is needed to be able to practice this experiment, even for a minute. They will also be able to confirm his assertion of how it is impossible to divide the attention if the mind is already poisoned by the process of corruption. Further, they will be aware of a new and surprising energy that can become available and accumulate if the efforts are successfully sustained, and that such experiences provide an unequivocal experience of self-knowledge.

[1] Rodney Collin, The Theory of Celestial Influence (London: Vincent Stuart Publishers Ltd, 1958), p198-199.

Another powerful factor he references in the process of personal reconstruction is the immediate experience of the actual sensation of the body. When combined with an intentional use of the ability of imagination, an exceptional vivid experience of living becomes accessible. It is interesting to note that he also regards intentional imagining as a natural excretion of the mind.

We see once again how a division into two emerges as a fundamental prerequisite, as Collin considers regeneration relative to the function of movements and sensations:

> *The higher part of the sensational function knowingly registers the physico-emotional 'weather' of the organism. One has the sensation of one's movements, the sensation of one's sensations, physical awareness of the body and of more or fewer of the processes passing in it. This is the 'feeling of oneself', of one's physical existence in certain surroundings at a certain time, which, if seriously cultivated, observably produces a very strong and valuable emotion. But again, except in rare and accidental moments, it requires the greatest possible attention to maintain the 'separation' between the registering sensation and the manifold feelings and impulses registered, which all the time tends to rush together into one vague and unobserved sensation of 'I'.*[1]

As we can see, attention plays a crucial role in terms of the manifestation of the process of regeneration related to mental registration and physical sensations. Collin is unequivocal that it is only when attention is deliberately focused and sustained that the process of regeneration is possible.

It is in the sexual-emotional function of man that we encounter the last and most challenging aspect of regeneration. As in all other regenerative contexts, action begins with a division, a separation. It is the usual flow of emotional desires, attractions and longings that Collin regards as waste matter, which becomes the subject of processing, alongside intense attractions and repulsions. Because ordinary human emotions operate at such a high speed, emotional reactions to impressions manifest before there is an opportunity to detect, confront and work with them.

It is because man operates in arrears that Collin emphasises the necessity for his objective to be of a permanent character. It is only when one's emotional aim has such a permanent anchor that the necessary and

---

[1] Rodney Collin, *The Theory of Celestial Influence* (London: Vincent Stuart Publishers Ltd, 1958), p200.

friction-filled struggle between destructive and constructive forces can take place. The key to the generation of the consciousness that characterises the regenerating process lies precisely in such confrontational friction.

By separating a higher objective from the habits and limitations of body and personality, hidden weaknesses, justifications and self-indulgences become gradually more visible in the light of an increased consciousness. Likewise, one's longings, capacities and aspirations are also more accessible. Collin compares this process to the changes matter must undergo in order to go from being opaque to being radiant. The preconditions of being able to shine with one's own light is that one has acquired the ability to be illuminated by another body:

> ... a man wishing to develop must first become translucent, that is, he must expose all sides of himself without reserve to the penetration of another man's consciousness, that of his teacher. He must lose his solidity, become invisible and unrecognized, be seen only by another's light. This very exposure and penetration may then prove the means enabling him to know himself and in the end to acquire permanent consciousness of his own.[1]

Perhaps not surprisingly, Collin draws a parallel between the three stages, opacity, translucence and radiance, to three different states of matter, namely mineral or cellular, molecular and electronic. In Collin's perspective, an increased consciousness will lead to an increased freedom to penetrate worlds that would otherwise appear invisible. In the event of such penetration, ordinary concepts of what is near and far will be completely transformed. Our ordinary consciousness, operating at the 'cellular' level, is characterised by the fact that we relate to objects. However, a consciousness that benefits from the freedom of molecular level also includes relationships between objects, as what constitutes the distance between objects is mostly of a molecular nature. The practice of divided attention is what Collin points to as the key that opens the doors to a higher world through which one can gain a vivid understanding of the practical importance of regeneration:

> The man who begins to learn how to divide his attention deliberately between his own body and the object or person he is dealing with, that is, who is simultaneously aware of himself and his surroundings, does in

---

[1] Rodney Collin, The Theory of Celestial Influence (London: Vincent Stuart Publishers Ltd, 1958), p201.

fact begin to live in a world of relationships, in the molecular world. He has begun to be self-conscious. He has begun to grow a soul.[1]

There is little doubt that Gurdjieff's call to put oneself in the position of others assumes that one has access to such a molecular world. Another example of the consequence of living in such a world of relationships is Mrs. Staveley's support of the different original impulses to the creation of the International All & Everything Conference, where people from different lineages of the Gurdjieff work meet to share their questions and insights.

By reading between the lines of Collin's depiction of this triad, one cannot help but notice that entering the molecular world means getting beyond the stage of personal preoccupation where we are polluted by imagination, fantasy and dreams in the labyrinth of illusion, and that only in the molecular world can harmony in all shades begin to find fertile ground and optimal growth conditions. Whether human beings can be expected to live harmoniously together, even those of the same race, class and creed, is addressed by Gurdjieff in the form of a fascinating story:

> *"... when the results of the Very Saintly Labours of the Essence-Loving Ashiata Shiemash had already begun to blend with the processes of what is called their 'inner' and 'outer' being-existence, and when thanks to this, data for the Divine impulse conscience, surviving in their subconsciousness, gradually began to share in the functioning of their 'waking-consciousness', then the being-existence both personal and reciprocal began to proceed on this planet also, almost as it does on the other planets of our great Universe on which three-brained beings exist.*
>
> *"These favorites of yours also then began to have relations towards each other only as towards the manifestations varying in degree of a UNIQUE COMMON CREATOR and to pay respect to each other only according to the merits personally attained by means of 'being-Parktdolg-duty', that is, by means of personal conscious labours and intentional sufferings*
>
> *"That is why, during that period, there ceased to exist there the said two chief maleficent forms of their ordinary existence, namely, their separate independent communities and the division of themselves in these communities into various casts or classes.*

---

[1] Rodney Collin, The Theory of Celestial Influence (London: Vincent Stuart Publishers Ltd, 1958), p202-203.

"At that time, also, there upon your planet, all the three-brained beings began to consider themselves and those like themselves merely as beings bearing in themselves particles of the emanation of the Sorrow of our COMMON FATHER CREATOR.

"And all this then so happened because when the actions of the data of the Divine being-impulse begun to participate in the functioning of their ordinary waking consciousness and the three-brain beings began manifesting themselves towards each other, solely in accordance with conscience, the consequences was that masters ceased to deprive their slaves of freedom, and various power-possessing beings of their own accord surrendered their unmerited rights, having become aware by conscience and sensing that they possessed and occupied these rights and positions not for the common welfare but only for the satisfaction of their various personal weaknesses, such, for instance, as 'vanity', 'self-love', 'self-calming', and so on.

"Of course, at that period also, there continued to be all kinds of chiefs, directors and 'adviser-specialists', who became such chiefly from difference of age and what is called 'essence-power', just as there are everywhere on all planets of the Universe on which there breed three-brained beings of various degrees of self-perfecting, and they then became such, neither by hereditary right nor by election, as was the case before this blissful Ashiatian epoch and as again afterwards became and even till now continues to be the case.

"All these chiefs, directors and advisers then became such in accordance with the objective merits they personally acquired, and which could be really sensed by all the beings around them.[1]

The distinction between essence and personality was central to Collin's approach to human psychology. In short, personality is something inflicted on a human being from the outside – a kind of outer construction. Mainly through imitation, one acquires a repertoire to orient one's organism to the outer environment. On the other hand, essence represents the true objective nature of man and is associated with its organic body and actual physical chemistry. The importance of planetary conditions in the formation of essence is also central to Collin's understanding and account. As a result of the sensitivity of different glands, they act as a receiving apparatus, as previously mentioned, and they also have implications for the formation of different essence-types. In addition, he assigns great

---

[1] G. Gurdjieff, All & Everything (Aurora Oregon: Two Rivers Press Edition, 1993), p384-385.

importance to the role of blood in the understanding of essence. Collin connects what a human being essentially is to all the blood that flows through his life, from the fetal stage of birth to the final draw of the last breath.

> *In every moment, the composition of the bloodstream dictates his mood; the totality of his life-blood, bearing the final sum of the influences that have contributed to his being, is the man... The trouble is that no one knows what the sum is. No one knows himself objectively.[1]*

When a man's subjective self-image, backed by invented attitudes, overtakes his essential potential, a maze of illusions is created and maintained where the distinction between its different sides sinks into a foggy landscape with a seemingly keyless abyss. When Collin makes us lift our gaze and see that there is a way out of this landscape, he reminds us that the word 'personality' is derived from the Latin word 'persona', which means mask, as worn by an actor. When personality is in a constructive position, it stands between essence and the world outside. According to Collin, the personality is a type of psychological skin that can protect a person's inner life from unnecessary stresses and distractions. At the same time, it can act as a medium through which man can adapt to the world outside himself.

Collin envisioned a human life as a circle in which essence constitutes the content of the sphere, while personality, located on the outer side of the sphere, can be reflected onto the sphere's surface. He further believed that we can deepen our understanding of the nature of personality if we can realise that what is reflected is what a human does not absorb.

> *What is most obvious about a man is what he rejects and the particular manner in which he rejects it. He is recognized by what he does not yet understand, by that which separates him from the rest. This is his personality. When he really understands and absorbs something, it enters into him and becomes part of his essence. It is then no longer apparent to others as his personality – it is he, and he is it. The separateness characteristic of personality has disappeared.[2]*

In the same way that the digestion of food does not reach the human bloodstream before it is sufficiently refined, neither does an impression

---

[1] Rodney Collin, The Theory of Celestial Influence (London: Vincent Stuart Publishers Ltd, 1958), p206.
[2] Rodney Collin, The Theory of Celestial Influence (London: Vincent Stuart Publishers Ltd, 1958), p207.

reach essence until it is digested through personality. In other words, personality is the organ of digestion for experience.

In Collin's view, man's inability to distinguish between personality and essence is the root cause of many human abnormalities. And the greater the predisposition a being has about himself, the crazier it gets. The solution to the dilemma is to become aware of oneself and one's surroundings. Only in that way can one become aware of who one is not and who one is. Or, in other words, to see what's on the outside and the inside of oneself. Through such insights, one can free oneself from the patterns of behavior locked up for years, through pretence and imitation, which made it impossible to experience freedom and new energy and prevented necessary advances. All efforts not rooted in the discovery of oneself, but based on an illusory identity, will at best be shattered by a given confrontation or, at worst, lead to annihilation.

For a person who finds himself in a developing phase, personality must take on a passive role in which it serves essence. Conversely, spending natural energy earning an imaginary self-image will stop all internal growth. Again and again Collin highlights the necessity of the one and only legitimate instrument – self-remembering.

We've previously looked at how Collin connects the glands to the bloodstream and nervous systems. He sees cultivation of self-consciousness as an extension of the workspace of these functions.

The ability to experience sensations associated with new compounds in the nervous system are an aspect of self-consciousness, comparable to the experiencing of sensations of body heat through the bloodstream. Likewise, as the total flow of blood in a man's life constitutes its essence, the overall time of self-consciousness constitutes its soul. Referring to how discernible such moments are in ordinary man's life, he concludes that man does not have a soul, but can, through inner work, acquire one.

His considerations and reflections on ordinary psychological theses are also interesting. In his opinion, these are better regarded as forms of psychiatry, because they really relate to conditions associated with the illness of the soul or the lack of soul. True psychology, on the other hand, is the study of the art of developing a soul.

Such a study implies that, through increased consciousness, one penetrates greater worlds, experiences greater forces, acquires higher ideals and thereby is put in front of higher opportunities. Not least, such study involves facing painful and challenging incidents in a new way that will nourish and enrich essence. Although Collin does not elaborate on the meaning of 'new way', there can be no doubt that it means no longer explaining, justifying or otherwise evading a truth, because it is truth that causes essence to grow.

In order not to provide a too-simplified impression of the conditions of growth of essence, it is necessary to remember that there are different types of essence. Collin writes:

> What is true food for saturnine essence is useless for martial and vice versa. Feats of endurance which will enrich one man's essence may blunt another's, while subtleties by which this other's grows sensitive are merely enervating to the first. Thus each man must begin to feel for himself what feeds his essence, what makes him more himself.[1]

When we look a little later at the types of essence, it will be possible to get a more detailed idea of what this entails.

Consciousness basically depends on a certain fine matter produced in the body. This production assumes a digestion of food, air and impressions. Because the material is of molecular nature, it is unstable, volatile and difficult to keep together. In other words, they follow the same laws as any other free matters in a molecular state.

For this free matter to come under control, it must come under the influence of attention. Only then can it become the potential vehicle of self-consciousness. In order to hold or accumulate this matter, will is required. A will that man mostly does not possess. Given the difficulty of directing and keeping attention and considering the volatility of molecular material, perhaps Collin's illustration will provide some insight into the challenges and difficulties of self-consciousness. When this matter is not transformed into self-consciousness, it often leaks out of us in the form sex-energy as negative emotions or some healthy variant. According to Collin, it often leaves us in some form of fascination, as by a task, thought, sensation, or a book we read.

To explain the function of attention, he begins by showing how even finer and more productive kinds of work must be regarded as forms of fascination, even if attention has a direction for a certain period of time, such as demanding manual work or giving a speech. Obviously rooted in Fourth Way school terminology and Ouspensky's *In Search of the Miraculous*, he refers to how the ordinary expenditure or diffusion of this

---

[1] Rodney Collin, *The Theory of Celestial Influence* (London: Vincent Stuart Publishers Ltd, 1958), p210.

fine matter can be categorised in three different ways. Attention can float from object to object, captured through attraction or held in a desired direction within a limited time. The reason why they must all be characterised as mechanical is that the degree of attention is only sufficient to be able to relate to one thing at a time.

> *He can be aware either of the person to whom he is speaking, or of his own words, he can be aware of someone else's distress, or of a pain in his own body; he can be aware of a scene or of his own thoughts. But except on very rare occasions he is not aware simultaneously of his own words and the person to whom he is addressing them; of his own pain and someone else's; of a scene and his thoughts about it. Thus all man's awareness in his ordinary state may be classed as 'fascination'. For either becoming aware of some outside phenomenon he loses awareness of himself; or becoming aware of something in himself he loses awareness of the outside world – that is, he becomes 'fascinated' by one thing, inner or outer, to the exclusion of everything else.*[1]

As an example of an exception to the usual lack of divided attention, Collin points to certain circumstances where the extraordinary power of sensations is associated with love and sex. He characterises such experiences as a foretaste of the next consciousness. Through intentionally dividing the attention between oneself and the outside world, the fine matter of awareness is prevented from straying off in one direction, and can provide a very concrete experience of thinking, feeling and acting in relation to the world outside oneself, and thus one can gradually learn to remember oneself. What was initially only a moment, through effort can increase in frequency and duration.

One of several strange aspects of self-remembering Collin mentions is that no one can attempt to practice it until they have had it explained. Nor can it be repeated or sustained without effort. Moreover, if one forgets the idea of divided attention or self-remembering, no other type of effort can prevent one from sinking back into a state of fascination, where again attention can be related only to one thing at a time.

He points out that even if one brings close attention to tasks such as physical awareness of one's body, deep emotions, visualisation or mental exercises, it may not result in divided attention and self-remembering, because all this can be practiced with one-sided attention. In other words, one can be fascinated by a task.

[1] Rodney Collin, *The Theory of Celestial Influence* (London: Vincent Stuart Publishers Ltd, 1958), p212.

Finally, Collin highlights a curious psychological trick derived from Ouspensky's *In Search of the Miraculous*. If one associates self-remembering with something one has previously heard or come across the moment one is first presented with the idea, the experience of the content of the idea will be impossible. It simply loses its power and the idea disappears. Only under the assumption that the idea is allowed to appear brand new and at the same time is taken seriously will it be able to produce a condition that envisages life in a whole new way.

Collin says that the feeling man has, when he first comes across the idea that self-remembering is the answer to all life's challenges, is both right and wrong. If he masters practicing self-remembering, everything will look different. The problem, however, is that he does not adequately see his inherent resistance and lack of capacity. To be able to remember himself permanently, or even regularly, requires significant upheaval in a person's life. He must not only forsake his register of negative emotions and all kinds of fears, but also all that helps to make him feel comfortable with things the way they are. But first and foremost, the wish to be able to remember himself must be permanent. Such a reconstruction involves being able to endure oneself and others, no matter how painful and demanding it will turn out to be.

Another fundamental predisposition Collin highlights is an exaggerated belief in the ability to change oneself, others, or a situation. The ability to remember oneself decreases proportionally with the amount of effort one makes to maintain such a self-image.

He also does not hide that this is a years-long work, which in time will prove to be more possible if one divides the attention in three. He clarifies his illustration of what he calls full self-remembering using the law of three, in which any result or phenomena requires three powers.

In this model, one's organism faces the immediate situation to which it is exposed, while under the influence of something at a higher level than itself. As an example of what the third factor might be, he mentions, among other things, a teacher, one's school, the Sun, and some greater power in the universe, God. However, he clearly states that the responsibility for the design of such a third force is something that rests on the individual's shoulders.

As he further expands this perspective, he includes different worlds while complementing the triadic lawfulness:

> *Man's situation, his problems, surroundings, difficulties exist in the material, cellular world – this is passive force: the fine energy of consciousness directed by his attention exists in the molecular world – this is active force: and that which can resolve the eternal struggle between these two worlds can only derive from a yet higher world – the world of the Sun, the electronic world. Like sunlight which unites and interpenetrates everything, both creating and dissolving individuality, this third factor must be such that in remembrance of it the rememberer is united to his surroundings, he both acquires and loses separate individuality.*[1]

Whether self-remembering is related to external or internal tasks, what is important are the three aforementioned factors for a transformation, which in time can create a permanent crystallised vehicle of self-consciousness – a soul.

Rodney Collin's text on human psychology covers many topics which are central in Fourth Way psychology and his in-depth and detailed handling of subtle aspects deliver a substantial contribution. For example, his triadic perspective on self-remembering opens the door to all six processes. It is in this context that he highlights that self-remembering for regeneration is the only true form:

> *... man must place those hidden and higher powers first, himself and his soul passively at their service, invoking as result that plentitude of life and light to which alone this process yearns.*[2]

He has a number of distinctive approaches in his in-depth examination of the relationship between self-remembering and memory. If one sees a person's life as a circle, ordinary memory is an impulse that only moves in one direction in time and that occurs provided that there is a certain degree of consciousness. Memory can therefore be said to be an element of potential self-remembering. Collin develops a perspective based on this. Relative to the human's one-dimensional physical lifeline, his essence is two-dimensional in the sense that it brings all the points in his lifeline together simultaneously, whereby a surface is created. Relative to this surface, the human soul will appear as a three-dimensional solid:

---

[1] Rodney Collin, *The Theory of Celestial Influence* (London: Vincent Stuart Publishers Ltd, 1958), p215-216.
[2] Rodney Collin, *The Theory of Celestial Influence* (London: Vincent Stuart Publishers Ltd, 1958), p216.

... it would not only connect all the different points of his life and all the surface of his essence, but it would join these two quite other possibilities and forces existing in another dimension.[1]

Further in his perspective, Collin imagines that a human being at a given time is conscious, depicting its circular lifeline as a warm point that spreads in both directions. Due to limitations in our perception, which always moves forward, memory will be linked to the past. The further one moves away from the moment of the aforementioned consciousness, the weaker this impulse will appear. He highlights that a common notion of memory is that it crumbles and disappears on an equal footing with other material objects. However, according to Collin, memory is a phenomenon that is not subject to the laws of time. When memory is lost it may be due to negligence or starvation. He characterises such causes as passive.

Memory is actively replaced through imagination and lying. Collin further explains that memory lost by negligence remains intact but hidden and therefore recoverable, while memory subjected to lying is permanently destroyed. Both lies and mechanical imagination create distortions. Once replaced by the warped version, the original impulse becomes unavailable.

In the same way that a free blood circulation has implications for the organs of the body, Collin argues that a free circulation of memory in the long body of man has implications for the health and growth of essence.

The periods or individual events in one's life that one does not want to remember can contribute to blockages. Such obstructions can only be deliberately corrected by will and understanding. It is possible to consciously re-enact a scene from the past by attentively unrolling memory and keeping attention in one's senses, including moods. However, this does not mean that missed opportunities or other missteps are corrected. It only means that through the intentional use of imagination one has re-established consciousness in the past. If sufficient points in a person's circle of life become 'heated' by consciousness, Collin imagines that essence is affected and even, over time, the substance of his soul:

Though of course the task of heating something of more dimensions from something of less – a disc from a wire, or essence from personality, for instance – must be an immense one. If further, heat were to be transferred from the surface of essence to the solid of the soul, the same disproportion would be apparent. In fact, such a method of heating is

---

[1] Rodney Collin, The Theory of Celestial Influence (London: Vincent Stuart Publishers Ltd, 1958), p216.

manifestly impractical. And in the same way, the idea of creating consciousness in the soul exclusively from below, so to speak, runs counter to all human belief and all human experience.[1]

It is through man's own efforts to become conscious that Collin sees the possibilities of coming under the influence of a consciousness from above. If even just the idea of consciousness penetrates into the essence of man, it may be sufficient for it to tirelessly seek help in people who are more conscious than himself.

Even the man who has only acquired the most basic traits of the soul can, in his view, be put in touch with an unlimited cosmic creative energy that is a source of heightened consciousness. The soul can bring man to an association with matter in the molecular state and thereby the infinite world of molecular energy. It can be argued that an analysis of structure is not the description of the state of things. In this case, however, Rodney Collin's thoughts and ideas were rooted in his own experiences and were impacted by his close and dynamic relationship with Ouspensky which spanned many years. The importance of this relationship can shed light on the apparent paradox that the man who can do nothing by himself nevertheless must do everything by himself. Ouspensky's influence provided Collin with the opportunity to develop his consciousness himself.

As for the effect of different levels of consciousness, then moments of consciousness in the circle of the body of life will result in a stronger memory in the remaining part of life, and will theoretically create impulses that move backwards in the direction of the moment of birth. However, the effect of consciousness that has begun to penetrate essence has different characteristics. In addition to having a certain duration, it has the corresponding reliability, in that it exhibits a stability which means it cannot abruptly disappear. In Collin's terminology, it will radiate heat in all directions within the sphere of essence. A consequence of this, as exemplified by Collin's experiences with Ouspensky, is described as follows:

... the contact or presence of a man with such an essence may actually increase the awareness of those who come within his sphere of radiation or influence.[2]

---

[1] Rodney Collin, The Theory of Celestial Influence (London: Vincent Stuart Publishers Ltd, 1958), p219.

[2] Rodney Collin, The Theory of Celestial Influence (London: Vincent Stuart Publishers Ltd, 1958), p220.

For a human being with a soul, or an inner substance that has become warm, consciousness has become permanent and gained an ability to radiate over an extensive area. Collin believed that man's true history was written by the influence that this latter has had. It is interesting to note how the relationship between quantity and quality appears in this perspective: they were few but they had decisive importance for millions.

Rodney Collin considered objective laws associated with the interaction of human types very important. There is very little to be found about essence types in mainstream Fourth Way literature. Since the Fourth Way is primarily an oral tradition, this complex aspect is more likely to have been transmitted verbally than through written sources.

Whereas literature on essence types is very limited, there is a voluminous selection of books on personality-types. Some might argue that is just as well, given the quality of this literature. It is typically schematically over-simplified and superficial which is probably because what is presented is:

> ... using the system of classification developed in Robert Burton's teaching.[1]

Robert Earl Burton is a self-styled figure who for years has been accused of tailoring the idea-material of Gurdjieff, Ouspensky and Collin to create and maintain a luxurious and lavish way of life. Countless scandals and accusations of financial and sexual misconduct place him in a special position in a pseudo Gurdjieffian context. Throughout the history of mankind, one can find examples of this phenomenon where an individual with a self-constructed power apparatus in form of a cult dominates their surroundings with one goal only: unhindered exploitation for egoistic aims. No matter how much Burton leans on Collin's texts as a source of inspiration, his lack of attachment to a true authentic line in the Gurdjieff tradition will colour his attempts to further develop these ideas.

Much of this "human-type" literature can simply be regarded as propaganda for Burton's 'Fourth Way Business'.

Ouspensky made his views on types clear in a meeting on Monday October 4th, 1937. He said:

> Study of types is impossible on our level. Full appreciation of types needs a different level.[2]

---

[1] Susan Zannos, Human Types: Essence & the Enneagram (Red Wheel / Weiser, 1997), p2.
[2] P.D. Ouspensky, A Record of Meetings (London: Penguin Books Limited, 1992), p144.

The Theory of Celestial Influence

In *Beelzebub's Tales to his Grandson* Gurdjieff also expresses the need to be 'woken up' before one could take advantage of the doctrine of types:

> ... the learned beings of the planet Earth of that time were very well aware of what is called the 'law-of-typicality,' and that the three-brained beings of their planet are ultimately formed into twenty-seven different definite types, and also in which cases what had to be perceived and how it had to be perceived, and how they had to manifest themselves.[1]

Although Collin was aware of the history of theories of types, from Hippocrates to William Sheldon, they appear to have had no significance for him. There is no doubt that Ouspensky was resentful of revealing detail of his knowledge of types. It is also equally certain that someone from his innermost circle, in the period just before he died, was well versed about essence types. We have already seen that when Miss. R., with pen and paper, attempted to figure out the order of types present in the room, Ouspensky sharply interjected with Miss Q's missing place in the enneagram circle. This incident is a concrete example of how he conveyed knowledge of types even after he refused to respond to ordinary communication. The following can shed light on his attitude to and advice on how to approach the labyrinth of types:

> Miss S.: *When you like or dislike a complete stranger, has that anything to do with type?*
>
> Mr. O.: *No, only imagination. In most cases based on associations.*
>
> Miss S.: *But can we ever see type?*
>
> Mr. O.: *We can sometimes, but that is quite a different question. For instance, you can have experience of certain types and when you meet them a second time or a third time, you may recognise them. That is the only way we can come to an understanding of types. Suppose you knew somebody and saw how they act in certain circumstances. Later you meet somebody you think is like them and then you find him in the same circumstances and you see he acts in the same way. That means you will have guessed right.*[2]

Without examining the necessity of a requisite level in order to study types, we can be sure that part of such limitations relates to the lack of insight into the existence of rampant imagination and associations.

---

[1] G. Gurdjieff, All and Everything (London: Routledge & Co, Kegan Paul Limited, 1950), p468.
[2] P.D. Ouspensky, A Record of Meetings (London: Penguin Books Limited, 1992), p207.

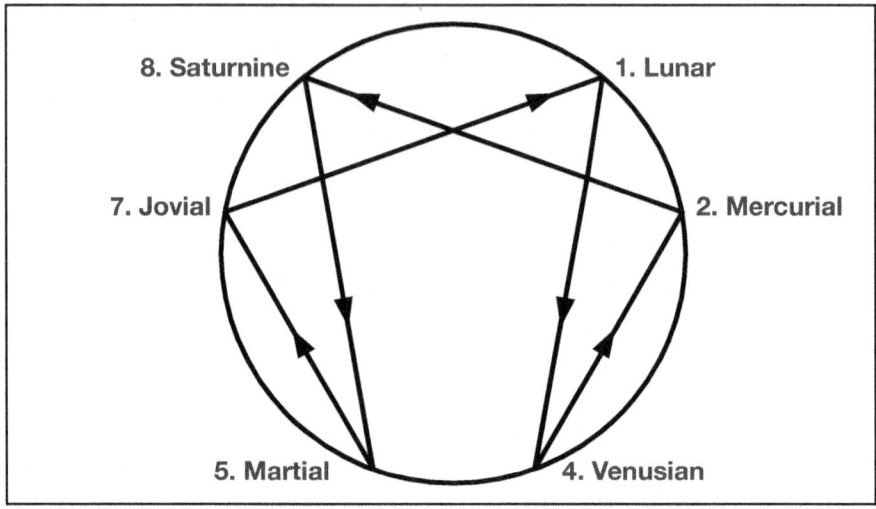

Figure 4. The Enneagram and Planetary Types

By applying the nine point circle that he had previously used as a template for the location and relationships of the planets, he introduces a model that both represents mankind and at the same time corresponds with the different planetary types (see *Figure 4*).

In the same way that the inner circulation represented an order of place and circulation of light in the original model, the same points now represent an order of types and the movement among them.

Because the inner movement does not follow the outer circle that represents time in the linear sense, it becomes clear that the circulation of types is neither temporary nor something that develops in time. At the same time, this movement visualises how circulation brings all parts and ages of the life of humanity together and forms a unity. For the individual, this inner movement represents the possibility of escaping from the limitations related to individual type by breaking the seals of other types and acquiring different characteristics absent in mankind in the form of types:

> *The obstinate lunar type must acquire the warmth and sympathy of the venusian: the lazy venusian must cultivate the quickness and agility of the mercurial: the restless mercurial must learn the breadth and wisdom of the saturnine: the introspective saturnine must achieve the courage and vigour of the martial: the destructive martial must acquire*

the ease and attraction of the jovial: and the intriguing jovial must relearn the cool instinctive certainty of the lunar – on a higher level.[1]

Collin suggests that this movement is of a cosmic nature, that the various characteristics are defunct in the individual as tendencies, and that if one can take advantage of them it implies a personal progression:

... the first commandment on the way of development is for man to free himself from pretense and imitation, discover how he reacts, discover the nature of his type, and try to live accordingly. He must learn to be himself.[2]

A necessary key for a proper understanding of essence-types is that all are necessary, that no type is better than another or in any way beneficial in terms of development. In other words all types are equal, in the sense that they have the same potential. When one can put aside notions of preference, there is only one thing that stands out as significant: to become one's own type – completely. The path to such insight, however, is as fraught with challenges as most others.

Because pure types are very rare, Collin's approach is to envision that one's type possesses parts of the type that lie in front of and after one's own. The center type becomes the center of gravity rather than appearing as an exclusive single type. For example, Saturn has Mars ahead and Mercury behind and Venus is surrounded by Mercury and Lunar.

Surprisingly Collin does not mention that the combination of types is confined to a limited order in the enneagram. Through this approach it may be possible to verify aspects of the doctrine of types. For example, one does not find a Saturn with physically congenital Venusian features, or a Jovial with the attributes of a Mercury, etc. Such diametral contradictions are self-explanatory.

The three points 9-3-6 in the enneagram that are not directly affected by the internal circulation, represent the three types of nutrition, food, air and impressions, required by any individual, whether conscious or not. However, it is only when a human being becomes conscious of himself that these nutrients can be absorbed consciously.

For digestion to be complete, circulation through types has to contribute to types that need to become more visible becoming visible, or, depending

---

[1] Rodney Collin, *The Theory of Celestial Influence* (London: Vincent Stuart Publishers Ltd, 1958), p223.

[2] Rodney Collin, *The Theory of Celestial Influence* (London: Vincent Stuart Publishers Ltd, 1958), 223.

on type, becoming less demonstrative and less visible. In other words, self-consciousness and deeper understanding lead to a movement where one comes out of oneself, while at the same time penetrating deeper into one's higher parts. Through an ongoing accumulation of consciousness and acceptance of one's type, not least seeing the necessity of dying to sides of it, one can not only acquire necessary and deeper characteristics but also discover that this movement results in a reduction of limitations. Through work to accumulate experiences from different essence-types, experiences are gathered for the consciousness that are necessary bricks on the path towards the creation of a soul.

After his exploration of types in *The Theory of Celestial Influence*, Collin turns his gaze from human psychology to the shape of civilizations. From considering different types as functions in the cosmos of man, he turns his attention to a detailed study of human society. His first proposition is that the cells of civilization are made up by individual men. Collin again faithfully follows an analogous method, which not only turns out to be accurate, but also helps to connect different parts of the material he processes.

Farmers and workers are associated with cells in the digestive system that prepare nourishment for a holistic organism. As blood cells distribute important products to all parts of the body, traders are seen as a similarly important function in human society. In this perspective, the function of every cell in the human organism parallels human functions or professions within the organism of civilization. This idea was not Collin's own, but one he drew from the founder of cellular pathology, Rudolf Virchow, who had disappeared in the wake of the criticism he faced from the then positivist scientists. They had summarily characterised and dismissed Virchow's idea as too 'picturesque'.

Ouspensky, by the way, was strongly critical of elements of the positivism's ethos. In particular that something is explained ipso facto if it is reduced to its simplest element, an argument which is nowadays termed reductionism. Collin, however, with his previous experiences with the analogous method, had no qualms about adopting Virchow's view.

As an example of how individual man acts as a cell in a civilization, he highlights the caste system. Although this has both been distorted and perverted, he claims that in its original form it had true features. As specific examples he mentions medieval castes of priesthood, knighthood, burghers and peasantry, but also Hindu castes of brahmins, kshatriya, vaisyas and sudras.

The role that inheritance plays within the various castes becomes, through Collin's depiction, almost a template for the health of this tradition. When factors such as personal characteristics trump inheritance and help individuals move from one caste to another, he points to an element that ensures the system's functionality. He exemplifies that both in the twelfth-century Europe and in first-century Rome, such transitions were possible for individuals who were not only ambitious enough, but were also willing to accept greater responsibilities. The impossible barriers of exclusive castes, on the other hand, are characteristics of a lackluster functional ability in a society that has grown so rigid that change is the only natural resort.

Another sobering implication of this idea is the parallel he draws between how a civilization can be characterised by a singular function, in the same way that a human can be characterised by his instincts where food and drink are central, or by motor function where movement, travel and activity dominate. Likewise, man can also be guided by thoughts and theories or be dominated by his emotions:

> *It is possible to think of peasant-ruled states such as Albania; of merchant-ruled states such as 19th century England; of warrior-ruled states such as Sparta; and of priest-ruled states such as ancient Egypt, the Cluniac monastic empire in the 12th century, and modern Tibet.*[1]

In the same way that a human being can be under the influence of a developed reason and finer emotions, a civilization can be marked by healthy functions. Conversely, anything from a degenerated intelligentsia, a corrupt priesthood, a criminal proletariat or criminal politicians, will align to a human ruled by physical or mental illness. When Collin collects the threads, it provides an overview of the information, but also allows for new and often surprising perspectives:

> *Theoretically, however, we may say that – although each civilization will have its own special tastes, capacities and understandings – the perfect civilization would be one in which the different functional groups were arranged in an ascending hierarchy according to the fundamental fineness of the energy with which their duties were concerned. As we saw in human physiology, the function of breathing works with finer matter than that of digestion, blood circulation with higher matter than respiration, and the various nervous systems with*

---

[1] Rodney Collin, The Theory of Celestial Influence (London: Vincent Stuart Publishers Ltd, 1958), p229.

still more refined energy. By objective measurement the functions arrange themselves in this order. So with the functional groups of a civilization. Whether any such objective or organic order of castes has ever historically been achieved is of course a different and very doubtful matter.[1]

Here we see how Rodney Collin, firmly rooted in a scale of value demonstrable through human physiology and an analogue perspective, does not deviate an inch from his ideal human vision.

In order to clarify certain principles, Collin addresses the question of whether a state is ruled by one or another group. It is important to note that it is civilization and not the state that is the organic being. Whether or not a state can approximate a cosmos, a true civilization always corresponds to a cosmos. Whereas a state can, but doesn't have to, depend on conscious beings, a civilization cannot be founded without them.

When the English historian, Arnold Toynbee, wrote his twelve-volume analysis of the growth and fall of civilizations, it was considered a complex synthesis of world history. Toynbee's belief that ideas and methods to meet the challenges of a society stemmed from a creative minority that was later copied by a majority matched Rodney Collin's perspectives in several ways. Even though he had certain objections, there is no doubt that Toynbee's historical analysis was of importance to Collin's work in time-fixing and synchronising historical periods. For example, Toynbee traced the beginning of Western European civilization back to the time of Charlemagne in the 8th century, which Collin considered to be too early. Another aspect that obviously violates Toynbee's view is that Collin believed some civilizations were re-born several times, as indicated by certain heredity characteristics.

Collin compares the few people who gain decisive influence and represent the conception of a new culture with the sperm that, in collaboration with the ovum, facilitates the creation of a human being. Just as not all fertilisable sperm lead to fertilisation, he considers people with a similar level of being to those performing a crucial role to be significant:

... if they do not generate the culture, they heighten its tone, vivify and regenerate it, exactly as does abundant sex energy within the body which produces it.[2]

---

[1] Rodney Collin, *The Theory of Celestial Influence* (London: Vincent Stuart Publishers Ltd, 1958), p229.
[2] Rodney Collin, *The Theory of Celestial Influence* (London: Vincent Stuart Publishers Ltd, 1958), p231.

Collin aligns the difficulties of studying a the history of a foetus earlier than about eight days with the difficulties of being able to attribute the formation of a civilization to an individual. An interesting observation he expresses is that the more significant the individual is to the origin of a civilization, the more invisible he becomes historically. It is no coincidence that he uses Jesus Christ as an example, because for Rodney Collin he was the foremost of all founders. In order to gain a more holistic grip on Collin's understanding of the nature of civilizations, it is useful to familiarise oneself with his premises for inferences and assumptions:

> *If one higher man is to a civilization as the reproductive-cell is to human life, then we should expect a similar multiplication of the different phases of the life-cycle proportionately from one organism to the other. In man, gestation, childhood and the full term of life last 10, 100 and 1000 lunar months respectively. Continuing this logarithmic progression, we may propose 100, 1000, and 10,000 lunar months (or roughly 8, 80 and 800 years) as the corresponding phases of a culture. Remembering that the first phase or period of gestation is the 'invisible' one, passed in the mother's womb in the case of the embryo, and in some hidden incubation – in a monastery, in the desert, in some hidden 'school', or with some teacher in exile – in the case of the founder of a culture, then we see that these periods do appear probable enough.[1]*

Based on the aforementioned logarithmic progression, Collin concludes, among other things, that the period which inaugurates a culture by the founder inaugurating his inner circle of students or disciples into certain basic ideas takes eight years. As an example of formulations of doctrine within such a period of gestation, Collin refers to the law of Solon, the Gospels and the Koran, from the Greeks, early Christians and Arabs, respectively. The period when such basic ideas first find a physical expression, and which Collin also characterises as 'the lifework of the founder's immediate circle', is also eight years by his calculations.

It is behind this material, in the childhood of a civilization or its formation of personality, that he claims one can find knowledge of an esoteric nature.

To illustrate how an extraordinary cultural resurgence could take place over a strikingly short period of time, and then, at the height of its heyday, be wiped out, he references the replacement of Pythagorean culture in the

---

[1] Rodney Collin, *The Theory of Celestial Influence* (London: Vincent Stuart Publishers Ltd, 1958), p231.

sixth and fifth century B.C. by Romanesque civilization because there simply was not enough room for them both.

When a civilization loses its last remnants of connection to its original meaning and purpose it dies and all that remains are memorials of a bygone era. Collin regarded our Gothic cathedrals as such fragment of a once-living past.

Reminded that the length of a human life may be under planetary influence, he questioned whether a civilization's lifetime corresponds with some great cosmic rhythm. Collin believed Napier Shaw, the English scientist, expressed such a rhythm in his attempt to establish a timescale for the rise and fall of civilizations:

> *A period which embraces almost exactly an integral number of days, years, Sunspot periods and all the various lunar revolutions, would include almost everything external which can be thought of as affecting the earth's atmosphere. Such a period is 372 years... one half of a still longer period of 744 years.[1]*

The delay started after 372 years, or half of what was considered the full lifespan of a civilization, which aligned with his previous findings regarding a person's lifespan, where the logarithmic slowing down meant that less and less took place in each subsequent year. One reason why such a sliding transition may not be obvious is that the original and the foregoing came in the shadow of the dynamic and forceful actions of the new generation. As an example, based on his own time, Collin wrote:

> *... although the Renaissance Civilization is but four centuries old, its outlook and institutions are already half-eclipsed by those of its as yet unnamed successor.[2]*

On the other hand it does not seem to have surprised him that history connects two or three independent cultures together, not noticing that they have separate beginnings, careers and endings. The interlacing of the Early Christian, Monastic Christian and Medieval Christian civilizations is just one example of a cluttered relationship that illustrates how a culture can appear longer than it really was.

In the cases where one culture grows out of another, Collin believed that it is a phenomenon that takes place in a culture's third and fourth century.

---

[1] Rodney Collin, *The Theory of Celestial Influence* (London: Vincent Stuart Publishers Ltd, 1958), p232-233.
[2] Rodney Collin, *The Theory of Celestial Influence* (London: Vincent Stuart Publishers Ltd, 1958), p233.

He regarded such an event as analogous to the begetting of a human child, where the parents have reached an exceptionally high level and the child represents their highest achievable product.

As an example of how a new culture can originate from the previous, he refers to Medieval Christian culture, which in the eleventh century sprang out of Monastic Christian culture, through the influence and knowledge of the Mohammedan culture that expanded in Spain and the Middle East.

Perhaps not surprisingly, Collin believes that the birth of a culture is the same as any other birth; the ground must be fertile and otherwise possess all the feminine factors that make birth possible. On the other operational factor, he writes:

> *What we cannot calculate or foresee, however, is the active element in this begetting of a culture, the masculine germ. For, as we said, this can only come from a very high level of esoteric school, and in the person of an actual and extraordinary man – a founder of conscious spirit. Such impregnation we cannot simulate. We can only wait and watch, assured by history that somewhere and somehow the birth of a new culture must already be prepared.[1]*

Earlier, when we referred to Collin's ideas about the essence and soul of man, we saw that essence was the total amount of blood in his full life span, while the soul was the total number of moments in which he was conscious. To address the question of a culture's essence and soul he carefully considers the three traditional paths through which man should be able to learn to raise his own consciousness and develop an individual soul. A significant contribution to elucidating these questions is found in his own need for a fourth and alternative path, a path he himself followed.

Collin admits it is not easy to define the essence and soul of a culture. At the same time he points specifically to the keys to such an understanding: the monuments of a civilization, its institutions, laws and literature, as well as its way of conveying its ideas. The most obvious and least obscure essential qualities, he believes, are found in the poetic and artistic forms of expressions of a civilization, but also in its ideals, manners, clothing and weaknesses.

The cathedrals of Medieval Christian civilization, its ecclesiastical organisation and, not least, its dissemination of ideas through architecture,

---

[1] Rodney Collin, *The Theory of Celestial Influence* (London: Vincent Stuart Publishers Ltd, 1958), p234.

sculpture and rituals, are examples of Collin's rich and diverse illustrations of how different essences express themselves.

Referring to similarities found in civilizations widely separated by time and space he wrote:

> *There is a striking resemblance in the 'taste' of the times, for example, between the Parthian culture of the first centuries of our era and the early feudal age in Western Europe – both civilizations of hard-riding knights, of chivalry, of courts held in tents, and of a violent emotional people, at one moment passionately devoted to battle and the next to flower-gardens. Or again, between the Roman Empire of the second century and the British Empire of the nineteenth. The same essence expresses itself in characteristic literature. Think of the essence of the culture behind 'Beowulf' or the 'Chanson de Roland', for example, in contrast to that behind Shakespeare on the one hand or behind Tolstoy's 'War and Peace', on the other. All these works are lasting, they belong to all humanity. At the same time they are perfect expressions of the essence of one particular civilization at one particular age. Yet we must not be diverted here by difference arising from the age of a culture, for its essence is that which connects all its ages, which remains constant throughout its whole existence.[1]*

Through painstaking analysis, he shows how a human inherits culturally conditional essence influence over a period of seven hundred years, or twenty generations, which means that a human being has descended from a million individuals. According to Collin, this essence is in-born and permanent in the nature of culture; an essence in which each individual participates directly. Extending his analogy between individual man and culture, he concludes that it is the totality of the blood of a culture that is its essence.

Collin uses his analogue method with man as a starting point and concludes that the soul of a civilization is the sum of all human consciousness achieved within a culture. More specifically:

> *... at bottom, the soul of a civilization can be made of no other material than the souls of men, and that with which the souls of men connect.[2]*

---

[1] Rodney Collin, The Theory of Celestial Influence (London: Vincent Stuart Publishers Ltd, 1958), p236.
[2] Rodney Collin, The Theory of Celestial Influence (London: Vincent Stuart Publishers Ltd, 1958), p237.

Everything that lives and grows requires nourishment, including the soul of a civilization. In this context he introduces the three traditional paths through which man can learn to raise his consciousness that is the prerequisite for the development of an individual soul. The first of these roads is the path of the fakir, which is often associated with forms of asceticism. By mastering physical functions and pain, will is developed. This path, which requires neither understanding nor motivation, can, through bravery, contribute to the development of a soul.

The second way, which is characterised by coping with emotions, does not require understanding either, but here motivation is a decisive factor. Through the mastery of fear, fear is transformed into love. On this way, goodness becomes the key to a soul.

Mastery of the intellectual function is the hallmark of the third way. By transforming thoughts into understanding, purposeless thoughts become an indirect bridge to insights into patterns of cosmic laws. By considering the world according to higher principles, one escapes a subjective form of existence that is governed by likes and dislikes. By sacrificing self-deception, prejudice and inconsistency and by knowing the cause and motivations of one's actions, a soul can be created by wisdom.

The limitations and imminent dangers of these separate paths lie in the potential for different aspects of human structure to evade attention and remain an unexplored and undeveloped minefield. Collin offers possible examples of the desire of the past to remedy the aforementioned limitations. He regards the order instituted by Saint Francis as an attempt to unite asceticism with charity. Likewise, he considered the order instituted by Saint Ignatius Loyola as a combination of asceticism and philosophy, while the combination of philosophy and charity, he believes, can be demonstrated by Saint Vincent de Paul.

Compared to the three traditional ways, the fourth way is virtually invisible. In contrast to a one-sided focus, this doctrine requires that efforts simultaneously address moving, emotional and intellectual functions. In other words, a traveler on the fourth way must learn to be brave, good and wise. In the fourth way, for a long time, one incessantly loses one's grip and has to start over. This is a challenge one must also learn to accept in order to gradually move forward. In contrast to the other paths, where one withdraws from an ordinary way of life, the fourth way presupposes and encourages participation in everyday life.

RODNEY COLLIN

From one of Collin's historical perspectives, we can also get an impression of how varied and fleeting this direction has appeared. He writes:

> *Thus schools of the fourth way were undoubtably behind the designing and construction of the great Gothic cathedrals, though they had no special name and adapted themselves to the religious organisation of the time. For a time the Cluniacs sheltered them, for a time the Freemasons. In the seventeenth century, similar schools were responsible for much of the new scientific and medical research, sometimes under one name and sometimes under another. In the eighteenth century again, fourth way schools borrowed many of the discoveries of Greek and Egyptian archeology to clothe their ideas and their organisation, while some of their leaders – in order to penetrate the luxury-loving and sophisticated circles where they had work to do – might even appear in the guise of fashionable magicians or mesmerists.*
>
> *The fourth way endeavors to introduce consciousness into all sides of life, and its form is always connected with that which is most new, with that which prepares the future.*[1]

Because the fourth way constantly appears in new suits, consistent with the circumstances in its time periods, it is not so obviously recognisable. However, all the paths share the same function with regard to the development of a person's soul, at the same time as forming the nutritional basis for the soul of the culture in which it works.

As we have seen, Collin had a tendency to question almost anything and everything he encountered. We should therefore not be surprised that he draws attention to how, in the wake of the emergence, content and maintenance of culture, it is also diminished, narrowed and possibly crippled. Collin sought to access the soul of different cultures by identifying a culture's view of the universe. In terms of how one cosmos is merged into another, he forms a scale of value that makes it possible to identify their different God images. Beginning with how the infinite number of galaxies is contained within the Absolute and how the galaxies contain innumerable suns, he proceeds all the way down to the electronic level. Man's conception of God has at all times varied, not only from one culture to another, but also from man to man within one and the same culture.

---

[1] Rodney Collin, The Theory of Celestial Influence (London: Vincent Stuart Publishers Ltd, 1958), p241.

THE THEORY OF CELESTIAL INFLUENCE

Whenever the idea of an absolute of absolutes has been the basis for an attempt at a god-perception, this abstract idea was forced to develop into a more tangible context, because neither worship nor study are possible without names and images. Even when a galactic absolute formed the basis for godly image, as in the example of the Egyptian Khepra, portrayed as the creator of gods, the concept remains inaccessible to the everyman and, according to Collin, becomes available only to a priesthood or the Brahmin caste. However, when the level of the Sun forms the basis of a deification, humans may have a greater ability to experience a living relationship with the absolute:

> *Men can feel the warmth and light of the Sun, understand their utter dependence on it, intellectually study its nature, and emotionally rejoice in it as the source of life, seasons, the beauty of colour...*[1]

As concrete examples of gods on such a level, he referenced the Ra of Egyptians, the Apollo of Greeks and the Tonatiuh of the Mexicans.

As examples of degenerative aspects, he draws attention to how cultures declined in terms of what they perceived as the Absolute. In the late Greek and Roman world and the late Middle Ages, he highlights how planetary beings appeared as images of the Absolute. The pseudo-science of magic that arose from the 17th century sects, when planetary beings became the highest form of the Absolute, was a phenomenon that was associated with degeneration.

A culture associates higher powers with natural phenomena, such as thunder, rainforests and mountains, when their highest concepts are limited to the world of organic life. Referring to the worship of the Roman emperor and, more recently, Hitler, Collin clearly shows how worship of God can fall to a low point. The notion that microbes and bacteria transcend humanity or God is tied to the belief that the undeveloped human being can be the object of worship. Considering the body of civilization in a degenerative process according to the six processes, it becomes obvious that it is the triad of corruption that is in action, where a part of a whole acts without regard to the unity to which it originally belonged.

When examining the sequences or descent of civilizations, Collin was puzzled by significant differences in terms of ideal, capacity and understanding, despite the fact that the foundation sprang from the same

---

[1] Rodney Collin, *The Theory of Celestial Influence* (London: Vincent Stuart Publishers Ltd, 1958), p242-243.

racial stock. Even accounting for the psycho-social inequalities of Greeks, Romans, French and Italians, he does not find a satisfactory explanation for the significant difference in ideals and achievements. He was therefore prompted to investigate whether there could be a trace of any cosmic movement that could correspond to and explain these differences. Returning to his earlier calculations on the times of the universe, he saw that the time of a solar breath corresponds to the time it takes for Earth to shift its axis around a complete circle of fixed stars. The consequence of this is that the position of the Sun gradually moves through the whole cycle of the zodiac before returning to its original position after 25,765 years. This means that the celestial influence is an ever-changing influence that can affect cultures differently at different times. Collin seems particularly concerned with the emotional effect of this influence.

As he delves further into his timings, he finds that if the earthly hour of 20,150 years is considered an octave in which each note amounts to 300 years, then it corresponds to the period between the birth of a culture and its maturity. Through these calculations, he finds that in the last 2000 years of European history there is a theoretical chain of 84 different cultures which have been subject to different celestial influences.

According to Collin and backed up by archeological and geological records, a disaster took place on Earth. By his calculations, the galactic influences were the opposite to what they were in his day. He refuted Hans Hoerbiger and Immanuel Velikovsky's theories about the catastrophe in question, because they considered events in the Solar System to be random. In his opinion, such coincidences were as impossible as the collision of the internal organs of man. Anyway, for him this period raises questions that seem unanswerable and he concludes that an important key to human history has disappeared.

Among his extensive and detailed historical considerations, it is not surprising to find that his focus is predominantly directed towards the origins of man's search for his overarching cosmic position:

> *Somewhere between Altamira and Egypt, somewhere between 20,000 and 10,000 years ago, schools for the attainment of consciousness seem to have been established upon Earth. Somehow, men attracted the help of higher powers in the universe, were allowed to cooperate consciously in a cosmic scheme. This is the key which is lost. [...] When schools were first established on Earth, and began the immense task of opening the eyes of half-animal man to the nature of the universe and his*

possibilities in it, they must have acted openly. Such men could not have responded otherwise. School has been made invisible since. For some cosmic reason all traces of its first launching of conscious human effort have been wiped out. And ordinary man has been allowed, perhaps even encouraged, to think that he did everything unaided. This is part of his test, part of his possibility of reaching independent understanding.[1]

After noticing how artifacts from the Aurignacian period differed significantly from similar works in the Magdalenian era, Collin pondered whether human history corresponded to the development of human functions associated with the glands. The rough, static expression in the works of the Aurignacian period, which almost appeared anchored forever in the earth, in many ways aligned with the lymphatic world of Lunar, following Collin's conceptions. Likewise, he saw a connection with the thyroid-mercurial world and the violent motions of both humans and bison in their various actions to survive, masterfully depicted in Magdalenian artifacts.

He associated the slow building of civilizations of Egypt, Sumer and Ancient India with the parathyroid world of Venus. The subsequent table, representing human growth, which contains more examples than the ones we have chosen to mention here, takes us all the way to our own time. Although this is a very detailed model, there is no doubt that Collin was of the opinion that it was only in the basic phase and that it should be possible to develop it further.

When Collin considers the birth and re-birth of cultures in his descriptions of the sequence of civilizations, he emphasises not only that cultures replace cultures, but that they are nourished by an underlying esoteric source. Every time a new civilization saw the light of day, a reconstruction took place that meant that the needs of a new era were taken care of by a new form making a new beginning possible. But rather than seeing each civilization in a separate light and in contrast to the foregoing, Collin saw it all in a larger perspective: the life of humanity.

It is this holistic perspective that makes him emphasise the pulsating efforts that underpinned not only a renewal, but essentially a continuation of a new phase of human development. Thus, the beginning of a new culture, in his opinion, became a matter of life and death for the development of mankind.

---

[1] Rodney Collin, *The Theory of Celestial Influence* (London: Vincent Stuart Publishers Ltd, 1958), p248.

He indicates that the Greeks are the ancestral civilization of our Western culture. Although he does not dismiss past civilizations such as Egypt, Mesopotamia, India and China, he emphasises that they cannot be considered as belonging to the line of development of Western cultures.

Collin mentions Solon, Thale and Miletos in the context of the origins of our Western culture. However, he doesn't conclude what role they played and they appear as obscure figures in a shadowy landscape.

He seemed confident that the real founders and their impulses must have had their fertile ground in an already highly developed culture. Because the Egyptians had been in possession of a sufficiently concentrated body of knowledge, he believed that it was highly likely that the original impulse came from there. As an underlining of these assumptions, he reminds us that, according to Plato, Solon was taught by an Egyptian priest on a visit to Sais in 590 B.C. and, according to Clement of Alexandria, Pythagoras acquired his science from the same source.

When new directions in architecture and music appeared that reflected higher universal laws, Collin believed that the relationship between the Greeks and the instigators must have been of an esoteric nature. He also considered the growth of a civilization to be similar to that of the human organism, which follows a definite curve in which a single cell turns into millions.

It cannot have been surprising to him that the emergence of the new impulses resulted in the proportional reduction of Hellenisation. However, Socrates, Plato and Aristotle, by acting on the highest level of their culture, were able to introduce the balance necessary to avoid the emergence of destructive elements, a danger often latent in any significant process of change.

The Hellenistic culture ceased and no longer appeared as an independent organism when the Greek world succumbed to the new Roman civilization, after being overrun by the Goths. Collin compares this to how an old human gradually shrinks before coming to a complete stop. For him, the introduction to this new era is coloured by both doubts and facts.

When asked about the rise of Roman culture, he pointed to the fact that at the beginning of the fourth century B.C. the school of Epicurus at Samos existed, as well as the school of Stoics in Athens. However, it appears unclear to him who brought their knowledge to the city of Rome. On the other hand, he was well aware that, from its very beginning, the Roman civilization was under the influence of both Epicureanism and Stoicism.

THE THEORY OF CELESTIAL INFLUENCE

According to Collin's perspective, it was within the maturity of Roman civilization that the man historically known as Christ was conceived. Within a few years, his original activities had not only formed the basis of a subsequent civilization, but also erected a foundation of ideals that had the strength to penetrate all subsequent cultures.

A sea of inequalities separated the Roman culture from the Greek one. The construction of roads and aqueducts became its monument and replaced the Greeks' construction of temples. The design of law and regulations became a more important guide than the importance the Greeks had placed on art and thought. The Roman marching legions took the place of philosophy as an instrument of expansion.

We won't go into detail about all the background material that he laid as the basis for his illustration of the sequence of civilizations of Europe, which, according to the law of seven, he considered an octave. We will settle for summing up some of the most important aspects of this theory.

The Romans were followed by primitive or early Christians who, in addition to being particularly preoccupied with 'spreading the word', paved the way for what would be their monument, The New Testament, before it declined and degenerated about eight hundred years after its conception.

The next link in the chain of cultures is Monastic Christianity. From a small circle led by St. Benedict in 529, a reconstruction, adapted to a new era strong enough to cross the first interval of this historic octave, took place. Values from earlier times were preserved and hidden from the anarchy and ignorance that characterizes the violent dark ages:

> *The physical grandeur of the ancient world was as it were reduced to molecular scale, like memory in the cells of the cerebral cortex, against a time when it might manifest openly once more.*[1]

Then, in the midst of monastic activities, there were produced what Collin considered illuminated manuscripts. Undermined by the external joys of life and an inner decay, as well as an excessive degree of protection, a voice that no longer had a message gradually became silent.

The subsequent Medieval Christians created churches and cathedrals in the wake of new found hope with consequent energy and effort and, in addition, transmitted their ideas through rituals and sculptures.

By the eleventh century, another re-cultivation took place, with schools actively turning to the world that led to the realisation of Medieval

---

[1] Rodney Collin, *The Theory of Celestial Influence* (London: Vincent Stuart Publishers Ltd, 1958), p255.

Christian civilization. With the abbey of Cluny in Burgundy as a source of inspiration, in cities across Western Europe, buildings were erected that reflected a new image of the universe, often with significant contributions from Freemasonry. Under the influence of a reformed monastic system, anarchy and brutal violence loosened their previously firm grip, leaving room for new growth. Different schools with common interests ensured sophistication and breadth. In Chartres they cultivated the art of medicine, in Reims, music, while Mont St. Michel became the headquarters of astronomy.

Another expression of interrelationship can be found in the envoys of people from Chartres and Cluny to Arab Spain, who returned with newfound knowledge of algebra, logarithms, astronomy, alchemy and the Koran. The Cluniacs, otherwise undoubtedly the founders of pilgrimage, contributed not only to an opportunity to acquire new knowledge about art, agriculture and various skills but, according to Collin, could create a deeper personal foundation and understanding of the importance of inner work. This can be appreciated by anyone who, in their own inner workings, has verified the importance of remodeling one's own intellectual function, which, after all, is the place were ideas are kept, weighed and refined in different ways.

The inexorable hand of time once again confirmed that what has a beginning also has an end:

> *The world which it had brought to birth became racked by monstrous persecution, dogmatic quarrel, the Inquisition. Thought became frozen by superstition and scholasticism. As always, that which at the beginning had stood for all that was new and hopeful, itself tried to stamp out change. Latent pressure grew. And nine hundred years from its foundation, the mobs of the French Revolution wrecked the great Abbey of Cluny so thoroughly that hardly a trace of its magnificence remains.[1]*

With the Renaissance came universities and schools and a prevalence of ideas through printed writings and paintings.

Cosimo Medici, neither an abbot nor a priest but a wealthy Italian banker, became a central figure in the formation of the Renaissance. Surrounded by artists such as Donatello, Ghiberti, della Robbia, and Lippi, while also acquiring Greek and Latin writings, he laid the foundation for a

---

[1] Rodney Collin, *The Theory of Celestial Influence* (London: Vincent Stuart Publishers Ltd, 1958), p258.

significant and open library. Under his influence, scholars, originally associated with Emperor John Paleologus, were gathered, with the result that everything they had of significant importance was well preserved in Florence when the Emperor Paleologus of Constantinople saw the city fall into the hands of the Turks in 1453. In Collin's view, the emperor's schoolmen were reluctant to accept Cosimo's approaches because they needed protection for a tradition. About Cosimo himself, Collin was inclined to assume the banker was either already part of a school or was looking for one.

A significant collaborative project between the Medici family and the emperor's learned men was the Platonic Academy. Although we know that its main function was to teach Plato's philosophy and challenge the scholars to develop a new understanding of the universe, Collin clearly stated that in retrospect one cannot know what really took place. However, the Academy gained traction in literature through Politan and Mirandola and artistically through Botticelli and Veroccio. But it also had an impact on the Reformation in Germany through Reuchlin and in London with the creation of the College of Physicians.

Collin mentions Leon Battista Alberti, not only as a father of the Renaissance architecture, but also as a concrete example of how the Renaissance could draw impulses from earlier times. Through one of the academy's teachers, Ficino, Alberti found inspiration to base his architecture on the divine proportions and the Pythagorean system of numbers. This was an important and formative phase of this historical period. Not on only did it connect figures like Michelangelo and Leonardo da Vinci while they were still very young, but with its technical innovations, art, ideals and perspectives on the concept of freedom, it had an almost invaluable impact on Western culture.

Collin calls the period from 1859 to 2636 the Synthetic. He describes this period, which includes Collin's and our own, as one in which ideas are transmitted through radio and cinema, and electromagnetic apparatus appear as the monuments. This was accurate for his time and now, many years after his death, we could make certain additions, but still not of such a nature that it would outdate his original ideas. Not only does Collin point out how one culture is based on another, but also that the source itself is of an esoteric nature.

In Collin's opinion, Ouspensky's dying admonition that everything had to be reconstructed in a larger context is also, to a significant extent, a legality that applies to a birth of a new civilization. Can Ouspensky's

307

abandonment of the system be seen as the creation of a seed that had the potential to contribute to a new civilization? Collin's hope for future generations clearly lies in our ability to embrace Ouspensky's message of reconstruction.

The planet we live on is threatened by the ignorance that is a consequence of the fact that so many of us have managed to evade a reconstruction. This is masterfully described by James George in *Asking for the Earth,* in which the Dalai Lama, in the foreword, points to the connection between the global crisis and an inner confusion.

Central to Rodney Collin's investigations of the characteristics of our culture were different aspects of time. In the same way the Renaissance, through the development of perspective-drawing, gave man the opportunity to project three dimensions through two dimensions, Collin believed a similar conquest of time would be the characteristic of the new era. Such a conquest would be its main feature and would contribute to its development. Around 1865, a number of technological innovations took place that in many ways would change people's relationship with time. Edward Muybridge's inventive experimentation with cameras placed in a row formed the origin of moving images, which could move not only at different speeds, but also backwards. This technical innovation, Collin argues, broke the illusion which man had lived with in time immemorial, that time moves in a uniform speed in one direction. When Graham Bell a few years later invented the microphone, man could reach innumerable people without the mediator of time, whereas before he was limited to a certain amount of people in a certain place. Before Edison invented the phonograph in 1877, it had been impossible to preserve sound-waves beyond the moment they reverberated.

As a result of these changes, Collin notes that mechanical movement implies time while, relative to human perception, electromagnetic movement is immediate.

The seed inventions of the Time-Age arose from the gradual discovery that mechanical motion and electro-magnetic motion were interchangeable. By changing electro-magnetic waves into mechanical motion, as in the cinema or phonograph, time was introduced where it had not entered before. By replacing mechanical motion by electro-magnetic impulses, as in the radio or telephone, phenomena were made instantaneous, which previously could only be accomplished by the aid of time. Even in medicine the replacement of natural drugs acting on the

organs by synthetic ones acting on cells, or by short-wave treatment
acting on molecules, was an attempt to speed up the process of healing
by transferring it to the faster time of a lower cosmos. All this implied a
new interchangeability between dimensions.[1]

Another characteristic feature of the new era that Collin points out as associated with the technological innovations of the time was the tendency for small federations to grow into larger units, as when Great Britain became united and Italy, Russia and Germany expanded.

This tendency appeared not only in the context of nations but could also be of a more local nature. In geographically limited areas where humans had previously found affiliation and identity in what was measured in terms of a day's journey, these were replaced as a result of the introduction of new forms of transport such as railways and eventually aircraft. As the world grew smaller, the original passionate patriotism was weakened, but at the same time it found new and expanded forms.

The creation of First International (International Workingman's Association) and the International Red Cross in 1864 are also examples of how former frontiers were overridden. Likewise, the formation of the International Postal Union in 1875. Around 1870, in the field of writing, there was a reconstruction of the past that clearly points in the direction of modern man. The young Nietzsche, the 42 year-old Norwegian writer Henrik Ibsen, Tolstoy, the somewhat older Victor Hugo, Hans Christian Andersen, Tennyson and Whitman all made mature literary moves that reflected a new era while revealing a connection to their homeland. The seriousness, breadth and depth of their writings led Collin to regard them as deeply religious people, liberatingly devoid of doctrines. Collin compared their influence in the contemporary political arena to the influence of the abbots and churchmen in the Gothic flowering.

Of the list of writers whom Collin considered more deeply religious, Walt Whitman is almost self-explanatory, however, for many the choice of Nietzsche is probably harder to understand. Not only because Collin fails to justify the choice, but because the perception of Nietzsche as a nihilist and if not the enemy of everything and everyone, then at least the enemy of morality and religion, is so widespread. We must therefore assume that Collin regarded Nietzsche's 'superman' and 'will to power' as his endeavor for a fundamental force that is laid down in man.

---

[1] Rodney Collin, *The Theory of Celestial Influence* (London: Vincent Stuart Publishers Ltd, 1958), p262.

An interesting perspective that comes to light when Collin compiles literature and economic theory also shows how his thinking and conclusions lean on different aspects of the six processes:

> ... *reconstructing the past is the first and essential step towards any real change in the future; as Karl Marx also realized when he prepared the way for bolshevism by reconstructing history on the basis of 'economic motive' and 'class struggle'. But Hugo, Andersen and Whitman worked upon time in the reverse way to Marx. Instead of eliminating the ideals which actually existed and ruled in the past, and replacing them with the lowest human motives of greed and violence, as he did, they attempted to put back into the past higher ideals than had actually prevailed there, or at any rate ideals more comprehensible to the new age. Thus their attempt, whether successful or not, was to regenerate the past, whereas that of Marx, again whether successful or not, could only serve to degenerate it.*[1]

Regarding the Church's role during this period, it was his conception that it was most concerned with preserving the purity of its rites and therefore did not assume a leading role in shaping the future as it had in earlier times. However, the freedom possessed by the poetic prophets of the time had the ability to create fertile ground for an openness and tolerance that enabled new thoughts and ideals to gain a sufficient foothold.

Another visible sign that the world had diminished was the growing public interest in religious texts from other regions. The German Oriental scholar Max Muller's initiative to process a number of Eastern holy writings meant that many gained access to Buddhist, Hindu and Zoroastrian texts, as well as books on Islam and a number of Chinese writings. A little after Muller introduced his ideas, in 1877, Madame Blavatsky established the Theosophical Society. With the idea that no religion is higher than the truth, she wanted to form a new synthesis that would unite different religious beliefs. When Dr. R. M. Buck in 1901 wished to create an objective psychology in which cosmic consciousness was central, it was a sign of the previous generation's ability to influence, but also an example of how this entire period stood before the ability to transcend the division of space by escaping the limitations of a one-dimensional time.

One of the major and underlying themes of Collin's studies of civilizations were questions related to the origins of the higher knowledge

[1] Rodney Collin, The Theory of Celestial Influence (London: Vincent Stuart Publishers Ltd, 1958), p265.

that nourished their design and content. In his opinion, the source of the rapid dissemination of ideas in the 19th century could be obscured, in that new ideas could be traced back to different sources, without any obvious means of communication.

However, one place that excelled, as we have mentioned before, is Rome. So many artistic works that would turn out to have future distinctive meaning were rooted there, both directly and indirectly. Collin does not seem to have any doubt that many of these works bore the hallmark of direct school knowledge. Goethe's complete reworking of Faust took place after his remarkable *Italian Journey* from 1796. Likewise, Collin highlights his *Theory of Colour* from the same period in Rome, where Goethe points out not only that light is the highest form of energy, but also that colours are corruptions or modifications of pure light. When the English poet Shelley, shortly after returning from Rome, expresses the same idea in one of his poems, Collin finds further support for the idea that Goethe, Shelley and others are pouring from the same source. He also found it striking that the German school of pre-Raphaelites originated in the same period which, incidentally, became the prelude to the English Brotherhood of pre-Raphaelites. As an artistic movement, it was not as unambiguous as one might infer from Collin's presentation. Their message was of both moral and artistic character and in that respect clear enough. They wanted to resurrect and embody the spirit of Christianity's original piety as it had flourished in the Gothic period.

Clark Maxwell's experiments in the 1860s, based on the new knowledge of electricity and magnetism, demonstrated various analogue connections between colour and sound and opened doors between rooms that previously had no connections.

The Rome-based group of Nazarenes, which we previously discussed in connection with Rodney Collin's search for traces of schools, was also under the influence of the new discoveries of the time. In their efforts to unite phenomena of the material and spiritual worlds, they leaned on newfound theories of light and vibration.

Collin highlights Henrik Ibsen's dramatic portrayal of Per Gynt, written near Rome in 1867, and Fredrick Nietzsche's *Eternal Recurrence,* written during his stay in Italy in 1881, as examples of the impact of new perspectives on the realm of time on literature. Obviously under the influence of the theory of electromagnetic vibration, Nietzsche refers to connections between human development, consciousness and recurrence. Collin suggests this work by Nietzsche had a decisive impact on Hinton and Ouspensky's contribution to a later reconciliation between modern science and the ancient ideas of eternity and regeneration.

Despite his year-long investigations and extensive collection of information, Collin acknowledges the limitations when it comes to drawing conclusions. The information he uses for his ideas, however, is consistent and well founded and forms the basis for his precise and simple statements:

> *Exactly what kind of a school existed in Rome between 1800 and 1880, from which so many creative ideas of the new age could emanate, we cannot know. Yet in all its traces we find the same understanding – light as the one creative and unifying force of the universe, the octave as the modification of pure light into form and colour, and time, recurrence, and the fulfillment of all possibilities as the three stages of man's ascent to the nature of light. So that if it be asked what is characteristic of the new age, and how may it be distinguished from the old, we can now answer: That which separates and divides belongs to the past. That which reconciles and unites belongs to the future. And the way towards unity lies through escape from time.*[1]

In Rodney Collin's presentations on the rise and fall of cultures, it is important to bear in mind that his underlying and fundamental attitude was that the perspectives he promotes were intended as background material for one's own observations, as only one's own observations and experiences can form the basis for an understanding that can be of real value. He stressed that this applied to his whole thesis. Not only do we hear an echo of Ouspensky's relentless imperative 'verify', but we are also face-to-face with the legality that is essentially the basis of transcendence from knowledge to understanding. Rodney Collin did not limit his own assessments. On the contrary. Therefore, those who attempt to familiarise themselves with the extensive and complex issues he raises will encounter significant challenges.

He forms his views on different cultures in the manner of an avid spectator to the large and small episodes of history. However, in order to embrace the breadth and depth of his insights, we must lift our gaze from a one-sided historical view and include a cosmos that holds more than just the events unfolding on our own planet Earth.

We will take a closer look at the details of human physiology, because they represent instruments designed to respond to and transmit functional

[1] Rodney Collin, The Theory of Celestial Influence (London: Vincent Stuart Publishers Ltd, 1958), p268.

mechanisms in the Solar System, more specifically movements and laws laid down in higher controlling cosmoses.

Collin has previously shown how different cosmoses align and how the parts of a smaller cosmos reflect and react to corresponding units in a larger one. As both man and planets are cosmoses, he considers the possible effect separate planets can have on man. We have also seen how the Solar System is identical to the glandular system, when unfolded in a spiral, and how this cohesion allows individual planets to control respective glands and thereby various functions of the human being.

As an example of the interaction between a planet and a human being, we find that the thyroid gland appears as the planet Mercury when one assumes that the human body is a replica of the Solar System. For Collin, Mercury seems to have a certain affinity to this gland and he assumes that it can control the function of voluntary muscular movement, including the ability to learn new movements and speed of reaction. Furthermore, he claims that the said muscle function is reflected in a scaled-down version in the head and facial muscles, the movements of which reflect a person's mental, emotional and physical life. It is through a similar and extended division of the head Collin bases his thesis that the thyroid gland, controlling the moving functions, is a consequence of a cosmic patten. He writes:

> ... the external forms of mouth, nose, eyes and ears are in their turn divided into three parts in which the intellectual, emotional and physical aspects of the corresponding functions are reflected. In the eyes, the shape and motion of the top lid particularly reflects the state of intellectual function, the eye itself the state of emotional function, and the lower lid the state of instinctive function. Similarly in the ears, the configuration of the upper part of the shell is connected with intellectual perception, of the entrance to the auditory canal with emotional perception, and of the lobe with instinctive perception. And again in the nose, exaggeration of the upper part represents predominance of intellect, of the middle part of emotion, and of the lower bulb and nostrils instinct: so that a straight nose, always regarded as a sign of beauty, in fact represents perfect balance between these three sides ... it is interesting to note that the skin is similarly divided into three different layers, with similar significance.[1]

---

[1] Rodney Collin, The Theory of Celestial Influence (London: Vincent Stuart Publishers Ltd, 1958), p271.

Another important aspect of the mouth, nose, eyes and ears is the distinction between relaxed, dilated and contracted state. The desire to limit the intake from the outside world is characterised by contracted state, while dilated state is an expression to the contrary. A more subtle aspect is the dilation of one orifice and the contraction of another. Collin claims this is the source of man's ability to discriminate and at the same time a source of the countless expressions that may result from different dilatations and contractions of the mouth, nose, eyes and ears.

He also suggests that varying degrees of contractions of the organs are connected with intellect, emotion and instinct. This is an indication of the thoroughness of his investigations. It is not possible to shed light on every detail of his thesis about the cyclic influence of the planets on the various glands and thereby their importance to human behaviour, however the following examples illustrate his diverse angles of attack.

The idea that the design of the body indicates different characteristics has probably followed man since time immemorial and has been emphasised to varying degrees throughout history. As far back as ancient Greece we find experiments in biological anthropology in Plato's 'scala naturae'. From a more recent time we have William Sheldon's somatotypes and constitutional psychology, a direction that was met with some interest in the 1950s, in which factors such as temperament, moral character and future potential were central. This theory has since been discredited.

Varying approaches have resulted in changing attitudes as to the importance of the body, which is at times completely disregarded. In sharp contrast to constitutional psychology, which considers behavior as a result of the body, we find psychoanalysis. Although it is doubtful whether we will find a psychoanalyst who will not admit that the body has its own language, it is equally doubtful they recognise the body as a cause in any context. There can be no doubt that Freud put language before body, in his theory that the solution to psychological problems lies in memory.

Although Collin makes no direct reference to historical sources regarding details of characteristic structures of the biological organism, it is reasonable to assume that some of the information originally came from Ouspensky. On the other hand, we have seen that his own capacity for reflection was astonishingly fertile and ingenious, above all in the way he handled the analogue method.

We have previously seen that Collin's attitude to astrology was characterised by scepticism about fortune-telling and prognostications, but that he was open to exploring its more fundamental features which he thought may have been lost. It seems likely that his research on physiognomy were connected with these investigations.

In order to prove the relationship between the moving function, the thyroid gland and the cycle of Mercury, it would be necessary to demonstrate how mankind as a whole was more operational, corporate, mobile and expressive at certain times within a timeframe of about three months. Collin believed that there were too many possible factors that would obscure such a short-term observation and concluded that Mercury's cycle was therefore unsuitable for his purpose.

Another and more general challenge encountered when studying planetary cycles is that one and the same phenomenon appears differently under varying circumstances:

> *It is a commonplace that men regard surgery or assault committed by an individual in one light, but surgery or assault committed by nations under the name of war in a quite different light. The scale changed, the phenomenon appears to our perception to be different in its nature.*[1]

Collin nevertheless believed that one could approach this problem through a well-founded knowledge of the functions of the individual human being and the effect of planetary stimulation on these functions. By utilising observations of individual man to develop a corresponding description of a more universal character, one can imply an image of the planetary cycle's ability to influence man.

For anyone who has studied different body/essence types, not only is Collin's argument credible but probably the most practical approach to verify the ability of planets to influence. The pattern of movement of a Mercurial type is so remarkably different from other types, not only in accordance with Collin's thesis about the properties of this planet, but so characteristic that it effectively eliminates the other types. It is, therefore, surprising that Collin does not mention the method of elimination as an indirect approach for verification.

Venus was the planet Collin associated with fertility. It is important to note that this was not limited to biological growth only, but also implicitly included the growth of communities in any biological form. Collin seems to think that one of the least intricate and recognisable impact-rhythms exists when parathyroid glands are under the direct and maximum influence of the planet Venus. Such a period will have consequences not

---

[1] Rodney Collin, *The Theory of Celestial Influence* (London: Vincent Stuart Publishers Ltd, 1958), p274.

only for the human organism, but also animals, fish, birds and plants in the form of increased growth of tissues. Referring to legend, he called such periods 'fat years' and the absence of such influence 'lean years'. Because an average person's lifetime is ten times longer than a Venus cycle, the effect of fecundity is distributed over a long period of time and is therefore difficult to detect.

Collin believed that, if his calculations were correct, lifeforms with an equal or longer life expectancy than the cycle would correspond proportionally to such a synodic period. It must have thrilled him when he discovered that the English zoologist, Charles Sutherland Elton, could demonstrate a distinct four-year rhythm of numbers, migration and epidemics among foxes and a variety of different rodents in distinct areas, such as Norway, Canada and Newfoundland.

Collin also drew attention to a 9⅔ year biological rhythm. This applies to the tent-caterpillar and chin bug, which attack fruit trees and cereals respectively. The same cycle was also detected among a number of animals, including Canadian lynx, muskrat and mink. It was also a pattern in the catching of salmon in New Brunswick. A rhythm he found particularly interesting, because it seemed to show an interrelationship between different scales, was built on the connection between the occurrence of ozone in the atmosphere and its stimulating effect on sex among all living creatures. Unfortunately Collin did not specify the scientific investigations that underlie this hypothesis, but gave the following elaboration:

> ... electronic radiation from the heavenly bodies produces molecular change in the Earth's atmosphere, while such molecular change in the atmosphere in turn produces cellular change in the organic bodies dwelling therein. In this way we can see the practical influence of celestial phenomena upon creatures living on the Earth's surface, and bridge the apparently insuperable gap between the movement of a planet and the individual impulses of a man, a salmon or a lynx.[1]

Regardless of what Collin's scientific sources were, if we take a closer look at some recent research about the relationship between ozone and fertility, we find several studies that support a correlation. An article published by Medical Gas Research refers to results that clearly indicate that ozone is emerging as a new adjunct therapeutic agent for female infertility.[2]

---

[1] Rodney Collin, The Theory of Celestial Influence (London: Vincent Stuart Publishers Ltd, 1958), p276-277
[2] Merhi, Zaher, et al. "Ozone therapy: a potential therapeutic adjunct for improving female reproductive health." Medical gas research 9.2 (2019): 101.

Another medical article concludes that ozone therapy may be beneficial for treating erectile dysfunction as a result of enhanced enzymatic activity in endothelial nitric oxide synthase levels.[1] Likewise, a botanical oil composition, including ozonated olive oil, is claimed to improve several aspects of men's sexuality from dysfunction to sexual arousal.[2]

However, the effect of ozone is ambiguous. A study conducted at the Max Planck Institute for Chemical Ecology on the question of how increased levels of ozone affect pheromone communication in different Drosophila species hypothesised that increased levels of ozone affected sexual communication in two ways:

> ...degraded pheromones might first result in lower levels of mating success within a population of a given species and second in the breakdown of mating barriers between closely related species.[3]

In his further investigations of a possible connection between the Venusian cycle of 585 days and the aforementioned cycle of 9⅔ years, he emphasised the diversity of rhythm that in itself reflects the infinite multitudes that form the variation of nature. Thus, it is useless to look for signs of increased fecundity by focusing only on the properties of parathyroid or other glands contributing to tissue-building. Collin identifies adrenaline as a contributor in a necessarily complex and multifaceted image that allows for and embraces the exchanges between different rhythms.

Cautiously leaning on his former reference to the legend of the fat and lean years, he wrote:

> Adrenal impulses by themselves, without the favorable conditions of 'fatness', tend to be sterile; while 'fatness' without the stimulation of mating resulting from adrenal activity, again fails to lead to prolific reproduction. So that if, as we supposed, the parathyroids are under the influence of Venus and the adrenals under the influence of Mars, we should expect conditions favoring fecundity to be produced when the maximum effect of these two planets coincided. The observed fecundity cycle of 9 2/3 years expresses just such a double conjunction. For at 3510 days the completion of six periods of Venus exactly coincides with the

[1] COLAKEROL, Aykut, et al. Effects of ozone treatment on penile erection capacity and nitric oxide synthase levels in diabetic rats. International journal of impotence research, 2021, 33.5: p1-8.
[2] Mansour, A., and Ammar Mansour. "A Botanical Nano Ozonated Erotic Oil Composition with Maximum Bioavailability for Men." MOJ Bioequivalence & Bioavailability 5.1 (2018): 29-31.
[3] Max Planck Center, How do increased levels of ozone affect pheromone communication in different Drosophila species?; Downloaded from https://www.ngice.mpg.de/8589/Project-6.

completion of four and a half period of Mars. The two influences 'shine together', so to speak, with the results which have been described and which we would expect.[1]

When Collin deepens his understanding of the relationship between the adrenals and parathyroids, the glands of passion and growth, emphasising that they are essentially of animal constitution, he draws on Huntington's previous observations. Huntington had discovered that the 9⅔–year cycle is not only gradually less distinct in the movement from mammals, insect and fish to trees and crops, but also in the opposite direction, from animals to human health. Therefore the circumstances that formed the basis of the cycle apparently had a particularly direct effect on animal vigour.

Collin believed that the cycle was difficult to recognise in the vegetable world due to it being overshadowed by stronger rhythms associated with lower functions, while a similar obscurity in regards to man was due to a mental and emotional modification in the form of reason, foresight, loyalty and aspiration. It is hardly surprising that he considered the latter to be a higher form of rhythm governing the mind and emotions. It was equally obvious that the features of this rhythm separated man from the animals and at the same time contributed to a flexibility in relation to the influential rhythms of Venus and Mars that formed the basis for his further individual choices.

Because all matter must follow its own inevitable laws, man as a cellular being can likewise not escape the growth and flux of cells associated with the Venusian cycle. However, Collin maintains it is possible for man to break out of a one-sided cellular existence and into a permanence beyond cycles. This potential, which resides within consciousness, opens the doors to what he calls a super cellular life.

Collin claims that humans, unlike animals, can develop a conscious relationship with the mechanical influence of Venus that otherwise constitutes an inescapable influence on all cellular life. One consequence of such an awareness is that, by becoming aware of the community he shares with plants and animals as a cellular being, man no longer considers them alien and incomprehensible. The appreciation of the beauty and wonder of the cellular world will also be an experience that in itself will help to increase the appreciation of the opportunity that lies in increased consciousness.

---

[1] Rodney Collin, *The Theory of Celestial Influence* (London: Vincent Stuart Publishers Ltd, 1958), p277.

Second in importance only to Jupiter, Mars was the most Roman of the gods. The origin of the name is disputed, but those who interpret the root of the word Mars to mean 'shining' view Mars as a solar divinity. However, Collin chose the traditional association of Mars as the god of war. Behaviour associated with war, victory, violence and uncontrolled actions Collin connected to the adrenal glands, where impulses such as fear and flight are directed by the medulla, while rage and pugnacity are controlled by the cortex. From this perspective, Collin considered 'war' to describe a sufficient number of people gripped by panic and others by anger – at the same time.

A highly unusual and original approach to the nature of war, and one worthy of reflection, can be found in the following statement:

> ... the first thing which it is necessary to understand about war is that all men are responsible for it, all men are guilty of the passionate reactions against others which, enormously multiplied and harnessed in a definite direction, make war possible. The motion of a certain gland produces 'passion' in man, and in his ordinary state of subjectiveness and illusion, this passion finds its outlet against others. This is man's ordinary state of being. And without a definite change of level of being, without a definite abandonment of a certain illusory sense of 'I', no men – however cultured, however 'liberal' – are exempt from this guilt.[1]

Passion is obviously a trait that manifests in everyone, but in different forms and with varying causes. Although some of Collin's examples may appear general, they nevertheless contribute to an unambiguous understanding that what may be cause and form for some is an impossible form and cause for others.

While women and food form the basis for disagreement among instinctive types, disagreement will arise among emotional types in religious issues and in different interpretations of the term 'justice'. Types with a clear intellectual inclination and who consider themselves tolerant, flexible and broadminded, tend to become unruly and strong rivals in questions concerning scientific theories, or in relation to their subjective interpretations of artistic and literary works.

It is no wonder mankind repeats its mistakes in this respect. Escaping such an inherent disability is a comprehensive exercise that requires room for manoeuver that few people possess. Only after a complete change of

---

[1] Rodney Collin, The Theory of Celestial Influence (London: Vincent Stuart Publishers Ltd, 1958), p279.

attitude towards oneself and others, that comes as a consequence of a deeper understanding of how our situation is conditional on different influences, can there be any liberation:

> ... *only when he fully realizes that neither he nor anyone else does anything but what they must do in the light of their being and their type; only when a certain fundamental illusion of his personality has actually died, will he become free of fighting and quarreling.*[1]

It doesn't take much to imagine how often and intensely we will end up justifying our negative opposition to others, even if we are in possession of some knowledge of our limitations. Collin also emphasises how challenging the transformation of passionate impulses is without the support of a school. From being the most characteristic and visible planetary manifestation, the mechanical passion, once transformed, will become virtually invisible. Considering how war has been one of our most faithful companions in human history, it does not feel like an exaggeration when Collin associates transformation and the omission of mechanical passion with miracles such as moving mountains. So rooted in man's common condition are the causes of war that its common explanations, upon close reflection, appear as permanent illusions, interwoven into a cluttered myriad of elements – interspersed with politics, religion, crime, lies and any number of 'convictions'.

According to Collin, the understanding that everyone, each in their own way, is responsible for the monstrosity of war, stems from the fact that no one can be said to be responsible. It is only when one realises that these claims relate to different levels of understanding, based upon each other, that these statements no longer appear as paradoxical and can become the starting point for yet another point of view.

That a planet, in certain aspects of its cycle, is able to create sufficient tensions on the earth's surface to cause man to contribute to war does not mean that this influence is the direct cause of a war. The crucial trigger point is a man's level of being. With a higher level of being, the martial cycle can contribute to a much-needed maturation process and a moment of heightened internal tension can be exploited to one's own advantage. Although Collin does not say it directly, there can be no doubt that he sees man's own contribution to this process requires self-investigation to provide the necessary motivation for change and escape from a previous mechanical pattern of reaction that invariably led to violence.

---

[1] Rodney Collin, *The Theory of Celestial Influence* (London: Vincent Stuart Publishers Ltd, 1958), p279.

The Theory of Celestial Influence

Based on a two-hundred-year period up to the mid-1950s, Collin believed there was a historical basis for a link between incidents of war and Mars' fifteen-year cycle:

> *Every fifteenth year, with extraordinary regularity, finds a number of the nations of Europe involved in wars between themselves, or in warlike adventures and disasters in other parts of the world. While the intermediate periods, if not exactly peaceful, nevertheless seem to bring the nearest approximations to peace possible in the present state of humanity and widespread lip service to peaceful ideals and aspirations. Perhaps the clearest indication of this cycle is that its peaks mark a general fashion of belligerent patriotism, while in its troughs even politicians tend to adopt a conciliatory and international attitude.*[1]

Collin believes that Mars' properties are highlighted and accentuated in the synergy between the cycle of Mars and the thirty-year cycle of Saturn. As we saw, in terms of the connection between the human glands and the different planets, Collin associates Saturn with anterior pituitary. One of the aspects of Saturn's influence on this gland is related to the impulse and power to dominate and master. As a result of man's deficient being, when this impulse cannot be exploited for his own benefit, he seeks to master and dominate not himself, but others. Collin further believes that it is reasonable to assume that the passionate urges caused by the stimulation of adrenaline, in combination with the aforementioned aspects of Saturn's influence on the anterior pituitary, leads to an exaggerated tendency to war every thirty years. If one considers the influence of Mars and Saturn's cycles as peak points, every third peak point, or forty-five years, will match a peak point in the nine-year rhythm of the asteroids. The impact of these influences will be characterised by a general economic and psychological depression with resultant crime.

One of the reasons Collin sees it as a challenge to identify the real nature of war is due to the many variations in which Mars' influence synchronises with other influences. Mars in combination with Saturn will lead to a war marked by domination and conquest, whereas when Mars is united with inflows from the asteroids, panic, barbarism and cruelty will be particularly prominent. Wars that can be put in the context of population growth are linked to Venus, while a modification of Neptune relative to the martial cycle can contribute to Holy Wars. Despite the very different consequences of the varying constellations, Collin concludes that the

---

[1] Rodney Collin, *The Theory of Celestial Influence* (London: Vincent Stuart Publishers Ltd, 1958), p281.

common denominator for all types of wars is destruction. Collin sees destruction as an inevitable common and useful cosmic process. Although in warfare it is practically always combined with crime, he emphasised that the nature of destruction is different from crime, which can never under any circumstances lead to fruitful results.

> *This distinction makes it possible to understand why the nature of war has baffled men throughout the ages, and it explains the evident unreality, for ordinary men, of a purely pacifist position. For the pacifist can never explain how it is that, although war seems absolutely futile and undesirable, nevertheless some of the strongest and noblest men take part in it, and often act then with much greater courage, loyalty, devotion and self-sacrifice than they do at any other time. Looking back into other ages, we sometimes find very high ideals upheld by a warrior class or knighthood. And in certain special conditions, the art of war could even provide the form for an esoteric school, as it did for the Knights Templars and for archery schools in Persia and India. If war itself belonged to the criminal process this would be quite impossible, for all taking part in it would become defiled. And one of the first conditions of all esoteric work is that it must not be touched by crime.[1]*

There must be many examples where the introduction of crime causes destruction to lose its original function. Collin indicates that fear, hatred and cruelty are at the root and the origin of other forms of causes.

Considering the extent to which the entangling of crime and destruction has taken place in the history of war, it is understandable that some might object to a depiction of war as purely destructive. Collin's illustration of this aspect of war by reference to the highly respectable Hindu scripture, *The Bhagavad Gita*, may facilitate a more open attitude and greater understanding of something that can initially appear controversial. When Arjuna asks to be relieved of the task of fighting his own kin, Krishna, his divine guide, responds:

> *Realise that pleasure and pain, gain and loss, victory and defeat, are all one and the same: then go into battle. Do this and you cannot commit any sin.[2]*

According to Collin, Arjuna exhibits the most advanced emotion a human being can have to war. Krishna's guidance, however, challenges

---

[1] Rodney Collin, *The Theory of Celestial Influence* (London: Vincent Stuart Publishers Ltd, 1958), p282.
[2] Swami Prabhavananda and Christopher Isherwood, *The Bhagavad Gita*, p44.

Arjuna to assume an even higher stance. Collin maintains that, as a crucial test, a person's relationship to war, as well as to sex, can show with mathematical precision who he really is.

A thought-provoking point of view Collin advances is how little human nature has changed since the time of Arjuna. However, one factor that has changed significantly is the capacity of man to kill. It is staggering how quickly we have gone from the time when people beat each other to death with clubs to technological solutions where a man can exterminate millions with just the touch of a button. Whether this power is wielded using the first cannons or the atomic bomb, Collin points out that it is in the same hands – those belonging to the unregenerated man.

The more Collin considered human history in light of the boundless mechanics in the universe, the more difficult it became for him to attribute an independence to man in relation to the energies he possessed. However, this does not imply a form of determinism, but rather a holistic view, in which higher levels know of and at the same time take into account both the limitations and inherent potential of men:

> ... *man's destructiveness must certainly be well known to and calculable by such higher power. The desperate danger of his enjoyment of unlimited energy is understood even by himself, let alone by any superior being. The penalty is obvious – what then is the possible prize? For we can hardly imagine a universe so devilish that danger goes unaccompanied by equivalent opportunity. Is it that by mortal danger man is being forced on to some great decision and some great jump in conscious development, which he could never have faced except in emergency?*
>
> *We do not know. But the idea is difficult to avoid.*[1]

Despite the fact that Collin used the same principles as in the study of Mars and Venus, he did not expect Mercury, with its influence on the thyroid gland, to produce a clear form of universal restlessness. As we have already mentioned, he believed that the mercurial cycle was too short to reveal anything definitive. What he discovered, however, was a restlessness associated with a nine-year rhythm tied to the stock market and price developments. Shifting his considerations from a statistical perspective to an emotional language, opened up new insights. The alternating optimism, pessimism, initiative and depression that naturally take place in the most

---

[1] Rodney Collin, *The Theory of Celestial Influence* (London: Vincent Stuart Publishers Ltd, 1958), p283-284.

industrialised parts of the world, he considered an underlying force of unrest that characterised the people involved in this mercantile activity.

According to Collin's calculations and based on Kepler's third law, the orbital period of a celestial body at a given distance from the sun is about 1700 days, and a planetary mass moving at such a rate will take exactly nine years to complete its synodic period. He went on to recognise even more periodic rhythms of time and by compiling his previously prepared table of synodic periodicity in light of octaves, he demonstrated that the asteroids appear at *re* in the first octave with a period of 27 years. When he then expanded this perspective by including additional octaves, the number of years is doubled at *re*, thereby revealing a further rhythm of 54 years that is more or less of the same character as the previous ones. In addition to highlighting the importance of asteroids as influences, he also notes how this forms the basis for specific historical events. Dates such as 1813, 1865 and 1919 coincide with market changes in American wholesale prices. Coal and iron production as well as industrial wages were all affected in the same periodicity.

Collin saw aspects of the asteroid's function as an expression of a disturbance and restlessness that could manifest without taking into account a whole. In a cosmic context it would not take into account the rest of the Solar System. On a human level, he considered this influence a psychological poison of a criminal nature, such as when it manifested in the context of modern industrial economics and especially life in larger cities, where depression, fear and panic are common.

Because nothing abnormal and underdeveloped has the ability to regenerate until it is restored, Collin sees crime, healing and conquest as part of a cycle.

Collin seems to attribute a share of the healing of the aforementioned turmoil to the planet Jupiter. This planet is equipped with an extensive system of satellites whose size, distance, revolutions and speeds are so coincident with the Solar System that Collin assumed they were both constructed according to identical laws. Therefore he believed that Jupiter's system has to possess a large number of frequencies that operate in a similar interaction.

A parallel to Collin's earlier image of the Solar System, in which the different glands of man reacted to the influence of different planets, can be found in his explanation of Jupiter's role in the aforementioned cycle:

Jupiter by its place in the Solar System appears to emit a 'note' or frequency which activates the posterior pituitary gland and produces in it a corresponding rhythm. But by the same laws Jupiter's moons will produce faint harmonics which affect all the other glands. Although each of these other glands will be chiefly controlled by the influence of its 'own' planet, it will also in a very much less pronounced way react to the influence of the corresponding moon of Jupiter, since each of these emits a frequency harmonically related to a certain planet but nearly six octaves higher. This calculation gives us quite a new idea about the significance of a planet's satellites in relation to man. If each planet controls one of his functions, the number of that planet's moons controls the interaction of that particular function with others, its power of harmonizing with others.[1]

Because only Jupiter and Saturn possess a complete system of moons, Collin concluded that the pituitary gland, in both its functions, stands in a peculiar position in terms of being able to influence all other functions of the body and the organism in its entirety. He attributed masculine and feminine characteristics to posterior and anterior lobes, respectively, because posterior has an overall, unifying and controlling function, while the anterior weakens and limits mismatches.

Like the anterior and posterior lobes, with the aforementioned characteristics almost acting as a father and mother to the body's other glands, he also considered Saturn and Jupiter to have similar maternal and paternal roles relative to their respective system of satellites.

For example, in his detailed research on questions about how Jupiter promotes functions of a healing and harmonizing nature, he was as keen to detect individual influences as more elusive consequences that affected millions of humans, often linked directly to quantified rhythms of years. Because everything, one way or another, is affected by a universal process of corruption, Collin believed that everything was also in need of healing and not least because a process of regeneration presupposes that the starting point is not abnormal. In other words, healing is a preparation for regeneration.

When Collin linked Saturn to the concept of conquest, it was because he sought to detect connections between this planet's influence on the anterior pituitary and characteristic and coinciding features of the gland itself. Not only did he point out that human types can be characterised as

---

[1] Rodney Collin, *The Theory of Celestial Influence* (London: Vincent Stuart Publishers Ltd, 1958), p291.

Saturnine and that a prominent anterior pituitary is reflected in bodily form and a characteristic psychology, but he also refers to how certain countries, in different historical eras, manifest Saturnine features.

Such a distinctive feature is the urge to dominate. Given Britain's spread from the seventeenth to the nineteenth century, it is not surprising that he points to the British as an example of a dominant nation, closely followed by the Germans, who in 1870, 1914 and 1939, with active atrocities and massive destruction, can be considered a nation that in its utmost ambition sought world domination.

To substantiate his preconditions that different types of influences can generate and then achieve a decisive maximum, Collin once again turns to historical facts. The Greeks under Alexander, the Tartars under Genghis Khan and the Spaniards in Mexico under Cortes are all examples of historical phenomena in a time span from 332 B.C. to 1525 A.D., which resulted in an incredible expansion.

The French Napoleon and the Hitler of the Germans are self-evident examples from a more recent era. Collin argues that dominance, as an underlying impulse, does not necessarily manifest in the form of warfare, and illustrates the point by pointing to the commercial expansion of the Venetians in the 14th century and the Dutch in the 17th century.

A number of the consequences of such underlying causes were not only unexplained by any logical reasoning, but sometimes even seemed on the verge of something miraculous, such as when, according to Collin, less than 400 hundred Spaniards could defeat the vast Aztec empire in two years.

Regardless of the attitude one may have to the participants in these various historical events, one must, in order to understand Collin's point of view in these questions, extend the boundaries of inquiry and try to understand the meaning of his statement:

... they do not do what they appear to do.[1]

In his perspective, the decisive importance of these patterns of action is mainly in Saturn's influence via the anterior pituitary gland. Central figures in these events are people who possess a type of talent for rhetoric, strategy and timing. A highly unusual and interesting approach to understanding the kind of sensitivity such people possess is found in his assertion that it

---

[1] Rodney Collin, *The Theory of Celestial Influence* (London: Vincent Stuart Publishers Ltd, 1958), p294.

is in the temperament of the people they surround themselves with that they develop their ability to listen to the planetary influence.

Another prominent feature of the anterior pituitary is its origination of what Collin calls synthetic thought, that is the processing and coordination that form the prerequisite for any theoretical or practical discovery or invention. By considering the enactment of advances in medicine in light of World War I and the corresponding progress in bacteriology, electronics and physics in the context of World War II, Collin provides us with a glimpse of the contours of a bridge between the urge to conquest and human knowledge and ingenuity.

Although it can be argued, rightly, that war stimulates ingenuity, Collin maintains the thesis that the pituitary is a deeper cause. An assertion he supports, among other things, with historical events that were synchronised with the thirty-year synodic period of Saturn.

We have previously mentioned how different cultures are influenced by planetary influences. Collin considered his own time period as part of one dominated by Saturn. The ingenuity that characterised this period, ranging from such varied inventions as the steam engine to the atomic bomb, leaves no doubt about the central position and importance of the intellect. If one is to point to a dominant and especially well-developed single trait associated with Saturn, it is the human intellectual function.

By noting how incompatible Saturn's prominent features are with the characteristic features of previous eras, we see, indirectly, how different periods have been inextricably linked to other glands and planets. Thus, for example, Collin shows how the colourful and jovial Renaissance is associated with Jupiter and the anterior pituitary.

About the Saturnine stimulation he writes:

> If in previous ages there had been no rest for men's muscles, now there was no rest for their minds. And the chief focus of all this stimulation, in any single man, was the anterior pituitary gland. Thus in a very real way, the present culture may be said to be especially under Saturn.

He continues:

> Every celestial stimulation which is brought to bear upon man is thus his opportunity and his danger. It opens new possibilities for him, but it also brings a new test of his being.[1]

---

[1] Rodney Collin, The Theory of Celestial Influence (London: Vincent Stuart Publishers Ltd, 1958), p296.

For Collin, the dark aspects of the Middle Ages with its speculative fantasies, persecutions, witches, etc., were examples of how weak beings handle a universal cosmic stimulation of the heart. Addressing the contemporary inability to deal with similar challenges of stimulation of the mind, he pointed to the increasing prevalence of mental madness, scientific superstition, the decay of thought into the trivial and conspicuous need for entertainment.

In response to such negative guidelines, Collin refers to the need to study examples of strong being. He highlights characters from his own time, such as Winston Churchill, Albert Schweitzer, Fridtjof Nansen, Jan Christian Smuts, Wilfred Grenfell and, of course, his own hero Pyotr Demianovich Ouspensky. But he does have reservations:

> *As in all periods, such heroes may be over-estimated or under-estimated. Some may be made over from what they were into what men need; others may teach men to need what they have made themselves. It does not matter. The hero of our time is the man who can reconcile all sides of life in one all-embracing view; who can understand, act, organise and make compassion manifest. Perhaps the archetype of such a man has not yet appeared, and all these are but his forerunners. In any case, they have helped to create conditions in which a man of to-day can find his conscience. Such is the work of heroes. And it is the work of the fourth way consciously and invisibly to produce them.*[1]

Collin might have included the following characters from our own time: Desmond Tutu, Martin Luther King Jr., and perhaps above all, Dag Hammarskjold.

Rodney Collin never saw the countless events that make up individual lives and human history as a reflection of a chaotic mess. He always viewed large and small events, both visible and invisible, in the light of the six processes. For him, these were not only so basic that they were inevitable, but it was also inconceivable that something could manifest independent of one or more of them.

In his perspective there also existed a seventh cycle, that not only ties all the processes together into a unified whole, but creates in its turn another cosmos: the cycle of sex, ordained by the planet Uranus.

---

[1] Rodney Collin, *The Theory of Celestial Influence* (London: Vincent Stuart Publishers Ltd, 1958), p297.

THE THEORY OF CELESTIAL INFLUENCE

Man's relationship with sexual drive is uniquely surrounded by myths, subjective attitudes and fantasies. This impulse, that has relentlessly commanded man at all times, manifests in multiple forms. It is the diversity of these results and the inability to detect their original source that contributes to confusion and loss of orientation. On the other hand, Rodney Collin's approach and understanding was, in addition to the information Ouspensky had gained from Gurdjieff, rooted in a cosmic perspective based on his study of the planet Uranus. It forms a holistic view that explains opportunities and limitations and how these find their natural place. In order to better understand why and how he gave Uranus the importance he did, it is crucial to know some of its fundamental features. He wrote:

> Unlike all the other planets, whose axes lie more or less at right angles to the plane of the Solar System, and which thus present chiefly their equators to the Sun and to their fellows, the axis of Uranus lies almost flat upon the plane of its orbit. This means that, alone of all the planets, it presents its two poles in turn directly to the Sun and to the Earth. Every eighty-four years its positive pole, illuminated by the full solar brilliance, shines vertically upon the Earth while its negative pole lies hidden and in darkness: in the intermediate periods it is the negative pole which so directly reflects the Sun's light towards us, and the positive which lies obscured in the direction of outer space. If the positive and negative poles of planets have some cosmic affinity for masculinity and femininity in general, then we can understand why Uranus – by reason of its unique movement – is the planet which governs the sex function in man, and further, why the alternating stimulation of the two sexes on Earth follows the eighty-four year rhythm which we clearly see in history.[1]

Collin uses clothing and fashion to illustrate sexual traits, because clothing is distinctive in its emphasis of sexual ideas, both for a historical period and for an individual. In other words, according to Collin, the way we dress becomes a kind of sexual signature that reflects our feeling and ideas about sex. Literature, art and poetry are also often carriers of sexually charged undercurrents and attitudes that mark out different historical eras.

Collin reveals how, in painting, it isn't only the motifs and content of the images that change over time, there is also a reflection of a historical change of attitude. With remarkable precision, he quantifies the time span

[1] Rodney Collin, The Theory of Celestial Influence (London: Vincent Stuart Publishers Ltd, 1958), p300.

for such changes. There is 40 years between Agnolo Bronzino's 'Venus, Cupid, Folly and Time' and the Fontainebleau school's swanky naturism. A corresponding distance is found between the latter and the inflexible soberness of Greco's female figures. Moreover, if we go back another 40 years, we meet Rubens' corpulent women, who almost appear as a personification of physical love. Here, in what can be considered a fragment of art history, the woman is portrayed in multiple roles, ranging from sensual promiscuity to an anemic weightless tenderness, via austerity and fleshy sensuality.

Collin saw a direct connection between these variations and how Uranus presents its two poles alternately to the Sun and to the Earth. We have so far focused on the feminine aspect of Collin's theories about the cycle of sex but, to understand the importance of the movement and positions of the aforementioned poles, we must include the masculine aspect. According to Collin, in the periods when women dress down, men dress up and vice versa. Rather than consider Uranus' 84-year cycle as an expression of variation between open and hidden sexuality, he emphasised that this is an alternation between a feminine and masculine age. This means that 42 years after a feminine phase, a masculine phase will enter, while a new phase for the feminine will begin 84 years after its previous beginning.

As examples of how masculine and feminine forces manifest in alternating periods, he refers to how the view of sex in the masculine period is characterized by honour, rivalry and morality, where sex is almost considered an exalted and hard-to-reach value worth fighting for. However, the feminine period is characterised by the opposite where the hard-to-reach is now openly available, accompanied by an undercurrent of invitations.

Collin exemplifies the characteristics of a masculine period in the cycle of sex ruled by Uranus by referencing the lengthy medieval poem, *Le Roman de La Rose*. In this work, characterised by both sensual language and hefty imagery, it becomes apparent that the woman is the subject of both defense and conquest. A literary touch is applied, through an allegorical form, that makes the poem appear to be a psychology of polite love.

Although Collin does not mention it, the popularity and prevalence of this work in the Middle-Ages serves as a confirmation of the period and an illustration of the sensitivity for these ideas during this part of the masculine span. As a complementary counterpart, Collin refers to 'The Garden of Earthly Delights', by Hieronymus Bosch, painted in 1505, immediately prior to a feminine peak in the sexual cycle of Uranus. In this painting, which is undoubtably Bosch's most energetic and complex work, man's restrictions are lifted through an all-encompassing invitation. Although the full meaning of this triptych may appear as a theological rebus, in this context it serves as a clear illustration of Collin's ideas. The feminine and masculine phases of Uranus' cycle can correspond to other planetary cycles in order to produce the countless attitudes, leanings and ideas associated with sexual expression, as experienced in multiple forms and interpersonal relationships.

Collin's statement that sexual cycles can correspond with cycles of war and crime is supported by the use of rape as a sinister, cheap and effective weapon in warfare. The Russian invasion of Berlin in 1945, ISIL's attack on Yazidi villages in 2014 and the countless and persistent occurrences on the African continent are examples from our own time of a practice that has washed in waves over humanity throughout history. There can be no doubt that the 2018 Nobel Peace Prize to Dr. Denis Mukwege marked a new understanding of sexual abuse in war. However, he didn't address the wider perspective in which these horrifying events can also seen as cosmic phenomena.

Another example of the consequences of the sexual cycle's combination with other planetary cycles is when sex is intentionally harnessed to serve the development of consciousness. The Kushan civilization of the second century and the Shaivite temples of the eighth century testify to teachings in which physical sensuality was a cornerstone of a mysterious experience of a union with God. Collin offers Persian Sufis as an example of a teaching where sex plays a significant role and the emotional aspect is especially emphasised.

It was Rodney Collin's firm conviction that sex, under given conditions, could serve as a bridge to man's highest form of consciousness. A fundamental premise is that both parties are of an essential sensuous physical type and that they are free from shame and any form of violence. Another precondition he included was that such interpersonal actions could only take place if Uranus' cycle was in a feminine phase.

The sexual revolution that originated in the 60s and 70s liberalised and individualised sexuality in much of the industrialised world. The Kinsey reports from the early 50s on the sexuality of American woman and men had, by then, already contributed to a new and public openness about sexuality. The availability of contraceptives, which were both cheap and safe, also contributed to a new liberalisation. All these factors seem to have engendered the opinion that sexuality is a prerequisite for quality of life and a right widely supported in much of the industrialised world. It is understandable that an ever-increasing awareness of body and sexuality has led to performance-anxiety affecting women and men. At the same time, such problems can be seen as the tip of the iceberg if we consider the broader significance and influence of sexuality.

Collin considers sexual energy a molecular phenomenon and points out that it carries a universal signature that, when it manifests in the form of physical offspring, corresponds to the cosmic image from which it originates. The battle over what attitudes we should have to inter-bodily relations takes place in multiple arenas of the community. Collin's view would indicate that a psychological approach, focused on social interactions, shaped by values, attitudes and social systems, is necessarily limited.

A person living up to the average life expectancy will die in a sexual atmosphere similar to that at their birth, because the 84-year cycle of sex, ruled by Uranus, is of approximately the same length. At the same time this means that the opposite atmosphere to that existing at the moment of birth takes place at the age of 40. This is, according to Collin, the period of a person's life where the understanding of sexuality is fullest and deepest and where the sexual atmosphere is at its most stimulating.

It is easy to imagine many people facing great challenges, or a significant dilemma, being at the mercy of the sexual atmosphere of their time and with no apparent choice but to manoeuver to the best of their ability within it. Consequently, Collin emphasises the necessity of understanding sex as the highest creative function, an understanding that can contribute to a harmonisation of the other functions of the human being:

> ... whether in the creation of children in the physical image of their parents, in the creation of the arts, or simply in the creation of the individual's true role in life. Unfortunately, in many people, far from harmonising other functions, sex obstructs them, interferes with them, prevents them carrying out their proper task. It must be remembered that sexual energy is the finest energy normally produced and conducted through the human body. This means that it is also the most volatile, the most difficult to store or keep under control. Like a supply of high octane petrol, its presence represents both a source of immense power and potentiality, and also a constant danger of catastrophic explosion. At any moment it may leak into the mechanism of other

functions, and like such petrol leaking into a heating system or into a storeroom, suddenly give rise to spontaneous fires which in a few seconds can destroy long-accumulated stocks of other materials and even damage the basic structure of the building. Usually, however, these violent and destructive manifestations of sexual energy are directly or indirectly traceable to a negative attitude towards sex in general – that is, to suspicion of it, fear of it, or to a cynical, brutal or obscene sense of sex. For such negative attitudes prevent sex from finding its proper and natural expression and force its energy into channels and functions for which it is far too strong.[1]

If we are to believe Collin, much of the human expression of negativity, feverish imagination and lack of control is associated with sexual energy being forced into thoughts, actions and instinct, causing overload. Moreover he argued that an emotional understanding of sex as a harmonising factor does not release one completely from such negative forces. Instead it leads to neither wanting to justify them, nor pretending that they are usable, because the emotional aspect of one's understanding provides a deeper insight into the constitution and roots of such forces.

He emphasises the necessity of having sufficient self-control over one's sexual expression and, at the same time, expresses the danger of such control. The balancing point is delicate, as whether sex plays too big or too little a role can determine whether sex becomes a destructive or edifying element in a person's life. The danger of controlling and suppressing this creative energy is that such a significant waste of one's powers can leave no room for much else.

He compares the attempt to limit a scent to a restricted area of a room with 'keeping sex in its place'. The nature of the molecular state of matter and the speed at which sex operates make such a task impossible. Of such 'self-control' he says:

... the man who prides himself on being most self-controlled often spends far more thought, time, energy and ingenuity on sex than anyone else. He can never get sex out of his mind, and he is thus never able to consider any other side of life impartially. Every question, even the most trivial or academic, decides itself in him on the basis of the sexual opportunity it will offer or avoid. In this way his whole life becomes poisoned, and he sacrifices even ordinary opportunities and possibilities.

---

[1] 267 Rodney Collin, The Theory of Celestial Influence (London: Vincent Stuart Publishers Ltd, 1958), 302303.

Such a man is the most abject slave of sex; and with neither profit nor pleasure.[1]

He is equally unequivocal on the spectrum of consequences sex can have. Because this energy can be used for any purpose and manifest on all levels, it can break down a being physically, morally and emotionally. Likewise it can be combined with a man's highest aspirations. Because he considered that this energy could express itself on any level, he believed that everyone had to try, to the best of their ability, to get as much out of it as possible. At one point, he saw this gift in light of the biblical parable of talents, talents given by nature. It is in this perspective that he sees sex as a provider of a universal test or examination that is essential to a person's future possibilities.

As we noted in the chapter on *The Theory of Eternal Life*, Collin drew several lines between death and sexuality. In his *Theory of Celestial Influence* he considers the sexual act to be a foreshadowing of death.

Because sexual energy carries in it a complete cosmic image especially associated with each individual, the individual, by the release of energy during the sexual act, will be parted from himself. In Collin's opinion, a sexual ecstasy, in which contradictions are united and an experience of unity is proportional to the experience of annihilation, is a likely taste of what one can experience when death occurs. Losing and finding oneself at the same time is a dramatic common denominator:

> *... as man, parting from his seed in the sexual act, in the instant reveals and experiences his whole being, falls into oblivion, is seized with despair or transported with ecstasy, so may a man parting from his body in death be so revealed and rewarded – not for an hour but for a lifetime.[2]*

The more Collin was able to understand the legalities connected with sex energy and the various consequences of these, the more evident the mystery became. For him it was never a matter of reveling in the mystery – the deeper he penetrated, the deeper it got.

To demonstrate aspects of how the various functions of humans can be refined, Collin refers to Plato's statement: "souls seek the other half from which they were severed at creation." As previously mentioned, the sex function, provided it works normally, has the ability to create harmony

---

[1] Rodney Collin, *The Theory of Celestial Influence* (London: Vincent Stuart Publishers Ltd, 1958), p305.
[2] Rodney Collin, *The Theory of Celestial Influence* (London: Vincent Stuart Publishers Ltd, 1958), p305-306.

between the other functions. He notes that, in the quest for perfection, the sex function has a natural inherent ability to contribute characteristics that other functions may lack. He illustrates principles of attraction and marriage between men and woman through an analogous function in the world of chemistry:

> *The perfect shell being constituted of a definite number of electrons, sodium with one outstanding electron rushed irresistibly to embrace chlorine with one missing. On the other hand nothing could make sodium with its extra electron combine with other alkalis similarly composed. This was the principle of the marriage of the elements, and the basis of all chemistry.*[1]

We all know how we can be attracted, repulsed or simply indifferent to people, without any apparent reason. Collin attributes this not only to the ability of functions to recognise and calculate the factor of reciprocity found in each individual function, but also to make a calculation of the average and the total amount of factors. Fortunately, he argues, one does not have to leave this to the logical mind, because the sexual function is able to produce a precise calculation in a second or less. To show how legality exists at different levels of polarity, he uses the glandular system as an example.

The anterior pituitary carries masculine characteristics associated with reason, will, coordination, and the power to dominate the organism as well as its surroundings. The posterior lobe, on the other hand, exhibits clear feminine features, with its abilities to safeguard the inner working of the body, as well as its association with healing. Similar male and female role distribution is also found in the other glands and in their systems and functions. For example, in the adrenals, where the cortex and medulla are underlying sources of fight and flight respectively. Instinctively, a man or woman will seek their complementary counterpart based on what each lacks. It is when one's partner is accurately reciprocal in one function but not in another that sexual inconsistencies arise. This also explains, according to Collin, why some people do not find polyamorous situations abnormal, although they often experience the pressure of expectations, social conditions and criticism.

The modern human being, already significantly confronted by advertising, news media, influencers, coaching, the internet, etc., where a

---

[1] Rodney Collin, *The Theory of Celestial Influence* (London: Vincent Stuart Publishers Ltd, 1958), p306-307.

variety of male and female roles are projected, may be further impacted through their sexual nature. Such stimuli are, of course, not a modern invention but have followed man in various forms since time immemorial. Collin references imaginary sexual mental images, based on heroics from books and the products of the entertainment industry, all of which affect responsive and susceptible people. In his opinion, such pseudo-sexual creations and forms of expression foster pornography and will counteract and obstruct that to which one's true nature aspires.

The sexual instinct will continue its quest for a complementary counter pole until every function is simultaneously fulfilled. The unmet need will inexorably manifest through an attraction. And further:

> *An attraction will be felt with increasing intensity as the woman (or man) encountered approaches this ideal. A woman who is his complement or nearly his complement in all functions must always arouse in a man an inexhaustible sense of fascination and mystery, and must ever stand for him as an ideal, that is, as that by which he himself is made whole and perfect.*[1]

Collin warns against embarking on a hunt for the ideal partner, primarily because few of us possess a being strong enough to deal with the challenges associated with finding one's perfect complement. Daydreaming about the perfect companion will rob us of the ability to recognise what we want, simply because such a dream state is incompatible with being psychologically awake.

Collin sees a basic understanding of types as a clear precondition for understanding the relationship between the sexes. We have previously looked at the relationship between the glandular system and types, and also relative to essence. In the perspective of sex as the quest for perfection, Collin emphasises other significant features of the same types. Although each type can be attributed to both men and woman, Collin points out that three types are strongly feminine and three masculine. Lunar, Venus and Jovial make up the feminine aspect, while Mercury, Mars and Saturn make up the masculine portion. What is always perceived as the female or male ideal is reflected in preferred type in a relentless movement within the two groups and between the three types.

Firmly rooted in the history of painting, Rodney Collin saw what is visible to the naked eye, yet hidden sufficiently to escape the watchful gaze of art history:

---

[1] Rodney Collin, *The Theory of Celestial Influence* (London: Vincent Stuart Publishers Ltd, 1958), p308.

... the artist tends always to paint men of his own type, and woman of the type which most intensely attract him. And the successful artist unwittingly expresses the ideal types of his age, for precisely in the recognition of this lies his success. In this way, art very often reveals the fundamental laws of type much more clearly than life, where pure types are rare and the affinity between types are confused by imagination, convention, fear, pretense and material interests.[1]

Rodney Collin had no professional art history background, but he knew what he was looking for. Therefore, he could recognise what he sought when he found it, through a form of advantageous concentrated vision. In the recognition of the sequences of civilizations, traces of esoteric sources, or in objects of art, he demonstrated original and surprising approaches. The concrete examples that underpinned his understanding of types are weighty and convincing.

In both El Greco and Albrecht Durer pictures, he found tall ascetic and bony men corresponding with the Saturn type. The female characters were equally distinct Lunar types, with their round, meek and pale features. He found dazzling and colourful Jovial women and powerful and fierce Marital men in the work of both Rubens and Veronese. Likewise, in the art of Fragonard, Correggio and Boucher, he discovered the dynamic youthfulness of Mercurial men, along with lackadaisical and unhurried Venus women. Collin's assertion of who these artists preferred to paint and why can be verified indirectly by studying their self-portraits. He himself was never in any doubt that these combinations were natural and fundamental.

Considering the different types according to the enneagram, it becomes easy to visualise which types have maximum mutual attraction. Opposing each other on a vertically divided enneagram, we find Saturn opposite Lunar, then Jovial – Mercury, and finally Mars – Venus. Although these combinations indicate maximum attraction, Rodney Collin is again very clear that one should not necessarily approach this in a slavish and indiscriminate way. Although types with maximum attraction naturally gravitate towards each other sexually or in the form of friendship, such relationships are not necessarily suitable and satisfying. Collin elaborates:

Very often, if strong feeling exists, there will be a quality of transience, of the precariousness of love. And this may even bring with it a passion and desperation which can shake individual lives to their foundations.

[1] Rodney Collin, The Theory of Celestial Influence (London: Vincent Stuart Publishers Ltd, 1958), p309.

337

Under such stress a man or woman may suddenly throw away all that life has given them for a momentary satisfaction, knowing in advance that they can hope for nothing lasting or permanent from it. In such combinations there is often a sense of the tragic, the illegitimate. Weak characters, characters without roots, can be destroyed by them. And yet, for people of set and narrow lives, the very suddenness and violence of the passion may break through convention and open the way for new possibilities which could come to them in no other way.[1]

Another cosmic aspect of the psychological nature of types is an interrelationship movement in which, for example, Saturn moves towards Mars, then searches towards Jovial, etc., before eventually returning to its original position. Rodney Collin sees this circulation as an expression of a learning process, not only for the individual, but also as a movement in which humanity advances. In the chapter, *The Cycle of Sex*, Collin gives conspicuously few examples of how a type in front supports the one behind, and how the one in front supports the one arriving. Perhaps the reason was that he wanted to avoid stereotypical ideas that could easily overshadow the diverse approach such work can offer in practice.

Nevertheless, it seems natural here to contribute a few more examples to further clarify these ideas. By incrementally acquiring qualities that are naturally laid down in the type that is in front of you, one acquires not only new Essence qualities, but also greater understanding and tolerance of others and oneself. The predictable and moderate Saturn type that relies on a carefully constructed perspective can learn to become courageous. Mars, on the other hand, can tame his aggressive dedication by acquiring the generous and benevolent character traits of Jovial. The often colourful and exaggerated assertiveness of Jovial can, by acquiring Lunar's reserved and reflective calmness, learn something about not having to always burst out with everything with no apparent self-discipline. Lunar, with her restraint, can be inspired by the diverse passivity of Venus. The energetic ubiquitous Mercury can, in turn, be motivated to slow down and acquire the perspective of the systematic Saturn.

Although all types have distinct features, there is a wide spectrum of psychological characteristics within them. Therefore these examples are only a fragment of countless possibilities for learning at each stage in the circulation, because the combinations of the characteristics of different types are so vast and diverse.

---

[1] Rodney Collin, *The Theory of Celestial Influence* (London: Vincent Stuart Publishers Ltd, 1958), p310.

Collin describes an interesting phenomenon about circulation, when one partner acts as a leader by virtue of being a full stage ahead of the other. For example, where Saturn leads Mercury, Mars leads Saturn, etc. If such pair formations are able to keep up with each other in this movement, the mutual attraction will be maintained. Collin claims such relationships will be the most enduring and permanent.

Rodney Collin considered negativity, perversion, fear, greed and violence to be obstacles that make the experience of ecstasy and union impossible. He also truly believed that sex, under certain conditions, is a manifestation of the nature of higher consciousness and can contribute to internal growth:

> By pure sex, the ordinary man may gain in a moment what the ascetic denies himself for years to achieve, what the saint prays for a lifetime to feel.[1]

To acquire the insights possible through sexual union, understanding must penetrate all aspects of a person's life without restrictions. When the man and woman become a living mutual reminder of 'whence he came' and 'wither she must go', new doors open.

> Together they must remind each other of the beginning and the end, of the whole and of perfection.275

While the cycle of sex can be understood in the context of types and individuals, it was also clear to Rodney Collin that the celestial impulse for the cycle of regeneration is hardly traceable in relation to individual man. Based on his diagram of the human body, where the different planets placed along a line in a spiral correspond to the glandular system, he puts forward a theory that the planet Neptune plays a central role in the new forces and perceptions associated with the regeneration of man's whole being.

By comparing atmospheres of different planets in terms of gases and atomic weights, he saw that Neptune's methane gas has a lower atomic weight than the gases of the other planets. This contributed to his assumption that Neptune possesses the Solar System's most delicate transformation mechanism. Because Neptune is the furthest from the Sun, it consequently corresponds to the outermost gland of Collin's spiral-diagram, the pineal. As we have previously encountered, the function of this gland was poorly understood and there were many myths surrounding it. Its association with melatonin production was only discovered two years

---

[1] Rodney Collin, The Theory of Celestial Influence (London: Vincent Stuart Publishers Ltd, 1958), p311.

after Rodney Collin's death. Neptune's 165-year cycle means its influence on the the average human life is almost constant and hard to detect. Collin believed that Neptune's influence might be expressed through its effect on humanity rather than individuals.

Although he does not directly link the influence of Neptune with regeneration, it is likely that he would make that connection, based on his unshakable basic view that man is a self-developing organism in a holistic universe, characterised by reciprocal maintenance. Any possible correspondence between what he considered the Solar System's most delicate transforming mechanism and the possible inner development of man would be something well worth investigating.

Collin envisaged that such an influence could lead to an augmented interest in regeneration that peaked above and beyond the ordinary, to the extent that it led to actual transformation of some individuals. It would be unlikely that such individuals could be identified historically. But because such transformed people often formed schools and some such schools had a form of teaching that left an external trace, it would be possible to indirectly get an impression of the existence of such impenetrable schools and of some conscious men, even though the teaching itself remained hidden.

Collin does not directly link Neptune's cycle with favourable and unfavourable periods for such schools. It is nevertheless reasonable to assume that the phenomena he associates with these concepts coincide with Neptune's cycle – and indeed there are times when it is stronger or weaker with regard to the planet's conjunction with other forces in the universe. In his view, a school in adverse times will operate covertly, while in favourable periods, through external work and preparatory schools, its surface will be more detectable, even historically:

> ... *some of the men who have in themselves succeeded in achieving the aim of the school may even appear as famous figures, in the guise of priests, saints, architects, painters and so on.276*

Collin believed that best means of detecting the existence of favourable periods in history is through evidence of imitation schools and of a general interest in regeneration. This is because conscious people, who are a product of true schools, can neither be seen nor directly studied outside their own time. At best, they will be described by their contemporaries, so it is almost impossible to distinguish between what is an original and secondary source. Therefore, all we can know about a true school is that it must have possessed a degree of secrecy and anonymity.

Rodney Collin compares human requirements for regeneration to a seed's preconditions for sprouting. As the seed needs to be enclosed by earth, likewise man needs a space that excludes external disturbance.

A historical example of both secrecy and how original material is lost can be found in Collin's reference to a school led by the early mystic, Ammonius the Sackbearer, in Alexandria in the 3rd century. Three of his students, Herrenius, Origen the Christian and Plotinus had all agreed that none of the doctrine should be written down. When Herrenius broke this agreement, Origen and Plotinus felt a responsibility to correct false impressions. None of Herrenius' writings are thus preserved for posterity. Another example, not mentioned by Collin, of how original texts from this period were lost, distorted and later appeared in fragmented secondary versions, is Origen's symbolic expression of the union between the soul and God in the Song of Songs. Not only is this a fragment of the original text, but it is additionally only a variant, in the sense that it is translated into Latin.

Collin also suggested that schools may have leaked information intentionally to select individuals and that the respected physicist, Robert Fludd, may have been one of them. Fludd, who candidly declared that he did not belong to any school of regeneration but had only come into possession of its cosmological theory, nevertheless seems convinced that this material, including experiments he had witnessed, was exceptional. This led to a series of confrontations with the German mathematician, Johannes Kepler. In his work, *De Monochordum Mundi*, published in 1623, Fludd wrote that he had seen experiments performed by men:

> *... who, without doubt, are a thousand times to be preferred both to Fludd and Kepler in the mysteries of philosophy, and in their deep and true knowledge of cosmic harmony.*

Rodney Collin mentions Fludd because, apart from written sources, architecture and individual symbol-bearing works of art, the kind of information that Fludd possessed was important in order to form a theoretical, albeit fragmented, image of such schools.

Uncertain, but not discouraged, Collin notes that the first challenge in finding possible connections between Neptune's cycle and manifestations and renewals of schools of regeneration is that one does not know where to start.

He draws attention to the consolidation of the Gothic cathedrals around 1125 as the clearest expression of an outward manifestation of an underlying school of regeneration. He also notes that the Rosicrucian alchemical school becomes invisible after 1620. Based on these two dates, seen in the context of Neptune's 165-year cycle, the following dates emerged that he set in a linear historical perspective, showing several interesting correlations. B.C. 30, A.D. 135, 300, 465, 630, 795, 960, 1125, 1290, 1455, 1620 and finally 1785.

In 135 A.D. we find a noticeable revitalisation of Buddhism. Around the year 300, a new era for Christianity arises, associated with the cataclysm of the Roman world. Then St. Benedict at Monte Cassino, about a cycle later, formed the basis of the monastic system. About 630 Mahomet facilitated the spread of Islam from India, while Palma Sambhava, one cycle later, brought an esoteric influence to Tibet. The only dates Collin did not tie to a historic event, was year 30 B.C. and 1785. We assume that Rodney Collin was aware that Cleopatra died in 30 B.C., thus marking the end of ancient Egypt, but he obviously didn't consider it significant enough to include.

Something that must have puzzled him, but he chose not to interpret, was that the planet Neptune, at all the aforementioned times, was astronomically in the direction of the galactic center.

According to Collin's understanding there was no impulse that had more significance than the schools that were behind the construction of Gothic cathedrals in the early 12th century. Although these impulses had an impact on architecture, art, music, politics and various ecclesiastical rituals, Rodney Collin emphasized a very important point, namely that all these are by-products – an effect:

> *The men who actually produced these changes in external life and history, and whose existence we can verify, were probably not in schools at all. They may have been influenced or guided by school-men, or they merely have imitated others who already had this influence at second-hand.*[1]

Rodney Collin was in no doubt that those who stood behind and were the very source of these impulses were as invisible in their time as today, because their task was solely to help regenerate selected individuals who could create conscious souls themselves, a work so demanding that insulation was required. To shed light on the extent of such work, Collin imagined the following fascinating thought experiment.

---

[1] Rodney Collin, *The Theory of Celestial Influence* (London: Vincent Stuart Publishers Ltd, 1958), p317.

The Theory of Celestial Influence

If 50 suitable men come under the guidance of a human being whose only goal is the pursuit of consciousness, and if 50 people of the latter category come under the instruction of someone who has developed a conscious soul, on what level would that person have to be in order to be able to lead a school of 50 conscious people?

His response is as humble as it is instructive:

> *Again we can give no answer. But we can see from this principle that the greatest 'golden age' might indeed be created by no more than fifty conscious men, who in their turn might depend on the presence in the world at that time of one single man of an unknown but even higher level. In such historical roles as Christ, Buddha, Mahomet, we appear to see at least the trace of such latter men.[1]*

Despite the lack of insight into the activities of schools, Collin believed that the increased consciousness of their pupils would increase insight into what one can and cannot do. As a consequence, they will realise that they cannot change others but only change their own attitude. Collin points out that these practices create a freedom from illusion – a liberation which can release powers to use for what one *can* do. In addition to such subjective abilities, increased consciousness releases objective powers. The competence to intentionally place specific thoughts in someone else's mind is such an ability. Collin believed it fell outside the scope of *The Theory of Celestial Influence* and, therefore, only mentioned it as a fact. However, we previously pointed to concrete examples in the period shortly before Ouspensky's death, such as when Collin traveled to Mendham, U.S.A., to visit Madame Ouspensky.

Another aspect of the newfound insight into what one can and cannot do is the conviction that:

> *… each man's weakness can be absolutely relied upon.[2]*

Whether the power one comes into possession of through such insight is used for the benefit of oneself or another depends entirely on one's level of being. Rodney Collin highlights the essential distinction between the different qualities of power and being by referring to the fact that a strong man is not necessarily a good man. He further argues that a fundamental feature of all true schools is that the development of consciousness and being take place in parallel. He also reasoned that, for humanity as a whole, power cannot be allowed to outgrow being, ensuring true telepathic

---

[1] Rodney Collin, *The Theory of Celestial Influence* (London: Vincent Stuart Publishers Ltd, 1958), p318.
[2] Rodney Collin, *The Theory of Celestial Influence* (London: Vincent Stuart Publishers Ltd, 1958), p320.

abilities will not fall into the hands of immature people who would otherwise have been able to use them for their own gain. One of the greatest challenges associated with a parallel development of being and power is a person's self-image. Collin believed that revealing illusions related to how human beings perceive themselves is not only a necessary form of purification, but for many can also be the most demanding part of schoolwork.

It is clear that a person seeking to move from one level to another will experience challenges. A fateful point in this process is when a student does not have sufficient knowledge and understanding of the necessity of school discipline. On this threshold, the learner may not only harm himself but also others. However, if he gets through this step and acquires an understanding of the underlying principles and, not least, realises the dangers of abuse of newfound powers, it will be impossible for him to take certain steps in the wrong direction. For Collin, the greatest danger in the process, which in itself is an expression of failure in being, is that the development of consciousness stops for some reason.

Expanding on how and to what extent the cycle of regeneration is affected by the planet Neptune, Collin writes the following:

> *In favorable periods of this cycle ... the acquisition of new powers connected with increase of consciousness may become slightly easier. The problem of being, on the other hand, always remains exactly the same, and work on being is never easier or more difficult than at any other time. Moreover, while increase in consciousness may be only possible with the help of schools of regeneration, the problem of improvement of being is one that faces all men everywhere by the very fact of their birth into the world. It provides a test for every living individual, and unless this test is successfully passed, the question of schools and their possibilities does not even arise.[1]*

Rodney Collin saw that the dissemination of information about natural laws, the true nature of man and his possible evolution is the subsequent task of a school, secondary to the stimulation to regeneration. When he goes into more detail about the prerequisites and conditions associated with something having to die in order for something to be born, he again focuses not only on how significantly different the development of being and power is, but also on the consequences of a deficient parallel development. If one's old personality breaks down without a soul

---

[1] Rodney Collin, *The Theory of Celestial Influence* (London: Vincent Stuart Publishers Ltd, 1958), 321.

developing, a person can be subject to possession by another or insanity. If, on the other hand, a soul is acquired without first wiping out the old personality, one crystalises in a position where weaknesses are reinforced under the influence of new powers. Without pointing to concrete examples, Collin says such cases are thankfully rare.

The latter may explain how and why apparently enlightened individuals in sectarian and religious environments can acquire a position of power in which they exploit others sexually and economically. On the other hand, because such situations are unfortunately not so rare, a possible explanation is that such abusive individuals suffer from psychopathy.

One of the most important processes in a school is separating the acquired personality from the essence of man. School discipline can take different forms in a process that spans many years, depending on a teacher's nature and the student's starting point. The scale of methods is extensive, ranging from violent reproof to complete humility at the extremes. Alongside the outside impulses that a student receives through discipline, inner work for self-purification is also a decisive factor. This involves the removal of anything he himself does not want to remain permanent, such as harmful emotions and self-centered thoughts, including uncontrollable attachments and longings. Although Collin does not believe that physical purification is strictly required, disharmonious physical conditions and illness, leading to pain and inertia, can be a significant burden on a person's will and should not be overlooked. Not surprisingly, he considers the elimination of unnecessary suffering as an effect of physical purification.

It is necessary to deal with difficult and agonising challenges in what can be considered the reparation period in order to develop the ability to cement a certain state later. Collin stated unequivocally that such efforts must not be overemphasised when any kind of fixing is not desirable. The coping ability acquired will enable one to face future challenges without being bewildered.

The moment of the intersection between the last preparation and the final breath of the old personality can take many forms, but the content is timeless and immutable:

> *It may be the deed of a teacher, either gradual or in one terrible assault. It may perhaps be induced by some overwhelming pressure from life, which the pupil has voluntarily accepted or invoked. Hardship and sacrifice, spread over many years of preparation, may have reduced*

personality to a powerless wraith. Pain, prison, starvation, torture, abandonment or ruin – swallowed and not rebelled against – may equally destroy it … What is left has no position, no money, no family, no acquaintances, no ambition, no power of acting for itself. Many of these things may return to the pupil later in a different way. But at this moment – whether in school, in prison, or on the battlefield – he finds himself without anything and without any past. It is as though his body were placed naked on a desert island where it had no previous connections of any kind. For a little while he is as a new born child.[1]

Although the birth of a conscious soul is often seen in the context of the death of the old personality, Collin considered these to be two separate events. In his analogue imagery, he draws a parallel to the birth of a physical body where the source of consciousness is the active male element, while the Essence possesses the female role. It's hard to not notice that a number of the elements Rodney Collin refers to as essential aspects of the delivery of a soul resonate with his own situation during the days he was locked in the room next to the bedroom where Ouspensky lay dying:

Alone in his retreat or alone with his agony, he is thrown upon his own resources. Suggestions may be conveyed to him by his teacher, if he has one, by inspiration if he has not. But the way he carries them out, the methods he uses, and the conclusions he comes to, all derive from his own essence. Now he has to put into practice as intensively as he can all that he previously learned. In general, pain and repetition are fixative agents, and the exercises or experiences of which we speak use one or other or both principles to fix the soul in him and to set in it certain general attitudes, beliefs and principles … The repetition may equally consist in a Russian pilgrim's endless repeating of a prayer, or a prisoner's endless enduring of his routine. What is important is the attitude which accompanies them. For these experiences may indeed fix permanently in a man a certain attitude towards God, towards his fellow-men, towards his duty. And if they are sufficiently intense, such attitudes will remain with him for the rest of his life.[2]

The gradation of intensity that Collin refers to reflects the extent to which the preparatory work has contributed to liberation from connections to longings, casual thoughts, fears, ambitions, regrets, etc. In the discovery of such deficiencies, it is important to make the necessary

---

[1] Rodney Collin, The Theory of Celestial Influence (London: Vincent Stuart Publishers Ltd, 1958), p323.
[2] Rodney Collin, The Theory of Celestial Influence (London: Vincent Stuart Publishers Ltd, 1958), p324.

trade-offs and determine whether one is willing to live with such feelings and thoughts in the future. As we have already mentioned, Collin considered physical purification not strictly necessary. However, if such cleaning has been carried out in advance, a fixation in which one is able to carry every conceivable challenge could become affordable. It is only by such fixation, where one's understanding, natural and mastered learned properties are gathered into a whole, that a man knows who he is, what he believes in and how he must act in the future. As far as Rodney Collin could see, it was the processes that led up to these consequences of fixation, which constituted the work of a school of regeneration.

It is when Rodney Collin broadened his perspective on regeneration to include all six processes that he came to regard a true school of regeneration as unprecedented and incomparable to any other form of human society, in that it creates a cosmos. But because humans must take part in a higher cosmos to regenerate and the cosmos of Earth and that of nature is too slow, Collin sees only one solution. A school of regeneration can not only create the necessities and present the opportunities that are laid down in a cosmos, but these will be significantly faster than in the natural world, i.e., the world of nature and the Earth. In other words, a school is an artificial cosmos whose laws must be understood by those who administer it. Referring to an enneagramatic structure, Collin sheds light on aspects of such a cosmos:

> ... *its circle of life developing logarithmically in time; its informing triangle at the points of which three kinds of 'food' or inspiration from higher cosmoses enter and sustain it; the inner circulation which unites its different functions. All these motions cross and recross, and at their points of crossing definite phenomena are created – 'batteries' or 'organs' which are alternately charged and discharged according to the motions which pass through them. At one certain crossing within the cosmos, regeneration – that is, the escape of an individual 'cell' from a lower to a higher circulation – is possible.*[1]

Many of us will accept that we tend to attribute difficulties or unpleasantness to circumstances in which we ourselves are not to blame. However, we are inclined to view things differently when we believe we have contributed to something successful. Collin provides examples of how a student, relatively early on, through self-observation in an increased state of consciousness, can discover that what he seemed to do really

---

[1] Rodney Collin, *The Theory of Celestial Influence* (London: Vincent Stuart Publishers Ltd, 1958), p326.

happens to him. Not only his behaviour happens, but so do friendships, quarrels and loves, just like the physical characteristics received at birth.

When self-inquiry lifts us out of the self-image that reacted, defended, and rebelled at any suggestion of our inability to arrange our own life, it becomes possible to take advantage of the idea of role-playing.

It becomes a challenge to stick with a role that is pre-chosen when contradictory thoughts and feelings are triggered. When the distance between a role of accountability and irresponsible aspects of oneself is great, it is sincerity and understanding of one's own situation that becomes the motivating factor. Collin does not mention this latter aspect of individual psychology, most likely because it was self-evident to him, but also because he was focused on a higher level. He writes:

> *Yet, though what the pupil may learn from such experiments is unlimited, he is not the chief reason for them. They are the first preparations for a great drama, which – somewhere and at some time – will have to be performed. This drama represents the perfection of a cosmos.*[1]

In other words, role playing, with all its beneficial challenges, is but a fragment of a larger whole.

Rodney Collin makes significant claims for these schools. We get the impression that a school of regeneration must be something completely beyond comparison; something unique. Collin argues that neither common religious practice, philosophical methods nor social structures intended to upgrade the moral or cultural level of man can be compared with a true school of regeneration.

The constitution of cosmoses is unknown to ordinary man and its law remains invisible. Collin's interpretations of school as a cosmos are more detailed than we can account for here, but we will look at some basic features. Once again, the enneagram is his starting point, where its triangle, representing aspects of communication with the original impulse, is enclosed by the outer circle of linear time. (See *Figure 5.*)

Between points 9 and 3 we find the outflow from Higher School, between 3 and 6 the struggle with resistance, and between 3 and 9 the return to Higher School. In the outer circle we can see how and in what stages a school unfolds in time. In the first third of the circle, which includes the invisible presence of a school's ideas, we also find the first period of a teacher's confidential directions and guidelines to his students. At point 3

---

[1] Rodney Collin, *The Theory of Celestial Influence* (London: Vincent Stuart Publishers Ltd, 1958), p327.

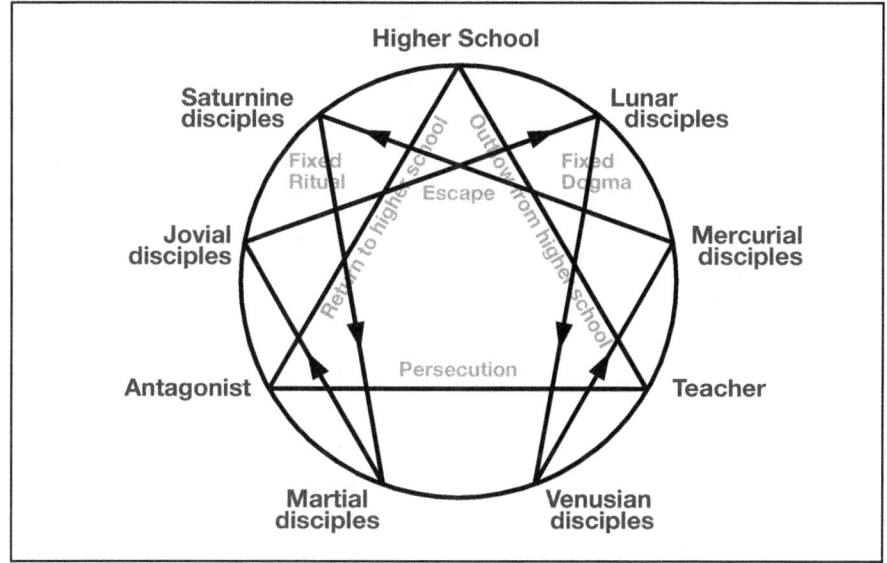

Figure 5. School as a Cosmos

the teacher will appear transformed. He will reveal his previous camouflage and clearly appear as a delegate of a Higher School. It is at this point that doubts in the group cease. However, it is also here that a powerful agitation occurs, both outside and inside the group. This resistance produces, through friction, the energy necessary to clarify every detail of the teacher's message.

Collin introduces an interesting suggestion that, seen in a logarithmic context, such a struggle could go on for several generations. Although this friction is required, this period is not at all without dangers. If the level of tension between two different aspects of the school becomes too high, the triad of corruption can take effect and destroy it all.

Because a school is a cosmos and any cosmos must necessarily contain all six processes, corruption must also have its place. However, corruption is never a school-product, but a costly challenge, which reveals its value by being neutralised. It is revealing that the common perception is that corruption is best fought by destruction. In contrast, the inner school will choose the process of regeneration. A school will only be able to overcome resistance as long as this secret knowledge is practiced.

As a result of the diversity of the universe, any cosmos is always in motion and many necessary processes are not clear to us. By expecting security wouldn't we deny life?

... sooner or later, someone connected with the school falls into temptation. Patience gives out – and he meets crime, not with regeneration, but first with destruction and then with other crime. In this way, a part of the experiment must always fail. The proportion between this failure and this triumph is the great unknown, the cosmic gamble in every school experiment.[1]

When we now return to the enneagram, we see that after persecution, between 3 and 6, the triangle once again touches the time circle. This is the point at which Collin envisioned that whoever had come to personify persecution reveals his role as a representative of Higher School, where the work of two transfigured individuals merges into a whole and where external and internal forms unite. Then a 'tradition' or 'church' arises. In the circle's time span, between points 6 and 9, these are developed until their last phase where a final return to Higher School (9) takes place. By juxtaposing the cosmoses of civilization and school, Collin concludes that they essentially make up a whole:

... since it is only the hidden presence of a school which makes a civilization really self-evolving and thus really a cosmos. 'Civilization' indicates the outer form, 'school' the inner meaning.[2]

Although Collin believed that the favourable times for a person's opportunity to change are periods when the triangle is close to the circle, he believed, as we have seen before, that it is the line that follows the enneagram's internal circulation that is decisive, not the circle of time.

By aligning the different types with the functions of a school, he demonstrates that, through an interchange between types, what he calls balanced 'supertypes' can develop. His holistic view is evident when he claims that this aspect of development contributes, within certain frameworks, to the general process of the development of the universe. Because the internal circulation is not only a movement from one type to another, but to a type at an ever-higher level than the previous one, Collin saw this not as a circular movement, repeating on one level, but rather as a spiral. The movement of the spiral is composed of all people of all types who have come under the influence of a particular school in all ages. In order to understand such a perspective, one must break out of a one-dimensional linear concept of time and apply the type of understanding we introduced when we explored Ouspensky's perspectives on time according

---

[1] Rodney Collin, *The Theory of Celestial Influence* (London: Vincent Stuart Publishers Ltd, 1958), p330.
[2] Rodney Collin, *The Theory of Celestial Influence* (London: Vincent Stuart Publishers Ltd, 1958), p331.

to *A New Model of the Universe*. To illustrate an interchange of types in such a spiral, Collin turned to biblical history:

> *The change from the belligerent, impatient Simon Peter who strikes off the soldier's ear in the Garden of Gethsemane to the wise, understanding, all-embracing, 'jovial' Peter of the Acts of the Apostles is an example of such a move.*[1]

It is precisely among the smallest details of Collin's theories about the form, function, prerequisites, and stages of schools that the key to a gradually growing understanding lies. For example, we can find definite meaning in the diverse intersections of lines in Rodney Collin's school-enneagram. Simply by focusing on the twelve points where the inner line crosses the triangle, we can form a clearer idea of the importance of details for an understanding of a school's form and function. About these crossings Collin wrote:

> *... definite 'monuments' or 'memorials' have to be created, from which forever after all men concerned with the school will be able to draw different kinds of inspiration, each according to his type, and which will serve as a signpost showing each how he must proceed. These twelve 'batteries' are symbolized in the drama of Christ by the twelve apostles, who establish a series of permanent ideals, to one of which each particular man at the particular point in his movement can aspire or make appeal. Gradually, these 'batteries' are supplemented by concrete expressions of the work of the school in lasting form – on the outgoing side of the triangle by the four Gospels, on the lower side by conflicting 'creeds' and 'dogmas', on the returning side by great cathedrals, rituals and works of art.*[2]

Collin regarded various later additions to the Christian tradition where elements such as the formation of 'orders', 'reformations' and even 'heresies' are included as constituent parts of the 'batteries'. The question of whether these 'batteries' are sometimes charged in the form of regeneration, or whether these additions are an expression of forms of corruption, can be viewed more holistically. Since any cosmos must necessarily hold all six processes, the challenge for each individual is to adopt an inner position where any step on the road becomes an opportunity, no matter what form it takes.

---

[1] Rodney Collin, *The Theory of Celestial Influence* (London: Vincent Stuart Publishers Ltd, 1958), p331.
[2] Rodney Collin, *The Theory of Celestial Influence* (London: Vincent Stuart Publishers Ltd, 1958), p332.

All in all, the inner line makes twelve crossings of the triangle, where each passage illustrates how individual types provide and receive energy from the original creative vitality of Higher School.

The external appearance of a school, characterised by entrenched attitudes that both attack and defend other aspects, is demonstrated in the intersections outside the triangle. Completely detached from the informative content and meaning of the triangle, these points represent the inability of the Form to carry content. We have previously seen how, in a triad of corruption, Form is in an active position, while Life is parked in a passive location. This is exactly what happens when a group or organisation becomes more important than the work itself. Collin gives examples of what the crossings outside the triangle represent, including the ridicule of rituals from some quarters within the Christian tradition and the cultivation of dogmas as well as organisations. He found further examples of the fixed bodies outside the triangle, which can possess neither consciousness nor understanding, in Paul's first letter to the Corinthians, which deals with strife in churches and is a clear warning against division.

The point at which the lines intersect within the triangle represented to Rodney Collin the very purpose of a school. It symbolised the place where, at any point in a school's life, anyone who met a school could escape – die and be reborn.

Collin's active search for traces of schools, particularly during the first half of the 1950's, contributed to his understanding of their development, form and function. However, his deepest insights and detailed knowledge found fertile ground in the challenges he faced from the moment Ouspensky unequivocally declared that he had abandoned the system and elaborated:

> You must reconstruct everything. Everything must be remade from the beginning.[1]

Collin perceived this as an impulse launched from Higher School and as nothing less than a significant crossroad in human history. The extent to which this potential was exploited was a different question. Until his death he maintained the conviction that Ouspensky's transformation performed the function of opening a door to higher realms. Both Ouspensky and Gurdjieff stood as examples of men who became instruments of higher powers by being themselves fully and sacrificing themselves completely for the Work. That Collin was not surprised by Ouspensky's dramatic

---

[1] Rodney Collin, *The Theory of Conscious Harmony* (London: Watkins Publishing, 1977), p110.

statement, not only says something about how close their cooperation was, but also something about Collin's spiritual maturity. Well versed in the principles of the fourth way, with a strong conscience, a powerful intellect and a quest for the truth, the way lay open for him to explore the nature of school beyond the threshold of Ouspensky's door.

When Rodney Collin gathers up the threads in the final chapter of *The Theory of Celestial Influence*, man appears at the center of a cosmic backdrop that is difficult to understand in a three-dimensional perspective. Here, as in *The Theory of Eternal Life*, death is regarded as a consequence of such intense energy that ordinary man is simply wiped out, but where one with sufficiently developed consciousness should be able to participate. As we have seen, it is Collin's various timescales, related to the cellular, molecular, and electronic world that are of crucial importance for a deeper insight into hitherto hidden realms.

On a cellular level, we see that the human body renews itself by cells dying and new ones coming to life. Because the form remains the same, we can say that the renewal consists in repetition. Thus, an uninterrupted circle of death and rebirth is underway. The transformation from young to old becomes visible after countless insignificant and imperceptible changes that take place with each individual rebirth. To the question of what causes this continuity, Collin replies:

> *It is the relation of cosmoses, and the relation of dimensions. The time of the cell is made up, not of generations of molecules, but of their recurrence, that is of their fifth dimension. The time of man is made up, not of generations of cells, but of their recurrence, their eternity.*[1]

Using his analogue method, Collin examines the underlying laws that are prominent when an ending life produces effects that in turn become causes of future rebirth. Each step in the renewal of the human body at the molecular and cellular level shows that the forgoing was and is identical. Such newly created molecules are not only a spitting image of the previous ones purely materially, but also occupy the exact same location in the cell in which it operates. He also found similarly identical parallels on a cellular level. For both levels, the moment of death and rebirth were similarly identical and inseparable. When Collin transfers this same lawfulness to man, he draws the conclusion that, at the very moment of death, man is reborn in exactly the same position that he was previously in. Likewise, all

---

[1] Rodney Collin, *The Theory of Celestial Influence* (London: Vincent Stuart Publishers Ltd, 1958), p335.

the effects he or she had earlier on their surroundings are inherited. About the causal relationships and the process itself he says:

> *In the moment of death, the pattern of these effects, transformed by this cosmic lightning into a single sign, is struck through time upon the waiting embryo. This is the secret of what happens to man's essence at death. It causes the same body to be born again, in the same place, of the same parents, at the same time. Such a possibility cannot belong to ordinary time, that is, to man's fourth dimension. It can only belong to his fifth dimension, his recurrence, his eternity. Death and conception are one in eternity. Each man's life lies in time, but the sum of his lives lies in eternity. The point at which one life joins the next is the point at which time joins eternity.[1]*

Although the imprint of a human life automatically carves out the form and content of its next image, this does not preclude change. Abetted by a consciousness, death will involve opportunities, as we have pointed out in our previous review of *The Theory of Eternal Life*.

The process of acquiring new understanding has always been associated with resistance. Although humans have an inherent desire for new insights, they often not only lack the necessary knowledge, but confuse knowledge and understanding - thinking they are the same. Thus, the possibility for understanding is limited and opportunities for insight are further disrupted. It is through a concrete experience of an idea that it can appear as something else. Collin's theory of an immediate experience of a fifth dimension is thus linked to a concrete experience of an inner perception due to expanded consciousness.

In connection with his investigations of the consequences of various effects, he claims that one of the few effects that can have a direct and decisive significance in a person's life is their attitude towards new knowledge.

Other seemingly significant events that may occur he explains in a simple but comprehensive way. Events that lie within the moment themselves, but which have no roots in the past, are considered accident.

Events whose causes accumulate in the past through a continuous tendency manifested in time are defined as a product of temporal cause and effect. Events which cannot be traced back to anything one has or could have done, because they occurred before one had begun to create causes, such as date and place of birth, and parents, Rodney Collin

---

[1] Rodney Collin, *The Theory of Celestial Influence* (London: Vincent Stuart Publishers Ltd, 1958), p336.

personally considered fate. The fact that such causal relationships were outside of time was not in doubt, but he drew no firm conclusion that these were directly linked to recurrence, a certain life, lives, or eternity. In his last category he created the space necessary to include all possibilities. He wrote:

> *Theoretically, a fourth class of events is also possible for a man. In this case, the cause lies neither in the present, nor in the past, nor even in recurrence. And only if we begin to understand the almost inescapable hold which his fate has over every side of a man's life, shall we realise that from his point of view such events will be miracles. In this way it becomes clear that if a man wants to study the possibility of recurrence personally, he has particularly to study his own fate, and to begin to distinguish the kind of events which belong to this fate.*[1]

Inspired by Ouspensky's groundbreaking insights into realms behind linear times, Rodney Collin continued his explorations of his own visions of man in eternity, where the destiny of a human life, previously looked at in a circle, enters reality as a stretched-out spiral. Small and large events in human life are recorded in parallel in the different areas of the spiral, down to every minute detail – repeatedly. The reason we do not remember such past events is as obvious as the reason why we do not remember details from our current existence, lack of consciousness. However, with a consciousness of a certain intensity, it will be possible to influence, by heat, parallel points in the under and overlying place of the spiral.

Because transferring heat in such circumstances requires a temperature higher than that achieved by conduction, Collin argues that transfer must take place by radiation. In any case, the point is that if the heat development is sufficient, it will help to create memory in another life.

Challenged with the impossibility of proving his theory, Collin put forward the idea that a human being possesses a faculty capable of recognising his fate. He acknowledges a number of preconditions for this ability to operate. One is that it can only work if one has sacrificed every kind of negative imagination about oneself. Another assumption is that one must achieve a certain degree of impartiality to one's destiny.

In a less detailed picture, Collin concludes that through increased awareness in this life consciousness spreads in all directions. This means that both the past and the future are included in eternity as well as in linear time. This may seem a little unusual, because the future and the past are

---

[1] Rodney Collin, *The Theory of Celestial Influence* (London: Vincent Stuart Publishers Ltd, 1958), p338.

normally associated with linear time, whereas eternity is conceptually different from passing time, in the sense that it is not of an endless duration. However, it resonates well with a statement from Jacob Boehme:

Time is found inside eternity.

And Aristotle's saying:

That which constitutes the enclosing limit of the whole universe and embraces the infinite period and the infinity of all things is eternity.

A significant aspect of Collin's considerations around recurrence is that time ceases to be a measurable entity. This means that the cohesion of different individuals in recurrence remains untouched by each individual's lifespan. Regardless of time and with a meeting point as a common denominator they are equal and complete. From the perspective of man's many lives, represented in the spiral of recurrence, their spirals are interwoven and each spiral crosses at the same relative spots on the individual spirals. Collin's perspective, however, is more comprehensive than that. In addition to the intersection of spirals, he argues that different interpersonal energy levels can contribute to different meanings and consequences:

... by purely physical contact, by community of thought, by sensuality and physical attraction, and by the highest love, reverence or pure sex. Still more important, all these reactions may be blindly undergone, or consciously experienced. Perhaps this can change, and if it could, then everything would both appear the same and yet be utterly different.[1]

From the perspective of the fourth dimension, measured in the extent of time between birth and death, one may come to consider the fifth dimension as an endless reliving of the fourth dimension. Collin uses the fact of the difference between the days, moments, months, and years that make up our linear time to demonstrate a possible perspective on the fifth dimension. By recognising that the different units through which we identify time are experienced with various depths and intensities, it becomes possible to consider linear time as something other than a monotonous line without a thickness and another way of perceiving the fifth dimension. Not surprisingly, Collin links this intensity and depth to man's level of consciousness. Increased consciousness is, in his view, the only prerequisite for being able to penetrate the fifth dimension. With the

---

[1] Rodney Collin, *The Theory of Celestial Influence* (London: Vincent Stuart Publishers Ltd, 1958), p341.

many different elements that make up possible interpersonal touch points in the spirals of recurrence, consciousness transcends and transmutes all.

From one perspective the unimaginable amounts of interconnections each individual forms in their lifetime are so intricate that they do not appear as a diverse volume, but as a solid. About this dimensional viewpoint, Rodney Collin writes:

> *The total of all the recurrence-spirals of all human beings produces the solid of humanity, in the same way that the recurrence of all cells produces the solid of a man.*[1]

When he takes a closer look at this solid in a metaphorical perspective, it appears as a tapestry, composed of inconceivable elaborate weaving that, through the warp, holds all the threads together in one direction, representing eternity. By introducing colours, the different threads came to represent not only their different properties, but also different levels of energy. Through these instruments, Collin was able to highlight significant periods and events in humanity. Such periods were characterised and dominated by moving skills and sensations, intellectual activities, or pure physical existence. Areas with elements of threads that exceptionally distinguished themselves from the others, and which in every way were consistent with the whole design of the solid body of humanity, represented the existence of men and women with conscious souls and conscious spirits.

Rodney Collin's creative ability, which always served a higher purpose, has once again come to light. As we have seen on a number of other occasions, the path between his abstract mental images and his anchor to concrete life has often been short. Here too:

> *... those threads are threads only in our metaphor. In fact they are alive and their total mass is alive. They are the cells and capillaries and nerves of a body, the Adam Kadmon of the Kabala, Mankind.*[2]

Dealing with images in the context of recurrence within probable and understandable frameworks requires some mental resilience. The next and even more challenging step Rodney Collin appears to take in his stride, this time stepping behind the recurrence. The big questions about man, mankind, human relations, life, death, and cosmic universal laws had become part of him and consumed him incessantly. The basis of his drive

---

[1] Rodney Collin, The Theory of Celestial Influence (London: Vincent Stuart Publishers Ltd, 1958), p342.
[2] Rodney Collin, The Theory of Celestial Influence (London: Vincent Stuart Publishers Ltd, 1958), p342.

was not only the depth of his insights and thereby his convictions, the diversity of his knowledge also constantly opened new doors.

When the idea that aspects of the logarithmic scale would lead the way in the pathless land behind recurrence, it was the depth of his openness about more than four dimensions and the breadth of knowledge that would prove decisive. As he had already explored in *The Theory of Eternal Life*, it is possible to consider man's life course in the form of a circle, because it has no beginning, since birth is a kind of extension of death. It was a door out of and at the same time an entrance into a cellular existence. Related to an expanded perspective on the logarithmic scale he had originally assumed for the circle of life, Collin questioned whether there can be another door that shares the same threshold between death and conception:

> *... it began not at zero but at one. And at earlier stages on it, beyond one, must lie one-tenth, one-hundredth, one-thousandth, to infinity. In other words, the same scale must have continued from somewhere else, outside the circle of physical life, and thus even outside the spiral of its repetition.*[1]

Founded on his earlier theory that different stages in the circle of life occur through compressed processes with an increase in speed, he concludes that an alternative door out of the life circle must necessarily lead into a faster state of matter.

As the process around birth operates at a slower rate than at conception, then the process around human individuality before conception and cellular matter, by following the logarithmic scale, will continue at an ever-increasing speed. After reaching molecular matter, it will enter an electronic state. About this logarithmic journey towards the unknown, Collin wrote:

> *We have to imagine the signature of man, his pattern or fundamental nature, impressed first upon a vehicle resembling air, and second upon a vehicle resembling light. That is to say, we have to imagine the individuality of man attached to a soul without a body, and even to a spirit without a soul.*[2]

Almost in the same breath as he proposes this reversal and disintegrating process, he emphasises the limitations of our ability to imagine. Stuck as we are in our physical organism, our imagination is limited by our sensory

[1] Rodney Collin, The Theory of Celestial Influence (London: Vincent Stuart Publishers Ltd, 1958), p344.
[2] Rodney Collin, The Theory of Celestial Influence (London: Vincent Stuart Publishers Ltd, 1958), p345.

apparatus. As an example of the extent to which we are rooted in our physical form of existence, he points to the connection between physical union and our sex function. Likewise, he questions what our emotional function would be without a body. Even our logical thought depends upon having a physical body to be able to check results in a physical world. In order to prepare for states after death and before birth, it is necessary to develop intentional imagination. Through training and inner work, one can gradually cultivate this ability and become acquainted with characteristics, powers and possibilities that, from the cellular level, will be considered incomprehensible and miraculous.

As death and transformation is man's inexorable fate, all he can change is his consciousness, a change that has decisive significance and far-reaching consequences. According to Collin, the disintegration of man's cellular body to a molecular world represents his advent into eternity or recurrence, while an entry into the sixth dimension and a merging with the Absolute is related to the disintegration of his molecular body into the electronic world.

He regarded the principle of successive existence in different states of matter as a mechanical feature of the universe, free from individual merit or defect. On the crucial distinction between people on Earth, he wrote:

> *Their common possession of a physical body, with a head, two arms, and two legs, may in this world tempt us to discount the difference between conscious and unconscious man. In the sense that food goes in and words come out from both their mouths, Christ and the criminal are equal. It is only the disintegration of this deceptive body, and the passage of what remains into other states of matter, that reveals to us the vast gulf between sleeping man and him who has created a permanent and indestructible principle of consciousness.[1]*

It is now around 70 years since *The Theory of Celestial Influence* was published and it is reasonable to assume that some later scientific innovations would have had an impact on some aspects of his views. In his day, Rodney Collin always sought support in what he considered to be relevant research. However, it is important to note that he considered a one-sided scientific method to be limiting, and that it is necessary to view man and his inner life from the same perspective as the universe, and vice versa.

---

[1] Rodney Collin, *The Theory of Celestial Influence* (London: Vincent Stuart Publishers Ltd, 1958), p346-347.

According to Collin, there are two ways of acquiring knowledge. The scientific one, in which one classifies phenomena by induction and then tries to derive laws and principles from them. The second method, deduction, in which, through specially designed studies one tries to understand principles and laws that one has perceived, had revealed or somehow discovered. While the first approach can be attributed to the ordinary logical mind of the human being, the second springs from a potential human function that is usually out of action, because it lacks sufficient nervous energy and intensity. However, when this higher mental function comes into effect, it reveals laws in action through the appearance of the phenomenal world as products of those laws. By recognising and acknowledging these two methods of knowing, Collin sought, in *The Theory of Celestial Influence*, to build a bridge between and reconcile these different forms of approaches.

Another example of a bridge builder between science and the Fourth Way is the English Professor Meredith Thring who, at the request of Henri Tracol, prepared a detailed scientific justification of Gurdjieff's cosmology that not only encompasses the beginning of the world, but even includes the division of the atom. Another is the American Dr. Keith Buzzell. His contribution is unique, not only because of his medical background and intellectual capacity, but because his research has a breadth and a personal depth. He presents many facets of Gurdjieff's ideas that can only come from first-hand experience, including the necessity of the application of the higher mental capacity.

Why did Collin and Ouspensky have such a deep interest in recurrence? One possibility is that it may have been prompted by experiences they had in a higher mental state. A characteristic approach of this method of knowing is that it begins with 'laws' and attempts to reach 'facts', while the logical approach does the opposite.

Recurrence is not a part of Gurdjieff's teaching but Ouspensky did not consider it to be contrary to Gurdjieff's ideas. In a rather strange conversation they had, Gurdjieff did not deny the phenomena, but emphasised the dangers of bringing the topic to the fore. People might not make the necessary efforts today if they were presented with the idea of a new opportunity at a later stage. Unfortunately, most of us may have to admit that Gurdjieff has a very good point, but it still doesn't address Ouspensky's central questions. Asked directly about recurrence, Gurdjieff said:

This idea of repetition … is not the full and absolute truth, but it is the nearest possible approximation of the truth. In this case truth cannot be expressed in words. But what you say is very near to it. And if you understand why I do not speak of this, you will be still nearer to it. What is the use of a man knowing about recurrence if he is not conscious of it and if he himself does not change?[1]

It was of tremendous importance to Ouspensky that Gurdjieff had recognised his fundamental premises for recurrence, and he felt that Gurdjieff had thereby given him something substantial that he could not take back.

The future showed that I was right, for although G. did not introduce the idea of recurrence into his exposition of the system, he referred several times to the idea of recurrence, chiefly in speaking of the lost possibilities of people who had approached the system and then had drawn away from it.[2]

For Rodney Collin, the great task in life consisted of building a bridge between all the possibilities of the universe that man carries within himself and the mechanised human being who was created through a relentless response to stimuli. He believed that only through such a bridge could creation become conscious of its own origin and all its infinite promises be fulfilled. Although such a process is essentially an individual undertaking grounded in a longing, at the same time it is also part of a larger exchange of all-encompassing ideas and energies. Those ideas are often made available through practical cooperation with others, where we are confronted not only with our various and often contradictory sides, but also with a new point of view from whence we can see that, in the process of transformation, we are primarily our own enemy.

The Theory of Celestial Influence is one of Rodney Collin's many contributions to a better understanding of man's position and possible relationship with the universe. Whether one makes use of it in the process of forming an understanding and insight into one's own life in the universe, is up to oneself.

---

[1] P.D. Ouspensky, *In Search of the Miraculous* (London: Routledge & Kegan Paul Ltd, 1969), p250.
[2] P.D. Ouspensky, *In Search of the Miraculous* (London: Routledge & Kegan Paul Ltd, 1969), p251.

APPENDIX

This appendix was a programme Rodney Collin designed in Mexico that formed the basis of some of the studies in his groups in the mid-1950s. They were also sent to some close acquaintances in Europe such as Maurice Nicoll. The programme came to me in connection with Joyce Collin-Smith handing over various of Rodney Collin's surviving papers, including the correspondence she had had with him.

PROGRAMME OF STUDY

INTRODUCTION

This tradition teaches us to study ourselves, our fellows, and the universe from different points of view, under different laws. All are correct, but each requires separate study and understanding. Combining the understanding of these different laws, we come to a more balanced estimation of man – including oneself, including one's neighbour – to a more living understanding of the universe, including nature, including God.

Gradually all fits together. We hope in the end to combine all our different understandings in one single vision. But that can only happen if we come **to live** these understandings, **to be them**. And then (with luck or grace) only by the working of a higher illumination in us.

Meanwhile, remember that you cannot understand something in another until you understand it in yourself: and you cannot measure its significance in yourself until you measure its significance in general.

We will study man

> as unity,
> as duality,
> as trinity,
> as a play of seven and twelve,
> as multiplicity.

For each study to be as objective as possible, try to see in that particular way:

> Yourself.
> Your companions (but you must not speak about this).
> Men in general (but you cannot if personal likes and dislikes enter).

365

Some world smaller or larger than man (a cell, an organ, humanity, nature, the earth, the solar system).

Remember that this study is **for yourself**, and for you to find yourself. It is not to impress your companions, or your leader, nor – heaven forbid! – for you to impress yourself.

Only if you do it honestly, sincerely and truthfully, and you do begin to find yourself, you may somewhere and somehow become of use. That's all

Appendix

UNITY

The study of unity is the study of God.

So if you think of man as a unity, or humanity as a unity, you think of divinity in them. Don't try to force what is human and material into this vision. Because you cannot. You will only hurt your mind.

And if you cannot glimpse this unity, or somebody else cannot, don't blame yourself and don't blame them.

Just be quiet, and be patient, and from time to time remember God.

————————

Yet, we can affirm that there is a unity. One being and one energy which impregnates all; all matter can be resolved eventually into electronic force. In this unity there is no contradiction, no doubt, no ignorance; all is known instantly; everybody shares everything.

————————

Try to understand unity.

Imagine and study the properties of:

> air,
> light,
> order,
> timelessness,
> love.

————————

DUALITY

True	False
Real	Imaginary
White	Black
Light	Dark
Myself	Not myself
Inside	Outside
Up	Down
Motion	Matter
Waking	Sleep
Life	Death

Think about these contraries; how to resolve them?

Ordinary man lives inside out.

He lives in constant forgetfulness of what is real – **constant forgetfulness of his own existence.**

He lives in constant remembrance of what has no reality – **constant remembrance of his own self-importance.**

He **does** exist – both physically and in other ways. Yet ninety-nine per cent of the time he actually feels himself as the centre of the universe, actually believes the true significance of things lies in the way they affect him. This is illusion.

Unconsciousness plus illusion is sleep.

Sleep infinitely prolonged is death.

To wake up and live everything has to be reversed:

> **Remember** your true existence.

> **Forget** your self-importance.

Remember yourself and forget yourself – always and everywhere.

———————

Begin with the body.

Begin by feeling the existence and behaviour of the body.

Soon you will have to admit that usually you **are not aware of its existence** unless it is stabbed by some penetrating pain or pleasure.

APPENDIX

Yet at the same time its state affects your mood, your beliefs, your whole picture of the world. If its blood is moving fast and its pores are open after exercise, then you feel eager, optimistic, enterprising. If it is torpid, with accumulation of poison in the pancreas, you feel pessimistic, depressed, disillusioned. If it has an excess of nervous energy, you want to interfere with everyone; if it is exhausted of nervous energy, you feel irritated by every demand made upon you. Its states happen, and your moods happen with them. This is to be in the power of chemistry. When the chemistry of the body – unrecognised – dictates your state, this is mechanicalness.

In these conditions, **when one is the body, and the body is unconscious,** there are no higher possibilities.

First, **you** must become conscious of <u>it</u>.

Recognise what is happening in the body, and that it **is not you.** Learn when you must exercise it, when keep it quiet; when feed it; when starve it; when allow it to sleep; when rouse it in the small hours – in order to keep it sensitive, alert, and obedient to **you.**

But with sympathy and understanding, not with violence or contempt. As much as you become conscious of it, it will become conscious of itself. Then you will realise what a wonderful organism it is, how sensitive, how ingenious, how capable of work and sensations of which you never dreamed. You will see that it is an image of the universe.

Study simple anatomy and physiology if they help; and **never, never** interfere with natural breathing.

So begin by studying duality in relation to the physical body.

How much does the physical body unconsciously direct you?
How much do you consciously direct the physical body?
How often?
How long?
How completely?

369

TRINITY

Body	Soul	Spirit
Red	Yellow	Blue
Water	Air	Fire
Sound	Heat	Light

What does it mean to remember one's true existence?

It means to remember oneself as a trinity – since everything real in the universe is created by three; since God is a trinity, and He made man in His own image.

Remember that you are **body**, **soul** and **spirit**.

The **spirit** lives in eternity; exists outside time; knows the complete truth about you; shares divinity.

The **body** is limited by space and time; measures everything by its sensations, in relation to its type; and from the point of view of its situation in the present moment.

The soul should form a conscious bridge between spirit and body; make man into a conscious unity; enable the body to consult the spirit; the spirit to direct the body to consult the spirit; the spirit to direct the body as its instrument.

But the soul obviously does not yet exist in this way. It exists at present only as a focus of vague feelings and intuitions, easily obscured by considerations of comfort, fear and material advantage.

_____

Study the teachings about body, soul and spirit in different traditions:

In ancient Egypt:

Khat (a leaping fish which is at home in water but not in air).

Sekhem (an owl which is at home in air but not in light).

Ikh (a hawk which flies straight into the sun).

Among the Platonists:	Soma, Psyche, Nous.
In the Gospels:	Soma, Psyche, Pneuma.
Among the Alchemists:	Corpus, Anima, Spiritus.
Among the Sufis:	Jism, Nafs, Ruh.

_____

Appendix

How is the soul formed?

By attention, by self-remembering, which focuses the higher principle of **consciousness** in the body. The fine matter which carries consciousness is the matter of the soul. By constant attention, by constant self-remembering, this fine matter accumulates, crystallises, forms a permanent vehicle.

Self-remembering

Can you look out intentionally through your eyes while aware of the light shining above your head? What looks out, what is aware? The soul. A moment of self-remembering brought it there.

Self-remembering momentarily brings the soul into conscious being; puts it in memory of body and spirit simultaneously. The three parts are aligned. Moment of equilibrium. Moment of stillness. Moment of truth.

Each person must create self-remembering for himself – alone, among companions, in a crowd; in work, in leisure, in love; always and everywhere.

Conscience is the voice of the spirit, heard in the body, heard in the heart. It can only be heard when the soul is present, only in a moment of self-remembering.

The voice of conscience can be heard only by listening; disregarded it becomes silent; obeyed, it speaks with more and more authority.

True development is measured by the degree to which a man is obedient to his own conscience. For this means the degree to which body responds to spirit, the degree to which a man is **one**.

Everything about the soul is a paradox.

It is made by attention, yet Christ said: "Take no thought for your soul." It is made by self-remembering, yet Christ said: "Whosoever shall save his soul (psyche) shall lose it, and whosoever will lose his soul for my sake shall find it."

The law of the soul is "what you give you get." It is made of the fine matter of attention; the more attention is consciously given to others, the more is

371

generated, and the more the soul grows. The more heat a fire gives out, the more air it sucks in and the hotter it becomes.

Trying to keep one's soul for oneself is always doomed to failure. It is like trying to keep opened wine to drink next day – next day it is vinegar.

Self-remembering shows how to acquire a soul; conscience shows how to give it away.

––––––––––

The <u>body</u> judges by distance (far or near) and by stimulation (pleasant or unpleasant). A man a hundred yards away is of no importance for it; a man one yard away fills its world. An event a month away has no importance; an event a minute away takes all its attention. Stimulation which produces warmth is pleasant; stimulation which produces burning is unpleasant. The body's judgments are subjective, and not valid for any other point of the universe.

The **spirit** measures by **goodness, truth, honesty, beauty, perfection, order.** It reacts in the same way to these qualities and their absence, whether

> in oneself or in others;
>
> in this room or in China;
>
> now or a thousand years ago.

The spirit's judgements are objective and valid always and everywhere.

The embryonic soul can be wedded either to the judgment of the body or the measure of the spirit. This is its free choice. Naturally without attention the soul and its feelings support the body's judgment. Self-importance is the result of the soul supporting the body's sense of itself as centre of the universe. Wonder is result of the soul supporting the spirit's sense of truth and order.

Only by effort, by attention, by self-remembering, by love, can the soul be re-wedded to the spirit, and so lead the body instead of being led by it.

Try to study practically:

> The unaided perceptions of the body (senses);
>
> The pure perceptions of the spirit;
>
> The effect of the soul (emotions) joined to either.

––––––––––

APPENDIX

When you have the feeling of body, soul and spirit, remember how these three elements (like every other triad) can combine in six different ways to produce six different processes:

Growth

Decay

Purification

Sin

Healing

Regeneration

How do these processes come about in the relation of body, soul and spirit?

Change the scale from individual man to humanity:

Man	Mankind
Spirit	The spiritual hierarchy
Soul	Esoteric school
Body	Chemical man

The creation of esoteric schools on Earth is exactly the same task as the creation of soul in individual man. For these schools are to enable physical man to listen to the guidance of the spiritual hierarchy, and the spiritual hierarchy to help and regenerate physical man.

The individual soul and the true school of wisdom both establish communication – **communication** between body and spirit. If this is forgotten, everything is forgotten.

Thus all through the ages, the hierarchy – working through schools – transmits into human life images of the working of cosmic laws. For example, in:

the alphabet	architecture	art
astronomy	dance	decoration
games	festivals	legends
music	philosophy	popular proverbs
religious ritual	special customs	the theatre
	all science	

Study any of these deeply enough and you will find the trace of schools.

More especially, the hierarchy arranges performances of the redemption of man. From time to time, members of the hierarchy are born into human life, and there act out the drama of their own redemption, helping their disciples and companions to imitate them in lesser roles. Try to recognise these dramas in history and study them.

Remember that all that is said about the relation of **body**, **soul** and **spirit** is equally true of the relation between the hierarchy, schools and physical man.

APPENDIX

HARMONY (seven and twelve)

Everything is created by the law of trinity, and develops by the law of harmony. Develops according to a rhythmic pattern whose image has been given to us in the musical scale. To the three notes of a cord, four more are added to make an octave; then five half-tones to complete the scale. Scales multiply and interact to produce the whole web of creation.

Let us use this pattern as a basis to study the physical body, **our own**, by direct observation.

The tones of the octave are its **functions**, in the order in which they develop. The half-tones are the five senses which feed these functions.

do		Intuition
	-do/	Touch-Taste
re		Digestion
	-re/	Orientation
mi		Movement-Breathing
fa		Blood-Circulation
	-fa/	Hearing
sol		Thought
	-sol/	Smell
la		Projection
	-la/	Sight
si		Reproduction

Intuition is the function which brings us knowledge from before birth, from another octave.

Touch and taste make the first way of perceiving our surroundings. They are different degrees of the same sense. A baby puts things into its mouth to know them. Touch and taste prepare for the function of **digestion**.

Orientation is the sense of up, down, left and right, before and behind, and of distance. Perceiving our surroundings in this way prepares for **movement**.

Movement and breathing are two aspects, inner and outer, of the same function.

Blood-circulation is self-contained and continuous – it needs no external sense to feed it.

Hearing prepares the way for thought. As we hear, so we think. Sound waves are of the same nature as thought waves. Thought can be inner noise or inner music.

By **smell** we recognise what other things project. If the sense of smell were sufficiently developed, we should distinguish the subtle acids secreted by the pores for every emotional change.

Projection is the function by which a man who is nervous projects nervousness, who is confident projects confidence, who is angry projects anger, who is affectionate projects affection. It is very important to study this function, and begin to project intentionally instead of accidentally.

Sight is the finest and most perfect of the senses, for it gives intimation of the **whole**, a whole cosmos. And the function of reproduction is concerned with the creation of a new cosmos – in every sense.

Try to study the working of each of these senses and functions separately. A week for each pair. Study their interaction and combination. Observe how they work with or without **attention**.

If you do this seriously, you will know a great deal about the physical body and about yourself.

———————————

Observe the play of seven and twelve everywhere:

Esoterically:	12 apostles; 7 churches which they founded.
Naturally:	12 months of the year; 7 ages of man.
Astronomically:	12 elements in the Solar System (Sun, Moon, Mercury, Venus, Earth, Mars, Asteroids, Jupiter, Saturn, Uranus, Neptune, Pluto) of which 7 are visible to the naked eye.
Politically:	North America divided into three countries, Central America into seven countries, South America into about 12, etc., etc., etc.

Take the law of seven and twelve on another scale.

By slow shifting of the earth's axis, each year at the spring equinox the Sun is seen a little behind the point where it was the year before. Gradually, in 25,000 years, it seems to pass round the whole heaven and return to the same place. Its path is divided into twelve parts, and it takes 2160 years to pass through each.

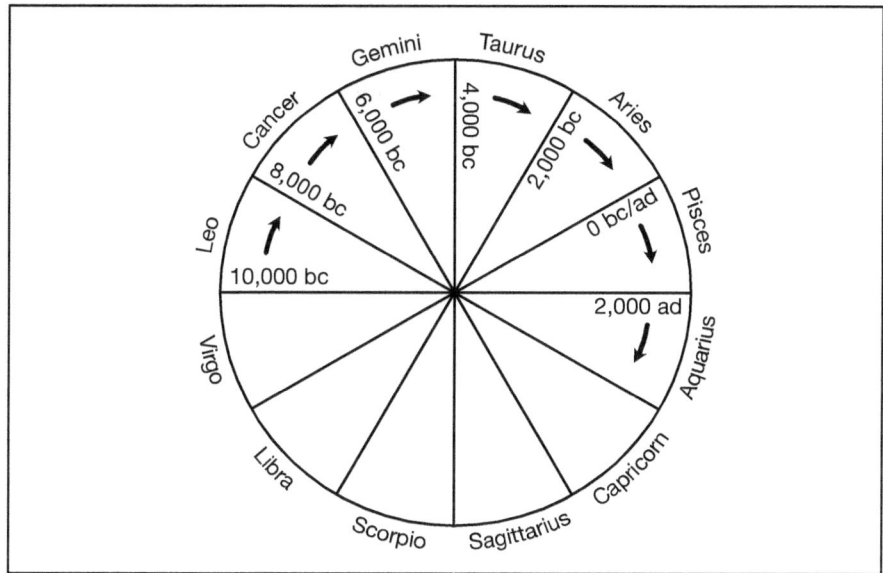

Figure 6. The Zodiac and the Ages of the Earth

These parts are distinguished by the signs of the **zodiac**. Naturally when the Sun seen from the Earth is in one sign, the Earth seen from the Sun is in the opposite sign.

The ancient names for these signs have great meaning, and suggest to us how cosmic work on great and small scales is linked into one plan. For each sign means a new **month** for the Earth, a new **age** and **task** for mankind, a new revelation from the hierarchy.

Thus when the Sun was in Geminis (6000-4000 B.C.), divinity and its work was represented by the heavenly twins, Castor and Pollux; when it was in Taurus (4000-2000), by a bull (Assyria); when it was in Aries (2000-0 B.C.), by a ram (Egyptian Khum). The ritual of bull-fighting or bull-killing, for instance, dates from the time when the Sun was passing from Taurus to Aries.

In the same way, when the Earth was in Capricorn (8000-6000 B.C.), she and her role were represented by a goat (Pan); when in Sagittarius (6000-4000 B.C.), by a centaur; when in Scorpio (4000-2000 B.C.), by a scorpion (Assyria), or scarab (Egypt); when in Libra (2000-0 B.C.), by a figure holding the scales of justice.

At the beginning of our era, the Sun entered Pisces and the Earth Virgo. The fish became the symbol of Christ and fishermen, his disciples; a virgin became symbol of the Earth, and Christ born of a Virgin, the sign of its redemption.

Study everything, remembering that **all has meaning in relation to the great work.**

———————

APPENDIX

MULTIPLICITY

All life is created by the interplay of the law of Trinity and the law of Harmony. Between them they produce multiplicity.

When understanding of these laws is present, we see multiplicity as **order** – as in nature, as in the heavens. When understanding of these laws is lost, we see multiplicity as **chaos**.

Chaos is the absence of recognition of law, absence or discrimination.

See chaos in yourself – when there is no discrimination of functions, of levels, of origin, when all kinds of impulses are confused, when all are taken equally as 'I'.

See chaos in the world – when laws are not recognised; when all sides of human life are mixed, without discrimination; when all six processes (growth, destruction, purification, crime, healing and regeneration) are taken on the same level.

––––––

To make order out of chaos:

first **watch**,

then **measure**,

finally **choose**.

Nothing can be altered (in yourself or outside) until it is seen impartially and accepted. Everyone wants to start by changing something. This is like trying to rearrange the furniture in a dark room without turning on the light. First you must turn on the light and take stock.

Watch, watch, watch.   Observe, observe, observe.

Gradually begin to measure what you see – not according to how it effects you, but according to laws. Learn not to start every sentence with the first person. Begin to see law everywhere. See the operation of higher laws and lower laws; of conscious influences and mechanical influences. Measure – larger, smaller, older, younger, finer, denser.

Measure, measure, measure.

When you begin to recognise the difference between mechanical and conscious, reaction and will, the way of the world and the way of the hierarchy, begin to choose.

In every moment there is choice – if you are awake.

But choice is not between doing something and not doing it; choice is connected with:

Seeing a third possibility
Seeing the right way of doing or not doing

In sleep there is either/or; waking is connected with **how, why, for what motive**.

So ask yourself continually:

> What about my aim?
> What about body, soul and spirit?
> What about harmony?
> What about self-remembering?
> What about vanity?
> What about conscience?
> What about God?

Mexico 1955

BIOGRAPHICAL NOTES

Terje Tonne came in contact with Gurdjieff's ideas in the early 1970's. Together with his wife, he has led a group in Oslo for 35 years. He has had a long close relationship with professor Meredith Thring, George Cornelius and Joyce Collin-Smith.

He is the author of *The Gurdjieff Puzzle Now*, Nevada City, CA: Gateways Books, 2001and *Were sich verliert, der findet sich,* Lotos, Verlagsgruppe Random House. GmbH.

He is a retired conservator with expertise in fire damaged paintings.